Teaching
Elementary
Reading
Today

Teaching Elementary Reading Today

WILMA H. MILLER
Illinois State University
Normal, Illinois

Holt, Rinehart and Winston
New York   Chicago   San Francisco   Philadelphia
Montreal   Toronto   London   Sydney
Tokyo   Mexico City   Rio de Janeiro   Madrid

Photo credits: pages xxii, 28, 62, 84, 110, 170, 180, 198, 212, 226, 248, 300, 314, and 350: National Education Association, Joe Di Dio; page 12: HRW photo by Suzanne Szasz; page 138: © Beryl Goldberg; page 272: HRW photo; page 382: Freda Leinwand, from Monkmeyer Press Photo Service.

Library of Congress Cataloging in Publication Data

Miller, Wilma H.
  Teaching elementary reading today.

  Includes bibliographies and index.
  1. Reading (Elementary) I. Title.
LB1573.M533 1984   372.4'1   83-10757

ISBN 0-03-059342-5

CBS COLLEGE PUBLISHING
Holt, Rinehart and Winston
The Dryden Press
Saunders College Publishing

Acknowledgments

Figure 1-1: Reprinted with the permission of Arista Corporation.

Pages 56–57: The recipe for alphabet pretzels is from *First Steps to Reading* by Carl Braun and Allan R. Neilsen. Reprinted by permission of Braun and Braun Educational Enterprises.

Figure 5-1: From *McGuffey's Electic Primer* by William H. McGuffey, Van Antwerp, Bragg and Co., 1881. Revised by American Book Company. Reprinted with the permission of American Book Company.

Figure 7-1: From *Reading Mastery I: DISTAR Reading*, Take-Home Book A. Copyright © Science Research Associates, Inc. 1983, 1974, 1969. Reprinted by permission.

Figure 7-2: From the *Phonetic Keys to Reading* series. Reprinted by permission of The Economy Company.

Figures 9-1 and 17-2: From tests in the *Wisconsin Design for Reading Skill Improvement* series. Reprinted by permission of Learning Multi Systems, Inc.

Figure 11-1: Reprinted by permission of Wendell K. Simpson and Harriet S. Simpson.

Pages 267 and 285: Excerpts from the book, *Reading Diagnosis Kit*, 2nd ed. by Wilma H. Miller, © 1978 by The Center for Applied Research in Education. Published by Parker Publishing Company, Inc., West Nyack, New York.

Figures 16-1, 16-3, 16-4, and excerpts on pages 322–327, 331: From *The Reading Activities Handbook* by Wilma H. Miller. Copyright © 1980 by Holt, Rinehart and Winston. Reprinted by permission of Holt, Rinehart and Winston, CBS College Publishing.

Figure 16-2: From *Exploring American Neighbors*, rev. ed. Copyright © 1967 by Follett Publishing Company. Reprinted by permission of Allyn and Bacon, Inc.

Figure 17-1: Sample item reproduced by permission. Copyright © 1978 by Harcourt Brace Jovanovich, Inc. All rights reserved.

Appendix I: From "The New Instant Word List," by Edward Fry, *The Reading Teacher*, December 1980. Reprinted with the permission of Edward Fry and the International Reading Association.

Appendix II: From "Word Lists—Getting It All Together," by Robert L. Hillerich, *The Reading Teacher*, January 1974. Reprinted with the permission of Robert L. Hillerich and the International Reading Association.

To my beloved mother

Preface

Research has indicated that it is often the teacher's role, rather than the method or methods which are used, that most greatly influences the quality of elementary reading instruction. Therefore, it is imperative that teachers of reading in the elementary school be as competent as possible. Only with very well-trained and well-motivated teachers will the teaching of elementary reading be as effective as it should be. It is vitally important that each student who leaves the elementary school be as capable a reader as his or her potential will allow. It is hoped that this textbook can enable both preservice and in-service teachers to become excellent teachers of reading.

This textbook was written primarily for prospective elementary-school reading teachers. It should be very effective as the major textbook in an elementary reading methods or language arts methods course. However, it contains countless teaching strategies and concepts that should prove of equal value to experienced elementary teachers of reading as well as to reading specialists. Elementary school administrators should also find this textbook a valuable source of information.

This edition was primarily designed to be practical and, therefore, contains numerous classroom-tested teaching strategies. Although relevant research studies are presented, this textbook places more emphasis on the ways in which research can be implemented in the teaching of elementary reading. This textbook was also designed to be as comprehensive as possible. It covers all the major areas in elementary reading instruction as thoroughly as possible within the confines of a single textbook.

Because both preservice and in-service teachers need to be aware of the many aspects of the reading process, the textbook opens with a brief description of reading. The next chapter explains in great detail the many strategies that parents can use in the home to present prereading skills to their children prior to school entrance. This chapter is the result of a course the author has taught for a number of years. Chapter 3 describes in practical detail how to present reading readiness and beginning reading skills in the nursery school and kindergarten.

The next four chapters are devoted to discussing some of the major approaches to elementary reading instruction. Chapter 4 describes how to implement the very useful language experience approach in the teaching of prereading and beginning reading skills. The fifth chapter explains how to implement the basal reader approach, the most commonly used approach in the elementary schools today. Chapter 6 discusses how to use individualized reading effectively in an elementary-school reading program. The seventh chapter describes phonic approaches and presents the phonic elements and generalizations in detail.

Chapter 8 explains the significant contributions that the science of psycholinguistics has made to the teaching of reading. The next chapter explains diagnostic-prescriptive reading programs and reading management systems in detail. Chapters 10 and 11 tell how to implement what this author believes to be excellent reading programs for both the primary and intermediate grades.

The next three chapters are devoted to improving competency in the important reading skills. Chapter 12 describes how to improve both sight and meaning vocabularies, whereas Chapter 13 provides many strategies for improving ability in structural analysis and contextual analysis. Chapter 14 explains the four main levels of comprehension—literal, interpretive, critical, and creative—and provides numerous ideas for improving ability in each.

Chapter 15 discusses the ways in which elementary reading instruction is organized in contemporary schools. The sixteenth chapter is devoted to the special skills that are needed for effective reading in the content areas of social studies, science, and arithmetic. Chapter 17 describes the standardized and informal ways that can be used to ascertain a student's reading progress. Chapter 18 is devoted to strategies for teaching children with unique needs in the elementary school. It was written as a direct result of the passage of U.S. Public Law 94–142, which mandates that all handicapped children be mainstreamed into regular classrooms as much as possible. It describes how to teach reading in the regular classroom to children who are visually or aurally handicapped, to learning-disabled children, to slow-learning children, to blind and low vision children, and to deaf and hard-of-hearing children.

The author wishes to thank her undergraduate and graduate students at Illinois State University for providing some of the practical suggestions included in this edition, and also Carla Kay, the Project Editor. She also wishes to express her special gratitude to her mother, who, at the age of seventy-nine, not only typed the entire manuscript but was also an unfailing source of inspiration.

Wilma H. Miller

Normal, Illinois
October, 1982

Contents

CHAPTER

The Nursery School and Kindergarten Reading Programs   29

CHAPTER **4**

The Language Experience Approach   63

CHAPTER **5**

The Basal Reader Approach   85

What Did She Do Wrong?   85

CHAPTER **6**

Individualized Reading   111

What Would You Have Done?   111

CHAPTER **7**

Phonics and Phonic Analysis   **139**

CHAPTER

The Contributions of Psycholinguistics   171

Do You Think That This Should Have Happened?   171

CHAPTER **9**

Diagnostic-Prescriptive Reading Programs and Reading Management Systems   181

Why Did She Feel This Way?   181

CHAPTER **10**

A Recommended Primary-Grade Reading Program   199

Why Was This Better?   199

CHAPTER **11**

A Recommended Middle-School Reading Program   213

Why Was This Better?   213

CHAPTER **12**

Developing Sight and Meaning Vocabularies   227

What Should She Do?   227

CHAPTER

Improving Ability in Structural Analysis and Contextual Analysis   249

Why Was This Better?   249

CHAPTER **14**

Developing Ability in Comprehension   273

What Did She Learn?   273

CHAPTER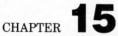

Ways of Organizing Elementary Reading Instruction   301

Why Was This Wrong?   301

CHAPTER **16**

Teaching Reading in Content Areas   315

Why Was This Better?   315

CHAPTER **17**

Appraising Progress in Reading   351

CHAPTER **18**

Teaching Reading to Children with Unique Needs   383

Teaching Elementary Reading Today

The reading process

What Would You Have Said?

As Paul Williams entered Mrs. Goodman's office, he was quite nervous because he knew that he had to make a good impression on her if he were to be hired as a new fifth-grade teacher at Truman School. Mrs. Goodman was the director of personnel in the school system, and she had a reputation for asking tough questions. However, Paul felt quite well prepared to answer any of her questions, especially those about reading instruction, for he believed that he had taken a very good reading methods course at his university the previous year.

Nevertheless, he found that he was not well prepared when Mrs. Goodman asked him to explain his view of the reading process after only a few minutes of preliminary conversation. She asked him if he could explain the role of saccadic movements in reading, and Paul really wondered what they were. Mrs. Goodman also asked him how he felt about using a computer to study the eye movements of disabled readers to determine the number of their fixations and regressions and to examine their return sweeps. Paul thought a computer was used for calculation—not to study eye movements during reading.

As he apparently knew nothing

about the role of eye movements in reading, Mrs. Goodman then asked Paul questions about the role of sight words, phonic analysis, structural analysis, and contextual analysis in the reading process. At least he knew something about phonic analysis that he thought made some sense, but he was totally unable to answer Mrs. Goodman's question about the ability of a student to comprehend material effectively without being able to pronounce a number of the words in the reading material. He wondered how a person could read effectively if he or she couldn't even pronounce all the words correctly in the reading material. Moreover, Paul really couldn't explain the differences between the four levels of comprehension—literal comprehension, interpretive comprehension, critical reading, and creative reading.

By the end of that unfortunate interview, Paul was certain he had a lot to learn about the complex reading process. He was not at all surprised when he did not receive the fifth-grade teaching position at Truman School. However, after you read this chapter carefully, you will never be placed in Paul's situation, for you will understand the major elements that comprise the reading process.

EYE MOVEMENTS

It is important to understand at the outset that reading is a complex process that even today is not completely understood by researchers. However, researchers have attained a fairly good understanding of the less complex aspects of the reading process by this time. It is also important to note that the reading process as described in this chapter is an accumulative, interrelated process in which each element is at least to some extent dependent upon the previous elements.

The role of the eye movements is the first aspect of the reading process. This visual aspect of reading must occur before a person can reach the higher levels of reading. Eye movements during reading have been studied scientifically since the early part of the nineteenth century. One of the first efforts involved attaching an instrument to the eyes that recorded movements on a smoked drum. However, about 1907, Raymond Dodge formulated the corneal reflection method, which involved bouncing a beam of light off the eye and directing the reflection into a camera with moving film. The light ray then produced a streak on the film that accurately showed each movement of the eyes.[1]

After Dodge's discovery of the corneal reflection method, a number of cameras using this approach were built. One such camera, for example, was about ten feet long and five feet high. This camera was constructed by Miles A. Tinker and his associates at the University of Minnesota. Its use helped them discover much of what is known today about the role of eye movements in reading.[2]

At the present time, eye movements are being studied with sophisticated on-line computer systems. A small computer is connected to a cathode ray tube, which is used to display the text that the person is to read, and to an eye-tracking device, so that complete data on the person's eye movements can be recorded. The reading material is changed very rapidly while the person is reading it. A photograph of one type of device used for studying eye movements is illustrated in Figure 1-1.

According to the result of the studies of eye movements, as a person reads, his or her eyes move along a line of print in quick jerks that are called *saccadic movements*. This term comes from the French word *la saccade,* which means "jerk" or "jolt." As the moving eye is blind for all practical purposes, a person is not able to read during these jerking movements, but instead reads at pauses, which are called *fixations*. While a person is reading, the eyes pause or fixate more than *90* percent of the time and move less than *10* percent of the time. A typical fourth-grade student pauses or fixates about five times while reading an average line of print. Even a good adult reader can see only about 2.65 words at each fixation.

When a person is unable to recognize a word while reading, his or

[1]Raymond Dodge, "An Experimental Study of Visual Fixations," *Psychological Monographs, 8* (1907): 1–95.

[2]Miles A. Tinker, "Eye-Movements in Reading," *Journal of Educational Research, 39* (December 1936): 241–277.

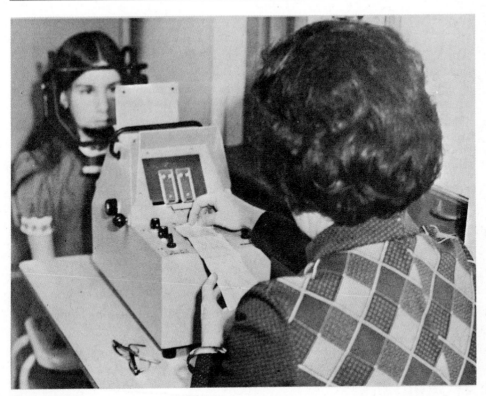

Figure 1-1

her eyes move back along the line to examine the word more carefully in what is termed a *regression*. Regressions can be useful because every reader needs to examine difficult or unknown words carefully from time to time while reading. If elementary-school students make an excessive number of regressions while reading any type of material, that material probably is too difficult and may be on their frustration reading level. It is also important to remember that beginning readers normally make many more regressions than do typical good older readers.

While reading in English and in most alphabetical languages, a reader's eyes move along lines of print in a left-to-right movement which is called *left-to-right progression*. When a reader's eyes reach the end of a line of print, they move to the next line in a sweeping movement in what is termed a *return sweep*. Eye movement photography has indicated that some disabled readers may have no true return sweep but may return to the beginning of the next line by a series of regressions from right to left.

While a person is reading silently, his or her eyes often move ahead of the point of understanding, and this forward movement is called the *span of recognition*. The span of recognition for an intermediate-grade student usually averages a word or slightly less than a word. You can determine the width of your own span of recognition by having a friend cover the end of a line of print that you are reading silently with an index card. By recalling the words read in advance, you can determine how far ahead you have read while part of the line was covered. You might be interested to know that a reader normally can improve his or her reading rate by shortening the length of each fixation or by increasing the length of the span of recognition.

The vast majority of classroom teachers of reading need not be concerned about studying the eye movements of their students. Most average and above-average readers have satisfactory eye movements as a result of reading adequately. On the other hand, as most below-average readers improve their basic word identification and comprehension skills, their eye movements usually improve simultaneously. Usually, eye movement photography would take place in a university reading clinic with severely disabled readers in order to locate the duration of their fixations, the number of their fixations and regressions, the length of their span of recognition, and the adequacy of their directional attack and to find indications of their difficulties in visual functioning.

THE WORD IDENTIFICATION TECHNIQUES

The next aspect of the reading process is the use of the various word identification techniques. However, the effective use of the word identification skills is closely related to eye movements. Word identification is the process of obtaining the pronunciation and meaning of the words that a person encounters while reading. Within word identification are the subskills of sight word recognition, phonic analysis, structural or morphemic analysis, picture clue usage, and contextual analysis. Although a detailed description of each of these skills appears in later chapters, for clarification a brief description is found in this chapter.

Sight word recognition is used when a reader recognizes a word instantly by its total shape or form. Sight word recognition consists of a number of subskills, one of which may be the use of configuration or drawing a frame around the word to emphasize its unique shape or form.

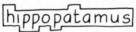

Sight word recognition also consists of certain unique characteristics such as ascending and descending letters in a word. Some of the unique characteristics within a word, for example, the double *o* in the word *look,* may be irrelevant cues because many other words such as *book, cook,* and *took* also contain a double *o.*

The acquisition of a sight word bank receives emphasis at the initial stages of reading in such elementary reading approaches as the basal reader approach and the language experience approach. Students in the elementary school should have a large stock of sight words if they are to be effective readers, for they cannot stop to analyze each word while reading. A number of disabled readers in the later primary and intermediate grades have a very poor stock of the basic sight words.

All words cannot be recognized by sight at first exposure to them. As a means of approaching an unknown word, a reader should try to determine its pronunciation and meaning by another word identification technique such as contextual analysis, structural analysis, or phonic analysis. Eventually, most words should become part of the student's sight word bank so that they do not have to be analyzed each time that they are met.

The first one or two letters of a word usually are the most useful in sight word recognition. When people read from left to right, they obviously see the beginning of the word first. The end of the word is the next easiest to notice, and the middle part of the word seems to be the most difficult for most people to notice. In addition, the upper half of the word usually is somewhat more useful in sight word recognition than is the bottom half. If you examine the word *puppy,* you will see that this is true.

DUDDY

| | | /   (puppy)

Phonic analysis is a very important word identification technique that also is presented at the initial stages of reading instruction in most approaches. Phonic analysis involves determining the pronunciation and meaning of unknown words by associating phonemes (sounds) with the graphemes (symbols) that represent them. As English is supposed to be about *85* percent phonetically consistent, phonic analysis is a useful word identification technique for a number of words. However, it is not useful in decoding such words as *mother, father, said, were,* or *our.* Phonic analysis may be somewhat more effective in a language that is completely phonetically regular such as Italian or Finnish. Through phonic analysis the student learns to understand the use of consonants, consonant blends, consonant digraphs, vowels, vowel digraphs, diphthongs, phonograms, and spelling patterns.

Structural or *morphemic analysis* is another word identification technique that is first presented at the beginning stages of reading in most approaches. This is the process of obtaining the pronunciation and meaning of an unknown word from the use of word structure or word parts. It consists of the understanding of the use of base or root words, prefixes and suffixes (affixes), inflected endings, contractions, syllabication, and accent. Many of these subskills of structural analysis can also be used for vocabulary improvement at the middle-school level.

Picture clues is a word identification technique that is used in several beginning reading approaches. In this technique the child associates a picture with an unknown word located on the same or a nearby page. For example, a child can learn to associate the written symbol *dog* with a picture of a dog that is found on the same page. Picture clues can be useful but should not be overemphasized. For example, the beginning reader must not rely so heavily on picture clues that he or she does not learn to recognize the printed words. Although picture clues undoubtedly are the most important in beginning reading, they also have relevance and can clarify concepts in the middle school in such content areas as social studies and science.

Contextual analysis or context clues are useful for a reader attempting to determine the meaning, and less often the pronunciation, of an unknown word from the sentence, paragraph, or passage in which it is located. Contextual analysis is not an effective word identification technique when there are many unknown words in the reading material. However, in most other instances it is the most effective technique of word identification that an efficient reader can employ. In fact, the efficient reader can learn the meanings of countless words by the use of context. The variety of context clues includes experiential clues, synonym clues, previous contact clues, association clues, comparison clues, and contrast clues.

It is important to remember that effective word identification techniques always should lead to effective comprehension. This is why word identification techniques must never be overemphasized at the expense of effective comprehension. In fact, many contemporary reading specialists believe that a person can make some errors in word identification or decoding and still comprehend the reading material quite effectively.

ASSOCIATING EXPERIENCES WITH THE SYMBOLS THAT REPRESENT THEM

The next aspect of the reading process sometimes is called the *associative task,* associating experiences with the symbols that represent them. Many printed symbols are graphic representations of oral language symbols that, in turn, represent actual objects. As an example, the printed symbol *table* is a representation for the oral symbol

/table/, which in the English language represents the actual object of any type of table.

For the associative aspect of reading to be truly effective, a reader must be able to interpret the exact shade of meaning that each symbol represents. Many words have slightly different, subtle shades of meaning depending upon their use in context. This concept is termed the science of *semantics*.

In the English language, most abstract words have many different meanings, whereas scientific words usually have one or several. To illustrate this concept, consider that, according to one dictionary, the word *call* has approximately twenty-five different meanings when used as a verb and eleven different meanings when used as a noun. On the other hand, the scientific term *osmosis* has only two different meanings.[3]

Because the associative aspect of reading is very closely related to the meaning-vocabulary knowledge that is always required for effective comprehension, a student who is weak in this aspect of the reading process also may have difficulty with comprehension. For example, because culturally different students sometimes have had different experiences and oral language models from those found in the middle-class-oriented basal readers, they may be weak in the associative aspects of reading. This may be one reason why such students sometimes have difficulty in comprehending basal readers effectively.

LITERAL AND INTERPRETIVE COMPREHENSION

The next aspect of the reading process is comprehension or understanding. However, successful comprehension usually depends at least to some extent on effective word identification techniques and always depends upon the possession of a rich, varied meaning vocabulary. Reading without comprehension is not considered to be reading by most reading specialists. Instead, reading without understanding can be called *word-calling, verbalism,* or "barking at the words." Comprehension also involves prediction of the content of the reading material. Through prediction the reader asks questions and sets purposes for reading, whereas comprehension means getting the questions answered and satisfying the purposes for reading.

Because comprehension undoubtedly is the most complex aspect of the reading process, even reading specialists who have studied it in detail are not yet completely certain of its components. There have

---

[3]*Webster's Seventh New Collegiate Dictionary* (Springfield, Massachusetts: G. & C. Merriam Company, 1963), pp. 118–119, 597.

been various models of comprehension formulated. However, most reading specialists agree that there are several levels of comprehension that can be described.

The lowest level of comprehension is called *literal* or *factual comprehension* or *simple recall*. This level of comprehension consists of the subskills of answering a question correctly from the reading material, reading and carrying out directions, placing a number of items in correct sequence, locating directly stated main ideas, finding significant details, and locating irrelevant details. Comprehension can also be related to the various levels of the *Taxonomy of Educational Objectives*. For example, literal or factual comprehension corresponds to the knowledge or translation levels of the *Taxonomy*.[4]

Literal comprehension begins to be important at the earliest stages of reading instruction in most approaches. However, it should receive less stress as a student progresses through the upper primary grades into the intermediate grades. Literal comprehension often receives too much emphasis in contemporary elementary schools.

A higher level of comprehension is called either *interpretive comprehension* or *inferential comprehension*. Interpretive comprehension is a thinking process performed by interpreting what is read, inferring from what is read, reading between the lines, drawing conclusions and generalizations, predicting outcomes, summarizing, locating the author's mood and purpose, and locating implied main ideas. Interpretive comprehension is thought to correspond to the interpretation or extrapolation levels of the *Taxonomy*.[5]

Interpretive comprehension is also stressed from the earliest stages of reading instruction in such methods as the basal reader approach and the language experience approach. However, it should be increasingly emphasized as a student progresses through the elementary school.

CRITICAL READING

Some reading specialists consider the next higher aspect of the reading process to be *critical* or *evaluative reading,* whereas other reading specialists consider it to be a high level of interpretive comprehension. Although this author considers it to be a separate entity, you may find it very difficult to differentiate between interpretive comprehension and critical reading.

In any case, critical reading involves evaluating or judging what is

---

[4]B. S. Bloom, M. D. Engelhart, E. J. Furst, W. H. Hill, and D. R. Krathwohl, *Taxonomy of Educational Objectives,* Handbook I: *Cognitive Domain* (New York: David McKay Co., Inc., 1956).

[5]Bloom and others, *Taxonomy.*

read in terms of some specific criteria that the reader has formulated through previous experiences or reading. It consists of the subskills of differentiating between fact and fantasy, comparing reading material from different sources, judging the accuracy and truthfulness of reading material, and recognizing various propaganda techniques. Critical reading is closely related to critical thinking and corresponds to the evaluation level of the *Taxonomy*.[6]

In the past, elementary schools generally have done a rather inadequate job of teaching critical reading skills, but these skills are now being presented and reinforced more effectively than they were in the past. Critical reading skills should be stressed from the beginning stages of reading instruction. Although a number of adults do not critically analyze what they read, this skill is indispensable in a democratic society such as ours.

CREATIVE READING

The highest level of the reading process can be called *creative reading, applied reading, integrative reading,* or *assimilative reading.* In any case, creative reading is the application of what one reads to one's own life for problem solving. It also is any way in which reading can be followed up to create some new type of process or product. Creative reading probably corresponds to the application or synthesis levels of the *Taxonomy*.[7]

Creative reading should begin to receive emphasis at the earliest stages of reading instruction. Students in the elementary school can apply the knowledge and attitudes gained from reading through participation in creative writing of prose and poetry, role playing, dramatic play, cooking and baking activities, art activities, construction activities, and rhythm activities.

HOW YOUR VIEW OF THE READING PROCESS MAY INFLUENCE YOUR TEACHING OF ELEMENTARY READING

Most contemporary elementary reading approaches emphasize many of the aspects of the reading process. In most of these approaches, no one aspect of reading is overemphasized at the expense of the remaining aspects.

---

[6]Bloom and others, *Taxonomy.*

[7]Bloom and others, *Taxonomy.*

No elementary reading approach places emphasis on improving the student's eye movements because a reader's eye movements usually become more efficient as his or her other reading skills and reading fluency improve. However, all reading approaches stress most of the word identification techniques to some degree, though in several reading approaches, the word identification skill of phonic analysis may be overemphasized. If you think of any of the word identification techniques as being of primary importance, you may overemphasize decoding or word pronunciation at the expense of comprehension of what is read.

Some elementary reading approaches do not stress comprehension at the initial stages of reading instruction but later on as the basic word identification skills are mastered. Because comprehension is of vital importance, it always should receive much emphasis. In addition, if you are cognizant of the importance of comprehension, you will not be unduly concerned if a student miscalls several words while reading orally if he or she effectively comprehends what is read. Critical reading and creative reading also should receive much more emphasis than they now do in some elementary reading approaches. They are too important not to receive much stress in all of the primary and intermediate grades.

Generally, no single aspect of the reading process should be emphasized to the exclusion of the others. No single elementary reading method is the most beneficial for the majority of elementary-school children. Most children at this level should have extensive instruction and reinforcement in the word identification techniques of sight word recognition, phonic analysis, structural or morphemic analysis, picture clues, and contextual analysis. The reading process should include many different types of experiences for vocabulary improvement. Students always should see the necessity of understanding what they read. Finally, if it is appropriate, students should evaluate what they read and apply the reading to their own lives.

SELECTED REFERENCES

Dallmann, Martha, Roger L. Rouch, Lynette Y. C. Char, and John J. DeBoer. *The Teaching of Reading.* New York: Holt, Rinehart and Winston, 1982.

Hall, MaryAnne, Jerilyn K. Ribovich, and Christopher J. Ramig. *Reading and the Elementary School Child.* New York: D. Van Nostrand Company, 1979, pp. 5–9.

Lamb, Pose, and Richard Arnold. *Teaching Reading.* Belmont, California: Wadsworth Publishing Company, 1980, Chapters 1, 2.

Otto, Wayne, Robert Rude, and Dixie Lee Spiegel. *How to Teach Reading.* Reading, Massachusetts: Addison-Wesley Publishing Company, Inc., 1979, Chapter 2.

Ransom, Grayce A. *Preparing to Teach Reading.* Boston: Little, Brown and Company, 1978, Chapter 1.

Robeck, Mildred C., and John A. R. Wilson. *Psychology of Reading: Foundations of Instruction.* New York: John Wiley & Sons, Inc., 1974, Chapter 1.

Smith, Frank. *Understanding Reading.* New York: Holt, Rinehart and Winston, 1982.

Spache, George D. *Investigating the Issues of Reading Disabilities.* Boston: Allyn and Bacon, Inc., 1976, Chapter 3.

Zintz, Miles V. *The Reading Process.* Dubuque, Iowa: William C. Brown Company, Publishers, 1980, Chapter 1.

SUGGESTED ACTIVITIES

1. State how your view of the reading process has changed as a result of reading this chapter.
2. If your university has a reading clinic that studies eye movements, observe the records of the eye movements of able, average, and disabled readers.
3. Determine the width of your span of recognition by having someone cover with an index card the end of a line of print that you are reading silently.
4. Discuss the comparative importance of completely accurate word identification in relation to effective comprehension with less than totally accurate word identification.
5. React to this statement: If I can pronounce all the words in a passage written in Finnish, I can read material written in this language.

Developing prereading
skills in the home

CHAPTER 2

What Would You Have Told Her?

Ever since Colleen was a small baby, Mrs. Sullivan had wanted her to learn to read very well when she was in school. When Colleen was about three years old, Mrs. Sullivan began to ask some of her friends what she could do to help Colleen learn to read before she started kindergarten. As none of her friends seemed to know what to do, Mrs. Sullivan really didn't make much effort to teach Colleen to read until she was four years old.

About that time, Mrs. Sullivan read an advertisement in the Sunday supplement in the local newspaper, which was promoting a record and some workbooks that could be used to teach preschool children how to read in their home. Mrs. Sullivan eagerly ordered the record and the workbooks even though they were quite expensive and waited for them to arrive so that she could begin teaching Colleen how to read.

When the materials arrived, Mrs. Sullivan noticed that they mainly emphasized phonics, something that she didn't know very much about. She decided to use the materials with Colleen anyway as they must be worthwhile because they had been published.

After Mrs. Sullivan had used this program with Colleen for several weeks, she noticed that Colleen was getting rather restless each day when the phonics lesson was presented. Although Colleen objected to doing the drills found in the material, Mrs. Sullivan continued the lessons for several months. Finally, she had to discontinue them when Colleen had a temper tantrum every time Mrs. Sullivan got the materials out.

By the time Colleen entered kinder-garten at the age of five, Mrs. Sullivan had given up ever teaching her to read at home. Colleen had even told her mother that she never wanted to learn to read anywhere because it was so dumb. When Mrs. Sullivan talked to Colleen's kindergarten teacher, Ms. Owens, in September, she was very upset to learn that Colleen was not interested in any type of reading readiness activity. Ms. Owens could not understand this until Mrs. Sullivan told her how she had tried to teach Colleen to read at home with a phonics record and phonic workbooks when she was four.

Ms. Owens then explained to Mrs. Sullivan that there are many more effective ways of presenting a preschool child with reading readiness and beginning reading skills at home than by using formal phonics materials. Some more effective ways of doing this are reading to the child, developing the child's background of experiences, improving the child's oral language, using the language experience approach, using visual discrimination and auditory discrimination activities, providing cooking and baking activities, using various types of art activities, teaching the letter names by association, and teaching words by sight. Ms. Owens told Mrs. Sullivan that she would have been glad to tell her how to work with Colleen in presenting beginning reading skills if she had been asked.

After you read this chapter carefully, you will know many prereading activities to provide for your future children at home and many activities to suggest to parents who ask you what they can do in their home to improve reading readiness and to present beginning reading.

SOME GENERAL CHARACTERISTICS OF THE PRESCHOOL CHILD

It may be helpful at the outset to review very briefly some of the physical, cognitive, and social-emotional characteristics of the young child.

Obviously, a newborn baby spends most of his or her time sleeping, with the periods of being awake increasing each day. A baby begins to focus on nearby objects at about six weeks of age, after which his or her motor control begins to increase. After this time, babies can hold their heads upright and can control their arm and head movements.

During the child's first three years, his or her body proportions, height, and weight change considerably. Heredity and environment usually affect the child's motor development and cognitive development. By the time the child is three years old, he or she usually can run well, stand on one foot, ride a tricycle, draw simple pictures, manipulate objects, and button and unbutton clothing.

The late Jean Piaget, the famous Swiss child psychologist, is credited with much of the contemporary understanding of the cognitive development of young children. He has stated that the child is in the *sensorimotor stage* of development from birth until about two years of age. This stage consists of such substages as the development of reflexes, the adaptation and refined adaptation of innate abilities to environment, the accommodation of new experiences, experimenting and discovering, and cognitive inventions.[1]

The older preschool child of four or five begins to grow less rapidly and begins to develop more adultlike proportions. Most children of this age are very active although they often still need frequent rest periods. A child of this age usually has not established lateral dominance or handedness and appears ambidextrous. Most children of this age usually have better large muscle control than they do the fine motor control that is required for drawing and writing.

The child of four or five exhibits many social-emotional characteristics that make him or her very enjoyable to work with and very interesting. Some of these characteristics are the ability to imitate, a lively imagination, excitability, independence, nonpredictability, the enjoyment of challenges, and self-awareness. However, a child of this age also is likely to be impatient and to have a fairly short attention span, especially when some activity is not very interesting or challenging.

Piaget has stated that the child of four or five usually is in the

---

[1]Jean Piaget, *The Origins of Intelligence in Children* (New York: International Universities Press, Inc., 1952).

preoperational stage of development.[2] This stage of development begins at about the age of two and lasts until the child is about seven. The preoperational stage is characterized by beginning symbolic functioning when the child is able to use symbols to represent concrete objects. It also includes classification in which a child sorts objects according to their discriminating characteristics. In addition, the child in this stage has some concept of time and space. Moreover, this stage includes the understanding of serial relationships in which the child is able to use one or several dimensions to arrange items in correct sequence.

Although most preschool children have the characteristics that have been very briefly described in this chapter, it is obvious that there are many differences among preschool children of the same age. That is why every young child always must be considered as an individual by his or her family members.

RELATION OF CERTAIN ELEMENTS IN THE HOME ENVIRONMENT TO SUCCESS IN PRIMARY-GRADE READING

It is obvious that there is a great variation in the home environment provided for the preschool children in our contemporary society. A number of fortunate children are provided with an excellent home environment from the time of their infancy onward. These children are cared for by loving, supportive parents, who provide much in the way of the significant prereading experiences that are discussed later in this chapter. Although it is certainly not always true, many of these children enter nursery school or kindergarten possessing many prereading skills and a real desire to learn to read, and sometimes they already possess the ability to read at a primary-grade level.

On the other hand, there are a number of preschool children in our society who unfortunately do not have the kind of home environment that lends itself to the effective development of reading readiness and beginning reading skills. Such children may live in black inner-city neighborhoods, in Chicano neighborhoods, in rural areas, in Appalachia, on reservations, in working-class neighborhoods, and in middle-class or upper-class neighborhoods. They also may come from broken homes.

There are many reasons why such children do not live in a home environment that is conducive to subsequent reading achievement. Sometimes their parents are not financially able to provide activities

---

[2]Piaget, *The Origins of Intelligence.*

and materials that develop reading skills and present beginning reading skills. In other cases, their parents may simply be too busy with a myriad of other responsibilities to provide the individual attention that the child needs. In many cases, however, parents simply do not know what types of activities and materials can be used at home to improve reading readiness and present beginning reading. Many of these activities are inexpensive and are not time-consuming. Yet their use can greatly improve the quality of a child's home environment in relation to the degree of reading success that the child will have in school.

A number of research studies over a period of many years have found that the type and quality of home prereading experiences prior to school entrance have greatly influenced children's subsequent first-grade reading achievement. Some examples of these home prereading experiences were reading to the preschool child; parents who were interested in reading themselves; reading materials in the home; trips to interesting places; and the use of manipulative materials in the home such as crayons, scissors, paints, paper, and a chalkboard. Such studies have been conducted by Millie Almy,[3] Esther Milner,[4] William Sheldon and Lawrence Carrillo,[5] and Marjorie Hunt Sutton.[6]

Although none of these studies is current, they probably could be replicated with similar results today. One can conclude from them that children who have had a variety of prereading experiences prior to school entrance often will achieve more success in beginning reading than children who have had few opportunities to do so. Although this is often the case, you should remember that it is not always true.

Much of the emphasis on teaching beginning reading skills in the home has resulted from several research studies conducted by Dolores Durkin of the University of Illinois.[7] In a study in California, Durkin studied forty-nine children whom she determined to be early readers in first grade. Later she conducted a larger replication study in New

[3]Millie Almy, "Children's Experiences Prior to First Grade and Success in Beginning Reading," *Teachers College Record, 51* (March 1950): 392–393.

[4]Esther Milner, "A Study of the Relationship Between Reading Readiness in Grade One Children and Patterns of Parent-Child Interaction," *Child Development Abstracts, 25* (1951): 189.

[5]William Sheldon and Lawrence Carrillo, "Relations of Parents, Home, and Certain Developmental Characteristics in Children's Reading Ability," *Elementary School Journal, 52* (January 1952): 262–270.

[6]Marjorie Hunt Sutton, "Readiness for Reading at the Kindergarten Level," *The Reading Teacher, 22* (January 1964): 234–239.

[7]Dolores Durkin, *Children Who Read Early* (New York: Teachers College Press, 1963).

York City. In each study she interviewed the families of the early readers to determine the kinds of prereading and beginning reading activities in which they had participated in their homes before entering first grade.

Durkin discovered that the early readers in both research studies often had engaged in informal reading activities such as learning by sight the letter names and words that interested them. The early readers often had older brothers and sisters who had helped them learn to read in an informal way. In addition, it is very interesting to note that the early readers were members of all different social classes and were of all intellectual levels. Durkin discovered that the early readers in her studies generally retained their initial advantage in reading through the intermediate grades. Perhaps most significantly, this was especially true of the slow-learning students.

It is significant to note at this point that there is one simple activity that can be provided in the home that probably is the single most influential factor in a child's subsequent success in beginning reading. This is simply reading to the preschool child on a daily basis from a variety of sources such as books of nursery rhymes and various types of children's trade books.

A family member can begin reading to a baby at as early an age as less than a year. Even though the baby obviously does not gain any real information from the reading at this age, he or she can begin to associate books with a pleasurable activity such as being held in the parent's lap. Of course, the older preschool child from about the age of two years on benefits considerably more from being read to because he or she understands the story content better, enjoys examining the pictures, and learns some of the characteristics of print such as the left-to-right movement.

As part of the requirements of a class I have taught for a number of years entitled "Pre-First Grade Readiness and Reading," my students work on a one-to-one basis with a four-year-old or five-year-old child on reading readiness development. Unfortunately, some of the children with whom my college students have worked had never heard a book or story read to them before they were helped by the college students.

PREREADING ACTIVITIES PARENTS
CAN PROVIDE IN THE HOME
PRIOR TO SCHOOL ENTRANCE

There are a multitude of prereading activities that parents may wish to use to improve the child's prediction ability by having him or her predict the story content from the title or predict what events the child thinks will happen next in the story. The parent also can sometimes ask the older preschool child literal, interpretive, or critical comprehension questions about the material, being careful not to ask the child to overanalyze the material.

It is very important for the parents and other family members to provide their preschool child with a positive reading model. The parent who values reading and seems to enjoy reading materials such as books, magazines, or newspapers can be a very positive force in motivating the young child to want to learn to read. Such a positive adult reading model may not be found in a number of the culturally different families in our society. This absence may somewhat account for the culturally different child's lack of motivation to learn to read well.

It is also important for the preschool child to own a few books, if possible. These can be inexpensive paperback books or more expensive hardcover books. The important thing is for a preschool child to listen to his or her own books if possible.

One prereading activity that often is overlooked by parents is that of taking their preschool child to the local public library and helping him or her select appropriate trade books that can be checked out and then read aloud to the child at home. Most older preschool children are fascinated by the children's section of the library and very much enjoy selecting appropriate trade books with the help of a family member or the children's librarian. Many preschool children with whom we have worked in college classes in reading readiness development also very much enjoyed receiving their own library card when this was possible.

Activities to Develop Experiential Background

There are many different types of prereading activities that can develop experiential background. Perhaps one of the most useful of these is the taking of family trips of various types. These trips need not be expensive or difficult, but instead can consist even of a picnic in the park. Here are some of the types of excursions that my students have used with preschool children: a trip to a dairy farm, the zoo, a pet shop, a shopping mall, the grocery store, a greenhouse, a museum, a park, the fire station, the police station, the post office, McDonald's, and an ice-cream store. Obviously, there are many other kinds of family trips such as camping trips, trips to the seashore, trips to a lake, and trips to an amusement park that parents can take their children on.

Note: Any family trip is more valuable if some of the specialized vocabulary that represents what will be seen is discussed briefly in advance. Then these vocabulary terms can be discussed on the trip itself. All vocabulary discussions should, of course, be informal and enjoyable for the preschool child. Part of the follow-up to a family trip sometimes can be the dictation of a language experience story, as is very briefly described later in this chapter and described in detail in Chapter 4.

Television also can be used as a means of increasing a preschool child's experiential background. Although most commercial television programs are not very useful for this purpose, a few may be. On the other hand, such television programs as "Sesame Street," "Captain Kangaroo," and "Romper Room" usually are very valuable in improving the preschool child's reading readiness and in presenting some rudimentary initial reading skills. "The Electric Company" may be useful in teaching reading skills with a very few children at the kindergarten level.

As you may know, "Sesame Street" was designed to improve the reading readiness skills of culturally different children. However, it probably has been more effective in improving the reading readiness skills and beginning reading skills of middle-class children because they often watch it more regularly, and their parents often are more involved in helping them benefit from the program. In fact, a number of kindergarten teachers seem to feel that "Sesame Street" has been the main reason why a number of contemporary children enter kindergarten more nearly ready to read or indeed perhaps already reading. Critics of "Sesame Street" sometimes say that it is too fast-paced for young children. However, I think that preschool children themselves are the best judge of its worth. Countless parents of preschool children have told me that their children very much enjoy watching "Sesame Street" and apparently benefit from watching it from the age of two or three onward.

Activities to Improve Awareness of Reading

There are several activities that improve awareness of reading although they could equally well be placed in another category. One of these is the use of alphabet books and alphabet blocks to learn the letter names. As will be explained in detail later, it is important for the preschool child to learn the letter names by association. An alphabet book and alphabet blocks can be a useful early vehicle for this purpose.

The preschool child also may benefit from pretending to read simple trade books from about the age of two on. The child can learn from this activity that a reader's eyes move from left to right across the page when a family member shows the child that print goes from left to right. This prereading skill is called left-to-right progression.

The preschool child also may benefit from learning how to interpret a picture from an appropriate trade book critically and creatively.

Such picture interpretation activities pave the way for future interpretive and critical comprehension of material that the child reads himself or herself at the elementary-school level.

Activities to Improve Competency in Oral Language

In the past a number of research studies have found that a child's facility in oral language is very much related to his or her probable success in primary-grade reading. Therefore, informal activities that improve the child's oral language ability obviously are often very helpful. Incidentally, oral language facility also is a very good indicator of a child's mental ability. Thus, the mentally handicapped preschool child often has very delayed oral language development.

In any case, it is very important for the family members of a preschool child to use acceptable sentence structure and a varied, colorful vocabulary if possible. A parent who stresses vocabulary development, especially from firsthand experiences, is likely to help his or her child improve oral language usage.

After a family member has read or told a story to the preschool child, the child can be asked to retell the story. Not only does the retelling technique enhance the child's oral language development, but it also enhances his or her comprehension ability. As an example, retelling is used as a technique to assess comprehension ability of the material that older children have read for themselves.

The dictation of language experience stories is an excellent way for parents to help their preschool child improve many aspects of reading readiness and informally teach beginning reading skills in a very pleasurable way. Chapters 3 and 4 contain detailed directions on how to implement the language experience approach. However, when the language experience approach is used at home, the child should be involved in some type of interesting experience such as a trip, an art activity, or a cooking or baking activity. Then the child dictates an account of the experience to the family member who transcribes it, using manuscript handwriting on a piece of chart paper or traditional paper. The family member and the child then read the story together aloud while the parent points out interesting sight words, letter names, and other linguistic features found in the story. The child often illustrates the story. After the child has dictated and illustrated several stories, they can be reread and compiled into some type of booklet.

I have worked with many parents who have used the language experience approach very effectively with children as early as three years of age to improve various prereading skills as well as to teach simple beginning reading skills. Most of these parents have reported a high degree of success with the use of this approach. Most preschool children very much enjoy the language experience approach because it is highly motivating and very interesting.

A few children do not enjoy it, however, and therefore this approach should be discontinued after several unsuccessful attempts.

Activities to Improve Visual Discrimination Ability

As is explained in more detail in Chapter 3, visual discrimination ability is a child's ability to differentiate visually between concrete objects, geometric forms, various patterns, letter names, and words. Visual discrimination ability is especially related to success in a beginning reading approach that places heavy emphasis upon sight word recognition.

Activities to improve a preschool child's visual discrimination ability probably can begin with some children around the age of two or three when they group various small objects such as blocks by an attribute such as color. Children of this age also usually enjoy scribbling on a chalkboard or a large sheet of paper.

Older preschool children can engage in somewhat more difficult visual discrimination activities such as discriminating between various geometric forms, copying geometric forms from models, and reproducing geometric forms from memory. Parents can also encourage dot-to-dot exercises on the chalkboard and other types of chalkboard activities. Parents may wish older preschool children who seem interested to discriminate between various letters and between various words. Here are several examples of this type of activity:

w	bwc
d	ddb
cat	cat jump baKe
stop	stop spot stop

Activities to Improve Auditory Discrimination Ability

As is explained in more detail in Chapter 3, auditory discrimination ability is a child's ability to discriminate between various environmental sounds, between the phonemes (sounds) contained in words, and between various entire words. Auditory discrimination ability is very much related to success in a beginning reading program that puts heavy stress on phonic analysis.

When the typical preschool child is about three years of age, the parent can take him or her on a walk around the neighborhood to listen for various environmental sounds such as the wind blowing, dogs barking, birds singing, or the movement of traffic. The parent also can purchase one or more of the commercial records containing various environmental sounds that are mentioned in Chapter 3. However, perhaps better, the parent can make cassette tape recordings of various sounds that the child is to identify, such as running water, a door closing, the sound of sandpaper, or any other common household sounds. A cassette tape recording for older children can require the child to discriminate between sounds of varying intensity and pitch.

When the typical preschool child is about four years of age, a family member can present the auditory discrimination skill of rhyming words. Usually this concept will have to be demonstrated to the child as he or she has no understanding of the term *rhyming*. Nonsense words are acceptable for this activity also. Here are several examples:

bump, dump, fump, hump, lump, mump, pump, sump, tump
bat, cat, dat, fat, hat, lat, mat, pat, rat, sat, tat, vat

Although many parents may not wish to do so, a parent can help the child learn to discriminate between various sounds (phonemes) and between various words. As is indicated later in this chapter, this is an area that has been overemphasized by parents with preschool children. Therefore, you should indicate to parents that they should approach this area with caution.

Activities to Promote Initial Reading Skills

There are a number of activities that promote initial reading skills that undoubtedly could be included in other categories as well. The parent can teach the older preschool child to recognize his or her first name by sight and subsequently to print it in correct lowercase manuscript letters. Most children learn to print their first names at home but do so in uppercase (capital) letters as in this example.   JANE
They then must relearn to print their names in kindergarten, sometimes much to their disgust. Normally it is better for the preschool child to learn to do it correctly at home. Here is a copy of the uppercase and lowercase letters written correctly in the way in which they are taught in most, but not all, contemporary kindergarten classrooms:

Aa Bb Cc Dd Ee Ff Gg Hh Ii

Jj Kk Ll Mm Nn Oo Pp Qq Rr

Ss Tt Uu Vv Ww Xx Yy Zz

The parent also can present by association first the lowercase letter names and subsequently the uppercase letter names. Most parents teach their preschool child the "alphabet song" at home. Although this procedure is acceptable, it is much better for the parent to teach the preschool child to associate each letter name with its printed counterpart. Normally only one or two letter names should be presented at a time, with considerable repetition to ensure that the child remembers them. At the beginning stages of this instruction, it probably is most effective to teach the child the letter names that are in his or her own first name. There is no one sequence for teaching the letter names that has been found to be the most effective. However, usually it may be better for the parent to teach the lowercase letter names first and the uppercase letter names later.

Several research studies have found that letter-name knowledge is the most predictive factor of subsequent primary-grade reading achievement.[8],[9] This is probably the case because the child who learns the letter names effectively often has a good linguistic aptitude that makes all reading-related tasks fairly easy. He or she probably also lives in a home environment that emphasizes learning to read. At the same time, I recommend teaching the letter names by association to older preschool children who evidence interest in this activity because letter-name knowledge is helpful in any beginning reading program to a greater or lesser extent.

Some preschool children around the age of four are ready to learn some interesting words by sight. They frequently learn such words by exposure to them on television or by asking questions about words that their family members answer. Words such as these are quite typically recognized by older preschool children: *STOP, McDonald's, K-Mart, Hardees, Santa Claus, Christmas,* and *ice cream.* They also may recognize the names of other stores or can labels. Older preschool children also can learn sight words at home from language experience stories by the use of a word bank, as is explained in Chapter 4. Parents are very much encouraged to develop their child's interest in learning words by sight at home, for the child then will retain these words on school entrance and will not have to learn them by another technique such as phonic analysis.

Manipulative Activities

There are a limitless number of manipulative activities that parents can encourage their preschool child to engage in at home that mainly are designed to improve his or her fine motor coordination. Some of these art activities also can be used along with language experience stories. As an example, the child either can illustrate a dictated language experience story or he or she can do the illustration first and then dictate one or several sentences about it.

---

[8]Donald D. Durrell, Alice Nicholson, Arthur B. Olson, Sylvia R. Gauel, and Eleanor B. Linehan, "Success in First-Grade Reading," *Journal of Education, 140* (February 1958): 1–49.

[9]Guy L. Bond and Robert Dykstra, "The Cooperative Research Program in First-Grade Reading Instruction," *Reading Research Quarterly, 2* (Summer 1967): 5–141.

One art activity that preschool children have enjoyed very much is drawing letters and words in instant chocolate pudding on a shiny type of paper such as butcher paper. Many of the preschool children that my students have worked with have found this to be a favorite at-home activity. They have enjoyed licking their fingers as much as they have enjoyed drawing in the pudding!

There are many other art activities that can be used at home with preschool children. Here are a few of them: fingerpainting on shiny butcher paper, drawing on a chalkboard, construction activities, using colored chalk, using water colors, cutting and pasting activities, and making collages. In fact, there are as many creative art activities that can be used with preschool children as there are creative parents.

Older preschool children also may enjoy and benefit from various types of tracing activities of the letter names of sight words. They can trace over glitter letters that have been sprinkled over glue, trace over sandpaper letters, trace over felt letters, or use a sand tray or salt tray.

Cooking and Baking Activities

One type of activity that parents often do not consider as a pre-reading activity consists of cooking and baking activities. However, these activities improve the child's experiential background, help him or her carry out directions, and pave the way for subsequent creative reading in school.

Sometimes a family member can write a simple recipe on a piece of tagboard or on a sheet of paper. The child then can be helped in reading and following this simple recipe. Often the simplified recipe can contain rebuses (pictures) for some of the ingredients in the recipe that otherwise would be too difficult for the child to read. Here is an example of a simple recipe for deviled eggs containing rebuses that an older preschool child can read and follow with help:

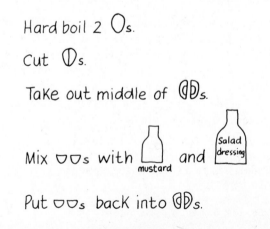

Older preschool children are able to participate in numerous cooking and baking activities at home with some parental supervision and help. Here are some of the activities that my students have used successfully with older preschool children: baking and frosting cupcakes, only frosting cupcakes, baking cookies from scratch or from a mix, boiling and dyeing Easter eggs, carving a jack-o'-lantern, baking pumpkin seeds, making deviled eggs, baking bread, making instant pudding, and making letters from pretzel dough.

Writing Activities

As has been mentioned previously, a chalkboard in the home is a very useful device for a preschool child. The child of two or three can begin scribbling on it and making the lines and circles that later will form the manuscript letters. A chalkboard is equally useful when the child is beginning to print his or her first name and other sight words that he or she can recognize. The chalkboard often is a better alternative than a large sheet of paper because it offers the young child a better opportunity to use the large muscles.

When the older preschool child seems to have adequate fine motor skills, he or she can be taught to print his or her first name. As was mentioned earlier, the parent should provide the child with a correct model of his or her first name by using lowercase manuscript letters, with the exception of the uppercase first letter. If possible, the child should learn to print his or her first name on the chalkboard first. Later the child can practice it on a sheet of paper or label drawings that he or she has made. Although some children are ready to learn how to print their first name at the age of four, this is not true of all of them. Some cannot make much progress in this activity until the age of five.

If the preschool child seems to have very good fine motor coordination, the parent may want to have him or her learn to print the lowercase letters, the uppercase letters, and sight words that he or she can recognize or is learning to recognize. Sometimes writing the letter names or sight words can help the older preschool child to retain them, for it seems to add a kinesthetic reinforcement to the learning.

Physical Activities

Although physical activities are often recommended as one means of improving a preschool child's overall reading readiness, it should be stated that research has not found a conclusive relationship between competency in various physical activities and the child's subsequent success in primary-grade reading. Yet I recommend that parents encourage their preschool children to engage in appropriate physical activities for several reasons. Perhaps the most important one is that the typical child very much enjoys physical activities. Then, too, it may be that physical activities help develop the child's motor coordination and hand-eye coordination, which may, in turn, develop his or her visual perception ability.

Here are some physical activities that older preschool children can do with parental supervision: throw and catch a large ball, throw and catch a beanbag, run, jump, hop, skip, and use a balance beam in various ways.

Some Other Suggestions for Parents

Parents can be given several other suggestions that may aid in their child's subsequent degree of success in primary-grade reading.

As much as possible, the parents should encourage and satisfy their child's natural curiosity. It is very typical for preschool children to ask such questions as these: "Why is the sky blue?" "Why is grass green?" It is especially important that the parents try to answer the child's spontaneous questions about letters and words conscientiously.

A parent should, of course, attempt to provide the preschool child with adequate nutrition and rest. Unfortunately, that is not always done, and the lack of these essentials is found not only in culturally different homes. It is not uncommon for a preschool child to have inadequate rest in a middle-class home. For example, when the movie *Helter Skelter,* the story of Charles Manson's life, was broadcast in a large Midwestern city from ten until midnight on a school night, many kindergarten children apparently were allowed to stay up and watch it.

Any home activities that promote self-reliance, persistence, and a sense of responsibility will help to promote the child's subsequent reading success. Reading is a very difficult developmental task for many young children, and it requires a high degree of persistence for success.

Here is the most important advice that can be given to parents of preschool children about improving prereading skills and presenting beginning reading skills in the home: Keep the sessions very brief, informal, and interesting. If your child seems disinterested in any activity, switch to another activity or forget about the sessions altogether for a while. Make the activities interesting, and help to build your child's self-esteem.

WHAT SHOULD PARENTS OF PRESCHOOL CHILDREN AVOID DOING?

These are some things that parents should avoid:

> Avoid using any type of formal phonics program. Such a program may interfere with the child's school reading program and may cause confusion.

Do not present initial reading skills before the child is four years old. Very few children younger than four benefit from any activities but the most informal prereading activities.

Never pressure a child into any type of prereading or beginning reading activities. The preschool child usually is the best judge of his or her ability to profit from any type of prereading or beginning reading activity.

Never compare a preschool child with his or her siblings or peers. Too many parents want to teach their preschool child to read only so that he or she compares favorably with the children of their friends and neighbors.

SELECTED REFERENCES

Anselmo, Sandra. "Improving Home and Preschool Influences on Early Language Development." *The Reading Teacher, 32* (November 1978): 139–143.

Dallmann, Martha, Roger L. Rouch, Lynette Y. C. Char, and John J. DeBoer. *The Teaching of Reading.* New York: Holt, Rinehart and Winston, 1982.

Flood, James, and Diane Lapp. *Language/Reading Instruction for the Young Child.* New York: Macmillan Publishing Company, Inc., 1981, Chapter 2.

Lapp, Diane, and James Flood. *Teaching Reading to Every Child.* New York: Macmillan Publishing Company, Inc., 1983.

Vukelich, Carol. "Parents Are Teachers: A Beginning Reading Program." *The Reading Teacher, 31* (February 1978): 524–527.

Vukelich, Carol, and Judith A. McAdam. "Mothers' Ability to Predict their Children's Reading Readiness Skills." *The Reading Teacher, 32* (December 1978): 345–347.

Zintz, Miles V. *The Reading Process.* Dubuque, Iowa: William C. Brown Company, Publishers, 1980, Chapters 16, 17.

SUGGESTED ACTIVITIES

1. Select a preschool child of about three or four years of age. Read an appropriate trade book to the child, and ask the child to use one of the prediction strategies included in the chapter.
2. Take a preschool child on an excursion. Follow up the visit with a simple language experience story.
3. View the television program "Sesame Street." Discuss your view of it with some of your peers.
4. Try one of the cooking or baking activities mentioned in the chapter with an older preschool child. If you wish, make a rebus recipe for the experience.

The nursery school and kindergarten reading programs

Why Should This
Have Happened?

During the entire summer, Cindy had
eagerly been anticipating entering Mrs.
Paulson's morning kindergarten class
at Northlakeland School. Although
Mrs. Janowski, Cindy's mother, felt
somewhat guilty because she had not
provided Cindy with as many home
prereading activities as she probably
should have, Mrs. Janowski felt fairly
sure that Cindy was a bright, well-ad-
justed five-year-old child who would
very much enjoy kindergarten and
profit from its many interesting, varied
experiences.

After Cindy had been attending kindergarten for several months, her
mother noticed that she was a little
unhappy on school mornings just before
the school bus arrived. However, Mrs.
Janowski did not think too much about
it. After another month, however, Cindy's mother became very worried when
Cindy began having a stomachache on
many school mornings. She also stated
emphatically each morning that she
did not want to go to kindergarten that
day.

Shortly thereafter, Mrs. Janowski
visited Mrs. Paulson's kindergarten
class and was very surprised to notice
that all of the children were learning
to read by some type of very structured, intensive phonic approach. Although most of the children in the class
seemed to be catching on to the material presented in this program fairly
well, there were about eight children
who did not seem to know what was
going on. Cindy was one of these children. She seemed to be totally unable
to grasp the fairly difficult phonic concepts that were being presented.

Mrs. Janowski was equally surprised to notice that the kindergarten
classroom seemed to be as structured
and rigid as a traditional first-grade
classroom of the past. Mrs. Janowski
had always believed that a kindergarten was a fairly unstructured place
with many enjoyable activities. Mrs.
Paulson also seemed too concerned
about presenting a myriad of phonic
elements and rules really to enjoy
teaching her class of twenty-eight children. Mrs. Janowski wondered if the
phonic program was really worth all of
the effort. She knew that it certainly
was not worth the trouble for Cindy.
All summer long the child had looked
forward to going to kindergarten, and
now she disliked it so much that it
made her ill to go.

Later that morning Mrs. Paulson
explained that the phonic program had
been selected for all of the kindergartens in the school district. She further
explained that Cindy probably did not
have the necessary auditory discrimination ability to profit from the program. Mrs. Janowski asked the
kindergarten teacher what kind of attitude Cindy would have toward school
in several years if she disliked it this
much already. Mrs. Paulson could not
answer that question.

After reading this chapter, you will
know the elements of a kindergarten
reading program that probably would
have motivated Cindy to enjoy school.
This reading program would have enhanced her self-esteem and would have
presented appropriate beginning reading skills.

PRESCHOOL EDUCATION PROGRAMS

There are a number of different types of preschool education programs which are found in our contemporary society. Although it is fairly difficult to differentiate between the various kinds of educational programs that take place before kindergarten, this part of the chapter attempts to describe their history and characteristics very briefly.

The *nursery schools* are one kind of early childhood educational program. The first nursery schools, which were found in the slums of London, England, provided physical, intellectual, social, and emotional care to poor children from three to five years of age. The first nursery school in the United States was the Merrill Palmer School of Motherhood and Home Training, which was located at Columbia University. The first nursery schools in this country emphasized intellectual development.

During the 1920s the idea of nursery school education became somewhat more common in the United States. Most of these private nursery schools were attended by children from affluent families. However, during the depression of the 1930s the federal government provided funding for many nursery schools. Nursery schools also were fairly common during World War II, when a number of mothers worked outside of the home.

Although this usage is by no means universal, the term *nursery school* today generally denotes a type of preschool education for children from about two through four that consumes only part of the day. A nursery school often is privately owned and operated and usually must be licensed. It frequently is run by a private individual, several individuals, or a church. From my observations in a number of different nursery schools, it can be stated that their quality varies from mediocre to very good. A contemporary nursery school often places emphasis on the development of cognitive ability, physical ability, socialization, prereading activities, and other prelearning activities.

Another type of preschool education program is called a *day care center*. The first day care center was established in Paris, France, in 1844. Later, in this country, one was established in 1854. Both were mainly to provide help for working mothers. A day care center cared for the physical needs of children of working mothers from the middle and lower classes. During the late 1930s and early 1940s day care centers began to include some educational programs instead of just caring for the physical needs of the children.

As the term is commonly used today, a day care center is a facility in which a child from infancy through the age of four is cared for, often for an entire day. Some children, for example, arrive at a day care center at six o'clock in the morning and stay until six o'clock in the evening. During the day, the children typically eat several meals, take a nap, engage in play, and may or may not engage in a variety of prelearning activities.

From my observations, the quality of contemporary day care centers varies enormously. Some are merely custodial agencies with very little supervision and less learning. Others are much better. A day care center may be run by a private individual, several individuals, a place of employment, a community agency, or a franchised corporation. No parent ever should place his or her child in a day care center without observing its program very carefully.

Today a few preschool children attend the *Montessori School* in their community. Maria Montessori was a medical doctor who worked with mentally retarded children. In the early twentieth century she began working with poor children. She used sensory/tactile materials with these children and also presented early reading and writing experiences to them. Montessori visited the United States in 1912, and subsequently the American Montessori Association was started here. Later the sensory/tactile materials of Montessori were criticized as being too rigid and structured.

Montessori Schools were not in favor again until the early 1960s. Since then, a number of communities have established these preschools under the direction of specially trained teachers. A Montessori School is very structured and emphasizes sensory/tactile experiences in which the child participates independently to a great extent. Because the tuition at a Montessori School is not inexpensive, these schools usually are attended by children of fairly affluent families.

Other contemporary preschool children attend *Head Start Programs*. Project Head Start was begun in 1965 with federal funds to help economically improverished children attain the cognitive development and experiential background needed for school success. A subsequent program that also was federally funded was *Project Follow Through*. This program was similar to Project Head Start except that it also contained a parent-home aspect. Both of these programs attempted to provide poor, minority preschool children with services that were designed to improve their intellectual, social, nutritional, and medical conditions.

Because both of these programs were started in some instances without a sufficient amount of preplanning, some of the early programs did not achieve their desired results. Perhaps this was especially so because the personnel who staffed these early programs were not very well trained. However, measurement devices such as the 1976 National Assessment of Educational Progress Report found that a number of these programs were having a positive effect on the cognitive development of disadvantaged preschool children. It continues to be important that such programs be monitored very carefully to ensure that the money that is spent on them is well invested.

THE DEVELOPMENT OF PREREADING AND INITIAL READING SKILLS IN PRESCHOOL EDUCATION PROGRAMS

At this point it may be helpful to consider the importance of developing prereading and initial reading skills in any of the preschool education programs that have been described previously.

Prereading and beginning reading activities can be stressed in an informal way in any of the preschool education programs that were mentioned earlier for those children who seem to be ready for them. In most instances, these activities would be similar to the home prereading experiences that were mentioned in Chapter 2. Examples of these activities are reading to the children regularly, excursions for developing experiential background, picture interpretation, oral language and vocabulary improvement, the language experience approach, visual discrimination activities, auditory discrimination activities, teaching the letter names by association, manipulative activities, cooking and baking activities, the recognition and writing of a simple sight words, and enjoyable physical activities.

As in the case of prereading and initial reading activities in the home, any of these activities should be presented on an individual or small-group basis only to those preschool children who are ready for them. These, of course, usually would be older preschool children around the age of four. Any prereading or beginning reading activities in a preschool education program always should be interesting and informal and should promote the child's self-esteem. There obviously is no place in any preschool education program for any kind of formal reading instruction except for a very rare linguistically adept older preschool child. However, even such a child can profit just as well from an informal beginning reading program such as the use of the language experience approach with some instruction in letter-sound relationships.

THE HISTORY OF KINDERGARTEN

Kindergartens as they are known today have a history dating from the early nineteenth century in Germany. The first kindergarten was developed by Friedrich Froebel, and it was based on a religious philosophy that stressed integrating each child with God, nature, and other people. The curriculum included gifts that were manipulative objects to develop sensory and perceptual skills, occupations that were manipulative activities, mother's plays that were songs and games, and nature experiences that involved the child in outdoor activities. Teachers were not allowed to introduce any formal reading, writing, or arithmetic instruction.

Some kindergarten teachers who were trained in Germany immigrated to the United States during the middle nineteenth century. The first kindergarten in the United States was established by Margarette Schurz in Watertown, Wisconsin, in 1855. Other German-American kindergartens were established in this country during the 1850s and the 1860s. However, the first English-speaking kindergarten was established by Elizabeth Peabody in 1860 in Boston. Apparently this kindergarten was mainly established for the socialization of young children.

The kindergartens in the United States from approximately 1920 through 1960 apparently had several purposes. One major purpose was to give the child socialization experiences that would enable him or her to interact more effectively with his or her peers. Unstructured play also comprised an important part of the kindergarten curriculum of that time. Any reading readiness activities that occurred during that time in kindergartens were incidental and informal. Certainly no kind of formal reading instruction ever took place in the typical kindergarten of that era.

When the USSR launched its space satellite *Sputnik* in 1957, this event had a tremendous impact on all American education, as you may have already heard. It compelled American educators to look carefully at our school systems to find ways in which they might be improved. One change was placing more curricula at lower levels than before.

Therefore, more kinds of academic learning began to take place in the typical kindergartens of the 1960s. These, of course, included the teaching of beginning reading skills in kindergarten, often to all children. Kindergartens no longer consisted of a classroom primarily for socialization experiences, but sometimes became like the first grades with a structured curriculum and classroom organization. This has continued into the present, as will be explained in detail shortly.

CHARACTERISTICS OF CONTEMPORARY KINDERGARTENS

It is difficult today to describe a typical kindergarten reading program because there are great differences among the contemporary kindergarten classrooms. However, a few generalizations can be made about them.

Certainly the kindergarten with a main focus on socialization has mainly disappeared from the current scene. Virtually every kindergarten today places some emphasis on the development of reading readiness skills and/or beginning reading skills. The kindergarten in what I call an "intermediate position" stresses reading readiness development, using a vast array of prereading experiences such as those mentioned later in this chapter and in Chapter 2.

In addition, this "intermediate position" classroom also presents beginning reading skills in a predominantly informal way to those children who are ready for it. Such a kindergarten reading program often utilizes the language experience approach and teaches children to remember some sight words as well. Letter names and letter-sound relationships are taught. However, such phonic skills usually are presented in the context of words instead of in isolation. This kind of kindergarten classroom is activity-oriented and emphasizes interesting, varied experiences. It is a classroom in which play and socialization still are important, yet academic learning also is included for those children who are ready for it. This type of kindergarten classroom normally considers the needs and interests of individual children and promotes their self-esteem. In this kind of kindergarten, reading readiness skills and beginning reading skills merge gradually, and it is difficult to determine at what point reading readiness ends and reading instruction begins.

Note: This is the type of kindergarten reading program that is recommended by the writer. She has been privileged to visit a number of such kindergarten classrooms.

On the other hand, there are a number of contemporary kindergartens that are very much like first-grade classrooms. Initial reading instruction is presented in such a classroom to all children whether or not they are ready for it. Sometimes this instruction is by the use of a formal phonic approach such as *Alpha Time* or DISTAR. (See Chapter 7.) However, it also can be by the use of a basal reader series *or* some other type of formal approach.

When such a formal reading program is used in kindergarten, no concern is given to a child's mental maturity or auditory discrimination ability. Instead each child is expected to learn to read by the prescribed program. Some children do learn to read very well in kindergarten from a formal approach. However, other children experience failure from the beginning and learn to dislike all reading-related activities. In this kind of kindergarten there may be limited time for all those informal prereading and beginning reading activities that are really enjoyable for young children. The teacher also is somewhat more inclined to become a more structured teacher in this type of kindergarten classroom simply because of the requirements imposed by the reading program.

Judi Lesiak has reviewed a number of research studies dealing with learning to read in kindergarten. She stated that the research on formal reading instruction in kindergarten is fairly limited, with relatively few studies comparing structured kindergarten reading programs with more traditional or informal kindergarten programs. Lesiak wrote that the research she reviewed indicated that children can and do learn to read in kindergarten. However, she said that the research did not indicate what methods and materials were the most effective for teaching kindergarten reading. Lesiak further emphasized that the research did not suggest that a structured program should be used for teaching reading in kindergarten. She concluded that more research is needed that might determine the longitudinal effects of reading instruction in kindergarten and what types of children benefit the most from this instruction.[1]

CHARACTERISTICS OF TRANSITION CLASSROOMS

Some school districts today have a transition classroom for those children who have completed kindergarten but are not yet ready to enter first grade. These children probably lack the maturity and/or reading readiness skills to succeed in a traditional first-grade classroom. It is felt that it might damage the self-esteem of the children to have them repeat kindergarten. Then, too, some parents become quite disturbed when their kindergarten child "fails sandbox" and may begin to pressure them into succeeding. In addition, the child who repeats kindergarten may have little opportunity to learn the more advanced prereading skills that he or she probably is capable of mastering.

On the other hand, the typical transition classroom takes the child from where he or she is and works intensively to prepare him or her for a traditional first-grade classroom. Usually most of the prereading activities that are mentioned later in this chapter and in Chapter 2 are presented in the transition classroom. In addition, beginning reading skills usually are presented. Sometimes these are the beginning reading skills that are presented by the reading program selected for the school district.

The school districts that have used transition classrooms generally have reported a high degree of success with them. Usually the child then enters first grade well prepared to deal with the reading program and usually is successful with it.

ASSESSING READING READINESS SKILLS

A child's reading readiness skills should be assessed during kindergarten or beginning first grade in order to know which reading readiness skills and/or beginning reading skills should be presented to or reinforced with the student. These skills are visual discrimination,

---

[1]Judi Lesiak, "Reading in Kindergarten: What the Research Doesn't Tell Us," *The Reading Teacher, 32* (November 1978): 135–138.

auditory discrimination, letter-name knowledge, letter-sound relation-ships, sight word knowledge, writing activities, oral language usage, articulation ability, sequential ability, laterality, picture interpreta-tion, motor coordination, and social-emotional adjustment.

Usually it is most effective to try to assess a child's reading readi-ness by both formal and informal means. The formal assessment of reading readiness can involve one or more of the following measures: a reading readiness test, a group or individual intelligence test, a test of visual perception ability, a test of auditory discrimination ability, or a learning methods test. However, the informal assessment of a child's reading readiness usually is equally effective and occurs during an unstructured observation or structured observation, with the use of some kind of checklist by the kindergarten or first-grade teacher.

There are a number of reading readiness tests that are currently in print. Most of these tests should be given to a fairly small group of children—about twelve to fifteen. As young children are not accus-tomed to taking tests, they usually need more supervision than do older children.

Most reading readiness tests measure a child's competency in un-derstanding word and sentence meaning. These skills are evaluated by having the teacher read a definition of a word or a sentence and then asking the child to mark the appropriate picture on the test. Most such tests evaluate a child's auditory or listening comprehension, a skill that is supposed to be related to success in beginning reading. Visual discrimination ability is measured by asking the children to match geometric figures, letters, or words and by asking them to copy a number of geometric figures. Most of the reading readiness tests also evaluate the child's knowledge of the capital and lowercase letters. One reading readiness test evaluates the child's learning rate to de-termine how rapidly he or she can learn to recognize words in an actual beginning reading program.

Most of the reading readiness tests yield subtest scores and some type of total readiness rating. In general, the individual subtest scores usually are not very good predictors of primary-grade reading achieve-ment for individual children. Prediction of primary-grade reading achievement is somewhat better when the total readiness rating is used. Prediction of primary-grade reading achievement is the poorest at either end of the range of scores and is least reliable for children at the low end of the score. This indicates that the total reading read-iness test score can be used with the most confidence for children who receive an average total score.

It also is important to understand that the number of items in any subtest on a reading readiness test is too limited for use in making a diagnosis of the child's competency in that prereading skill. Then, too, a subtest with the same title on one reading readiness test may be quite different from a subtest with the same title on another reading readiness test.

Total reading readiness test scores usually correlate about .60 to .70 with subsequent first-grade reading achievement. In other words, the score from a reading readiness test is a helpful, but not foolproof, predictor. Therefore, it always is absolutely essential to supplement any reading readiness test with some type of careful teacher observation. Structuring the teacher observation by using a checklist such as the one found in this chapter is helpful. A child's score from a reading readiness test *never* should be used as the only criterion for placing a child in a reading group or in a classroom.

The following list of reading readiness tests is not all-inclusive, but is only illustrative of the reading readiness tests currently in use.

CTBS Readiness Test. Monterey, California: California Test Bureau/McGraw-Hill Book Company. This test contains six different subtests. Several of them are letter names, letter sounds, visual discrimination, and sound matching.

Clymer-Barrett Prereading Battery. Princeton, New Jersey: Personnel Press. This test evaluates letter-name knowledge, word matching, discrimination of beginning and ending sounds, form completion, and sentence copying.

First Grade Screening Test. Circle Pines, Minnesota: American Guidance Service. This is a group test for detecting probable learning difficulties. It evaluates intellectual and perceptual abilities as well as social and emotional adjustment.

Gates-MacGinitie Readiness Skills Test. Lombard, Illinois: Riverside Publishing Company. This test evaluates listening comprehension, auditory discrimination, visual discrimination, following directions, letter recognition, visual-motor coordination, auditory blending, and early word recognition.

Harrison-Stroud Reading Readiness Profiles. Lombard, Illinois: Riverside Publishing Company. This test evaluates use of symbols, visual discrimination, context clues, auditory discrimination, use of context, and auditory clues and letter naming.

Macmillan Reading Readiness Test. New York: Macmillan Publishing Company, Inc. The subtests are a quantified rating scale, visual discrimination, auditory discrimination, vocabulary and concepts, letter names, and visual motor skills.

Metropolitan Readiness Tests. New York: The Psychological Corporation. These tests evaluate auditory memory, rhyming, letter recognition, visual matching, school language and listening, and

quantitative language in Level I. They measure beginning consonants, letter-sound correspondences, visual matching, finding patterns, school language, and listening in Level II.

Murphy-Durrell Reading Readiness Analysis. New York: The Psychological Corporation. This test evaluates visual discrimination,
auditory discrimination, letter name knowledge, and learning rate.

In addition to a reading readiness test, a test of visual perception
ability may be given to those children in kindergarten or first grade
who seem to be especially weak in visual perception or visual discrimination ability. The most common such test is as follows:

Frostig Developmental Test of Visual Perception. Monterey, California: Publishers Test Service. This is a group test of five aspects of
visual perception.

In addition, there is a test of auditory discrimination ability for
children who seem to be especially weak in this prereading skill. Here
is this test:

Wepman Auditory Discrimination Test. Palm Springs, California:
Language Research Associates. This evaluates the child's ability to
determine whether two spoken words are the same or slightly different.

A few contemporary school systems use group intelligence tests in
kindergarten or first grade instead of a reading readiness test. An
individual intelligence test also might be used with children who have
probable learning problems. Because intelligence and readiness for
reading seem to be closely related, it is possible to use an intelligence
measure. However, in most instances the writer recommends that a
valid reading readiness test be used for the formal assessment of reading readiness because such a test more closely evaluates the skills
that are required for beginning reading. Intelligence is not generally
considered quite as important in beginning reading as are such reading-related skills as knowledge of letter names and letter sounds. Intelligence does, however, become much more important at the upper
primary-grade level and subsequently, when more abstract intelligence is required for comprehension.

Some kindergarten and first-grade teachers also have the child draw
a figure of a man, woman, boy, or girl to assess a measure of the child's
intelligence. This is an acceptable informal way of doing this. Here is
the name of this test, which can serve as a measure of the child's
nonverbal intelligence:

Goodenough-Harris Drawing Test. New York: The Psychological
Corporation.

Another test that is used by some first-grade teachers contains a series of teaching lessons with subsequent testing to determine the possible appropriateness of the various methods (visual, phonics, kinesthetic, and combination) for the beginning reader. Here is the address of this measure:

Mills Learning Methods Test. Fort Lauderdale, Florida: The Mills Center.

Many reading specialists, including this writer, believe that the typical kindergarten or first-grade teacher can assess a child's reading readiness skills at least as effectively as any standardized reading readiness test. Therefore, it is imperative always to use some type of formal measure and informal teacher observation to evaluate most effectively a child's competency in the various reading readiness skills so that as prescriptive a reading readiness program as possible can then be provided.

Although a teacher can evaluate a child's competency in the various reading skills without using a checklist, a checklist does add some precision to the evaluation of these skills. Therefore, it usually is important, especially for an inexperienced kindergarten or first-grade teacher, to use some type of structured checklist to aid in this evaluation. Good checklists are found in the teachers' manuals of most basal reader series, in most professional books on reading, and in many reading readiness test manuals. One is included in this book (pp. 40–43) that can be used in its present form or modified in any way in which you wish.

It obviously is very important for the kindergarten or first-grade teacher to act upon his or her observation of a child's reading readiness attainment. If the child seems weak in a number of different areas of reading readiness, any type of formal reading program should be postponed until the child attains more prereading skills. However, an informal beginning reading program such as the language experience approach can be used with such a child. Many subsequent cases of reading disability could be prevented if a formal reading program were not begun before children were ready for it. I believe the lack of reading readiness attainment before initial reading instruction to be one of the more common causes of reading problems in the elementary school.

On the other hand, if a child is weak in only one or several of the prereading skills, he or she probably can be presented with a beginning reading program. However, the kindergarten or first-grade teacher should still attempt to help the child improve his or her competency in these prereading skills by using some of the strategies and materials that are included later in this chapter.

Child's Name

CHECKLIST OF READING READINESS ATTAINMENT

	Good	Fair	Poor	No Opportunity to Observe
A. Experiential Background				
1. Seems to have been exposed to a wide variety of firsthand experiences.	____	____	____	____
2. Seems to have heard stories read or told on a regular basis.	____	____	____	____
B. Oral Language and Vocabulary				
1. Is able to speak in complete sentences.	____	____	____	____
2. Is able to speak in compound or complex sentences.	____	____	____	____
3. Usually uses precise descriptive vocabulary terms.	____	____	____	____
4. Can dictate an interesting, individual language experience story.	____	____	____	____
5. Enjoys participating in such activities as sharing time, conversation, role playing, and dramatic play.	____	____	____	____
C. Visual Perception and Discrimination				
1. Is able to discriminate between various geometric forms.	____	____	____	____
2. Is able to discriminate between such letters as *c* and *i* or *b* and *d*.	____	____	____	____
3. Is able to discriminate between such words as *run* and *jump* or *was* and *saw*.	____	____	____	____
4. Understands that reading goes from left to right.	____	____	____	____

    5. Is able to draw an acceptable figure of a man, woman, boy, or girl.   ____   ____   ____   ____

    6. Is able to complete a fifteen- to eighteen-piece puzzle independently.   ____   ____   ____   ____

D. Sight Word Recognition
    1. Is able to recognize about six to eight or more words by sight that are found in his or her daily environment.   ____   ____   ____   ____

    2. Can recognize his or her own first name.   ____   ____   ____   ____

    3. Can recognize most words that are taught by sight one day after they were presented.   ____   ____   ____   ____

E. Auditory Discrimination
    1. Is able to discriminate between environmental sounds of varying pitch and intensity.   ____   ____   ____   ____

    2. Is able to rhyme words.   ____   ____   ____   ____

    3. Is able to discriminate between the various phonemes (sounds).   ____   ____   ____   ____

    4. Is able to discriminate between words that differ by only one phoneme, such as *tub* and *tug*.   ____   ____   ____   ____

F. Letter Names and Letter-Sound Relationships
    1. Is able to give the names of most of the lowercase alphabet letters.   ____   ____   ____   ____

    2. Is able to give the names of most of the uppercase alphabet letters.   ____   ____   ____   ____

    3. Is able to use consonant substitutions, such as changing *bump* to *jump*.   ____   ____   ____   ____

    4. Is able to give the long and short sounds of most of the vowels.   ____   ____   ____   ____

G. Writing Activities
   1. Is able to print his or her own first name correctly.   ___   ___   ___   ___
   2. Is able to copy sight words correctly that he or she can recognize.   ___   ___   ___   ___

H. Sequence Ability
   1. Is able to retell a story in correct sequence that he or she has heard.   ___   ___   ___   ___
   2. Is able to dictate a language experience story in correct sequence.   ___   ___   ___   ___

I. Picture Interpretation
   1. Is able to interpret a picture from a reading readiness workbook or trade book correctly.   ___   ___   ___   ___

J. Laterality
   1. Is able to differentiate between his or her right and left hands.   ___   ___   ___   ___
   2. Is able to differentiate between his or her right and left feet.   ___   ___   ___   ___

K. Motor Coordination
   1. Is able to catch a large ball with ease.   ___   ___   ___   ___
   2. Is able to walk a balance beam.   ___   ___   ___   ___
   3. Is able to jump with both feet off the ground.   ___   ___   ___   ___
   4. Seems generally well-coordinated when playing games.   ___   ___   ___   ___
   5. Is able to use such materials as crayons, scissors, paste, and paint brushes.   ___   ___   ___   ___

L. Social-Emotional Adjustment
   1. Appears to be self-reliant.   ___   ___   ___   ___

2. Is able to follow simple
   directions. ____ ____ ____ ____

3. Appears to have a positive
   self-image. ____ ____ ____ ____

4. Is able to work and play
   well with other children. ____ ____ ____ ____

5. Is able to concentrate on
   something that interests
   him or her for at least
   fifteen minutes. ____ ____ ____ ____

Overall Assessment of Reading Readiness

_____

_____

_____

PREDICTING COMPETENCY IN BEGINNING READING

There have been several research efforts to try to determine those young children who probably will have difficulty with beginning reading skills. Obviously, the purpose of this prediction is to locate such children so that proper intervention strategies can be prescribed for them.

Three researchers chose ten tests that could be given at the kindergarten level to determine a child's readiness for formal learning in school. They discovered that six of these tests could be used to locate the children who would have great difficulty in school by the end of second grade. These six tests were the Bender Visuo-Motor Gestalt Test (a test in which the child reproduces nine geometric figures), the drawing of a human figure, auditory discrimination ability, classifying or placing items in categories, the presence of reversals, and word recognition.[2] According to the researchers, first-grade teachers should be able to learn how to evaluate children by using these tests so that they could use diagnostic-prescriptive instruction of prereading and beginning reading skills.

---

[2]Jeannette Jansky and Katrina DeHirsch, *Preventing Reading Failure* (New York: Harper & Row, Publishers, 1972).

Robert Hillerich also developed a testing procedure for four- and five-year-old children, which he called "Prediction with Diagnostic Qualities" or "PDQ." The test that Hillerich researched evaluated children on these prereading skills: auditory discrimination, listening comprehension, attainment of vocabulary, ability to categorize, ability to use such relationship words as *in* and *on*, picture sequence ability, oral language development, following oral directions, and filling in an omitted word in a sentence by using oral context. Hillerich administered his test to children entering kindergarten. The kindergarten teachers then used the test results in their teaching to try to remove the children's deficits. At the end of first grade, the reading achievement of these children was compared to a control group of first-grade children who were not given the test. Hillerich found that the children who had taken the test and had been exposed to correct diagnostic-prescriptive prereading instruction outperformed the children in the control group.[3]

Since the time of Hillerich's original study, he has revised his test and helped to develop teaching materials that are designed to present and reinforce those reading skills in which a child has been found to lack competency. The skills that Hillerich and others assess and reinforce are as follows: auditory discrimination ability, instructional language, following oral directions, listening comprehension, sequencing, oral language development, general vocabulary, categorizing, using oral context, and letter form discrimination. The program is called *Ready Steps* and includes a test, a game box, many different types of cards, a poster pad, an activity pad, duplicating masters, and a teacher's guide. The entire program is published by Houghton Mifflin Company.

DEVELOPING READING READINESS AND INITIAL READING SKILLS IN KINDERGARTEN AND FIRST GRADE

This part of the chapter provides strategies and materials for improving competency in the major prereading and beginning reading skills. In addition, each of these skills is defined in some detail in this chapter. However, you will notice that the strategies contained in this chapter overlap in some cases with the home prereading activities that were included in Chapter 2. Many of these activities are equally applicable for use at school.

[3]Robert L. Hillerich, "A Diagnostic Approach to Early Identification of Language Skills," *The Reading Teacher, 31* (January 1978): 357–363.

Developing an Experiential Background

It is important for the kindergarten child to have as rich an experiential background as is possible. This is very important so that the child can effectively interpret the reading material found in basal readers, trade books, and other sources. Without a rich experiential background, the child will have great difficulty effectively comprehending the reading material. The development of a good experiential background is especially important for a child from a culturally different home environment because this child may not have participated in the type of experiences that are typically found in the middle-class home and often are required for successful comprehension of reading material at school.

Here are some techniques and materials for improving a child's experiential background in kindergarten and beginning first grade.

> Read or tell an interesting story to the class at least once each school day. This is extremely important in building an interest in learning to read and in developing improved linguistic ability.
>
> Take the class on as many educationally worthwhile school excursions as possible. Such excursions can be to places like a farm, a dairy, a shopping center, a zoo, a police station, a fire station, the post office, a museum, a bakery, the children's section of the local public library, the airport, a pet shop, and a grocery store. Before taking the trip, discuss what may be seen and later have a follow-up discussion. These two discussions should emphasize vocabulary development as much as possible.
>
> Acquire one or more classroom pets such as fish, turtles, hamsters, or gerbils for the children to observe, to learn about, and to care for.
>
> Have interest centers in the classroom where the children can work independently or in small groups. Interest centers can include a library corner, an arithmetic corner, a science corner, a writing center, listening posts, games, and many different types of toys.
>
> All types of cooking and baking activities are very good for improving experiential background. A number of contemporary elementary schools have a kitchen which can be used for this purpose. Appropriate activities for kindergarten include baking cookies, baking gingerbread men, making instant pudding to use for painting, baking cupcakes, frosting commercial cupcakes, making peanut brittle, and making fudge. A very interesting suggestion in this area is the making of "Frosted Funnies." The recipe for these is found in the book *The Little Witch's Black Magic Cookbook*.[4]
>
> The children can view films, filmstrips, videotapes, and slides in various areas to improve their experiential background.

---

[4]Linda Glovach, *The Little Witch's Black Magic Cookbook* (Englewood Cliffs, New Jersey: Prentice-Hall, 1972).

The children can listen to records and cassette tape recordings to build experiential background. A typical child in kindergarten can learn to operate a cassette tape recorder independently after a period of some instruction.

Commercial kits such as the following can be used to improve experiential background:

Ready Steps. Boston: Houghton Mifflin Company.

Peabody Language Development Kit. Circle Pines, Minnesota: American Guidance Service.

Happily Ever After. Reading, Massachusetts: Addison-Wesley Publishing Company, Inc.

Improving Oral Language and Vocabulary

Competency in oral language and a rich meaning vocabulary are very important to a child's subsequent success in first-grade reading. A child who does not have a good mastery of oral language and a good meaning vocabulary normally will have some difficulty in beginning reading skills. The child from a culturally different environment or a minority group or the bilingual child is quite likely to be rather weak in both oral language usage and meaning vocabulary. The slow-learning child also usually has difficulty with these two skills. Normally, then, these groups of children need to have great emphasis placed on oral language development and meaning vocabulary development in kindergarten if they are to make the optimum amount of progress in primary-grade reading. Here are some activities to improve competency in oral language and develop a larger meaning vocabulary.

Have one child dictate a language experience story, or have a small group of children dictate a language experience chart. Detailed directions for using the language experience approach are found in Chapter 4.

Have one-to-one conversations with each child whenever possible. These individual conversations also help in building the child's self-esteem.

It is especially important that culturally different children be given a program of planned sequential verbal bombardment.

Use picture books that match language symbols and illustrations to present meanings of words and phrases. They are especially useful with non-English-speaking children. Some of these books that repeat language patterns are especially useful. An article by Margaret Moustafa has an excellent list of picture books that can be used for oral language development.[5]

Have small groups of children engage in activities such as sharing time, conversations, role playing, dramatic play, and creative dramatics.

[5]Margaret Moustafa, "Picture Books for Oral Language Development for Non-English Speaking Children: A Bibliography, *The Reading Teacher, 33* (May 1980): 914–919.

Teach the child to speak into a cassette tape recorder and then listen to the recording. Most kindergarten children very much enjoy learning to operate a cassette tape recorder.

Teach the child to use the oral cloze procedure. Give a sentence orally with an omitted word, and have the child supply any word that makes sense in the sentence. Here is an example: Jimmy would like to have a ＿＿＿ for his birthday.

All the direct experiences such as school excursions and all the vicarious experiences such as the use of multimedia aids, which were mentioned in the preceding section, usually are very good for vocabulary improvement if this skill is carefully stressed as part of the experience.

According to an article by Carol Lauritzen, oral literature makes an excellent transition from being a listener to being a reader in first grade. To use this method first present a story, poem, or song to the children. Then the children are invited to join in. Next the material can be presented to the children either on a chart or in a duplicated form, and they are asked to read along. If able, they then read the material on their own.[6]

Improving Visual Perception and Discrimination

Although there are some differences between the terms *visual perception* and *visual discrimination,* a number of reading specialists use the two terms interchangeably. However, theoretically there is a slight difference between the two terms. *Visual perception* may be defined as selecting and organizing the sensory data that a person receives visually. On the other hand, *visual discrimination* may be defined as differentiating between the likenesses and differences in words, letters, geometric forms, or various kinds of patterns. Visual discrimination is sometimes thought of as part of the larger concept of visual perception.

Two other terms that are sometimes used in this area of prereading skills are body image and laterality. *Body image* may be defined as the child's knowledge of his or her body parts, such as head, eyes, ears, mouth, nose, trunk, arms, and legs. *Laterality* may be defined as the child's knowledge of the left and right sides of the body, for example, knowing the left and right hands and the left and right feet.

There have been many research studies on the relation between visual perception training and success in reading readiness and primary-grade reading. Very briefly, it seems that training in visual perception usually does not influence reading readiness attainment or primary-grade reading achievement significantly. However, visual discrimination activities that are reading-related, such as discriminating between letters and between words, seem to be more important than less reading-related activities, such as discriminating between geometric forms.

I believe that visual perception and discrimination activities that are not truly reading-related may be acceptable as *a beginning point* for those students who are very weak in this area. Therefore, the strategies and materials that are included in this section are presented in a generally easy-to-difficult sequence. If the child appears very weak in visual perception and/or visual discrimination ability, you should select suggestions from the early part of the strategies. On the other hand, if the child appears more confident in this area, you should select ideas from the latter half of the list.

Make templates to help the child learn to draw such geometric figures as a circle, a square, a rectangle, and a triangle. To make a template, take a piece of cardboard or plywood, and draw the geometric figure on it. Then cut the figure out. Have the child place the template on a piece of paper and trace around it to make the geometric form.

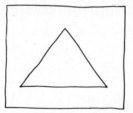

After the child has traced geometric figures for some time, have the child copy them from models and later reproduce them from memory. You can use such geometric figures as a circle, a square, a rectangle, triangles, and diamond shapes.

Draw some simple, incomplete pictures on the chalkboard or on a duplicating master. Have the child complete each incomplete picture. You can use such pictures as a cat without a tail, a house without a chimney, a person without a head, or a tree without a trunk.

Have the child work with parquetry blocks to improve visual discrimination ability.

Show the child several examples of geometric forms that have been constructed out of tagboard. Then cover them and have the child tell the shapes in the order in which they were presented.

Have the child attempt to assemble simple and then somewhat more difficult jigsaw puzzles. A puzzle containing only four pieces may be sufficient for a child in nursery school or kindergarten who has very poor visual discrimination ability. However, a typical child in kindergarten should be able to assemble a jigsaw puzzle consisting of ten to fifteen pieces. You can make your own simple puzzle by locating a picture, pasting it on a piece of very heavy cardboard or very light plywood, and cutting it into as many pieces as you wish.

Have the child use pegboards to improve visual discrimination ability.

Have the child string beads of various colors. You can give the child simple drawings to follow in the bead stringing. For example, draw three red circles, two blue circles, and three green circles on a sheet of paper, and ask the child to reproduce this pattern by following the model.

Have the child use the chalkboard for various types of chalkboard exercises to improve visual perception and visual discrimination. Some examples are copying and drawing geometric figures, dot-to-dot exercises, and completing incomplete figures.

Have the child participate in all types of tracing, cutting, and pasting activities. Most types of art-related activities are beneficial in developing the child's visual perception ability.

Have the child learn to use the balance beam to improve motor coordination. You can buy a commercial balance beam or construct one out of a piece of wood. The child can use the balance beam in several ways such as walking heel-to-toe forward and backward.

Have the child practice figure-ground relationships by placing some simple figures embedded in a ground on the chalkboard or on an activity sheet. Then have the child locate and color in the figure. This is supposed to be related to reading because on a printed page each word is considered to be a figure and the background on the page is considered to be the ground.

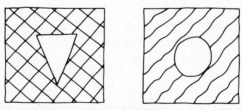

Have the child throw and catch different sizes of balls and beanbags.

To develop visual perception ability, select a ball about the size of a baseball. Suspend this ball at eye level from the wall, and begin to swing it slowly. Have the child follow the swinging ball with his or her eyes. Such a type of swinging ball is called a Marsden ball.

Have the child attempt to combine the various geometric forms such as a circle, square, rectangle, and triangle into various types of pictures.

Have the child make his or her own body into the shape of a letter. Obviously, letters such as *t, c, i,* and *l* are especially useful in this activity.

Construct a small obstacle course in the gym or outside that the child must use. Such an obstacle course can involve the use of a balance beam, boxes, chairs, or inner tubes.

Place some nonlook-alike letters on the chalkboard or on an activity sheet, and have the child place an *X* on the letter that is different. Here are several examples of this type of activity:

w   e   w w
l   l   a l

Place some look-alike letters on the chalkboard or on an activity sheet, and have the child place an *X* on the letter that is different. Here are several examples of this type of activity:

b   b   b d
g   q   g g

Place some nonlook-alike words on the chalkboard or on an activity sheet, and have the child place an *X* on the word that is different. Here are several examples of this type of activity:

run   pen run   run
jump   hit   jump jump

Place some look-alike words on the chalkboard or on an activity sheet, and have the child place an *X* on the word that is different. Here are several examples of this type of activity:

saw   saw saw was
stop   spot stop stop

Have the child print simple scrambled words in correct order. Here are several examples of this type of activity:

nur   run
edb   bed

Improving Auditory Discrimination Ability

There are several terms that are somewhat related to the general area of auditory discrimination ability. *Auditory discrimination* may be defined as the ability to discriminate between the likenesses and differences in the phonemes (sounds) that are heard in words. Another somewhat related term is *auditory synthesis,* which is the blending of a series of sounds into a recognizable word. On the other hand, *auditory memory* or *auditory span* may be defined as concentration on and then imitation or reproduction of sound sequences such as tapping, numbers, or words.

There have been a number of research studies on the relationship between auditory discrimination ability and success in primary-grade reading. Very briefly, it can be stated that competency in auditory discrimination usually is very important to success in any type of formal phonic program. (See Chapter 6.) It is probably also equally crucial to success in any basal reader approach that places considerable emphasis on phonic analysis as a word identification technique. (See Chapter 5.)

Normally if a child in kindergarten or beginning first grade appears to be very weak in auditory discrimination ability, it is best not to expose such a child to any type of program that places great stress on letter-sound relationships at the beginning stages of reading. Instead it is usually better to place more stress on sight word recognition with such a child while attempting to improve his or her auditory discrimination ability if possible.

It also is important to note that children who speak a nonstandard dialect such as the black dialect were thought in the past to be usually very weak in auditory discrimination ability. However, it is now known that most traditional auditory discrimination tests are biased against the dialect of such children and do not present a true picture of their auditory discrimination ability.

The strategies that are included in this section for the improvement of auditory discrimination ability are presented in a generally easy-to-difficult sequence. If a child appears very weak in auditory discrimination ability, you can select ideas from the early part of the list. However, if the child seems to have more competency in the area, you can select ideas from the latter part of the list.

Take the group of children on what can be called a "sensitizing experience" to promote auditory awareness. Have the children listen for various environmental sounds such as a bird singing, the wind blowing, or the sound of traffic.

Read nursery rhymes and other books with rhyming patterns, such as Dr. Seuss books, to a group of children. Have them listen for and subsequently repeat the rhyming patterns that are found in this material.

Obtain some pictures that represent minimal pairs or words that differ by only one phoneme. Place each pair of pictures on a table or desk, and ask the child to locate the one of the two pictures whose word you pronounce. For example, from the pair *man* and *pan*, ask the child for the pan.

Have the child practice rhyming words. You probably will have to illustrate this concept to the child as he or she otherwise may not know what the term *rhyme* means. Nonsense words also are acceptable for this activity. Here is an example:

bump, dump, fump, hump, lump, mump, pump, and sump.

Show the child or a small group of children several objects. Have the child indicate the one object that begins with a different sound from the other objects. Here are some objects for the phoneme /b/: ball, balloon, doll, bell, or button.

Have a group of children play a picture-name matching game. Put pictures in the chalk tray along the chalkboard. Have a child name one of the pictures (rat), and have another child find a picture whose name rhymes (bat).

Have the child formulate rhymes, using the names of people and rhyming them with other words. Here is an example:

I saw Bill.
Take a pill.

Formulate some two-line rhymes, and have the child complete each rhyme orally. Here are several examples:

Jim is a very fine boy.
For his birthday he would like a new_____.
I am sorry that the red baby fox
Got caught in that big _____.
Look at my black cat.
He is trying to catch that big _____.

This activity can be recorded on tape. Pronounce a list of words, and have the child indicate the one word in the list that begins with a different sound from the others. For example, here is a list of words for the phoneme /m/: *man, mother, money, neighbor, monkey, moon,* and *mine.*

Have a group of children indicate if their first name begins with the same sound as that of a word such as *mother.* They can indicate this by standing up, raising a hand, or clapping their hands. Children with names such as Mary, Mark, Marty, and Marilyn would make a response to the word *mother.*

Select some pictures from a picture file. Have a small group of children identify the pictures that begin or end with a certain sound.

Have a small group of children name objects that they can see in the classroom that begin or end with a certain sound. Objects in the classroom for the phoneme /d/ might be a door, a desk, a doll, or a dish.

Have a group of children make a bulletin board for a sound in the initial or final position. Have the children cut out or draw objects for that sound and label the pictures. As an example, pictures for the sound /b/ might be a ball, a balloon, a boy, a baby, or a bell.

Ask a child to give some words that begin with the same sound as his or her first name. For example, a child named David might give the words *did, donkey, doll, do,* and *dish.*

Show the child a number of pictures, and have him or her point out each picture that begins with a certain phoneme such as /t/.

This activity can be recorded on tape. Present pairs of words, and ask the child whether the words are alike or different. Here are some word pairs that can be used in this activity:

tub—tug
like—like

This activity can be recorded on tape. Present pairs of words, and have the child state if they begin with the same sound. Here are several examples of this activity:

> run—red
>
> pump—tent

This activity can be recorded on tape. Present pairs of words, and have the child state if they end with the same sound. Here are several examples of this activity:

> bump—lip
>
> dog—wish

Make some letter cards out of tagboard. Blindfold a child, and have the child select a letter card. Remove the blindfold, and ask the child to give a word beginning with that letter. If the child is correct, the card can be kept. The child that has the most cards at the end of the activity wins.

There are a myriad of materials that can be used to improve auditory discrimination ability. These materials are in the form of cassette tape recordings, records, duplicating masters, and filmstrips. The following list of commercial materials is not all-inclusive but rather just illustrative of the types of commercial materials that are available.

> *Auditory Training*. Chicago: Greystone. This is a group of records.
>
> *Gateway to Good Reading*. Kankakee, Illinois: Imperial Publishing Company. This is a tape-centered program with student activity sheets.
>
> *Auditory Perception Records*. San Rafael, California: Academic Therapy. These are three records.
>
> *Auditory Discrimination in Depth*. Boston: Teaching Resources. This is a training program.
>
> *Sounds Around Us*. Glenview, Illinois: Scott, Foresman and Company. These are records.
>
> *Sounds for Young Readers*. New York: Educational Record Sales. This is an album of three records.

Left-to-Right Progression

Left-to-right progression is a prereading skill in which the child is aware of the fact that in the English language print is read from left to right. It is a skill that most children in kindergarten should be able to accomplish.

Here are several strategies that can be used to improve ability in left-to-right progression.

> Make a cumulative class calendar that can be placed on a bulletin board. This calendar can be on a seasonal theme each month. For example, in October each date can be placed on a pumpkin made of orange construction paper. A different child each day can have the job of placing the date in the correct place on the calendar. The teacher can use this type of calendar to demonstrate clearly left-to-right progression. An alternative is a weather calendar in which an illustration of the proper weather for the day is placed on the calendar, such as an illustration of the sun, clouds, an umbrella, or a snowman.

Show children with your hand that reading begins on the left-hand side of the page of a book or an experience chart when you read aloud to them.

Place a red mark on the left-hand side of the paper on which the child is printing letters or words to show him or her that the left side is the starting point.

Select a comic strip and cut it apart. Have the child place it in left-to-right sequence. If you wish, it is helpful to paste each frame of the comic strip to a piece of cardboard and then laminate it.

Sequential Ability

Sequential ability is the child's ability to retell a story in sequence that has been read or told to him or her, or orally to place a number of steps in correct sequence. This is a very difficult prereading skill for the average child in kindergarten to master. Therefore, it is usually best to begin by placing only two or three steps in correct sequence and later progressing to several more steps.

Here are several strategies that can be used to improve ability in sequential competency:

Select a comic strip that illustrates good sequence and cut it apart. Paste or glue each frame of the comic strip to a piece of cardboard, and laminate it so it will be more durable. Have the child put the cut-apart comic strip in correct sequence. If you wish, the child can also tell the story of the comic strip as he or she is placing it in correct sequence.

Take the class or a group of children on an excursion or trip. Have the children dictate a language experience chart stressing correct sequential order of the events that happened during the experience.

Select a series of pictures that illustrate some type of event that can be placed in correct sequential order. Have the child then place this series of pictures in correct sequence, telling the story from the picture as he or she does so.

Have the child tell about a personal experience such as getting ready for school in the morning or getting ready for bed in the evening. Such a personal experience should be recounted in correct sequence.

Laterality

Laterality is the child's ability to differentiate between the left and the right sides of his or her body. Here are some strategies for improving competency in this prereading skill:

Have the children play the game "Simon Says," in which they are given directions for discriminating between the left and right sides of their body, such as left and right hands and left and right feet.

Have the child show knowledge of the left and right hands by raising the proper hand, or snapping the fingers on the proper hand.

Have the child show knowledge of the left and right feet by hopping on the designated foot or raising the designated leg.

Letter-Name Knowledge and Sight Word Recognition

It is important for children in kindergarten to learn both the lowercase and uppercase letter names by association. It is helpful in most beginning reading approaches for the child to have a name to call a letter so that it can be referred to conveniently. Letter-name knowledge also is quite predictive of success in primary-grade reading, partly because the child with good linguistic aptitude learns the letter names quite easily and goes on to learn to read quite easily. Although there is nothing particularly wrong with learning the alphabet letter names by rote as is done in the alphabet song, it is better for the child in kindergarten to learn both the lowercase and uppercase letter names by association. There is no one sequence that has been found by research to be the best for teaching the letter names. However, it generally is better to present the lowercase letter names first and the uppercase letter names later.

It is also helpful for the child in kindergarten to learn some words by sight. These can be environmental words such as those found on stores, restaurants, signs, or can labels. The kindergartner should also always learn his or her first name by sight. Language experience stories and charts also are a useful vehicle for the learning of words by sight. (See Chapter 4.) Labels that are placed in the kindergarten room—such as those on the door, a desk, or a table—also are useful in teaching sight words.

Here are some strategies for improving competency in letter-name knowledge and sight word recognition:

Use various tracing techniques to help the child learn the letter names such as felt letters, sandpaper letters, a sand tray, a salt tray, or glitter letters that are sprinkled over glue. The child can say the letter names as he or she traces them in any one of these media.

Use colored chalk to teach both difficult-to-remember letter names and sight words. Have the child choose his or her favorite color of chalk. Then write the letter name or sight word on the chalkboard. Have the child trace over the letter name or word, using the index finger and saying it aloud. Later the child can copy and subsequently write from memory the letter name or word.

Make letter pockets or word pockets out of strips of tagboard. Cut slits that will hold a letter card or a word card. Have the child look through a pile of letters or sight words that have been made from small pieces of tagboard. The child is to slip each letter card or word card into the strip of tagboard that matches it.

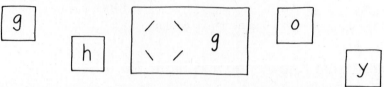

Use letter wheels to help the child learn to match the letter names. To do so, make two circles of tagboard, and laminate them for durability. Cut a window in the top circle, and write a letter name next to the window. Print letter names around the edge of the bottom circle. Put the two circles together with a brad. Have the child match the letters by turning the bottom wheel.

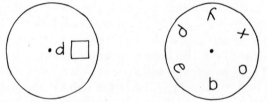

Teach the child to use picture clues by having a picture of an object and the printed symbol of that object on the same card.

If possible, have the child attempt to copy in manuscript handwriting each word that he or she is attempting to remember by sight.

Have the child construct a sight word card holder by stapling a piece of felt to a piece of cardboard about typing paper size. The surface of the felt will hold the sight word cards, which are made of tagboard, in place.

Have the children make a word bank in which to place their sight words. The word bank can be a metal file box, a shoe box, or some other type of container. Print each sight word on a piece of tagboard. The child then can place all of the sight words in the word bank and review them periodically. For more details on the use of a word bank, see Chapter 4.

Have the child or a small group of children make alphabet pretzels. Here is the recipe:[7]

1 cup lukewarm water	2 tsp. sugar
1 cake active yeast or	¾ tsp. salt
1 package dry yeast	
4½ cups all-purpose flour	1 egg yolk beaten with 1 tbsp. water

1. Preheat oven to 475°. Grease cookie sheet.
2. Combine water, yeast, and sugar. Let stand until yeast is dissolved.
3. Combine flour, sugar, and salt. Add to yeast mixture to form stiff dough.
4. Turn dough out onto floured counter and knead 8–10 minutes or until it is smooth and elastic.

---

[7]Carl Braun and Allen R. Neilsen, *First Steps to Reading* (Calgary, Canada: Braun and Braun Educational Enterprises, Ltd., 1980), pp. 65–66.

5. Oil a large bowl. Turn dough in bowl to oil both sides. Cover with clean damp cloth.
6. Let rise in warm place until double in size.
7. Punch down and shape into letters.
8. Place on cookie sheet. Baste each pretzel with egg yolk mixture. Sprinkle with salt.
9. Let rise again until almost double.
10. Bake for ten minutes until golden brown and firm.

Take a piece of tagboard, and fold and cut it as shown. Make a flip card so the child can match letter names. Place a happy face under the flip tab with the correct letter.

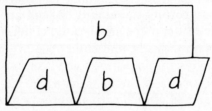

Improving Motor Coordination

Although research has not clearly established a relationship between a child's competency in motor coordination and his or her degree of success in primary-grade reading, physical activities are still recommended for most children in kindergarten. The vast majority of children enjoy physical activities, and they are good for them. Therefore, such activities can do no harm and may well be beneficial for children.

Here are some physical activities that can be used with children of this age:

running
galloping
jumping
walking a balance beam forward and backward
skipping
running an obstacle course
relays
Angels on the Mat
hopping
throwing and catching a large ball

Improving Social-Emotional Adjustment

Many of the daily activities included in the regular kindergarten program will help the child to attain the social-emotional adjustment that is important to successful reading achievement. Normally, no special activities need to be planned for this purpose. However, it is important to remember that learning to read is a difficult developmental task for most young children. Therefore, any activities that promote the child's self-reliance, persistence, sense of responsibility, and curiosity are useful.

However, here are some guidelines that you may want to consider:

Give children the opportunity to be responsible for their own behavior within the limits of their ability to do so.

Plan activities that will enable each child to experience success. This is especially important in building the self-image of culturally different, immature, and slow-learning children.

Accept each child as he or she is, and build upon his or her unique strengths while trying to compensate for his or her limitations.

Give each child classroom tasks to do, such as caring for the class pet, for a specific period of time without direct supervision.

ABOUT THREE CHILDREN IN KINDERGARTEN

As a means of synthesizing some of the information found in this chapter, examples of three children near the end of kindergarten will be briefly presented.

> David was given the Murphy-Durrell Reading Readiness Analysis near the end of kindergarten. According to the results of this test, he could name all of the uppercase and lowercase letter names and also knew the majority of the consonant and vowel phonemes. He also could learn and retain words very effectively. Moreover, he was proficient in most of the areas included on the Reading Readiness Observational Checklist. His teacher determined through careful observation and informal testing that David had several hundred words that he could recognize by sight. He also had good competency in the phonic analysis skills, which usually are presented during the first semester of first grade. When David enters first grade, he probably should be placed in a basal reader that is designed to be used during the last half of first grade. He also should be allowed to read individually from trade books on his instructional or independent reading level.
>
> Sandra was given the Metropolitan Readiness Test near the end of kindergarten. According to the results of this test, she was competent in word meaning and in knowledge of the alphabet letters. However, she seemed to be below average in visual perception and visual discrimination ability because she did rather poorly on the copying and draw-a-man subtests of this test. Her weaknesses in visual perception and visual discrimination ability were confirmed by teacher observation. As Sandra

was to be taught beginning reading skills in first grade by a formal phonic approach, her weaknesses in visual perception and discrimination might not be as significant as they would be if she were to be taught by the basal reader approach, which is generally at least somewhat more visually oriented at the beginning. However, her teacher gave Sandra a few of the work sheets from the *Frostig Program for the Development of Visual Perception,* which is available from Follett Publishing Company, 1010 Washington Boulevard, Chicago, Illinois 60607. She also gave Sandra some teacher-made activity sheets designed to improve her ability in discriminating and copying geometric forms, letters, and words.

Joey was given the Murphy-Durrell Reading Readiness Analysis near the end of kindergarten. According to the test results, he knew only a few lowercase letter names and no letter-sound relationships, and his learning and retention rate of unknown words was far below average. His teacher also further evaluated his reading readiness attainment by using the Reading Readiness Observational Checklist. According to the results of both formal and informal evaluation, Joey needed considerable reinforcement in visual discrimination and auditory discrimination. He also needed to have his experiential background widened. He was especially weak in all aspects of auditory discrimination. His teacher attempted to build Joey's experiential background by using some of the strategies mentioned earlier in the chapter. He also used the language experience approach with Joey on both a group and an individual basis. In addition, he gave Joey much reinforcement in auditory discrimination and visual discrimination by using some of the strategies suggested earlier in this chapter.

SELECTED REFERENCES

Dallmann, Martha, Roger L. Rouch, Lynette Y. C. Char, and John J. DeBoer. *The Teaching of Reading.* New York: Holt, Rinehart and Winston, 1982.

Durkin, Dolores. *Teaching Young Children to Read.* Boston: Allyn and Bacon, Inc., 1980, Chapter 3.

Flood, James, and Diane Lapp. *Language/Reading Instruction for the Young Child.* New York: Macmillan Publishing Company, Inc., 1981, Chapters 1, 5, 11.

Geissal, Mary Ann, and June G. Knafle. "A Linguistic View of Auditory Discrimination Tests and Exercises." *The Reading Teacher, 31* (November 1977): 134–141.

Harris, Albert J., and Edward R. Sipay. *How to Increase Reading Ability.* New York: Longman, Inc., 1980.

Karlin, Robert. *Teaching Elementary Reading.* New York: Harcourt Brace Jovanovich, Inc., 1980, Chapter 4.

King, Ethel M. "Prereading Programs: Direct Versus Incidental Teaching." *The Reading Teacher, 31* (February 1978): 504–510.

Lesiak, Judi. "Reading in Kindergarten: What the Research Doesn't Tell Us. *The Reading Teacher, 32* (November 1978): 135–138.

Montgomery, Diane. "Teaching Prereading Skills Through Training in Pattern Recognition." *The Reading Teacher, 30* (March 1977): 616–623.

Mountain, Lee. *Early Reading Instruction.* Providence, Rhode Island: Jamestown Publishers, 1981.

Past, Kay Cude, Al Past, and Sheila Bernal Guzmán. "A Bilingual Kindergarten Immersed in Print." *The Reading Teacher, 33* (May 1980): 907–913.

SUGGESTED ACTIVITIES

1. Visit a nursery school or day care center. Notice what type of prereading skills are presented in this facility if any are presented. What is your overall evaluation of the facility that you visited?
2. Visit a kindergarten. Would you call it an "intermediate position" kindergarten or a more formal kindergarten in which some type of true beginning reading program is presented?
3. Administer a reading readiness test or the Reading Readiness Observational Checklist contained in this chapter to a child in kindergarten.
4. Select a contemporary reading readiness test, and analyze it in terms of the following: name, author, publisher, date, subtests, administration time, correlation to primary-grade reading achievement, available norms, validity, reliability, and probable usefulness.
5. Record several activities on tape that were suggested in the chapter for developing auditory discrimination ability. If possible, use these activities with a kindergarten child who might benefit from them.
6. Construct several activity sheets for improving ability in visual perception and visual discrimination. Place each activity sheet on a duplicating master so it can be run off and used with children in kindergarten.

The language
experience approach

CHAPTER 4

Why Was This Better?

When Ben entered Mr. Jensen's fifth-grade class at Martin Luther King School in September, Mr. Jensen was appalled to notice that he was a virtual nonreader who had been socially promoted to the fifth grade despite a total lack of reading skills.

Upon examining Ben's cumulative folder, Mr. Jensen noticed that he had been presented with a widely used formal phonic approach in first grade. However, according to the records, he had failed to learn to read by this method. Later several other approaches had been used with Ben to no avail. He was presented with several other formal phonic approaches, a phonic/linguistic approach, and several basal reader series. However, after failing to learn to read by all of these different approaches, Ben developed a very negative attitude toward learning to read. He thus also had emotional problems in addition to a severe reading problem.

In wondering how best to help Ben, Mr. Jensen remembered that he had learned about the language experience approach in a reading methods course at college. He remembered that he had learned that this approach could be very useful with older nonreaders because it used their unique experiences, interests, and language patterns. He also knew that it was a very motivational approach with older nonreaders. Because Mr. Jensen always had taught at the middle-upper level, he never had had the opportunity to use the language experience approach with one of his students. However, he decided to try this approach with Ben.

To begin using the approach, Mr. Jensen attempted to determine some of Ben's unique interests so that he could dictate language experience stories about them. Mr. Jensen discovered through informal conversations with Ben and the use of an interest inventory that he was especially interested in participating in and viewing almost all types of sports. Above all, he enjoyed playing football and watching professional football games on television.

Mr. Jensen subsequently had Ben dictate language experience stories to him about various kinds of sports activities. Ben learned many sight words from these dictated experience stories and wrote each known sight word on an index card. Each of these words became part of his sight word bank, so he could review them periodically. In addition, Mr. Jensen taught Ben important phonic analysis skills, structural analysis skills, and the use of context from the language experience stories.

After several months, Ben was able to read successfully a few high interest, low vocabulary books about sports figures and sports activities. This ability increased his desire to learn to read better. By the end of the fifth grade, Mr. Jensen determined from formal and informal testing that Ben was reading at the late third-grade reading level. Mr. Jensen now knew that it was true that the language experience approach often was effective with older severely disabled readers.

After you have read this chapter, you will know how to implement this most useful approach successfully with beginning readers, older nonreaders in elementary school and high school, and adult nonreaders.

THE HISTORY AND PHILOSOPHY OF THE LANGUAGE EXPERIENCE APPROACH

As you will also see in later chapters of this book, most contemporary elementary reading approaches are based upon older reading approaches that have been modified and refined. This is also true of the language experience approach. For example, a modified form of the language experience approach was used in the 1920s, when experience charts were used for teaching beginning reading skills at the University of Chicago Laboratory School. Experience charts, as they were used at that time, were group-dictated stories that served as an introduction to reading skills in kindergarten or first grade.

However, the contemporary language experience approach containing both group-dictated experience charts and individually dictated or written language experience stories has been refined and publicized mainly by Roach Van Allen. He apparently began his refinement of this approach when he was in the Curriculum Division of the Harlingen, Texas, school system in the 1950s. Since Harlingen, Texas, is a border town, there were many Chicano children attending the school system, many of whom were bilingual and did not have the experiences that were required for comprehending the typically middle-class-oriented basal readers. Therefore, many of these children had difficulty achieving reading success in school. Van Allen noticed that the teachers who used a form of the language experience approach usually had more success in teaching initial reading skills to their students. He also noticed that these children subsequently enjoyed reading more than did children who were not taught to read by this approach.

After reflecting on the potential value of the language experience approach, Van Allen decided to recommend its implementation in some of the first-grade classrooms in San Diego County, California, where he had become director of curriculum coordination. By the early 1960s, Van Allen had crystallized the use of the language experience approach with this statement:

> What I can think about, I can say.
>
> What I can say, I can write or someone can write it for me.
>
> I can read what I have written or what someone else has written for me.
>
> I can read what others have written for me to read.[1]

Somewhat later Dorris M. Lee collaborated with Van Allen on a book that gave detailed directions for using the language experience

---

[1]Roach Van Allen and Gladys C. Halvorsen, "The Language Experience Approach to Reading Instruction," Ginn and Company contributions to *Reading,* No. 27 (Lexington, Massachusetts: Ginn and Company, 1961).

approach as a major way of improving the reading readiness skills of children as well as presenting beginning reading skills to them. Lee and Van Allen provided the following overview of language experiences in reading: sharing experiences, discussion experiences, listening to stories, telling stories, dictating, developing speaking-writing-reading relationships, making and reading books, developing awareness of common vocabulary, expanding vocabulary, writing independently, reading whole books, improving style and form, using a variety of resources, reading a variety of symbols, studying words, improving comprehension, outlining, summarizing, integrating and assimilating ideas, and reading critically.[2]

Van Allen and his associates conducted significant research on the use of the language experience approach in first-grade classrooms in San Diego County in the early 1960s. The results of this research are reported later in this chapter.

TERMS RELATING TO THE LANGUAGE EXPERIENCE APPROACH

It may be helpful in interpreting the remainder of this chapter to define some of the important terms relating to the language experience approach. According to Russell G. Stauffer, this approach may more accurately be described as the experience language approach because it utilizes both experiences and language in the creation of materials.[3]

In any case, *experience charts* comprise part of this approach. Experience charts are group-dictated accounts of experiences and activities. Although an experience chart can be dictated by an entire kindergarten or first-grade class, it is more common for it to be dictated by a group of children. There are several different types of experience charts that have been described by Lee and Van Allen. Several of these are the following: personal language charts that are a record of children's own language, work charts that are developed to give organization and guidance to classroom activities, narrative charts that are records of shared experiences of the group, and reading skill charts that provide teaching and practice of some specific reading skill.[4]

Experience stories are generally described as individually dictated accounts of an experience or an activity. Individual experience stories

---

[2]Dorris M. Lee and Roach Van Allen, *Learning to Read Through Experience* (New York: Appleton-Century-Crofts, 1963), pp. 33–35.

[3]Russell G. Stauffer, *The Language-Experience Approach to the Teaching of Reading* (New York: Harper & Row, Publishers, 1980), p. 2.

[4]Lee and Van Allen, *Learning to Read,* pp. 48–58.

often are used at periodic intervals in a kindergarten. Some children in late first grade and a number of children in second grade are capable of writing their own language experience stories. When this is done, the emphasis is placed upon the story content rather than upon the writing mechanics.

Language experience booklets can be either individually compiled or group-compiled. When an individual child has dictated or written a number of experience stories, they can be collected and bound into an individual booklet. However, when a group theme is chosen for the dictation or writing of stories, all these stories on the common theme also can be collected and bound into a booklet. More detail about the preparation of both individual and group language experience booklets is found later in this chapter.

USING THE LANGUAGE EXPERIENCE APPROACH IN THE HOME PRIOR TO SCHOOL ENTRANCE

As was briefly discussed in Chapter 2, the dictation of language experience stories is a fine way for a parent to help his or her preschool child improve a number of prereading skills and to present some important beginning reading skills in a highly motivating way.

When the language experience approach is to be used in the home, the preschool child first should engage in some kind of motivating experience such as a family trip, an art activity, a construction activity, or a cooking or baking activity. After the child has participated in the experience, he or she dictates an account of the experience to the family member who transcribes it, using manuscript handwriting on a chalkboard, a piece of chart paper, or a sheet of traditional paper. The family member and the child then read the story together aloud several times while the parent points out interesting sight words, letter names, and other linguistic features contained in the story. The parent also can print several important sight words from each experience story on a small card with a marking pen or a crayon. These words then are placed in the child's word bank for subsequent review. The preschool child usually wishes to illustrate each experience story with such art media as crayons, colored pencils, marking pens, or tempera paints. After the child has dictated and illustrated several stories, they can be reread and compiled into some type of booklet with a cover made of construction paper or cardboard.

Here are several language experience stories that were dictated by preschool children around the age of four to their mother, who transcribed them:

A Sled Ride

When it snowed I went on a sled ride with Bryan.
He is my friend.
Art pulled the sled.
We went too fast.
We hit a fence.
I fell off the sled.
Nobody got hurt.
We all built a snowman too.
It took a long time to make.
My hands and feet got real cold.
Then I went home.
It was fun.

Lassie My Friend

Lassie is my friend because he plays with me.
Let's go outside Lassie and play with Amy.
Let's go inside Lassie and take a nap.
And let's watch you on TV Lassie.

USING THE LANGUAGE EXPERIENCE APPROACH IN KINDERGARTEN AND FIRST GRADE

The language experience approach can be used to develop reading readiness skills and present beginning reading skills in both kindergarten and first grade. As was explained in Chapter 3, it is difficult to determine at what point reading readiness skills cease and initial reading skills begin. To encourage the development of these skills, the kindergarten or first-grade classroom should be stimulating and motivating in order to supply topics for experience charts and stories, especially for children who may come from an impoverished environment.

The kindergarten or first-grade classroom should contain a variety of motivating stimuli such as classroom pets, bulletin boards, art activities, construction activities, games, puzzles, story-starters, picture files, filmstrips, recorded songs, activity resource cards, listening posts, a science corner, and a library corner. The teacher may find it helpful to have access to a camera to take photographs of the children while they are engaging in various kinds of activities. For additional motivating experiences, school trips to such places as a farm, a zoo, the police station, the fire station, the post office, a dairy, a bakery, a candy factory, or a greenhouse can be arranged. All these experiences then create content for the children's charts and stories.

Procedures for Using Group Experience Charts

As was explained earlier, group experience charts can be dictated either in a small-group setting or the entire-class setting. Obviously, a group of children must have something interesting and meaningful to talk about if they are to dictate worthwhile experience charts. Group experiences such as school trips, classroom visitors, class demonstrations, trade books that have been read, or storytelling are just a few of the activities that can motivate experience charts. Before children dictate an experience chart, an interesting preliminary oral discussion about the topic should take place with as many children participating as possible.

After this oral discussion, the members of the group or class dictate the experience chart in sentences, with the teacher recording the story on the chalkboard or on a piece of chart paper. Usually, each sentence should end on the line as is shown in the illustration, especially at the initial stages of this approach. A number of reading specialists believe that the children's language should be transcribed exactly although correct spelling always should be used even though it may not reflect their exact oral language. However, other reading specialists believe that the language of the children should be altered to reflect Standard English usage. This issue is treated in detail later in this chapter. In any case, after an experience chart has been reported, it often should be rewritten in manuscript handwriting on a piece of chart paper if it originally was transcribed on the chalkboard.

A completed experience chart can be used in a number of ways to present prereading and beginning reading skills. In kindergarten and early first grade, the teacher usually reads the experience chart aloud once or twice to the children, emphasizing left-to-right progression by using a sweeping hand movement. Teacher reading of the chart may help the children to learn to recognize some words that they may not already know. Later, children can take turns reading the experience chart a line at a time or even the entire chart in a few cases. In any case, the teacher should help with the rereading as much as is needed.

A completed experience chart also can be used in a number of other ways. For example, the teacher can make letter cards, word cards, phrase cards, and sentence cards out of pieces of tagboard. Individual

children or several children can match the cards with the appropriate letters, words, phrases, or sentences.

In addition, one copy of the entire experience chart can be cut apart a sentence at a time, and the children can then try to reassemble the experience chart with or without looking at the original chart, depending upon their ability.

An experience chart also can be typed on a duplicating master, using a primary typewriter, and then duplicated so that each child has one or several copies to work with. As each child reads his or her copy of the experience chart, he or she underlines the words that he or she already is able to recognize. Each of these words then can be printed with a marking pen or typed on a small piece of oaktag or tagboard to be added to each child's *individual word bank*. This is a collection of the words that a child has recognized from reading experience charts and experience stories. The words in the word bank can be kept in a small container of some type such as a metal file box, a cut-down shoe box, or a candy box. In any case, the box should have a lid to avoid spillage. The word cards in a child's word bank can be used in a number of ways. The teacher, for example, can ask the children to find a word in their word bank that begins like the word *doll*. In addition, the child can locate words in his or her bank that end with a certain sound or that rhyme with a certain word. The child also can classify the words in his or her bank according to such categories as names of animals, names of places, names of colors, or names of things to do. In addition, Russell G. Stauffer has recommended that the words in a word bank be arranged on a *word card holder*. A word card holder is constructed by stapling a piece of felt to a cardboard 8 × 11 inches in size. The felt surface holds the word cards where they are placed.[5]

Auditory discrimination and rudimentary phonic analysis can be easily presented by using experience charts. The child can point to all the words on a chart beginning with the same letter and then give that letter name. Some children may be able to point to a word on the

---

[5]Stauffer, *The Language-Experience Approach*, pp. 118–119.

chart that rhymes with a word given by the teacher or point to words ending with certain consonants.

Informal instruction also can be given in structural analysis by helping children to notice such variant word endings on the chart as *s, ing,* and *ed.* Contextual analysis also can be presented by having children provide other words that would make sense in a sentence instead of the word that was used in the chart.

Procedures for Using Individual Experience Stories

Shortly after children have had some exposure to group experience charts in kindergarten and first grade, individual children should be given the opportunity to dictate experience stories. The motivation for these stories can take many forms. Unique individual experiences such as a family trip, a family pet, a gift, a holiday, or reaction to a picture may provide the basis for an individual experience story.

During the dictating of an individual experience story, the teacher may ask a few leading questions, being careful not to structure the story too much. Some teachers like to transcribe the story on an index card as the child dictates it, later typing it on a primary typewriter or writing it in manuscript handwriting. However, a sheet of paper or chart paper also can be used to record the stories. The child's language can be transcribed exactly or tactfully altered, as was described earlier.

Because it takes a great deal of time to transcribe individual experience stories in a kindergarten or first grade, some teachers use a teacher's aid, a parent volunteer, or an older child to act as a recorder some of the time. Such helpers need some brief instruction on the procedures for motivating and recording experience stories. Teachers also sometimes have a teacher's aid or parent volunteer type some or all of the individual experience stories.

After the child has dictated an individual experience story, the teacher reads it aloud for the child. Later the teacher and child read it together, and the child reads it alone when he or she is able to do so. The child underlines all the words in an experience story that he or she recognizes, and the teacher then writes each known word with a marking pen or types it on a piece of tagboard for inclusion in the child's individual word bank.

Each individual experience story can be used for improving a child's visual discrimination ability, auditory discrimination ability, beginning phonic analysis skills, initial structural analysis skills, and contextual analysis skills in the ways that were described in relation to experience charts. Some of these activities were matching letters and words, noting similarities in initial and final consonants, and noting different word endings.

Most children very much enjoy illustrating their individual experience stories by using such art media as crayons, marking pens, colored pencils, tempera paints, and finger paints. They also enjoy compiling a number of their stories and illustrations into a booklet, after making a cover for it. If you wish, the cover and pages of a language experience booklet can be laminated to improve its durability and appearance. An inexpensive spiral binding also can be placed on the booklet at the media center of many school districts. Bookbinding directions for making covers for experience booklets are available in a free booklet entitled *Cover to Cover,* which is available from Encyclopaedia Britannica Press, 425 North Michigan Avenue, Chicago, Illinois 60611.

EXAMPLES OF EXPERIENCE CHARTS AND EXPERIENCE STORIES

Here are some group-composed experience charts that were dictated in kindergarten and first grade:

> There is a turtle in our kindergarten room.
> The name of our turtle is Bobby.
> Bobby lives in a glass bowl with a rock in it.
> Sometimes the rock feels kind of slippery.
> Bobby likes to eat flies the best of all.
> Bobby is a green and black turtle.
> We hope that Bobby lives for a real long time.

> Last week our first-grade class went on a trip.
> We went to the zoo in a big yellow school bus.
> First we saw four big gray elephants with floppy ears.
> Next we saw a giraffe who had a very long neck.
> We hope that he never gets a sore throat.
> We saw a baby hippopotamus swimming in the water.
> We like the funny little monkeys best of all.
> We really had a fun day at the zoo.

> Our first-grade class took a trip to the fire station.
> We met the fire chief and his name was Mr. Martin.
> Mr. Martin showed us three red fire engines.
> One is a hook and ladder truck.
> That ladder really was long.
> Mr. Martin let each of us sit in the fire engine and ring the bell.
> We liked the spotted fire dog the best of all.
> He was black and white, and his name was Pyro.
> The firemen said that he was a Dalmatian.
> We had a lot of fun on our trip to the fire station.

Here are some individually dictated experience stories from children in kindergarten:

Cross-Country Skiing

We got cross-country skis from a store in Joliet.
We put on our skis.
We skied down the hill in the backyard.
We went in the gully and up the other side.
We had to watch out for trees and bushes in our path.
There were rabbit tracks in the snow.
Some people fell down—me and Gail.
We had to cross a little stream by stepping sideways.
Then we started to come home.

Cookies

The first thing we put in the bowl was butter and margarine.
The butter is more yellow than the margarine.
Then we put in sugar and stirred it with the mixer.
It got stuck in the mixer.
Then we put in the flour and oatmeal.
Then we put in the raisins.
We rolled the cookie dough into balls.
Then I had to smash them with a glass.
We baked them for 15 minutes.
Then we took them out of the oven.
After we let them cool, we ate some.
They were good.
Yum!

We Watched the Circus

We watched the people jumping in a circle where the guys lit it.
We saw the guys sitting on their knees so they can catch the ladies.
We saw the gorilla.
One guy put the gorilla on the swing.
He was trying to get down.
We ate cotton candy.
We were drinking Pepsi.
And I got a pink and blue mustache.

USING THE LANGUAGE EXPERIENCE APPROACH IN THE LATER PRIMARY GRADES

Dictated language experience charts and stories are an excellent way of improving reading readiness skills and initiating reading instruction. Often another method such as the basal reader approach, a formal phonic approach, or individualized reading is used later in first grade to teach or reinforce some of the word identification or comprehension skills. However, a variation of the language experience approach can continue through the end of first grade and into the remainder of the primary grades. At this time, however, the language experience approach gradually begins to relate to creative writing.

When he or she is able to do so, a child can write his or her own experience stories instead of dictating them to the teacher. This may occur during the first semester for a few first-grade children or not until second grade or later for other children. When a child has something interesting to write about, the teacher should encourage him or her to spell out the words phonetically to the best of his or her ability. However, a child can consult his or her word bank, a picture dictionary, or the chalkboard to locate the correct spelling of the words. Many reading specialists recommend that the story content be considered most important in first and second grades, with spelling accuracy becoming more important only at around the third-grade level. These specialists rightfully believe that if spelling accuracy is overemphasized when children first begin writing language experience stories, they become so interested in spelling accuracy that the content of the story is sacrificed in the process. Children in the latter part of first grade and early part of second grade often use invented spelling. In such invented spelling they usually spell unfamiliar words phonetically or in another way that seems logical to them. This concept is illustrated in the two language experience stories which follow in this section.

The sources for children's language experience stories are varied. Written stories can be motivated by actual experiences, stories or poems told or read to them, or, on occasion, teacher-assigned topics.

The following language experience stories were written by children in beginning second grade:

> Last nite my brother and I went trik or treating.
> I was dresst in a goest costume.
> My brother had on sum of my fathers old cloths.
> We got a lot of candy and had a lot of fun.
> We are going trik or treating agen tonite.

> I hav a black cat.
> Hiz name is Blacky.
> Sometimes Blacky runs away from home.
> But he always comes back home.
> I just luv Blacky.
> But I wish he woodnt run away from home.

USING THE LANGUAGE EXPERIENCE APPROACH WITH OLDER STUDENTS AND ADULTS

The language experience approach is extremely valuable with severely disabled readers in the intermediate grades and secondary school as well as with illiterate adults. In fact, it probably is the single most useful approach with adult nonreaders of all ages.

When the language experience approach is used with older non-readers or severely disabled readers, the methodology is similar to that used with beginning readers in kindergarten or first grade. However, the experiences on which the dictated stories are based are much more mature than the experiences of younger children. These experiences also reflect the person's unique interests or life-style. In addition, the language experience approach effectively reflects the unique language patterns of older nonreaders. These are the main reasons why the language experience approach is so effective in teaching beginning reading skills to older nonreaders. It reflects their own experiences and language patterns in a way not done in any of the conventional beginning reading approaches.

In using this approach with older nonreaders or severely disabled readers, we find the process is essentially the same as that used with beginning readers. The student dictates a language experience story, which is then typed by the teacher and later returned. The language experience stories are read aloud, and the various word identification and comprehension skills are taught and reinforced mainly from the story. In addition, the teacher can read a portion of material, such as the driver's training manual, to the student a section at a time and then discuss it. Later the student may dictate an account of the section that the teacher transcribes and types for the student to read back.

A number of teachers have reported that the language experience approach seems to be almost a miracle approach for older nonreaders and severely disabled readers who have failed to learn to read for many years by using any of the conventional reading approaches. Its usefulness with older nonreaders cannot be overemphasized.

SHOULD A CHILD'S LANGUAGE BE ALTERED BY THE TEACHER?

Some minority group children occasionally use vocabulary terms and elements of grammar that differ from Standard English. Many specialists in urban education believe that the teacher should transcribe a child's story exactly as it is dictated because altering the language can cause the child to feel rejected. After all, this is the language that the family members of the child use, and it is the language to which the child has been exposed.

However, some reading specialists believe that a teacher can alter a child's language as the story is being dictated if he or she has a very good relationship with the child and does it very tactfully. Still other reading specialists believe that the teacher should transcribe the story exactly as it is dictated but then can type two forms of the story. The second version of the story is written in Standard English. The child is then supposed to compare the two stories to notice how they are different.

In the past the author believed that it was best to transcribe each child's language experience story exactly as it was dictated to give the child a feeling of acceptance and success. However, after teaching countless minority group college students, she now believes that it probably often is more effective to alter very tactfully a child's dictated material to make it more nearly conform to Standard English. Virtually all of the minority group students that I have taught have convinced me that it is absolutely imperative for all minority group children to learn how to speak and write Standard English effectively if they are going to be able to compete in our society. These students further believe that the schools have an obligation to encourage the learning of Standard English as early as possible.

RESEARCH ON THE LANGUAGE EXPERIENCE APPROACH

One of the first research studies on the use of the language experience approach was conducted by Roach Van Allen and his associates in the 1960s in San Diego County, California. In this large-scale study, some first-grade classrooms used the language experience approach, others used the basal reader approach, and still others used individualized reading. The results of this study indicated that all three approaches resulted in good first-grade reading achievement for most students, but that the language experience approach resulted in a greater interest in reading on the part of most children as demonstrated by their responses to the San Diego Reading Attitude Inventory.[6]

Many of the research studies on the effectiveness of the language experience approach were conducted in the mid 1960s as part of the twenty-seven United States Office of Education federally financed first-grade studies, some of which continued through second and third grades. Although all these studies were attempting to find a single best method of teaching beginning reading skills, the results of the studies indicated that it often was the teacher who influenced a child's superior reading achievement instead of a method. However, most of the studies

---

[6]Roach Van Allen, Report of the *Reading Study Project,* Monograph No. 1 (San Diego, California: Department of Education, San Diego County, 1961).

discovered that the language experience approach was a very good beginning reading approach.[7]

One interesting study involving the use of the language experience approach in a summer migrant program from the kindergarten level through the second-grade level was conducted by Dan M. Baxley and Max Henton in Eloy, Arizona. These researchers planned a summer program designed to give migrant children all types of experiences leading to their dictating or writing language experience stories. The books written by the children were then used as the reading material for the entire class. Although no real effort was made to teach beginning reading skills, many of the children in this study did learn reading skills, and their attendance and language development improved during the course of the project.[8]

A very significant research study was conducted by John T. Becker with older severely disabled readers who were taught beginning reading skills by using their dictated language experience stories as the major material for reading instruction. The virtual nonreaders in this study were girls who were attending a Job Corps Center. They dictated language experience stories about what they wanted to do when they completed their Job Corps training. Thus, their dictated stories were about becoming secretaries, beauticians, or waitresses, among other occupations. Later the girls wrote their own stories. Becker found that the language experience approach was a very effective way of teaching beginning reading skills to older severely disabled readers.[9]

To summarize, the language experience approach has been found to be at least as effective as, if not somewhat more effective than, other reading approaches with beginning readers. It is also very useful with culturally different children and older nonreaders. The language experience approach is truly an excellent way to teach beginning reading skills.

UNIQUE STRENGTHS OF THE LANGUAGE EXPERIENCE APPROACH

The language experience approach has some unique strengths that make it the superior way of improving reading readiness skills and

[7]Guy L. Bond and Robert Dykstra, "The Cooperative Research Program in First-Grade Reading Instruction," *Reading Research Quarterly, 2* (Summer 1967): 5–141.

[8]Dan M. Baxley and Max Henton, "The Eloy Story—A Report from the Eloy Elementary School Summer Migrant Program for Kindergarten Through Second Grade," Champaign, Illinois: ERIC/RCS System, ED 067 217.

[9]John T. Becker, "Language Experience Attack on Adolescent Illiteracy," *Journal of Reading, 16* (November 1972): 115–119.

teaching beginning reading skills. One of its major strengths is that it enables students to use their own experiences as the major material for reading instruction. As an example, culturally different children may not have had the experiences that are portrayed in published reading materials and, therefore, they may have difficulty in interpreting the material. However, because the language experience stories always reflect the children's experiences, they can be easily interpreted by the children. The use of their own experiences is especially important for adults because published beginning reading materials are usually too immature for them.

Another advantage is that language experience stories use the reader's own language patterns. In most cases, readers can read their own language patterns more effectively than they can read the language patterns found in published reading materials. This is particularly helpful to culturally different children and nonreaders.

According to an article by Carol N. Dixon, language experience stories can be used effectively as a diagnostic and evaluative tool in planning an instructional program for an individual student. She has formulated a language experience checklist in which the child's performance is evaluated in such areas as these: watches when words are written down, paces dictation, pauses at the end of phrases or sentences, uses an appropriate title, attempts to read back, and uses global and refined language.[10]

As an integrated approach to language arts, the language experience approach effectively stresses the interrelationships among the four language arts of listening, speaking, reading, and writing. The dictated stories are a bridge between oral language and reading at the beginning stages. Later, child-written materials stress the relationship between reading and writing.

The language experience approach is very useful for linguistically gifted children because they can write experience stories very effectively in the early primary grades. Some children, for example, can write their own experience stories near the beginning of first grade. This obviously encourages both their creativity and their competency in creative writing.

The creativity of all the children who use this approach is greatly enhanced. Taking an active role in their own learning, children dictate and write interesting experience stories and illustrate them creatively. Even the covers of the language experience booklets often reflect the creativity of the children. Children who have used the language experience approach extensively are often adept at other forms of creative writing and often exceed children who have used other reading approaches in the quality and quantity of their writing.

---

[10]Carol N. Dixon, "Language Experience Stories as a Diagnostic Tool," *Language Arts, 54* (May 1977): 501–505.

The language experience approach presents prereading experiences that are reading-oriented. For example, a language experience story can be used to teach the prereading experiences of left-to-right progression and the beginning reading skills of letter recognition and sight word recognition. Therefore, the language experience approach makes the transition from reading readiness skills to beginning reading skills very gradually and should be followed.

Through this approach children learn that "reading is talk written down." Although talk involves more than this because of the part that facial expressions, body language, and intonation play in speech, the child should understand this concept to understand the reading process.

The language experience approach uses writing as an aid to word identification. When children write a word that they have recently learned to recognize, a kinesthetic or tactile reinforcement is added to the identification of the word, thus aiding in its retention.

The language experience approach appears to create an interest in reading because the experience stories capitalize on the children's own experiences and are written in their own language patterns. Thus, the stories often are more meaningful to the children who wrote them than are the stories found in the basal readers.

SOME LIMITATIONS OF THE LANGUAGE EXPERIENCE APPROACH

The language experience approach has several limitations that the teacher should be aware of before using it as a sole approach to teaching beginning reading skills. However, many of these limitations are unimportant when the language experience approach is used in combination with other more structured approaches such as the basal reader approach or a formal phonic approach.

Without question the most important limitation of the language experience approach is its lack of sequential skill development, especially of the word identification skill of phonic analysis. However, this limitation is most important for average and below-average readers because a number of above-average readers can learn the word identification techniques independently outside of a structured program.

The lack of structure in the language experience approach restricts its use as a major approach to beginning reading instruction by inexperienced teachers. Most such teachers need the guidance provided by the manuals of a more structured reading approach. Quite often, beginning teachers have not developed sufficient knowledge of the reading process to teach it to beginning readers without guidance.

Implementation of the language experience approach requires considerable time for the dictating and transcribing of experience charts and experience stories. However, this limitation often can be overcome at least to an extent by using teacher aides, volunteers, or older students to take down the experience stories and by using parent volunteers or secretarial help to type them.

To function most effectively, the language experience approach presupposes that primary-grade classrooms are well equipped and that teachers are able to provide enriching experiences for the children. The approach is based on the concept that each child will be exposed to interesting topics for talking and writing. Therefore, the children must have a motivating classroom environment, the opportunity to go on educationally worthwhile school trips, and available materials with which to construct their language experience booklets. Each classroom should also be supplied with an abundance of trade books, reference books, basal readers, and supplementary books.

USING THE LANGUAGE EXPERIENCE APPROACH WITH SPECIAL CHILDREN

The language experience approach has been used successfully with several different types of special children. For example, it has been very useful in improving the reading readiness skills of educable mentally handicapped and trainable mentally handicapped children. It also can be used to teach such children beginning reading skills. For example, several of my graduate students used the language experience approach successfully with trainable students of high-school age, whose IQs averaged about 50. These students dictated individual language experience stories about various aspects of traffic safety. They were able to read their stories fairly effectively and learned some rudimentary reading skills from them. Each student also illustrated his or her language experience story. This approach was very motivating for the students who used it.

The language experience approach also has been used effectively with children who are deaf and hard-of-hearing. When this approach is used with such children, they sign and vocalize experience charts and stories. Normally, deaf and hard-of-hearing children do not use connectives and articles as do most young hearing children. They use a telegraphic syntactical encoding of ideas instead. Many specialists in deaf education seem to believe that the language experience approach holds great promise in teaching reading skills to deaf and hard-of-hearing children.

The language experience approach also has been used to teach blind children how to read. When a blind child dictates a story, he or she realizes that oral language can be saved in the form of Braille. Therefore, Braille immediately has a use for the child, and he or she finds that learning to read and write is not a chore but rather a discovery of how to help order the child's world of experiences. The language experience approach presents Braille as a way of storing a child's ideas. Later, when the child is familiar enough with Braille to read trade books, he or she will discover that Braille also unlocks the ideas of others.

You are encouraged to consult the references at the end of this chapter for detailed directions on how to use the language experience approach with various groups of special children.

WHERE CAN MORE INFORMATION BE FOUND ON USING THE LANGUAGE EXPERIENCE APPROACH?

There are several excellent sources that you can consult for detailed directions on how to implement the language experience approach. Here are the titles of some professional books that are devoted entirely to the use of this approach:

Hall, MaryAnne. *Teaching Reading as a Language Experience*. Columbus, Ohio: Charles E. Merrill Publishing Co., 1982.

Lee, Dorris M., and Roach Van Allen. *Learning to Read with Experience*. New York: Appleton-Century-Crofts, 1963.

Stauffer, Russell G. *The Language-Experience Approach to the Teaching of Reading*. New York: Harper & Row, Publishers, 1980.

Van Allen, Roach. *Language Experiences in Communication*. Boston: Houghton Mifflin Company, 1976.

The teaching aids that can be used in kindergarten and the early primary grades to help implement the language experience approach mainly have been formulated under the direction of Roach Van Allen in collaboration with Richard Venezky and Harry Hahn. These authors devised a program called *Language-Experiences in Reading* (LEIR), which was published by Encyclopaedia Brittanica Educational Corporation of Chicago in 1976. According to the authors, LEIR is a supplementary reading program that uses each child's language and experiences. The program is designed to be used in grades one through six, and each box for the primary grades contains a teacher's guide, daily lesson plans, filmstrips, reading selection cards, story-starters, recorded songs, and listening activities. Although this program is designed for use through sixth grade, it probably would be most useful in kindergarten and first grade.

Roach Van Allen and Claryce Van Allen also have developed an aid that contains many useful examples of how to use the language experience approach. Here is the title of this aid:

Van Allen, Roach, and Claryce Van Allen. *Language Experience Activities*. Boston: Houghton Mifflin Company, 1982.

SELECTED REFERENCES

Askland, Linda C. "Conducting Individual Langu
ries." *The Reading Teacher, 27* (November

Chapman, Barbara Holland. "LEA Solves Synt
Speaking Child." *The Reading Teacher, 31*
151–153.

Curry, Rebecca Gavurin. "Using LEA to Teach
Read." *The Reading Teacher, 29* (December

Garcia, Ricardo L. "Mexican Americans Learn T
Experience." *The Reading Teacher, 28* (Decem⎽ ⎼⎽⎼⎼). ⎽01–⎽05.

Johnson, Terry D. "Language Experience: We Can't All Write What
We Can Say." *The Reading Teacher, 31* (December 1977):
297–299.

Karlin, Robert. *Teaching Elementary Reading.* New York: Harcourt
Brace Jovanovich, Inc., 1980, pp. 203–215.

Lapp, Diane, and James Flood. *Teaching Reading to Every Child.* New
York: Macmillan Publishing Company, Inc., 1983.

Pienaar, Peter T. "Breakthrough in Beginning Reading: Language
Experience Approach." *The Reading Teacher, 30* (February 1977):
489–496.

Stauffer, Russell G. "The Language Experience Approach to Reading
Instruction for Deaf and Hearing Impaired Children." *The
Reading Teacher, 33* (October 1979): 21–24.

Wiesendanger, Katherine D., and Ellen Davis Birlem. "Adapting
Language Experience to Reading for Bilingual Pupils." *The
Reading Teacher, 32* (March 1979): 671–673.

FILM

Stauffer, Russell G. "The Language-Experience Approach to Teaching
Reading." Newark, Delaware: Instructional Resource Center of
the University of Delaware, 19711. This is a 16-mm, color film
that is 45 minutes long. It can be rented for a week for $45 or
purchased for $425.

Van Allen, Roach. "Reading: A Language Experience Approach." Bir-
mingham, Alabama: Promethean Films South, Post Office Box
26363, 35226. This is a 16-mm, color film that is 33 minutes
long. It can be rented for $42 for three days or purchased for
$423.

SUGGESTED ACTIVITIES

1. Try using the language experience with an older severely disabled reader or nonreader to teach beginning reading skills.
What did you find to be the unique advantages of using this
approach with such a person?

2. Take a reaction picture to a school kindergarten or first-grade
class. Have a child dictate a language experience story to you,

it in manuscript handwriting. Then type the story
primary typewriter. If you wish, collect the typed lan-
e experience stories from the other members of your
ass, and then bind them into a booklet. Give the completed
booklet back to the kindergarten or first-grade class to read
and keep.
3. Observe a language experience lesson with a group-dictated
   experience chart in kindergarten or beginning first grade. Did
   the procedures vary from those explained in this chapter?
4. Select a rather immature child in kindergarten who needs individual help. Provide the motivation for several individually
   dictated language experience stories. Transcribe each story,
   and use it in some of the ways mentioned in this chapter.
   Have the child illustrate each story and make a cover for a
   language experience booklet. Compile all of the dictated stories into a booklet for the child.
5. Take a group of children in kindergarten or beginning first
   grade to an interesting place in the neighborhood. When they
   return to school, have the group of children dictate an experience chart and transcribe it for them.
6. Help a child in kindergarten or beginning first grade make
   either a word bank or a word card holder.

The basal reader approach

What Did She Do Wrong?

When Ms. Bernstein began her first teaching position, she was assigned to a second-grade class at Larkin School in a large city in the Far West. Unfortunately, she felt rather poorly prepared to teach reading although she had at least learned some of the major characteristics of the basal reader approach in her one undergraduate reading methods course.

When she examined the basal reader series that had been selected for use in all of the classrooms in Larkin School, Ms. Bernstein was rather appalled by how extensive the materials were. The series contained teachers' manuals, many levels of children's readers, many types of practice books, duplicating masters, filmstrips, cassette recordings, posters, word cards, discussion cards, reading games, and several types of tests. Ms. Bernstein really didn't know how to use all these materials.

First Ms. Bernstein divided the children in her class into three groups—an above-average group, an average group, and a below-average group. She then attempted to present all the new vocabulary suggested in the teachers' manuals to the children in each group. In addition, she tried to ask all the comprehension questions contained in the manuals, teach all the reading skills for each lesson, and provide all the enrichment activities suggested for each lesson.

After several weeks of attempting to do all these things, Ms. Bernstein was nearly ready to resign her teaching position. By that time she was exhausted from attempting to provide all the activities included in the teachers' manuals to the children in all three reading groups. She was shocked to realize that she had not even used any of the multimedia aids that were included with the basal reader series.

Unfortunately, Ms. Bernstein had not learned about the true usefulness of a basal reader series in her reading methods course. She should have learned that the manuals should be used only as a source of teaching suggestions. A manual should not be followed in detail if the suggestions are not appropriate for the particular children with whom the teacher is working. Ms. Bernstein should have been taught that no teacher can ask all the comprehension questions or present all the enrichment activities contained in a basal reader teachers' manual. Neither can any teacher use all the supplementary materials that are provided with a basal reader series. A basal reader series can be very helpful to a teacher of reading, especially a beginning teacher, but it never should dictate his or her entire reading program. This is a misuse of an inherently good reading program.

After reading this chapter, you will understand what the major characteristics are of the basal reader approach and how to use it most effectively in your future classroom. Then you never should have the difficulties in implementing this approach that Ms. Bernstein encountered during her first year of teaching.

THE HISTORY OF THE BASAL READER APPROACH

As with many elementary reading approaches, the contemporary and widely used basal reader approach is based on an older but somewhat similar reading approach.

The basal reader approach originated with *McGuffey's Readers,* which were first published in 1840 and which were the most commonly used materials for the forty years following. As one can see from examining the reproduced pages of the *McGuffey's Readers* (Figure 5-1), they were very similar to the contemporary phonic/linguistic readers that are described in Chapter 7. However, they also presented moralistic values, and this is not commonly done today, at least not in exactly the same way. The *McGuffey's Readers* used stories, parables, moral lessons, and patriotic selections to teach reading as well as to help children grow up to be good citizens. They also used graduated sentence length and vocabulary control.

However, the forerunner of the basal reader approach as it is known today was the *Elson-Gray Readers,* which were published about 1930. In these readers silent reading was greatly emphasized as it is in the current basal reader approach. This method emphasized graded readers, with controlled vocabulary and sentence length. The basal reader approach remained in almost total prominence until about 1960, when phonic approaches began to be more commonly used. However, even today basal readers are used as a major method for teaching reading skills in approximately 90 percent of all primary-grade classrooms and about 80 percent of all middle-school classrooms in the United States.

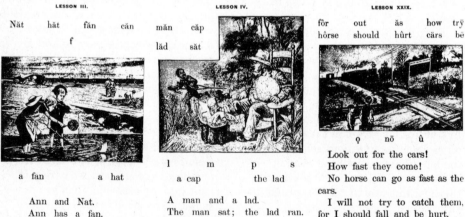

FIGURE 5-1

A BRIEF OVERVIEW OF THE BASAL READER APPROACH

The basal reader approach is, in general, a set of reading materials that attempts to present and reinforce all the word identification and comprehension skills. And, therefore, it can be called an *eclectic reading approach*. Although there are considerable differences between various basal reader series, the materials used in this approach do not emphasize any single reading skill at the expense of other reading skills. For example, all the word identification techniques of sight word recognition, phonic analysis, structural analysis, and contextual analysis are stressed from the initial stages of reading instruction. Students are given practice in responding to both literal and interpretive comprehension questions from the initial stages of reading instruction. In addition, critical reading activities and creative reading activities are stressed from the beginning. Particular attention is given to the child's use of the knowledge, insights, and attitudes gained from reading. Although quite a bit of the material in most basal readers is of the narrative type, contemporary basal readers are now emphasizing materials from the content areas of social studies, science, and mathematics much more than was done in the past, especially at the middle-school level.

When the basal reader approach is used as a major approach in kindergarten or beginning first grade, reading readiness skills are improved for those children who need them by materials such as various types of kits or reading readiness workbooks. (See Chapter 3.) Such materials emphasize visual discrimination, auditory discrimination, left-to-right progression, picture interpretation, oral language development, and the development of an experiential background.

In late kindergarten or beginning first grade, initial reading skills are presented by using soft-cover books, which used to be called *pre-primers*. This term has been replaced by the terms Level 1, Level 2, or Level 3 in most basal reader programs because they are now called leveled programs. Sometimes reading instruction is introduced by experience charts that teach the words that subsequently will be found in the appropriate beginning reading materials of the series. When experience charts are used in this way, the teacher structures the charts by asking the entire class or a group of children leading questions so that the necessary words are introduced. However, such contrived experience charts are not representative of the true language experience approach. (See Chapter 4.)

Word identification is usually taught by sight word recognition or picture clues in the beginning reading materials. After a group of children has progressed through several soft-cover books, they move on to the next level, which used to be called the *primer* level, and subsequently to the *first reader*. These materials may be in soft-cover or hardcover depending on the basal reader series. At these levels, word identification is presented by sight, picture clues, phonic analysis, and structural analysis. Reading for meaning is always stressed at these levels of the basal reader approach.

In the past there were two hardcover basal readers for second grade and two for third grade. However, in most new basal reader series there are many more readers at each of these levels. They may be available in hardcover or in soft-cover. As the typical contemporary basal reader series is a leveled program, it is usually difficult to equate the level designation on the basal reader with a reading grade level. This is done to discourage a teacher from placing a child in a reader designed for the grade in which he or she is enrolled even if the reader is too difficult or too easy for the child. In addition, the program attempts to avoid the stigma a third-grade child might feel in using a reader designed for the second grade. At the later primary-grade reading level, phonic analysis and structural analysis receive much emphasis and reinforcement. For example, the vast majority of phonic analysis skills have been presented and reinforced by the time a student begins the fourth-grade reading level.

At the intermediate-grade level, each grade level may have only one hardcover basal reader with a designation such as Level 12. Although the material is predominantly narrative, content materials are also found in the basal readers. Word identification techniques are refined at this level, and comprehension receives continuous emphasis. Additional sources for intermediate-grade reading are trade books, children's magazines and newspapers, supplementary books, content textbooks, and reference books.

Basal readers for grades seven and eight are now becoming more common than they were in the past. Thus, many basal reader series encompass the reading readiness levels through the eighth-grade reading level.

The basal reader approach usually features the division of each primary-grade class into three reading achievement groups—an above-average group, an average group, and a below-average group. At the beginning of first grade, the grouping usually is made on the basis of a child's score on a reading readiness test supplemented by teacher observation. In the upper-primary grades, the classification often is made as a result of the child's score on a reading achievement test and teacher observation. There are often two reading achievement groups at the intermediate-grade level. Although the teachers' manuals of all basal reader series recommend flexible, nonrigid grouping for reading, in practice teachers may be inclined to keep the reading groups too rigid, enabling few children to move to a higher group. This is mainly the case because the reading skills are presented in a very developmental, sequential manner.

The basal reader lessons are fairly similar in format in most of the series. A lesson often consists of some variation of the following procedure: development of a background of experiences for the story, presentation of new vocabulary terms, guided silent reading, purposeful oral reading, extending skill development, and enriching experiences.

Contemporary basal reader series have changed a great deal during the past twenty years. For example, more phonic analysis skills are now presented earlier than they were in the past. Previously, the basal reader approach did not emphasize phonic elements as much as it does at the present time.

Contemporary basal readers do not have the rigid vocabulary control that they had in the past. Because this vocabulary control was thought to be far too rigid, contemporary basal readers usually present more words at each reading level. However, the story content of the beginning basal readers still is rather uninteresting because of the limited vocabulary that can be presented at this level.

In the past many beginning basal reader stories were about family life in a typical middle-class suburban or small-town neighborhood. Today, however, a number of the stories reflect inner-city and minority group life. One can see many black, Oriental, Chicano, and Native American characters in contemporary basal readers. In addition, contemporary basal reader stories are much more likely to be realistic stories, fairy tales, or fables than was the case in the past.

Contemporary basal readers are also much more inclined to portray women and girls in active, nontraditional roles than formerly. One reason is that publishers have been greatly criticized recently for portraying men and boys as active and independent while portraying women and girls as passive and dependent. Today, therefore, one can see women portrayed as police officers or fire fighters and girls playing baseball or basketball. It is also much more common now in basal readers to see men and boys doing household chores.

Current basal reader series employ multimedia aids more than they used to. A contemporary basal reader series may consist of any or all of the following elements: a large chart-size beginning reading book, a reading readiness kit, a reading readiness workbook, paperback readers, hardbound readers, tests, practice books, filmstrips, cassette recordings, transparencies, reading games, supplementary readers, duplicating masters, word cards, posters, pocket charts, discussion cards, and writing helpers. Therefore, a contemporary basal reading series is very expensive for a school system to purchase. Usually, a school system must use a series for about five years for it to be economically feasible.

It also is important to note that there are considerable differences among the basal readers of different series that are designed for the same reading level. For example, a reader designed for use at the fourth reader level in one series may be much more difficult, in general, than a reader at a similar level from another series. In addition, according to studies using readability formulas, there are considerable differences among the difficulty levels of the material within any one basal reader. For example, the stories in a basal reader often do not increase in difficulty throughout the reader. That is, the material near the end of the reader is not necessarily more difficult than is the material near the beginning of the reader.

Some states in the United States have what is called state adoption of a basal reader series. State adoption indicates that the state board of education has selected approximately five basal reader series, and each school district in that state must adopt one of these series as its major method of teaching elementary reading. Obviously, the basal reader publishers concentrate very much on trying to have their series chosen as one option in a state adoption state. Several states having state adoption are Indiana, Arizona, and Texas. When one considers that a basal reader series might cost $10 million to $20 million before a single book is sold, one can see why basal reader publishers place a great emphasis on state adoption.

BASAL READER READING READINESS MATERIALS

Initiation of the basal reader approach often occurs during kindergarten or early first grade with the use of a reading readiness workbook or other reading readiness materials designed by the basal reader publisher. (See Chapter 3.) Only those reading readiness skills in which a child is weak should be stressed by using particular workbook pages or activities from a reading readiness kit. (See Chapter 3.) Such materials never should be used as an entire program.

A typical reading readiness workbook or other reading readiness materials are designed to develop or improve the prereading skills that may be related to success in beginning reading. Research has indicated that some of these prereading skills may be related to success in beginning reading whereas others appear to provide little empirical evidence to justify their development.

As an example, the prereading skill of visual discrimination is the ability to note the likenesses and differences in geometric forms, letters, words, and numbers. In an older, but still relevant, research study, Jean Turner Goins discovered little relation between a child's ability to discriminate between geometric forms and his or her subsequent ability to discriminate between look-alike words such as *spot* and *stop* and *was* and *saw*.[1] However, many commercial reading readiness materials still give children reinforcement in discriminating between geometric forms and patterns. Many children might benefit from reinforcement in discriminating between letters and between words. Overall, however, visual discrimination is well presented in commercial reading readiness materials.

On the other hand, auditory discrimination is not presented quite as well in commercial reading readiness materials. This skill needs to be improved mainly by other types of activities such as rhyming, discriminating between various phonemes, and learning letter-sound relationships. (See Chapter 3.) However, the reading readiness materials associated with basal reader series do attempt to have children recognize the beginning sounds of objects represented by pictures and do provide practice in various types of rhyming activities.

Left-to-right progression often is presented in reading readiness materials by providing a series of pictures that the child and teacher discuss in a left-to-right sequence. However, left-to-right progression also must be improved in other ways, as by cut-apart comic strips or the use of a cumulative calendar. (See Chapter 3.)

Picture interpretation is presented quite well in reading readiness materials. The workbook often offers a number of pictures that the teacher and child discuss together. The purpose of this discussion is to have each child interpret the picture critically and creatively. Picture interpretation activities are mainly designed to help children use the picture clues in the beginning stages of reading more effectively and subsequently comprehend better what is read.

Reading readiness materials also attempt to develop experiential background by presenting stimulating pictures and other types of activities. Yet reading readiness materials usually are not very effective in improving a child's background of experiences. The skill is improved much more successfully by the provision of firsthand and vicarious experiences. (See Chapter 3.)

A number of aspects of reading readiness, such as oral language, laterality, listening comprehension, motor coordination, self-confidence, and independence, must be developed mainly by the teacher without the use of the reading readiness materials that accompany a basal reader series. As was explained in detail in Chapter 4, the language experience approach is extremely useful in improving reading readiness skills and in presenting beginning reading skills.

---

[1]Jean Turner Goins, *Visual Perception Abilities and Early Reading Progress,* Supplementary Educational Monographs, No. 87 (Chicago: University of Chicago Press, 1958).

It also is important to remember that not every child in a kindergarten or first-grade classroom needs to have any exposure to the reading readiness materials that accompany a basal reader series. A child who is already reading or has attained sufficient reading readiness to begin a reading program obviously has no need of any type of commercial reading readiness materials. To use such materials with this type of child obviously is a waste of time and effort and also can be detrimental to the child.

Even if some type of commercial reading readiness material is relevant for use with a particular child, it should not be used in a routine manner. Only those workbook pages or activities that a child actually needs should be used. For example, if a child already has a high degree of competence in visual discrimination, it obviously is a waste of time for him or her to complete workbook pages devoted to improving ability in this skill. However, if the child needs additional practice in picture interpretation, the appropriate workbook pages may be useful for improving competence in this reading readiness skill. Unfortunately, this is *not* the way in which reading readiness materials typically are used in kindergarten or first-grade classrooms.

STRATEGIES FOR USING THE BASAL READER APPROACH IN THE PRIMARY GRADES

Employing the basal reader approach in the primary grades usually lends itself to the fairly extensive use of group work. Although it is possible to individualize reading instruction effectively while using this approach, this does not often occur in practice. Most often the word identification and comprehension skills are presented to a group of children. Therefore, first-grade teachers usually divide the class into three or four reading achievement groups near the beginning of the school year and base this division on reading readiness test scores and teacher judgment.

The teacher should choose basal reader materials that correspond to the reading level at which the majority of the children in each group are reading. For the above-average group in a first grade, this may be a reader that corresponds to the primer, first reader, or even second reader level. Normally, the children in the average group in first grade may receive beginning reading instruction by the use of the language experience approach or a preprimer or may be reading at the primer level.

Most children in the below-average group in first grade need additional prescriptive reading readiness training before being introduced to any type of formal beginning reading program. This reading readiness development may well include the use of the language experience approach or many of the reading readiness activities that were described in detail in Chapter 3. This reading readiness development also can use portions of the commercial reading readiness materials that accompany a basal reader series if such a procedure seems appropriate. Reading readiness improvement for children in the below-average group can take from one month to three months or more. I believe that the lack of sufficient reading readiness at the time reading instruction is begun is a major cause of subsequent reading disability, and that a child should never be introduced to reading instruction by using the basal reader approach until he or she is ready for it.

From the earliest stages of basal reader instruction, word identification is presented by a variety of different techniques. Picture-word association and sight word recognition may be used, although they do not receive the degree of stress in this approach that they did in the past. Instead, letter-sound relationships receive a great deal of stress from the beginning stages of reading instruction in most basal reader series. Obviously, letter-sound relationships are the beginning elements of phonic analysis. The typical basal reader series contains a comprehensive scope and sequence chart, which summarizes the phonic elements that are presented and reinforced in that series. Although it is difficult to generalize about the sequences in which phonic analysis skills are presented in most basal reader series, here is one sequence that may be used: consonant sounds, short vowel sounds, long vowel sounds, consonant blends, vowel digraphs, phonograms, consonant digraphs, diphthongs, and *r*-controlled vowels.

When the basal reader approach is used in the primary grades, the appropriate phonic analysis skills are taught and reinforced in a small-group setting. To teach the phonic analysis skills, the teacher often uses some of the strategies contained in the manuals. These phonic analysis skills then are reinforced by having the child complete the appropriate pages from the regular basal reader workbooks or a special phonics workbook that accompanies the basal reader series. Such reinforcement also can utilize other phonic workbooks, commercial duplicating masters, other commercially available materials, or teacher-made activity sheets.

The typical basal reader series also summarizes the structural analysis skills presented and reinforced in its scope and sequence chart. At the first-grade reading level, simple suffixes such as *-s, -ed,* and *-ing* are attached to regular base or root words. Later in the primary grades, most of the additional common suffixes are presented and attached both to regular and irregular base words. Common prefixes such as *un-, re-,* and *en-* are presented at about the second-grade reading level. Readiness for syllabication is begun in first grade whereas actual instruction in syllabication often is begun in second grade. Instruction in accent is started in the later primary grades. Thus, most of the basic structural analysis skills are presented and reinforced in the primary grades.

Context clues are used very extensively in the primary grades by the basal reader series as part of the emphasis on reading for meaning. Readiness for dictionary usage and dictionary skills are also presented at the primary-grade reading level.

The basal reader approach places great stress on comprehension of what is read from the beginning stages of reading instruction. From the beginning reader level, children are given countless opportunities to answer literal, interpretive, and critical questions and to read creatively. In fact, each primary-grade basal reader manual contains so many comprehension questions at various levels that no teacher could reasonably be expected to ask them all during a basal reader lesson. Actually, to do so might be detrimental to the children because the material then would be analyzed more than is justified in the light of its content.

The traditional basal reader lesson follows some variation of a *directed reading activity*. It also can be modified by the use of some variation of a directed reading-thinking activity, a procedure in which the child sets his or her own purposes for reading and subsequently reads to satisfy these purposes or evaluate his or her hypotheses.[2] This procedure is described in detail in Chapter 14.

Here are the steps in a typical basal reader lesson. Of course, there is considerable variation in these steps depending upon the basal reader series.

Developing a background of experiences. In this step the teacher attempts to relate the basal reader story to the children's own experiences by showing a filmstrip, pictures, or concrete objects that clarify the story content or by helping the children to set purposes for reading the story by examining its title and speculating about the possible story content. The major purpose of this step of the lesson is to motivate the children to want to read the story and to help them read it with the maximum amount of comprehension and enjoyment.

Presentation of new vocabulary. This step of the basal reader lesson is subject to some controversy. In the past, the teacher was directed to present selected new vocabulary terms found in the story in context by writing them in sentences on the chalkboard or on a sheet of chart paper. However, this presentation may have harmed a student's desire to use his or her own word identification skills in unlocking the pronunciation and meaning of the new words. Therefore, today some basal reader series encourage vocabulary presentation by the teacher although a number do

---

[2]Russell G. Stauffer, *The Language-Experience Approach to the Teaching of Reading* (New York: Harper & Row, Publishers, 1980), pp. 184–214.

not. It is probably true that vocabulary presentation did tend to damage a child's initiative in using independent word identification skills.

Guided silent reading. During this phase of the lesson, the group of children reads the story silently under teacher direction. Although in the past the stories were read and discussed one page at a time, today many basal reader manuals recommend reading and discussing the entire story as a unit or in several units. The teacher tries to help the children formulate purposes for reading by posing questions before they read that they are to answer from their reading. Often it is preferable for the teacher to encourage children to formulate their own purposes for reading the story by predicting what will happen. This technique is a variation of the *directed reading-thinking activity* that was mentioned earlier.[3] After the children read each section of the story or the entire story, the teacher usually asks the group comprehension questions about it. The questions often should be on the interpretive or critical levels instead of only on the literal level. In the past teachers have asked children far too many recall questions.

Purposeful oral reading. While children do purposeful oral reading in the reading group, they have the opportunity to answer such questions as these:

Read the sentence that tells you how Susie felt when her dog got lost.
Read the paragraph that tells you how the North Woods look on a winter day.
Read the paragraph that tells you how grandmother felt when she received flowers for her birthday.

Audience oral reading is conducted when a child in the group prepares a short excerpt to read aloud to the others who have their books closed. Oral reading used in this way is very different from "reading around the circle." Round-robin reading or reading around the circle is often rather meaningless as each child in the group thinks only about what he or she is reading when it is his or her turn to read. A story about round-robin reading concerns Billy, whose teacher asked him to read the next paragraph aloud in the basal reader story that his group had just read silently. Billy read the paragraph aloud flawlessly, and his teacher then asked him to tell the group what the paragraph was about. Billy replied, "I don't know. I wasn't listening." Often oral reading of this type can become a rather valueless procedure.

Extending skill development. During this part of the lesson, the teacher presents the word identification or comprehension skills from the manual relating to that particular basal reader story, often using the chalkboard, chart paper, or the overhead projector. These skills later can be reinforced independently with basal reader workbook pages, other commercially available materials, or teacher-made activity sheets.

---

[3]Stauffer, *The Language-Experience Approach*, pp. 184–214.

Enrichment experiences. The last step of the basal reader lesson provides appropriate follow-up activities that add to each child's understanding of the concepts presented in the story. For example, the teachers' manual usually indicates related stories for the child to read independently or related filmstrips and recordings. Other suggested activities might be creative writing, art activities, construction activities, dramatic play, role playing, and cooking and baking activities. So many suggested activities accompany each lesson that the teacher should choose only a few rather than try to present them all.

As part of the basal reader approach in the primary grades, each child participates in independent or small-group activities while the teacher meets with other reading groups. Finding worthwhile independent activities probably is one of the most challenging tasks confronting both the experienced and inexperienced primary-grade teacher. Each independent activity should be meaningful, require little or no teacher supervision, and not be busy work. Today a number of children participate in activities at *reading stations* independently or in small groups. A reading station can be located in a carrel or can simply be several desks pushed together. Some activities that can be used at a reading station are playing a reading game, listening to a read-along cassette tape and following along in a book, completing a commercial or teacher-made activity sheet, doing creative writing, or practicing a reading skill in another way. Other activities that can be used on an independent or small-group basis in the primary grades, depending upon the reading ability of the children, are independent reading of trade books, completing workbook pages or activity sheets, working with clay, art activities, and construction activities.

Although a number of primary-grade teachers mainly use *convergent independent activities,* they often should not do so. Any convergent activity requires one right answer and allows no room for differences of opinion. Convergent activities are mainly stressed in workbooks and a number of commercial activity sheets. However, children should also have opportunities to participate in *divergent independent activities.* In a divergent activity a child can be creative while responding because no one specific response is expected. Some examples of divergent activities are writing language experience stories, art activities, construction activities, some game activities, and some activity sheets.

Here are several good resource books for locating divergent independent activities at both the primary-grade and intermediate-grade reading level:

Paul C. Burns and Betty D. Roe, *Reading Activities for Today's Elementary Schools* (Chicago: Rand McNally College Publishing Company, 1979).

Wilma H. Miller, *Reading Correction Kit* (West Nyack, New York: The Center for Applied Research in Education, 1982).

————, *The Reading Activities Handbook* (New York: Holt, Rine-hart and Winston, 1980).

Evelyn B. Spache, *Reading Activities for Child Involvement* (Boston: Allyn and Bacon, 1982).

STRATEGIES FOR USING THE BASAL READER APPROACH IN THE INTERMEDIATE GRADES

The basal reader approach always must be considered only one of the reading experiences in which children at the intermediate-grade reading level should participate. Much individualized reading (see Chapter 6) and reading in the content areas (see Chapter 16) should always be used along with the possible employment of the basal reader approach.

Normally there is only one hardcover basal reader at the fourth reader level, fifth reader level, and sixth reader level. Today most basal reader publishers also publish one book at the seventh reader level and one book at the eighth reader level. Basal readers at the middle-upper levels usually contain some narrative-type material organized into units that can easily be supplemented by wide reading from other sources. In addition, they normally contain considerable information from such content areas as social studies and science. They often contain strategies for presenting content reading.

At the intermediate-grade reading level, the basal reader varies somewhat in format from that used at the primary-grade reading level. Most often, the teacher may attempt to develop a background of experiences for reading the story. However, new vocabulary rarely is presented because the students at this reading level are encouraged to use their word identification techniques to determine the probable pronunciation and meaning of unknown words. At this level students read silently, guided by teacher-formulated or, more importantly, student-formulated purposes for reading. Oral reading in the group setting is much de-emphasized at this level in comparison to the primary-grade reading level. There often is much group interaction at this level as the students react critically to the statements made by the other group members. The extending skills portion of the basal reader lesson mainly refines and extends many of the word identification and comprehension skills that first were introduced in the primary grades. The enriching experiences are similar in scope to those presented in the teachers' manuals at the primary-grade reading level.

Usually, two reading achievement groups are formed in each class to at least attempt to provide for the wide range of differences in reading achievement found at the intermediate-grade reading level. Although the range in reading achievement in a typical, heterogeneously grouped class in the later primary grades normally is about five or six grade levels, it extends to eight or ten or more grade levels in the later intermediate grades. It is obvious that two reading groups cannot begin to provide for the reading needs of such a wide range of reading levels. Therefore, considerable individualized reading must be done at the intermediate-grade reading level. It is interesting to note that although the typical middle-school classroom contains such a wide variety of reading levels, sometimes the teacher employs only one basal reader achievement group. Such a group obviously is an ineffective use of the basal reader approach, but this occurs because of the pressure to present so many other subjects at the intermediate-grade level.

A student in the intermediate grades always should read a basal reader and all other materials that are on his or her approximate *instructional reading level*—meaning that these can be read with about 95 percent or better accuracy in word identification and 75 percent or better accuracy in comprehension. It is meaningless to have a student in sixth grade read a sixth reader if his or her instructional reading level is at the fourth reader level. The same can be said of content materials. In the past far too many students have spent their entire school career reading on the *frustration reading level*. Therefore, such students have gained little from their reading and often have come to dislike all reading activities.

The basal readers that are designed to be used at the middle-upper reading levels are accompanied by practice books that are intended to reinforce appropriate reading skills. Although I believe that such practice books are usually less valuable and less needed in the intermediate grades than they are in the primary grades, a practice book can be useful if appropriate pages are selected to be completed by an individual child or the students in a group. Certainly, such a basal reader practice book never should be used in a cover-to-cover fashion.

The word identification skills that are presented and reinforced at the intermediate-grade reading level are mainly a refinement and extension of those skills that were presented and practiced in the primary grades. Because the vast majority of the phonic analysis skills were presented and reinforced at the primary-grade reading level, phonic analysis normally receives little stress at the middle-upper level, with the possible exception of some disabled readers. However, even some disabled readers need receive little instruction in phonic analysis if they have experienced little success in this skill in the past because a reader can be proficient without great competency in phonic analysis.

On the other hand, structural analysis skills are extended considerably at the intermediate-grade reading level. As an example, the meanings of many prefixes and suffixes are presented. The syllabication and accentuation of polysyllabic words also are presented at this level. Context clues often are very useful in determining the meaning of unknown words that intermediate-grade students meet in narrative and content reading. Students in the intermediate grades should have some direct instruction in using context clues effectively. This instruction and practice may well involve the use of variations of the cloze procedure. As dictionary skills are difficult for most children to master, direct instruction and motivated practice are needed for children to become proficient in their use. Basal readers designed for use in the intermediate grades also provide students with numerous opportunities to learn to use glossaries effectively.

Basal readers at the middle-upper reading levels place great stress on the improvement of interpretive comprehension skills, critical reading skills, and creative reading. At this reading level, literal comprehension normally receives much less emphasis than at the primary-grade reading level. Competency in the higher-type comprehension skills always should be stressed by using reading materials in addition to basal readers, such as trade books, supplementary books, children's magazines and newspapers, content textbooks, and reference books. Most middle-upper level classrooms do not use the predominantly narrative basal reader material every day. Instead basal readers may be used one or several days a week with the rest of the time being used for individualized reading or reading in the content fields. (See Chapters 6 and 16.) Much of the intermediate-grade reading material should be from trade books, other supplementary books, reference books, and such content books as social studies and science.

At the middle-upper reading level, children should learn to apply the study skills learned in basal reading to reading in such content fields as social studies and science. Contemporary basal readers at the middle-upper reading level make some attempt to do this. However, this instruction and practice must be supplemented by additional direct teacher instruction in most instances. Such study skills as locating the directly stated and implied main ideas, locating significant details, graph reading, map reading, summarizing, note-taking, and outlining should be presented and practiced at this level. Useful study techniques such as Survey Q3R, OK4R, or PQRST also can be presented at the intermediate-grade reading level. Some other strategies such as the oral reading strategy, C/T/Q strategy, and the question-only strategy may improve competency in content reading.[4] Details regarding these strategies are provided in Chapter 16.

Many students at the middle-upper reading level have difficulty in reading content textbooks because of the special reading skills that

[4]Anthony V. Manzo, "Three 'Universal' Strategies in Content Area Reading and Languaging," *Journal of Reading, 24* (November 1980): 146–149.

are needed and the specialized vocabulary, heavy concept load, and high readability level that are encountered in such textbooks. Although it is difficult for teachers at this level to cope with the content reading problems of many students, they should try to locate content reading materials on the student's instructional reading level. It is possible to present social studies and science by the unit method so that students can read about the unit topic from textbooks, trade books, supplementary materials, or reference books on their instructional or independent reading level. Some teachers rewrite material from the social studies or science textbook of the actual grade level so that disabled readers can read the rewritten material at their own instructional reading level. Portions of a content textbook also can be tape-recorded by the teacher, a teacher's aide, or an above-average student so that disabled readers can listen to the material and thus absorb its content.

Reading for pleasure, usually on the student's independent reading level, is extremely important at the middle-upper reading level. In the past, elementary schools have been fairly successful in teaching most students the important word identification and comprehension skills, but have been much less successful in teaching students to value reading for pleasure. If a student does not learn to read for pleasure at the intermediate-grade level, he or she normally never does this. Perhaps intermediate-grade teachers can best motivate students to read for pleasure by helping them select highly interesting, relevant materials that appeal to their emotions. Often such materials should be on the student's *independent reading level.* The student should be able to read the material with about 99 percent accuracy in word identification and comprehend it at a level of about 95 percent or better. Motivating students to want to read for pleasure is a very challenging and rewarding task that is extremely important both for the student and society.

USING THE BASAL READER APPROACH WITH SOME SPECIAL CHILDREN

Since the passage of Public Law 94–142, many types of special children will be mainstreamed into regular classrooms for at least part of each school day. The basal reader approach often is used at least fairly successfully with a number of these children.

The basal reader approach is used fairly often as a major approach for teaching reading to blind and low-vision children. The majority of the basal reader series are now available in Braille and large type at the American Printing House for the Blind, 1839 Frankfort Avenue, Louisville, Kentucky 40206. This is the case for the readers and the workbooks. An article by Marjorie Ward and Sandra McCormick provides many strategies for using these basal readers with blind and low-vision children in the classroom.[5]

According to a research study that was recently recorded, the basal reader approach also is by far the most commonly used method for presenting reading to hearing-impaired children. At least half of the teachers use the basal reader approach as the main means of instruction for hearing-impaired students.[6]

The basal reader approach often is used with other types of special children such as educable mentally handicapped, physically handicapped, and learning-disabled children. However, when one examines the content of contemporary basal readers, it is rather distressing to note that they usually contain very few handicapped children as the main characters in their stories. With the concept of mainstreaming now in general practice, basal reader publishers probably should attempt to include more handicapped children in favorable, realistic roles in their materials.

USING THE BASAL READER APPROACH IN A DIAGNOSTIC-PRESCRIPTIVE WAY

Although the basal reader approach is a fairly structured way of presenting elementary reading instruction, it also can be used in a diagnostic-prescriptive manner if the teacher chooses to do so.

When the basal reader approach is used in this way, a group of children do not have to read each story in a specific basal reader. Stories that are not relevant to the needs and interests of the children can be omitted. All the reading skills contained in a lesson in the basal reader teachers' manual need not be presented or reinforced if the children already have competency in those reading skills. Neither should all of the pages in a practice book be assigned to a child if he or she already has competency in those skills. A child should complete only those workbook pages that provide practice in a reading skill that he or she needs.

When the basal reader approach is used in a diagnostic-prescriptive manner, it should be easy for a child to move into another reading achievement group or another basal reader if he or she is ready for

[5]Marjorie Ward and Sandra McCormick, "Reading Instruction for Blind and Low Vision Children in the Regular Classroom," *The Reading Teacher, 34* (January 1981): 434–444.

[6]Patricia R. Bockmiller and Joan D. Coley, "A Survey of Methods, Materials, and Teacher Preparation Among Teachers of Reading to the Hearing Impaired," *The Reading Teacher, 34* (February 1981): 526–529.

such movement. If a child has been found capable of reading at a higher level than that found in his or her present basal reader, he or she should be able to move into another basal reader. Basal reader stories also can be read on an individual basis by children as part of the individualized reading plan. (See Chapter 6.)

Therefore, the basal reader approach can be a much more flexible approach than it usually is in practice. Its typical inflexibility is not inherent in the approach itself but rather is a result of the way in which the approach often is used.

RESEARCH ON THE USE OF THE BASAL READER APPROACH

As was mentioned in Chapter 4, during the mid-1960s twenty-seven first-grade research studies were funded by the United States Office of Education in an attempt to determine the best method or methods for teaching primary-grade reading. Guy L. Bond and Robert Dykstra compiled all the results of the first-grade studies in an article in the *Reading Research Quarterly*.[7] In general, the basal reader approach fared quite well in comparison with other beginning reading approaches such as the language experience approach or a formal phonic approach. Similar results were found when some of these studies were continued into second grade. However, the general consensus of all these studies was that superior primary-grade reading teachers did an effective job of teaching reading no matter what approach they used.

However, it also can be stated that the basal reader approach usually is the most effective when it is used along with other reading approaches such as the language experience approach or individualized reading.

ADVANTAGES OF THE BASAL READER APPROACH

Most certainly, the major advantage of the basal reader approach is its sequential and systematic presentation of the various word identification and comprehension skills. Because the basal readers and the accompanying manuals have been compiled and written by reading specialists who understand the complex reading process, a teacher who uses this approach can be assured that all of the major word identification and comprehension skills have been systematically presented

---

[7]Guy L. Bond and Robert Dykstra, "The Cooperative Research Program in First-Grade Reading Instruction," *Reading Research Quarterly, 2* (Summer 1967): 5–141.

and reinforced by the time a student has completed the basal reader designed for the middle-upper reading level. Research has indicated that some elementary teachers probably are not sufficiently knowledgeable about the various elements comprising the complex reading process to teach it effectively without the guidance that comes from the careful use of the basal reader manuals. These manuals are especially helpful to inexperienced teachers. This is why I recommend that such teachers usually use this approach along with several other approaches. (See Chapters 10 and 11.)

The basal reader approach stresses all the word identification techniques, with no single technique emphasized at the expense of the others. Although phonic analysis is receiving increased emphasis in contemporary basal readers in comparison to the readers of the past, the other word identification techniques, such as sight word recognition, structural analysis, and contextual analysis, also receive stress in this approach. The basal reader also stresses all the levels of understanding from the beginning stages—literal comprehension, interpretive comprehension, critical reading, and creative reading.

Contemporary basal reader publishers put forth a great effort to design readers that have an excellent format and greatly appeal to the majority of the students who are to use them. Most such readers are colorfully illustrated and contain the correct type size for their intended users. Their content also usually is fairly interesting to the students who are to read them. Current basal readers often contain good literature, sometimes even summaries of award-winning children's trade books, which will motivate the children to read. On the whole, the content and language of contemporary basal readers are much more appealing than they used to be. The basal reader publishers have made a concerted effort to keep the literary quality of their readers high and to use natural language as much as possible.

Basal reader publishers are now making a very limited effort to include handicapped persons in basal reader stories. As was explained earlier in this chapter, they need to make more of an effort to do this because so many children will be mainstreamed into regular classrooms for at least part of each school day as a result of Public Law 94–142.

As was mentioned earlier, the basal reader approach utilizes many helpful multimedia aids that can save the teacher time if they are used wisely. They are in the form of filmstrips, cassette recordings, transparencies, reading games, supplementary readers, duplicating masters, word cards, posters, pocket charts, discussion cards, and writing helpers. Many of these aids are very appealing and motivate students to improve their reading skills. However, they must be used carefully in a basal reader program that is both diagnostic and prescriptive, or they may become mere busywork.

LIMITATIONS OF THE BASAL READER APPROACH

A number of the limitations of the basal reader approach really are not inherent in the approach itself but in how it is actually used by some teachers.

Overdependence on the basal reader teachers' manuals may stifle teacher creativity if the manuals are used as a "Bible" instead of as a guide. Although the reading specialists who formulate basal reader series never plan on having their materials used in this limited way, in practice this sometimes happens. However, any teacher, whether experienced or inexperienced, can be creative while using the basal reader approach.

Another disadvantage that is not inherent in the approach is the use of rigid reading achievement groups. Sometimes, for example, a first-grade child is placed in the below-average group solely on the basis of his or her reading readiness test scores, not a completely valid criterion, and he or she may remain in that group throughout elementary school. Unfortunately, this may happen because the reading skills are presented in a sequential, developmental manner in the basal reader approach. Many of the reading skills build on previous skills at least to some extent. Therefore, children in the below-average group may have difficulty moving into a higher group because they have not yet learned some of the reading skills already learned by a faster group. Basal reader manuals always recommend flexible grouping and the use of other types of groups such as interest, research, and tutorial groups. (See Chapter 15.) However, in practice, the reading achievement groups in the basal reader approach often remain quite rigid, and the below-average reader may feel stigmatized in that group and consequently develop a dislike toward all reading activities.

The practice of some teachers of considering the basal readers as the only materials to which children should be exposed is another limitation that is not inherent in the approach itself. Children at all grade levels need numerous opportunities to read on their independent and instructional reading levels in trade books, in the basal readers of other series, in supplementary readers, in content textbooks, in reference books, and in children's magazines and newspapers.

In the past some administrators and teachers regarded the grade-level placement of a basal reader as an expectation that each child in that particular grade should read at that level. Fortunately, this is not so common today, and most children are allowed to read basal readers at the appropriate level. This practice has been enhanced because basal reader publishers have used levels instead of grade-level designations of their readers. These levels have not been tied to reading grades. However, even now some able readers may be required to use a basal reader that is below their instructional reading level, perhaps causing them to lose interest in reading. Perhaps even more harmful, students in the below-average group may have to read a basal reader that is one or more years above their instructional reading level. These children then are consistently reading on their frustration reading level, very likely causing them to dislike reading.

Recently there has been some attention paid to the images of the elderly in basal readers. The presentation of elderly people was found to be at least fairly positive with central elderly characters generally being healthy and active. However, considerable stereotyping appeared in the physical characteristics of the illustrations and in the types of jobs that the characters had.[8]

Vocabulary control, especially at the beginning stages of reading instruction, has been criticized in the past because the sentences obviously do not reflect the oral language patterns of first-grade children and, therefore, may cause language regression. As a result, reading specialists recently have tried to use the knowledge gained from the science of linguistics to make the language patterns in the basal readers more closely resemble oral language patterns, and this has helped to increase the appeal of the beginning basal reader stories.

LISTING OF THE COMMONLY USED BASAL READER SERIES

This part of the chapter contains a brief listing of the commonly used basal reader series. You can find additional information on them by writing to the following source:

Selector's Guide for Elementary School Reading Programs, Volumes
    I and II
EPIE Institute
475 Riverside Drive
New York, New York 10027

Basal Reader Series

Pathfinder
Allyn and Bacon, Inc., 1978
470 Atlantic Avenue
Boston, Massachusetts 02210

---

[8]Gail Cohen Taylor, "Images of the Elderly in Children's Literature," *The Reading Teacher, 34* (December 1980): 344–347.

American Book Company Reading Program
American Book Company, 1980
135 West 50 Street
New York, New York 10020

Ginn Reading Program
Ginn and Company, 1982
191 Spring Street
Lexington, Massachusetts 02173

Bookmark Reading Program
Harcourt Brace Jovanovich, Inc., 1979
757 Third Avenue
New York, New York 10017

Reading Basics Plus
Harper & Row, Publishers, 1976
10 East 53 Street
New York, New York 10022

Basic Reading Systems
Holt, Rinehart and Winston, 1980
383 Madison Avenue
New York, New York 10017

Houghton Mifflin Readers
Houghton Mifflin Company, 1981
2 Park Street
Boston, Massachusetts 02107

Laidlaw Reading Program
Laidlaw Brothers, Inc., 1976–1978
Thatcher and Madison
River Forest, Illinois 60305

The Macmillan Reading Program
Macmillan Publishing Company, Inc., 1974
866 Third Avenue
New York, New York 10022

Young America Basic Series
Rand McNally & Company, 1978
Box 7600
Chicago, Illinois 60680

Basic Reading Series
Science Research Associates, Inc., 1976
North Wacker Drive
Chicago, Illinois 60606

Scott Foresman Basal Reader Series
Scott Foresman and Company, 1981
1900 East Lake Avenue
Glenview, Illinois 60625

SELECTED REFERENCES

Aukerman, Robert C. *The Basal Reader Approach to Reading.* New York: John Wiley & Sons, Inc., 1981.

Farr, Roger, and Nancy Roser. *Teaching a Child to Read.* New York: Harcourt Brace Jovanovich, Inc., 1979, pp. 428–446.

Freedman, Glenn, and Elizabeth G. Reynolds. "Enriching Basal Reader Lessons with Semantic Webbing." *The Reading Teacher, 33* (March 1980): 677–684.

Karlin, Robert. *Teaching Elementary Reading.* New York: Harcourt Brace Jovanovich, Inc., 1980, pp. 47–50.

Legenza, Alice, and June D. Knafle. "How Effective Are Pictures in Basal Readers?" *The Reading Teacher, 32* (November 1978): 170–173.

McCutcheon, Gail, and Diane Kyle. "Characters in Basal Readers: Does 'Equal' Now Mean 'Same'?" *The Reading Teacher, 32* (January 1979): 438–441.

Pieronek, Florence T. "Do Basal Readers Reflect the Interests of Intermediate Students?" *The Reading Teacher, 33* (January 1980): 408–412.

———. "Using Basal Guidebooks—The Ideal Integrated Reading Lesson Plan." *The Reading Teacher, 33* (November 1979): 167–172.

Snyder, Geraldine V. "Do Basal Characters Read in Their Daily Lives?" *The Reading Teacher, 33* (December 1979): 303–306.

Zintz, Miles V. *The Reading Process.* Dubuque, Iowa: William C. Brown Company, Publishers, 1980, pp. 102–106.

SUGGESTED ACTIVITIES

1. In groups of three to five students, analyze a basal reader series in terms of the following criteria:

MANUALS

accuracy
reputable authorship
amount of detail
use of a scope and sequence chart
well-outlined lessons

READERS

titles
copyright date
format
story content
vocabulary control
appeal to minority groups and women
balance between fiction and nonfiction

WORKBOOKS
titles
ability to be done independently
ease of evaluation
format
reinforcement of appropriate skills

LIST OF MULTIMEDIA AIDS
usefulness
cost
probable availability

2. Teach a basal reader lesson to a small group of from two to five primary-grade or intermediate-grade students.
3. Compare the sequence of phonic analysis skills as they are taught in several sets of comparable basal readers.
4. If possible, listen to the presentation of a sales representative of a basal reader publisher. Such representatives often visit universities or school districts.
5. Visit an elementary classroom to observe a basal reader lesson. Do the steps in this lesson correspond to those outlined in the chapter?

Individualized reading

What Would You Have Done?

Mrs. Wascowicz was a sixth-grade teacher in a large city in the Southeast. For a number of years she had been concerned about the number of students in her sixth-grade class who could read fairly adequately but simply did not enjoy reading. However, she was especially concerned when a bright boy named Marty entered her class one September.

After examining Marty's cumulative folder carefully, Mrs. Wascowicz learned that he could read on about grade level. According to the folder, he had been given a number of standardized reaching achievement tests and several valid individual reading inventories. All these standardized and informal measures indicated that he could read at grade level. However, all the comments in the cumulative folder indicated that he simply was uninterested in reading. He generally did not do well in the basal reader achievement group and did not choose to read independently either.

Mrs. Wascowicz found both of these things to be accurate. Although Marty was capable of performing well in the basal reader achievement group, which used a sixth-grade basal reader, he was very uninterested in reading the material found in this reader. When Mrs. Wascowicz talked with Marty about this, she learned that Marty considered the material in the reader to be stupid and boring. After reflecting for some time on Marty's problem, Mrs. Wascowicz decided to allow him to read largely on an individual basis from self-selected materials that interested him. She found out that his major interest was in learning all that he could about motorcycles. With the help of the ele-

mentary librarian, Mrs. Wascowicz located a number of books on this topic. However, the librarian cautioned her that some of the books were on about eighth-grade reading level.

Marty chose several of the books to read independently, and he read them during several days when his former basal reader achievement group was meeting. Mrs. Wascowicz was able to find some time to meet with Marty in individual reading conferences, and during that time she discussed the books with him, asked him some comprehension questions, and had him do a little oral reading from the books. She was amazed to discover that because of his interest in motorcycles, he was able to read books even on the eighth-grade reading level with a fair amount of success.

After some time, Marty met with his basal reader achievement group about once a week to improve his critical reading skills and to learn some study skills. Because he continued to do largely individualized reading, he usually performed much better in the basal reader achievement group also. After a time, Mrs. Wascowicz added uninterrupted sustained silent reading (USSR) to her daily schedule. During this time everyone in the classroom, including the teacher, read self-selected materials for about thirty minutes. Marty enjoyed this period very much.

After you have read this chapter, you will know how to conduct an individual reading conference and how to use uninterrupted sustained silent reading in your classroom. This knowledge should help you motivate many of your able, but reluctant, readers to want to read—a very important and worthwhile accomplishment.

DEFINITION OF TERMS

It may be helpful at the outset to briefly define some of the terms that are related to the area of individualized reading because this is an area of reading in which there is considerable confusion in the way in which the terms are used.

Pure or *true individualized reading* takes place when the individualized reading plan is used as the major way of organizing an elementary classroom for reading instruction. As will be explained in detail later in this chapter, this plan presumes that each child seeks to read, can self-select his or her own reading materials, and can self-pace his or her own reading. Individual reading conferences, needs or skills groups, and record keeping are an integral part of this plan. When individualized reading is used in its pure or true form, it is the major mode of reading instruction in a classroom.

Modified individualized reading is individualized reading used along with another, more structured approach such as the basal reader approach or a phonic approach. In this way the more structured approach is used to teach the important word identification and comprehension skills while individualized reading is used to reinforce the reading skills and to motivate reading. As will be explained later in this chapter and in Chapters 10 and 11, modified individualized reading is recommended by this author because its use can eliminate the objections that often are voiced to individualized reading in its pure or true form.

A form of *diagnostic-prescriptive reading instruction* also can be made a part of individualized reading. Usually, when this is done, the basal reader approach or a phonic approach is used as the primary mode of elementary reading instruction. Then periodic individual reading conferences are used, during which the child reads portions of several basal readers or graded phonic materials to see if he or she possesses the competencies to be placed in a higher basal reader or phonic reader or workbook. Thus, when an individual reading conference is used in this way, the teacher diagnoses present reading skill strengths and weaknesses and subsequently acts upon the results of the diagnosis.

Personalized reading instruction, as is explained in detail later in the chapter, is somewhat more structured than is individualized reading. This is the case because the reading skill development is outlined by using reading skills checklists for each level from the reading readiness level through the sixth-grade reading level. Personalized reading does make use of individual reading conferences and various types of flexible grouping.

Contract teaching also is a form of individualization that sometimes is used at the middle-upper grade level. In contract teaching, the student agrees to do a specified amount of work during a specified period of time. The student then can arrange his or her own time schedule for completing this work. There often are several different ways in which the work can be completed also.

Programmed reading instruction also is a way of individualizing reading instruction. Programmed instruction is based upon the stimulus-response learning theory, which states that a subject will respond in a predetermined way upon the introduction of a stimulus. Normally, the reading skills are subdivided into small units and organized in a sequential manner when programmed reading instruction is used. This mode of instruction uses frames to present various aspects of the reading skills. Programmed reading instruction can take the form of teaching machines or workbooks. It can be a way of individualized reading instruction because the student can proceed through the frames at his or her own rate and can be directed to complete other frames if the material is not mastered. This concept is called branching.

Reading laboratories such as those published by Science Research Associates are another way of individualizing reading instruction. These are sets of materials that are graded. The student selects materials at the appropriate reading level and proceeds at his or her own pace through succeeding reading levels. Such reading labs are often used in an attempt to help individualized reading instruction at the intermediate-grade level.

A BRIEF HISTORY OF PURE INDIVIDUALIZED READING

Although individualized reading may sound like an innovative topic in elementary reading instruction, it, like many other contemporary plans and approaches, is based upon an older approach. A form of individualized reading has been in use in North American elementary schools for about sixty years.

Individualized reading probably gained impetus between 1910 and 1920 with the development of standardized tests in reading. These tests indicated the wide range of children's reading abilities in any single grade and the different rates at which children learn to read. These results showed educators that children should be allowed to learn to read at their own rate.

The actual forerunners of individualized reading as it is known today were organizational plans from several cities such as Dalton, Connecticut; Pueblo, Colorado; Winnetka, Illinois; and Madison, Wisconsin. In most of these plans, the students were given a unit of work in reading that each completed on an individual basis at his or her own rate of speed. Although the same material usually was covered by each child, the speed at which the material was completed varied.

Usually, the above-average students finished the work more rapidly than the average and below-average students.

However, individualized reading instruction was not widely used after the 1920s in elementary schools. In the early 1950s, mainly as a result of the writing of Willard C. Olson, a specialist in child growth and development, it reemerged. Olson correctly believed that reading development should always be considered a part of each child's total development and that each child is an individual who has a number of inherent needs that must be met. In relation to reading, Olson wrote that children desire to read, can select their own reading materials, and can pace their own reading.[1] These three needs formed the basis of the contemporary pure or true individualized reading plan of class organization. Not all reading specialists would agree that reluctant readers seek to read unless they are very much motivated by a teacher. However, most specialists would agree that children can select their own reading material and can pace their own reading with some teacher guidance.

In 1959, Jeannette Veatch wrote a book that provided an impetus toward individualized reading as it is practiced today.[2] Walter B. Barbe and Jerry L. Abbott also wrote a book that helped to promote individualized reading by using what may be a more useful term, *personalized reading*.[3] Other contemporary proponents of individualized reading are Lyman Hunt, Sam Duker, and Patrick Groff.

The versions of individualized or personalized reading vary greatly. Some versions use techniques such as reading skill checklists or reading stations. In fact, there probably are as many versions of individualized reading as there are creative and innovative teachers to implement them. Many, however, are at least partially based upon Olson's philosophy.

VARIOUS VERSIONS OF INDIVIDUALIZED READING IN THE PRIMARY GRADES

Success in a subsequent individualized reading program presupposes that a child has been exposed to many prereading experiences in the home, in preschool programs, and in kindergarten. It is especially im-

[1]Willard C. Olson, *Child Development* (Lexington, Massachusetts: D. C. Heath & Company, 1949).

[2]Jeannette Veatch, *Individualizing Your Reading Program* (New York: Putnam, 1959).

[3]Walter B. Barbe and Jerry L. Abbott, *Personalized Reading Instruction* (West Nyack, New York: Parker Publishing Company, 1975).

portant that the child has been read to extensively before being expected to succeed in an individualized reading program in first grade. This reading can take the form of picture books, trade books, fairy tales, and folktales of various types.

Then, before using an individualized reading program of any type, the teacher determines apparent reading readiness by using a combination of reading readiness test scores and observation in late kindergarten or early first grade. When the teacher has decided that certain individuals or small groups of children have attained sufficient readiness, they are introduced to beginning reading instruction.

Pure or True Individualized Reading

At the beginning of pure or true individualized reading, the kindergarten or first-grade teacher often uses the language experience approach before initiating actual reading. The teacher often decides on a *key vocabulary,* words needed to read most of the simple trade books that will be used in beginning individualized reading. These key vocabulary terms then are presented as sight words by using individually dictated language experience stories or group-dictated experience charts.

After a child learns to recognize the key vocabulary terms, the teacher helps him or her to select a simple trade book that he or she wishes to learn to read. If a child already can read, the teacher helps him or her to select a book on the instructional or independent reading level. In either case, the book should be very interesting to, and selected by, the child. The child then reads this first trade book silently on an independent basis while the teacher is working with other children in the class on an individual or small-group basis. When the child has read the book, he or she meets with the teacher in an *individual reading conference* to read a portion of the trade book aloud, answer a few comprehension questions about it, and share reactions to it.

After the individual reading conference, the child then selects another trade book on his or her instructional or independent reading level to read silently on an independent basis. Thereafter the child continues to select interesting reading material. Children build up reading skills gradually, attempting longer books when they are ready. In a trade book with approximately one hundred words on a page, you can have the child learn to turn to a page near the middle of the book and try to read it either silently or orally, putting one finger down on the desk or table for each unknown word. If the child meets more unknown words than he or she has fingers on one hand, the book can be considered too difficult. The child continues to meet with the teacher for individual reading conferences of about ten to fifteen minutes each two or three times a week. The teacher usually informs the children who have conferences that day by listing them on the chalkboard, on a piece of chart paper, or on a chart.

The individual reading conference is the primary contact between teacher and student in pure or true individualized reading. The conference is held so that the teacher can assess the child's reading progress and so that the child can receive the teacher's undivided attention and help. The teacher often begins the conference by asking the child about the book being read:

What is the name of the book that you have read?

Did you like this book? Why or why not?

Would you want to read another book like this one? Why or why not?

Tell me about the part of the book that you liked the best.

Who was your favorite person in this book? Why?

Is this a real or a make-believe story? Why do you think so?

Would you encourage a friend to read this book? Why or why not?

Next the teacher usually has the child read his or her favorite portion of the story aloud so that the teacher can assess the child's competency in the various word identification skills and fluency of oral reading. Usually, the teacher has the child choose a favorite portion of the story to read aloud although the teacher may ask the child to read a specific portion of the story aloud. During the oral reading, the teacher evaluates the child's weaknesses in the word identification techniques of sight word knowledge, phonic analysis, structural analysis, and contextual analysis. The teacher usually notes the child's specific difficulties in the various aspects of the word identification techniques so that they can be corrected later individually or in a needs or skills group. This type of group is explained later in this chapter. The teacher often writes the notes down at the conclusion of the conference.

As a part of the individual reading conference, the teacher then asks the child several comprehension questions about the trade book. Although some of them can be literal comprehension questions, many should require interpretive or critical responses. Before concluding an individual reading conference, the teacher may help the child keep a record of his or her reading. However, after competency is established in this procedure, the child usually can keep his or her own records independently.

It undoubtedly is possible to use a *group conference* in the pure or true individualized reading plan. When this is done, several children can bring the trade book that they have read independently to the group conference. If a question is asked about a word identification subskill, any child who wishes to can respond to it. However, if a comprehension question is asked in a group conference, it should have meaning to the entire group. For example, such questions could involve sharing the most exciting part of the book, telling about the most interesting character in the book, or summarizing the content of the book very briefly.

Record keeping is a very important aspect of individualized reading. Both the teacher and the child should keep careful records of each child's reading if the plan is to be implemented successfully. The records of the children at the primary-grade reading level can be quite simple. For example, the child may print the titles and authors of each book read. As a further record of a book, a child in the early primary grades may want to draw a picture of a favorite scene. In the second and third grades, a child may write a one-sentence summary of the book or his or her reaction to the book. At this level, the record keeping may be done on cards. Figure 6-1 is a sample reading card that was completed by a second-grade child. In addition to using reading cards, children in the primary grades can employ a number of other formats to keep a record of their reading: sheets of handwritten paper, scrolls, newsprint, folded manila paper, and the like. After some experience, children in the upper primary grades may want to design their own format.

To implement the pure or true individualized reading plan, the teacher must realize the importance of keeping detailed records of each child's reading. A number of teachers keep these records in some type of loose-leaf notebook or folder, with one sheet for each child. On such a sheet, the teacher can list the child's name, age, and standardized reading test scores and/or Individual Reading Inventory score. On the sheet the teacher then keeps a record of the date of each conference,

> The Snowy Day
>   by Ezra Keats
> This is a story
> about what one
> boy did on a
> snowy day. I
> really liked this book.

FIGURE 6-1

the title of the book read, the author, the child's specific word identification and comprehension skill needs as determined from each conference, and the child's interests as evidenced by the conference. Figure
6-2 shows a sample record sheet, which was completed by a teacher
for a third-grade child. Some teachers instead wish to keep some type
of running log of reading accomplished by the students who had conferences that day.

To help implement a pure or true individualized reading program
in the primary grades, some teachers have marked the back of each
trade book in their room with a different color of masking tape to
indicate the reading level of the book. If the trade books in an elementary school are housed in a central library, the librarian may be
able to provide some help in determining the approximate reading
level of a trade book. As was stated earlier, the child also can sample
the trade book himself or herself to decide if it is on the approximate
correct reading level.

As an additional help in conducting a successful individualized
reading program, some primary-grade teachers have formulated comprehension questions for the trade books housed in their classroom.

Name Beth Wright Grade 3 S.R.S. 4.2 I.R.I. 3.8				
Date	Title of Book	Author	Reading Skill Needs	Interests
10/14/83	Tamara and the Sea Witch	Krystyna Turska	needs help in critical reading	magic
10/17/83	Dear Sarah	Elisabeth Borchers	needs help in critical reading	travel
10/21/83	Wolf Story	David McPhail	creative reading	animals
10/28/83	Russian Fairy Tales	Afanas'ev Aleksandr	creative reading	fairy tales
10/30/83	Arthur's Adventure in the Abandoned House	Fernando Krahn	needs help in critical reading	adventure

FIGURE 6-2

These questions may be placed in a small file box for the teacher to refer to during individual reading conferences. This file of comprehension questions can be supplemented as the teacher reads additional children's materials.

It also can be stated at this point that the major emphasis in the pure or true individualized reading program always is on comprehension. This is especially true of the higher levels of comprehension in which the child applies and extends the ideas in the trade books.

Mrs. Larson's first-grade classroom is an example of the use of individualized reading in its pure or true form as a major approach at the first-grade level. Mrs. Larson's classroom is very well equipped and contains many trade books, basal readers, supplementary materials, language experience booklets, several reading stations, manipulative materials, a reading corner, a science corner, an arithmetic corner, several classroom pets, puzzles, reading games, and a simple writing center. Her room is large and spacious, which makes it fairly easy for the children to engage in independent activities. The elementary school in which she teaches also has a central library.

At the beginning of each school day during the second semester Mrs. Larson usually plans with her first-grade class, guiding their planning to some extent. She then helps the children prepare for their independent activities, independent reading, use of the reading stations, art activities, or construction activities, which are often related to their work in social studies and science. When Mrs. Larson has decided that all of the children in her class are prepared for an independent work period, she calls the first child who is scheduled for an individual reading conference on that day to come and join her in the conference area. Her approximate conversation with Ellen, an above-average reader, is as follows:

Mrs. Larson: What kind of a book have you been reading lately?

Ellen: It's a book about a deer and her baby who live in the woods.

Mrs. Larson: Can you tell me something about how the deer and her fawn lived?

Ellen: They ate the leaves and bark of some trees and drank water from a lake.

Mrs. Larson: What was your favorite part of the book about?

Ellen: It was when the fawn got bigger and lost his spots.

Mrs. Larson: Will you choose your favorite part of the book and read it aloud to me?

(Ellen selected a part of the book near the end and read three pages aloud. She mispronounced several words, including *fir* and *pier*.)

Mrs. Larson: Ellen, look at this word. That is an *r*-controlled vowel. Therefore, it does not have a short /i/ sound. What do you suppose the word is?

Ellen:	I guess the word is *fir,* not *fire.* I guess a fir tree must be a kind of tree. It looks from this picture like it's a Christmas tree.
Mrs. Larson:	Yes, a fir tree is a kind of evergreen tree. What is this other word?
Ellen:	It looks like *pire,* but I don't know what that means.
Mrs. Larson:	No, the word is *pier.* You know what a pier is?
Ellen:	Yes, it sticks out into a lake, and you tie a boat to it. It usually is made of wood.
Mrs. Larson:	Yes, it is. Have you written down the name of the book, the author, and your one-sentence summary on a reading card?
Ellen:	Yes, I have.
Mrs. Larson:	You really did well today, Ellen. I'm very, very proud of you. Remember to choose another book to read before the next time. I guess that's all the time that we have for today.

Modified Individualized Reading

A number of contemporary primary-grade classrooms use individualized reading as one important part of the total reading program, but they also employ other reading approaches in addition to individualized reading.

At the beginning first-grade level, the teacher often uses the language experience approach to present prereading and beginning reading experiences as well as to teach key vocabulary, as was explained earlier. At the beginning first-grade level, especially in a large class, it is very difficult for the teacher to present many of the word identification and comprehension skills on an individualized basis. Therefore, in a first-grade classroom that uses modified individualized reading, the teacher often employs basal readers or a formal phonic approach as the major method of teaching reading skills in a group setting. Then, as soon as some of the children have learned the most basic word identification and comprehension skills and understand what they have read, they can move into a mainly individualized reading plan, as was described earlier in this chapter. This type of transition usually occurs first in the above-average group, next in the average group, and last in the below-average group. When using a form of modified individualized reading, the first-grade teacher may employ reading achievement groups several days a week (see Chapter 5) and have the children read independently the remainder of the time, using self-selected materials and meeting with the teacher in individual reading conferences.

In the second and third grades, children who use some form of modified individualized reading often meet with their teacher one or two days a week to learn or review the appropriate word identification and comprehension skills. The rest of the week these children read individually, using reading conferences on a regular basis.

Although some of the proponents of individualized reading recommend the sole use of this plan in the primary grades, many reading specialists, including this author, recommend using modified individualized reading. Many elementary teachers recommend the use of individualized reading along with other reading approaches because it eliminates the limitations of pure or true individualized reading (to be described later in this chapter). Chapter 10 provides more detail on how to combine individualized reading with several other approaches in the primary grades.

Diagnostic Individual Reading Conferences

A few primary-grade classrooms that I have visited use diagnostic individualized reading conferences along with the basal reader approach to provide a more effective reading program than could be possible with the sole use of the basal reader approach.

For example, one first-grade teacher uses the basal reader approach as the major method of presenting the word identification and comprehension skills. However, she periodically has a diagnostic individual reading conference with each child in which she assesses the child's approximate instructional reading level and his or her specific reading skill strengths and weaknesses.

As a result of these periodic individual reading conferences, the teacher then may move the child into a different, usually more advanced, basal reader and/or basal reader achievement group. In addition, she may provide the child with additional group and/or individual instruction or reinforcement in any reading skill in which she has found the child to be weak.

Thus, this first-grade teacher uses diagnostic individual reading conferences to provide a more individually prescribed reading program for those children with whom she is working, while still using the basal reader approach as the major mode of reading instruction in her classroom. Such diagnostic individual reading conferences could be used equally well in any other primary-grade classroom that employs the basal reader approach and that has a teacher who is knowledgeable about the reading skills presented at the various reading levels.

Programmed Reading Instruction

Programmed and computer-assisted reading instruction also can be one means of individualizing reading instruction in a primary-grade classroom although this cannot be called individualized reading in any true sense. Programmed instruction is based upon a psychological theory developed by B. F. Skinner of Harvard University. Skinner formulated his variation of the stimulus-response learning theory and wrote a book about this theory entitled *The Technology of Teaching*.[4] In very simple terms, the stimulus-response learning theory is based on the concept that a subject will respond or react in a predetermined way upon the introduction of a certain stimulus. As an example, when a teacher holds up a flash card with a *d* printed on it in kindergarten or first grade, the child usually can identify it correctly.

In any case, programmed reading instruction can be presented by using a teaching machine, a talking typewriter, or a computer, all of which are called *hardware,* or with workbooks, which are called *software*. In programmed instruction, the content of a subject is outlined and divided into small units that are organized sequentially and are called *frames*. A student then completes each frame independently. After having been notified in some way that the frame is completed either correctly or incorrectly, the student either proceeds to subsequent frames or receives more reinforcement on the skill included in that frame.

Any type of programmed reading instruction is not truly individualized reading because each child essentially must proceed through the same content. Only the rate at which the child does so varies a great deal. However, programmed reading can be used fairly effectively in an individualized reading program to provide the child with the reinforcement that he or she needs in a specific reading skill.

VARIOUS VERSIONS OF INDIVIDUALIZED READING IN THE INTERMEDIATE GRADES

As at the primary-grade reading level, there are a number of variations of individualized reading that can be used at the intermediate-grade reading level. Before beginning any type of individualized reading program, the teacher usually has access to each student's approximate instructional and independent reading levels as determined from a valid standardized reading achievement test and/or Individual Reading Inventory. Obviously, such information helps the teacher aid the student in selecting materials to read that are on his or her level.

Pure or True Individualized Reading

Pure or true individualized reading is fairly easy to implement for a number of students at the intermediate-grade reading level because

---

[4]B. F. Skinner, *The Technology of Teaching* (New York: Prentice-Hall, 1968).

many of them have attained competency in the major aspects of the various word identification skills and comprehension skills by that time. A student at this level can self-select his or her independent reading materials from a myriad of sources such as trade books, basal readers, supplementary materials, content textbooks, reference books, and children's magazines and newspapers. These materials should reflect each child's unique interests as much as possible and usually should be on the student's instructional or independent reading level. However, if a student is especially interested in a topic, once in a while he or she can read material on the frustration reading level.

In the intermediate grades, students can engage in many types of independent activities while their teacher is working with other students in individual reading conferences or in needs or skills groups. Some independent activities at this level can include independent reading of trade books, basal readers, supplementary materials, content textbooks, reference books, newspapers, and magazines; the use of reading stations; various types of listening activities; workbooks of various types; commercially available activity sheets; teacher-made activity sheets; unit work in content areas; research groups; interest groups; peer teaching; and game activities.

When intermediate-grade students choose a book to read, they can test its reading level by choosing a portion near the middle and trying to read this portion silently to see if they can read it successfully. If it is too difficult, the student usually should select another book of interest to read. Most students in the intermediate grades will choose books on the appropriate reading level after some practice. Although students sometimes can read a difficult book if it is extremely interesting, most of the books that they select should be on their instructional or independent reading level. Thus, a student in the intermediate grades sometimes can read a book that is on his or her frustration reading level if it is very relevant. For example, a sixth-grade boy who is very interested in hang gliding and who is reading on grade level may be able to read a book on this topic at the eighth- or ninth-grade reading level. Each student then spends some of the reading period nearly every day reading self-selected, interesting materials.

The student meets with the teacher for an individual reading conference lasting ten to fifteen minutes several times a week. At the intermediate-grade level the student summarizes the reading material and gives his or her reaction to it. Once in a while the student may read orally as a check on his or her word identification and oral reading ability. However, this does not occur as often as it did in the primary grades. The teacher usually asks a few interpretive questions about the reading material.

Group conferences also are very useful when using pure or true individualized reading in the intermediate grades. Forming group reading conferences is assisted by having several students sign up according to topics such as biography, mystery, fiction, or various types of nonfiction. As at the primary-grade reading level, if a question is asked about base or root words, prefixes, suffixes, or syllabication, any student is permitted to answer it. However, comprehension questions in a group reading conference should be sufficiently general so that they apply to all the books read by the children attending the conference. They can be of types such as these: sharing the most interesting part of the book, sharing the most exciting part of the book, summarizing the book, sharing information about the author of the book, relating the book to contemporary life, or describing what all the books had in common.

Record keeping is an integral part of individualized reading in the intermediate grades, and it is imperative that both the teacher and students keep careful records if a program of pure or true individualized reading is to be successful. The students may keep a record of their reading on index cards or in a loose-leaf notebook. The record usually includes the title, the author of the material, a brief summary of the content, and, perhaps most importantly, an evaluation of the reading material. (See Figure 6-3.)

Obviously, the teacher also must keep careful records of the reading of his or her students if the pure or true individualized reading plan is to be successful in the intermediate grades. Although there are other forms, the teacher's records usually are kept in a loose-leaf notebook or folder and contain such information as this: the titles and authors of the books read, the number of pages in each book, the student's reaction to the material read, the student's specific reading skill weaknesses, and the type of each book (fiction, nonfiction, biography, sports, mystery, legends, myths, or poetry).

The Good Master   by Kate Seredy
   This book is about a boy named Jancsi who lives on a horse farm. It tells about life in Hungary. It has very nice pictures. I thought this book was pretty interesting, but it wasn't the best book that I have ever read. I might recommend it to a friend.

FIGURE 6-3

It is important at the intermediate-grade level for the teacher to attempt to broaden the scope of a student's reading from his or her present reading interests. As an example, at this level a student often may have an overwhelming interest in reading about horses. Although this obviously is acceptable at first, the student subsequently should be led into more diversified areas. Figure 6-4 shows a reading color wheel that can be used at the intermediate-grade reading level. This helps the student to widen his or her reading by indicating what type of books the student should read to complete the color wheel.

Mrs. Pamela King, an intermediate-grade teacher in central Illinois, uses the individualized reading plan very extensively. She has a number of unique ways of motivating her fifth-grade students to share the material that they have read individually. Here are some of them:

Ideas for Sharing Books

Make a poster to advertise the book.

Make a book jacket and write a statement to accompany it.

Write another ending for the story.

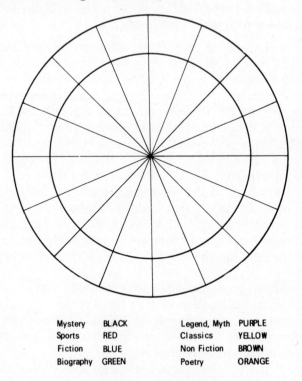

Mystery	BLACK	Legend, Myth	PURPLE
Sports	RED	Classics	YELLOW
Fiction	BLUE	Non Fiction	BROWN
Biography	GREEN	Poetry	ORANGE

Color edges of the circle proper color.
Print the author and title of each book
on the rest of the wedge.

FIGURE 6-4

Create a series of original illustrations for the story.

Write a letter to a friend recommending the book.

Use puppets to retell the story.

Write a simple version of the story to present to a younger child.

Broadcast a book review to a radio audience.

Make a "movie" of the book. This is a series of pictures drawn on a long roll of paper. The ends are fastened to rollers which are turned to move the pictures.

Choose special parts of the story and practice oral reading.

Act out a pantomime of the story.

Find out more about your favorite author and present a brief biography.

Write letters to authors about their books.

Construct a diorama to present a scene from the story.

Dress a doll to represent a scene.

Dramatize the story using stick puppets, papier-mâché puppets, puppets made out of paper bags, puppets made of cloth, hand puppets, or puppets with light-bulb heads.

One interesting technique for motivating students to read independently that can be used in any type of individualized reading program at the upper-intermediate-grade reading level is entitled "read a book in an hour." Although this is explained in detail in an article by Cyrus F. Smith, Jr., briefly it involves dividing a paperback book into chapters, giving a different chapter to each student for silent reading according to his or her reading level and then having each student tell the important events of his or her chapter to the rest of the group. Usually, the teacher acts as a discussion leader.[5]

It is crucial that students in the intermediate grades develop an interest in and a love of reading that lasts throughout all grades. However, students at this reading level do need additional instruction and reinforcement in some aspects of interpretive comprehension, critical reading, creative reading, the various study skills, and reading rate improvement.

Although intermediate-grade students may, therefore, meet in a basal reader group occasionally, they often do much of their narrative reading on an individual basis, using self-selected materials. Basal readers that are designed for use in the intermediate grades provide lists of materials to encourage individual reading.

Although many of the proponents of individualized reading may recommend the sole use of this plan in the primary grades, a number

[5]Cyrus F. Smith, Jr, " 'Read a Book in an Hour': Variations to Develop Composition and Comprehension Skills," *Journal of Reading*, 23 (October 1979): 25–29.

of reading specialists, including this author, highly recommend using modified individualized reading at the middle-school level. Many intermediate-grade teachers find the use of individual reading, along with the occasional use of basal reading and content reading instruction, to be very useful. Chapter 11 provides detailed strategies on how best to combine individualized reading with several other approaches at the middle-school level.

Other Variations of Individualized Reading

There are a number of other teaching strategies and materials that are sometimes called versions of individualized reading. A number of intermediate-grade teachers employ commercially available reading labs to enable students to read on their own level. Science Research Associates publishes the most widely used reading labs. These are boxed materials containing reading selections, comprehension checks, and other activities at various reading levels. The student then begins with materials at his or her approximate instructional reading level and subsequently proceeds to more difficult materials.

Contract teaching of reading in its various versions may be another way of individualizing reading instruction in the intermediate grades. This occurs when a teacher outlines a unit of work and the student promises to complete this unit of work within a specified period of time.

Often in contract teaching the student may choose a number of different teaching strategies or materials for any one aspect of the work. Supposedly, all the activities or materials designed to increase competency in any one aspect of the course content are fairly equitable. Thus, contract teaching does provide some options that serve to individualize reading instruction to some extent.

As was explained earlier in this chapter, programmed reading instruction also can be used to some extent to individualize reading instruction. Programmed reading instruction can take the form of teaching machines, computer-assisted instruction, or workbooks. However, programmed reading instruction is not as useful at the intermediate-grade reading level as it is at the primary-grade reading level because higher-level reading skills, such as interpretive comprehension and critical reading, are more difficult to program than are lower-level reading skills, such as phonic analysis. Some aspects of structural analysis and vocabulary development, however, lend themselves to programming.

USING NEEDS OR SKILLS GROUPS

Needs or skills groups are used quite often, especially in pure or true individualized reading, to present specific word identification or comprehension skills to a small group of students who have been diagnosed as needing help with the skills during individual or group reading conferences. As an example, a second-grade teacher may have noticed in individual reading conferences that five children in the class cannot discriminate between the short vowel sounds of /e/ and /i/. These children often apparently confuse these two sounds. The teacher then calls these children together in a needs or skills group to present these two short vowel sounds to them again.

The teacher also prescribes needed reinforcement in the use of these two vowel sounds in the form of commercial activity sheets, teacher-made activity sheets, workbook pages, tape-recorded materials, or games, which each child can do independently later. When the teacher has determined that the children in this needs group have gained competence in this aspect of phonic analysis, the group will be disbanded. Thus, the reading skill needs that are diagnosed by the teacher during individual and group reading conferences are the basis for the word identification and comprehension skills that subsequently are presented and reinforced in needs or skills groups. Although once in a while such skills are presented during individual or group reading conferences, this is done much more often in a group setting.

Besides needs or skills groups, other kinds of flexible groups often are used in both the primary and intermediate grades when a version of individualized reading is used. Such groups are research groups, interest groups, buddy groups, and peer teaching. More detail is found on all of these groups in Chapter 15.

SOME OTHER IMPORTANT CONSIDERATIONS IN ANY INDIVIDUALIZED READING PROGRAM

There are a number of other important considerations in any individualized reading program of which you should be aware. They are placed in this section of the chapter mainly for sake of convenience.

Especially when a program of pure or true individualized reading is used, it is important to have a large classroom with plenty of space. It normally would be quite difficult to conduct an individualized reading program in a small classroom. It also is important to have a sufficient number of tables and chairs that can be organized in various ways, depending upon the type of individual and group activities that are taking place in the classroom.

Reading stations or learning stations often are used in any type of individualized reading program. A reading station is a place where a child or a group of children can receive reinforcement in a word identification skill, comprehension skill, or study skill that has been presented previously. Often the skill is presented by using media such as cassette tape recorders or *The Language Master* at the reading stations. The use of reading stations can provide an effective structure for individualizing instruction.

When reading stations are used in a primary-grade or intermediate-grade classroom to individualize instruction, usually only about four or five reading stations should be set up initially until students become accustomed to using them. Performance objectives sometimes are used along with reading stations to determine what a student should be able to do after completing an exercise at a reading station. For example, if a child has completed an activity sheet that stressed discriminating between two short vowel sounds with the aid of teacher-taped directions using a cassette recorder, the child then should be able to discriminate successfully between these vowel sounds.

A reading station can be located in a commercial or home-constructed carrel. However, it also can be located on a table or by pushing children's desks together. It can even be a file folder that the child takes to his or her desk.

Many strategies can be used at reading stations to reinforce specific reading skills. Students usually should choose or should be guided to a reading station if they are weak in the specific reading skill covered by that station. Commercially available or teacher-made activity sheets that are covered by acetate or contact paper are useful for reinforcing competency in the word identification techniques. The directions for completing each of these activity sheets sometimes may be tape-recorded by the teacher so that the child can complete the activity sheet independently if he or she cannot read the directions. An activity sheet can stress sentence comprehension, paragraph comprehension, reading to follow directions, sequence ability, locating the main idea, or finding significant details.

Programmed reading materials also lend themselves very well to use in a reading station. Reading games that are self-correcting often are found at reading stations. Another common activity is read-along tape recordings. These can be commercial or teacher-made, and they have the student listen to the tape recording of a story while he or she follows along in a copy of the story or trade book.

Another important concept is this area is the differences that exist between individualized reading and *personalized reading,* a term credited to Walter B. Barbe, who wrote a book on this subject in collaboration with Jerry L. Abbott.[6] According to this very valuable book, personalized reading is somewhat more structured than is individualized reading.

Barbe and Abbott have formulated reading skills checklists for each level from reading readiness, first grade, and on through sixth grade.

---

[6]Barbe and Abbott, *Personalized Reading Instruction.*

Each checklist indicates to the teacher the reading skills that should be presented to and mastered by the average child at that level. These skills then can be presented and reinforced both individually and in small groups. These checklists cover the reading skills of sight word recognition, phonic analysis, structural analysis, dictionary usage, comprehension, oral reading, silent reading, and rate of reading. Similar reading skills checklists, along with suggested activities for teaching and reinforcing the various reading skills, have been authored by Barbe and others. These are found in spiral-back booklets at levels from the reading readiness level through the advanced reading level.[7]

Personalized reading is designed to make reading skill development more systematic than it is with individualized reading. However, a teacher using these checklists should remember that they are only indicative of the reading skills that a child should learn to use at various grade levels. They often are too easy for the above-average student at that grade level and too difficult for the below-average student at that grade level. Thus, the checklists are very useful for an understanding of the reading skills that could be presented to the typical student at each reading level.

It also is important to remember that a program of individualized reading that is to be truly successful requires certain teacher characteristics and student characteristics. The teacher, especially in a program of pure or true individualized reading, should be very knowledgeable about the reading process and be able to determine a child's reading skill strengths and weaknesses. He or she also should possess good organizational and managerial ability because success in individualized reading requires a high degree of competency in these characteristics. Children who are participating in individualized reading usually should be self-reliant and able to work successfully on their own for extended periods of time. In addition, they should be considerate of the rights of the other children.

Any program of individualized reading operates most effectively in a fairly small class. It generally is easiest to use individualized reading in a classroom of twenty or fewer students. It is undoubtedly most difficult when there are thirty or more students in the classroom. This probably is especially true at the lower-primary-grade reading level.

A technique that can be used effectively in any individualized reading plan is the *self-directive dramatization,* which was developed by the late Lessie Carlton and Robert H. Moore (professor emeritus) of Illinois State University. These educators defined the self-directive dramatization as "each child's original, imaginative, spontaneous in-

---

[7]Walter B. Barbe and others, *Reading Skills Check Lists and Activities—Readiness Level Through Advanced Level* (West Nyack, New York: The Center for Applied Research in Education, Inc., 1976).

terpretation of a character of his or her own choosing in a story which he or she selects and reads cooperatively with other children in his or her group which is formed for the time being and for a particular story only."[8]

Carlton and Moore conducted a research study, using the self-directive dramatization as a major reading approach, in an elementary school in an upper-lower- and lower-class neighborhood in a medium-sized Midwestern city. Carlton and Moore discovered that these students attained good reading achievement and a positive self-concept by using the self-directive dramatization on a regular basis.

To use this technique, encourage the children in the class to form groups, and tell them that each group is going to read a story and then act it out. Each group should consist of the same number of children as there are story characters. Each child in the group then reads the story or trade book independently or cooperatively. Although Carlton and Moore preferred that all the children in each group read the material cooperatively, each child probably can read the material independently if there are several copies available. After the children have finished reading the material, they decide which character they want to portray. Each of the groups subsequently dramatizes the story or trade book that they have read in front of the rest of the class. Since the self-directive dramatization is used to enhance creativity and imagination, each presentation should be spontaneous.

Imitative reading also can be used as a motivator in an individualized reading program. This is having the child read a book while listening to an accompanying read-along record or tape that is commercially or teacher-produced. Here are several sources of reading material with accompanying records or tapes:

Double Play and Triple Play Kits
Bowmar/Noble
4563 Colorado Boulevard
Los Angeles, California 90039

Venture Books
Garrard Publishing Co.
1607 North Market Street
Champaign, Illinois 61820

Instant Readers
Holt, Rinehart and Winston
383 Madison Avenue
New York, New York 10017

---

[8]Lessie Carlton and Robert H. Moore, *Reading, Self-Directive Dramatization and Self-Concept* (Columbus, Ohio: Charles E. Merrill Publishing Co., 1968), p. 13.

Troll
320 Route 17
Mahwah, New Jersey 07430

Contemporary Motivators
Pendulum Press
Saw Mill Road
West Haven, Connecticut 06516

There are a few other resources that can be used in any type of individualized reading program. One possibility for a teacher with limited library access is to purchase a kit on individualized reading from a source such as Scholastic Book Services, 904 Sylvan Avenue, Englewood Cliffs, New Jersey 07632. Another good source is *One-to-One,* Educational Book Division, Prentice-Hall, Inc., Englewood Cliffs, New Jersey 07632. Another resource is the *Personalized Reading Center,* Educational Division, Xerox Corporation, 245 Long Hill Road, Middletown, Connecticut 06457.

RESEARCH ON INDIVIDUALIZED READING

Most research studies have not defined individualized reading with enough precision to enable one to compare it with other reading approaches very well. Therefore, determination of its potential advantages is difficult. For example, some of the research studies that have attempted to evaluate the effectiveness of individualized reading in comparison with the basal reader approach have incorporated aspects of the basal reader approach or even a formal phonic approach into the reading plan, thus giving pure or true individualized reading more structure than it really should have according to its proponents.

Perhaps instead of trying to determine if pure or true individualized reading results in superior reading achievement in either primary or intermediate grades, it might be wiser to consider it a very useful way of organizing a class that can be used as either a major or a contributing reading method depending upon the interests, capabilities, and needs of both the students and the teacher.

THE ADVANTAGES OF INDIVIDUALIZED READING

The proponents of individualized reading claim a number of advantages for its use. Certainly these advantages are accurate and should motivate elementary-school teachers to use it as at least a very important part of their total reading program.

Individualized reading usually induces a great interest in reading and a love of reading on the part of the children who are using it. In my opinion, this is its major strength. An interest in reading usually leads to more reading on a child's part. Usually, the greater quantity of reading done by each student should lead to an increase in his or her word identification and comprehension skills because reading is a complex skill that often improves with motivated practice.

Individualized reading is very useful with reluctant readers, those students who can read adequately but choose not to. When such a student can self-select reading materials that interest him or her, that student usually is much more willing to read. Sometimes a reluctant reader is even able to read material on the frustration reading level if it is truly interesting.

Individualized reading may well develop the independence and self-reliance of the children who use it on a regular basis because they must read and work independently without direct supervision during most of each reading period. They also must learn a degree of self-discipline and concerns for the rights of others when using individualized reading.

Students who use individualized reading are able to read materials that are on their instructional or independent reading level. If a child is in a reading group, sometimes the material that is read may be too easy or too difficult for him or her because there is quite a range of reading achievement in any reading group. This is perhaps especially true in the case of the above-average group and the below-average group.

Students who use individualized reading may well make good progress in reading, for they can pace their own reading instead of being required to conform to the pace of a reading group, which may be considerably slower or faster than their own. The opportunity for increased reading achievement probably is particularly applicable to the bright children. These are the children who are near the top of each group and progress more rapidly than do the rest of the children.

Individualized reading always has a diagnostic-prescriptive emphasis because the teacher typically diagnoses a child's reading skill strengths and weaknesses during the individual and group reading conferences. Prescriptive reading instruction is then provided in the needs or skills groups, and reinforcement is prescribed when applicable. Because effective teaching of reading always should employ a diagnostic-prescriptive emphasis, it is apparent that individualized reading instruction certainly has merit.

Individualized reading is particularly adaptable to educational innovations. As an example, the multimedia aids that are used in individualized reading—such as listening posts, cassette tape recorders, and filmstrips—enhance an individualized reading plan.

In an individualized reading program, slow-learning students or disabled readers may feel less stigmatized about their lack of reading achievement than in a reading approach that employs more rigid and long-term reading achievement groups, as in the basal reader approach.

All students, but perhaps especially slow-learning students or disabled readers, benefit greatly from the undivided individual attention of the teacher on a one-to-one basis in the individual reading conference. Such undivided individual attention usually motivates a child and greatly enhances his or her self-concept.

The typical child is exposed to a variety of materials in an effective individualized reading program. These materials are in the form of hardcover trade books, paperback books, basal readers, supplementary readers, content textbooks, books of poetry, reference books, and children's magazines and newspapers. Such wide exposure will, one hopes, lead the child into a lifetime of reading interesting, informative material for pleasure.

THE LIMITATIONS OF INDIVIDUALIZED READING

Although the use of pure or true individualized reading has a number of limitations, these limitations can be eliminated when individualized reading is used along with other reading approaches such as the basal reader approach, a formal phonic approach, or programmed reading instruction.

As in the case of the language experience approach, the major limitation of individualized reading is the lack of sequential development of the word identification skills, especially the subskills of phonic analysis. However, this limitation may not be so critical in a more structured personalized reading program.

Another limitation of the sole use of individualized reading is the great amount of teacher time and effort required to conduct it successfully. If a teacher is to conduct frequent individual and group reading conferences, teach various flexible reading groups, keep adequate records of each child's reading and skill attainment, and plan worthwhile independent activities, it can be seen that this indeed is a very challenging task. The total use of individualized reading in the early primary grades usually is especially difficult when many of the children know few word identification strategies and are limited in the independent activities that they can do successfully without direct teacher supervision.

As was stated earlier, pure or true individualized reading is especially difficult to conduct in a large elementary-school class. It probably is most effective in a class with twenty or fewer students. Usually, it is exceedingly difficult in a class of thirty or more students.

Some elementary-school teachers, often perhaps inexperienced teachers, are not knowledgeable enough about the reading process to be able to teach it effectively without more guidance than is found in pure or true individualized reading. This is not so much the case with personalized reading. Undoubtedly, the lack of direction for sequential skill development is particularly acute in the early primary grades, when many children know so few of the reading skills. By the time students reach the intermediate grades, they usually are competent in most of the basic word identification and comprehension skills, and they can effectively decode unknown words.

The sole use of individualized reading presupposes that an elementary teacher can effectively diagnose word identification and comprehension difficulties in the individual and group reading conferences that are held with a student or students several times a week. However, this is not always the case owing to limited teacher time and inadequate knowledge of the complex reading process.

The elementary teacher must know the content and readability level of a wide variety of reading materials if he or she is to help a student effectively to select appropriate materials for reading. This requires that the teacher know the special vocabulary in the material, what type of comprehension questions to ask, and the approximate reading level of the book. However, the teacher can often receive the help that is required from the elementary-school librarian or media specialist.

Some contemporary elementary schools do not contain a central library, which is a prerequisite for the successful use of individualized reading. Elementary classrooms should have access to several hundred or more trade books, several basal reader series, supplementary readers, content textbooks, reference books, and children's magazines and newspapers.

Undoubtedly, some children do not possess the qualities that enable them to work independently for fairly long time periods without much direct teacher guidance. Such children may not profit greatly from the long periods of time in an individualized reading plan when they should be reading and engaging in other activities independently.

It also is quite difficult to provide meaningful independent work that is not busywork. This is especially difficult at the first-grade level, when most of the children have a limited reading ability. At all grade levels, however, it is indeed a very challenging task to provide meaningful independent activities.

Certainly, a program of pure or true individualized reading is not compatible with the personality characteristics of all teachers. A teacher who is to engage in this plan must possess excellent organizational ability and very good classroom management skills.

SELECTED REFERENCES

Barbe, Walter B., and Jerry L. Abbott. *Personalized Reading Instruction*. West Nyack, New York: Parker Publishing Company, 1975.

Criscuolo, Nicholas P. "Book Reports: Twelve Creative Alternatives." *The Reading Teacher, 30* (May 1977): 893–895.

———. "Effective Approaches for Motivating Children to Read." *The Reading Teacher, 32* (February 1979): 543–546.

Ekwall, Eldon E. *Teacher's Handbook on Diagnosis and Remediation in Reading*. Boston: Allyn and Bacon, 1976, pp. 155–167.

Farr, Roger, and Nancy Roser. *Teaching a Child To Read*. New York: Harcourt Brace Jovanovich, Inc., 1979, pp. 446–450.

Hall, MaryAnne, Jerilyn K. Ribovich, and Christopher J. Ramig. *Reading and the Elementary School Child*. New York: D. Van Nostrand Company, 1979, Chapter 10.

Harris, Albert J., and Edward R. Sipay. *How to Increase Reading Ability*. New York: Longman, Inc., 1980, pp. 104–109.

LaPray, Margaret. *Teaching Children to Become Independent Readers*. New York: The Center for Applied Research in Education, 1982.

LeGrand-Brodsky, Kathryn. "Television and Reading: Industry Initiatives." *Journal of Reading, 23* (October 1979): 9–15.

McGregor, Cavlyne U., and James T. Talbert, Jr. "Before You Prescribe . . ." *The Reading Teacher, 32* (December 1978): 279–280.

Moray, Geraldine. "What Does Research Say About the Reading Interests of Children in the Intermediate Grades?" *The Reading Teacher, 31* (April 1978): 763–768.

Otto, Wayne, Robert Rude, and Dixie Lee Spiegel. *How to Teach Reading*. Reading, Massachusetts: Addison-Wesley Publishing Company, Inc., 1979, Chapter 11.

Rhodes, Lynn K. "I Can Read! Predictable Books as Resources for Reading and Writing Instruction." *The Reading Teacher, 34* (February 1981): 511–518.

SUGGESTED ACTIVITIES

1. Conduct an individual reading conference with one child or a group reading conference with several children in the primary or intermediate grades after the child or children have read a self-selected trade book on an independent basis.
2. Visit a classroom and observe a teacher conducting an individual or group reading conference. Did he or she follow the guidelines outlined in the chapter?
3. Select ten trade books on a similar reading level. Type comprehension questions at the literal and interpretive levels for each trade book on a card. Give your cards to a teacher at the appropriate grade level to use in an individualized reading program.

4. Examine some of the materials that are used in an attempt to individualize reading instruction, such as programmed workbooks or reading laboratories.
5. Attempt to conduct a needs or skills group for several children who need instructional reinforcement in a specific reading skill.
6. Construct a teaching aid that can be used at a reading station, such as an activity sheet, a cassette tape, or a reading game.

On the chalkboard:

empty — emp'-t
employ — em-p
emerge — i' me
excess — ek-ses
excite — ek-sīt'
exclude — ek-sklo

Phonics and phonic analysis

CHAPTER 7

Why Did This Happen?

Mr. Marvin was a fifth-grade teacher at Edison School in a city in the Northwest. On the first day of school in early September, Mr. Marvin decided to have each student in his fifth-grade class demonstrate his or her oral reading ability by reading a portion of a fourth-grade basal reader story aloud. This story was from a basal reader series that the children had not used during the previous year. Mr. Marvin noticed from this activity that Jenny was one of the best oral readers in his new fifth-grade class.

Several days later Mr. Marvin briefly examined the cumulative folders of all the children in his class. From this examination, he was very surprised to notice that Jenny had scored considerably below grade level on the reading achievement test that had been given the previous May. He also was surprised to learn that she had been in the below-average reading achievement group in fourth grade. Before examining her cumulative folder, Mr. Marvin had tentatively planned to place Jenny in the above-average reading group as a result of her oral reading. However, now he did not know what to do.

In any case, Mr. Marvin tentatively placed Jenny in the reading achievement group that was to use a fifth-grade basal reader. He soon understood the reason why Jenny had scored so far below grade level on the standardized reading test that she had been given the previous year, and the reason why she had been in the below-average reading achievement group in fourth grade. Although Jenny had superior oral reading skills, she could answer virtually no comprehension questions about the material that she had read. She generally was not able to respond to literal comprehension questions and had even more difficulty responding to interpretive and critical questions. In addition, Jenny could not retell any of the story content that she had read, even with some prompting from Mr. Marvin. Several days later Mr. Marvin discovered that Jenny had still more difficulty in comprehending material from her social studies and science textbooks although she could pronounce the words in these fifth-grade level textbooks very well.

Mr. Marvin really could not understand how a student could read so well orally and yet could comprehend so little of what she read. He then talked to a first-grade teacher at Edison School and learned that Jenny had been taught early reading skills in kindergarten and first grade by a very popular phonic approach that put great stress on letter-sound relationships, phonic rules, and oral reading. The first-grade teacher then explained that this approach no longer was used at Edison School because the teachers had discovered that although it enabled some of the children to read above grade level in first and second grades, it also caused a few of them to become "word-callers"—children who can pronounce words very well but have little or no comprehension of what is read. This apparently was the case with Jenny.

After doing some reading from professional books, Mr. Marvin decided that he would encourage Jenny to do much self-selected silent reading from very easy, highly interesting reading material that she would really want to comprehend. He also tried to stress literal comprehension questions and the retelling technique with Jenny when he met with her in as many individual reading conferences as he possibly could fit into his busy teaching schedule. He also used the dictated stories that are part of the language experience approach. He mainly tried to stress the importance of always understanding what was read.

After several months, Jenny was usually able to answer literal comprehension questions about material that she had read. However, she still could not comprehend very effectively at the interpretive and critical levels. Mr. Marvin knew that it would take a great deal of time and effort to help Jenny learn to comprehend as well as she should.

After you have read this chapter, you should be better able to evaluate any formal phonic program with which you come into contact. You should always evaluate it in terms of its potential advantages and limitations for any particular student.

DEFINITION OF TERMS

It may be helpful at the outset to define briefly some of the most important terms that are found in the area of phonics and phonic analysis. However, you should be aware of the fact that reading specialists differ somewhat in their usage of the terms in this area.

The term *phonic program* usually refers to a basic or supplementary reading program in which phonic analysis is presented as the most important, if not the only, word identification technique. Such a program often emphasizes the decoding aspect of reading and may deemphasize comprehension of what is read. A phonic program of this type can be termed a formal or systematic phonic program. Although not all reading specialists would agree, for this book phonics is loosely defined as a method of teaching beginning reading skills.

Phonic analysis can be defined as a word identification technique in which a reader uses the association of phonemes (sounds) and graphemes (symbols) to unlock the pronunciation and meaning of unknown words that are met while reading. Although a number of reading specialists still call this word identification technique phonetic analysis, this author believes that phonic analysis is the most precise term. There are several types of phonic analysis, as will be described in detail later in this chapter. However, usually the words that children analyze phonetically should be in their speaking vocabulary so that they can use context to determine the exact meaning.

Phonemes can be defined as the sounds that occur in a language. There are approximately forty-four or forty-five different phonemes in the English language depending upon the differing views of reading specialists. When you see a written symbol such as /b/, you know that this is an example of a phoneme because the slash marks have been included.

A *grapheme* is the written symbol for a phoneme or sound. A grapheme can be composed of one letter or more than one letter depending upon the phoneme that it represents. For example, it takes the two letters *c* and *h* to represent the phoneme /ch/. Although not all reading specialists would agree, some of them believe that there are about 251 graphemes or different ways to spell the phonemes of which the oral English language is composed. Thus, you can see that English contains an irregular phoneme-grapheme relationship.

Phonemics can be defined as a somewhat narrower field of information about speech sounds than phonetics. Phonemics is that area of linguistic study concerned with the identification of the significant sounds of a language. On the other hand, the study of the actual sounds of a language is called *phonetics.*

Auditory synthesis or *blending* is the blending of individual phonemes, phonograms, or syllables to form recognizable words. It also probably can be called segmentation. Ability in auditory synthesis is very important to success in any type of formal phonic program. It is a very difficult skill for some children to master and requires considerable motivated practice.

Auditory span can be defined as a person's ability to reproduce digits or letters in a correct sequence. It also can involve the reproduction of certain sound patterns such as tapping. Auditory span sometimes is used as an indicator of intellectual potential. According to many trials with my college students, the typical adult can reproduce approximately nine or ten digits in correct sequence.

A BRIEF HISTORY OF PHONICS

According to the teachers' manuals of a number of contemporary formal phonic programs, their phonic materials are said to be innovative. Interestingly enough, phonic instruction that is not that dissimilar to contemporary phonic materials has been in use in elementary reading instruction for more than 180 years.

Phonic instruction apparently was introduced in the United States by Noah Webster in 1798, when he wrote the well-known *American Spelling Book.*[1] After this time, Horace Mann introduced the whole-word method of teaching reading, and phonic instruction was greatly de-emphasized. The whole-word method was predominant until the second half of the nineteenth century, when phonics again became

---

[1]Noah Webster, *The American Spelling Book* (Boston: Isaiah Thomas and Ebenezer Andrews, 1798).

popular. For example, Rebecca Pollard introduced a synthetic phonic method to schools in 1890. In 1912 the *Beacon Primer*[2] was introduced, as were the *Gordon Readers*[3] in 1918.

Around 1930 phonic instruction became less popular again with the introduction of the basal reader series, which placed stress on sight word recognition instead of intensive phonics. However, it is important to remember that although phonic instruction was de-emphasized during the 1930s and 1940s, it never was entirely replaced by the exclusive use of sight word recognition as is sometimes maintained.

Formal phonic programs of various types again became fashionable when in 1955 Rudolph Flesch wrote a very widely publicized and controversial book entitled *Why Johnny Can't Read and What You Can Do About It*.[4] In this book Flesch equated word pronunciation or decoding with reading and stated that if a person can decode or correctly pronounce a foreign language, he or she can read it. In other words, if a person can correctly pronounce Finnish, according to Flesch, that person can effectively read a book that is written in Finnish. However, according to the vast majority of reading specialists, this would not be possible because comprehension is the essential aspect of reading, and reading without comprehension is merely word-calling—certainly not really reading.

Numerous contemporary formal phonic programs are on the market today. There is a great deal of similarity between the major elements of current phonic programs and those dating from many years ago. Certainly, phonic instruction is quite fashionable today. Presently the practice is to present more phonic analysis elements and phonic generalizations earlier than was done fifteen or twenty years ago. For example, basal readers are presenting more phonic analysis skills than they did in the past. However, if phonic instruction continues to follow the pattern of the past, formal phonic programs may be out of style fifteen or twenty years from now. It is very likely that they then will later reappear in a form that is not too different from that used at the present time.

ABOUT FORMAL PHONIC PROGRAMS

As was stated earlier, there are many different formal, or systematic, phonic programs on the market. A few of these are revisions of older

[2]*Beacon Primer* (Lexington, Massachusetts: Ginn and Company, 1912).

[3]Emma K. Gordon, *Gordon Readers* (Boston: D.C. Heath & Company, 1918).

[4]Rudolph Flesch, *Why Johnny Can't Read and What You Can Do About It* (New York: Harper & Row, Publishers, 1955).

phonic programs whereas others have been formulated recently. Some of them are designed to be a total beginning reading program whereas others have been designed to be used as supplements to a basal reader series. Still others have been designed for special types of students, such as older disabled readers, learning disabled students, or educable mentally handicapped students.

However, most of the formal phonic programs contain some common features. For example, a formal phonic program emphasizes the pronunciation or decoding aspects of beginning reading. These programs usually do not emphasize comprehension to any great extent when a child is beginning to learn to read. Instead, the authors of such a program seem to believe that children will learn to comprehend what they read after they can "break the code."

The authors of most formal phonic programs apparently believe that phonic analysis is the most important, if not the only, word identification technique that should be presented to children. A formal phonic program usually places little emphasis upon the other word identification techniques of sight word recognition, structural analysis, contextual analysis, or dictionary usage and usually presents many more phonic generalizations (rules) than is done in the basal reader approach. In addition, these phonic rules are presented earlier in the beginning reading program than typically is done in the basal reader approach.

The authors of a formal phonic program usually recommend that such a program be presented in its entirety. They state that the program loses some of its effectiveness if it is not presented to all children in exactly the form outlined in the teachers' guide. They also indicate that the program is most effective when it is presented along with all the multimedia aids contained in it.

In addition, the authors of a formal phonic program usually advocate presenting the program to all the children in a kindergarten or first-grade class. It apparently makes little difference if the child has adequate auditory discrimination ability (the ability to hear the similarities and differences in sounds) and the necessary mental age to succeed in the program. Indeed, some reading specialists think that a mental age of seven may be a prerequisite for success in some types of formal phonic programs.

Moreover, the authors of some phonic programs apparently believe that their program is the one best way of teaching beginning reading skills to all children in kindergarten or first grade and to all severely disabled readers.

As was stated earlier, some formal phonic programs are considered to be total or basic, which means that such a program normally should constitute the entire reading program in a classroom with the possible exception of independent trade book reading. Normally, a total or basic formal phonic program should not be used along with the basal reader approach. On the other hand, some formal phonic programs are designed to be supplementary. Such programs contain no reading materials but should be used along with an approach that contains reading materials such as the basal reader approach.

There are approximately one hundred formal phonic programs. They are found in a number of different formats. Many of the total or basic formal phonic programs contain hardcover books, soft-cover books, workbooks, transparencies, filmstrips, cassette tapes, or records, among other multimedia aids. Supplementary formal phonic programs contain soft-cover books, workbooks, and various types of multimedia aids. Sophisticated multimedia aids such as computers and teaching machines of various types are being used to teach phonic skills in both total and supplementary phonic programs much more than was the case in the past. Therefore, a phonic program is likely to be more expensive today than it was in the past.

Both total and supplementary phonic programs differ in the order in which the various phonic elements and phonic generalizations are presented. In some programs, for example, the short or long vowel sounds are presented before the initial and final consonant sounds. However, it is important to remember that research has not yet determined the best sequence in which to present and review the phonic elements of consonant sounds, vowel sounds, consonant blends, consonant digraphs, diphthongs, or phonograms.

Total and supplementary phonic programs also differ somewhat in the stress that is placed upon comprehension at the initial stages of reading instruction. For example, some such programs place considerable emphasis on the comprehension of what is read at the initial stages of reading instruction whereas others place very little stress on comprehension. Instead they place their greatest emphasis on decoding or sounding out words.

Formal phonic programs also differ in the type of phonic analysis skills that are stressed. For example, some such programs emphasize analytic phonic analysis. As is explained in detail later, analytic phonic analysis teaches a child to take a total word and break it down into syllables or other chunks while attempting to sound it out. It is the type of phonic analysis that is also used in the basal reader approach.

Other formal phonic programs stress different variations of synthetic phonic analysis. As is discussed in detail later, synthetic phonic analysis involves blending individual sounds to form words or blending certain phonic elements within the word to form a complete word. As an example, if a child learns the phonic elements *ba, ca, fa, ha, ma,* and *sa,* he or she can use a final consonant *t* to form the words *bat, cat, fat, hat, mat,* and *sat.* The proponents of this type of synthetic phonic analysis believe that children then learn to decode words from left to right and that the consonant then never is sounded in isolation and thus is not distorted.

The use of *word families* is another variation of synthetic phonic analysis that is used in some formal phonic programs. Word families such as these may be presented in formal phonic programs: *-all, -alk, -at, -an, -ick,* or *-ill.* Then the appropriate consonant is blended at the beginning of each word family to form the words contained in that family. For example, the following words can be blended from the *-an* word family: *can, fan, man, pan, ran, tan,* and *van.* Proponents of word families correctly state that when a child learns one word family, he or she can form a number of words from that family. However, those who do not favor the use of word families correctly state that the consonant usually is distorted when it is pronounced in isolation and that a child tends to look at the end rather than at the beginning of each word, possibly causing subsequent reversals in reading.

The following basic or total and supplementary formal phonic programs are representative of those that are currently available. Many others could equally well have been included in this part of the chapter. For more detail on any formal phonic program, you should consult the teachers' manual or any of the materials contained in that program. Such programs often are available for examination in the curriculum laboratory or media center of a school district, an elementary school, or a university.

Alpha Time and Alpha One: Breaking the Code. Arista Corporation, 2440 Estand Way, P.O. Box 6146, Concord, California 94524.
This is an elaborate basic phonic approach. It has alphabet letter characters that are in the form of inflatable figures, pictures, filmstrips, records, wall charts, games, and workbooks.

DISTAR. Science Research Associates, North Wacker Drive, Chicago, Illinois 60606.
This total formal phonic program is intensive, fast-paced, and structured; and it involves sequencing, a procedure in which the teacher demonstrates actions that the children then imitate. The DISTAR alphabet is somewhat different from the traditional alphabet. (See Figure 7-1.)

Lippincott Basic Reading Program. J. B. Lippincott Co., 521 Fifth Avenue, New York, New York 10017.
This is a total formal phonic program that is designed for use in the first through the eighth grades. It stresses synthetic phonic analysis and writing. Because it presents some linguistic principles also, it often is called a phonic/linguistic approach. It contains folktales, fables, fairy tales, and imaginary episodes.

Open Court Basic Readers. Open Court, Box 599, LaSalle, Illinois 61301.

FIGURE 7-1

This is a total formal phonic program that emphasizes writing as an aid to word identification. It is a correlated language arts program. It contains soft-cover and hardcover reader workbooks, alphabet flash cards, wall sound cards, records, sound flash cards, word matching games, tracing sandpaper, and alphabet paper. The children use the chalkboard so that writing can be used as a kinesthetic reinforcement to word identification. The program stresses synthetic phonic analysis. The reading material includes Mother Goose rhymes, poems, fairy tales, and folktales.

Phonetic Keys to Reading. The Economy Company, Box 25308, 1901 North Walnut Street, Oklahoma City, Oklahoma 73125.
This is a total formal phonic program that is to be used through the intermediate grades. The long vowels are presented before the short vowel sounds, and consonant sounds are presented later. This program stresses analytic phonic analysis and comprehension. (See Figure 7-2.)

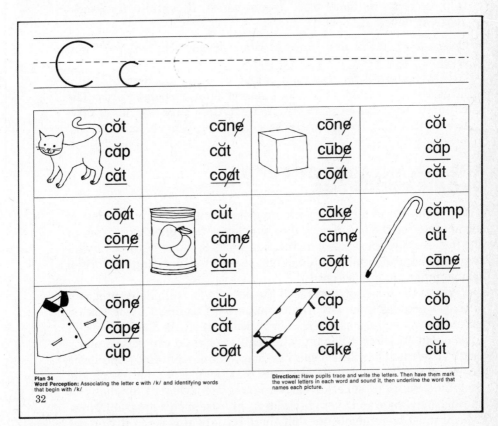

FIGURE 7-2

Phonovisual Method. Phonovisual Products, 12216 Parklawn Drive, Rockville, Maryland 20852.

This highly structured, total formal phonic program is designed to be used before the basal reader approach. The two most important elements are the consonant chart and the vowel chart. The initial consonant sounds, the final consonant sounds, and the vowel sounds are taught in that order.

Royal Road Readers. Educators Publishing Service, 75 Moulton Street, Cambridge, Massachusetts 02138.

This total formal phonic approach begins with regularly spelled words. It presents the short vowel sounds first and initial consonant sounds later. It is a fairly inexpensive program in comparison with many other phonic programs.

The SRA Basic Reading Series. Science Research Associates, North Wacker Drive, Chicago, Illinois 60606.

This is a phonic/linguistic program. The materials are fairly similar to those of an ordinary basal reader series. It contains five workbooks at Levels A, B, C, D, and E.

Speech-to-Print Phonics. Harcourt Brace Jovanovich, Inc., 757 Third Avenue, New York, New York, 10017.

All the materials for this total phonic program are contained in a large box. There are thirty-four sets of pupil-response cards. The children learn the letter names first and then have a series of fifty-five ear-training lessons with the sounds always included in words.

THE ADVANTAGES OF FORMAL PHONIC PROGRAMS

The proponents of formal phonic programs usually cite a number of advantages for the use of a total or supplementary phonic program at the initial stages of reading instruction. Indeed, many of these advantages are accurate and should be considered when deciding if a formal phonic program is to be used.

Perhaps the major advantage of the use of a formal phonic program is that it enables some children to become independent at unlocking unknown words very early in their school career. As English is said to be about 85 percent phonetically regular, a child can decode many English words when he or she has learned and can apply the basic phonic generalizations. It is also true that the use of a formal phonic program results in superior early reading achievement for many of the above-average and average children who use such a program. However, it must be remembered that these initial gains generally do not continue past the upper-primary-grade level.

Elementary school administrators sometimes are very much in favor of the use of a formal phonic program in the primary grades because of the superior initial reading achievement that results. They also may be in favor of the use of such a program because many parents of children in the primary grades are also very much in favor of the use of some type of total or supplementary phonic program. A number of parents erroneously believe that there would be no reading problems in the schools of our nation if more phonic analysis skills and phonic generalizations were taught. Actually, however, there are cases of reading disability even in countries that have a completely phonetically regular language.

Some who favor the use of formal phonic programs also state that other reading approaches do not present enough phonic elements and phonic generalizations to enable students to become competent in this very important word identification technique. They state that only through the use of a formal phonic program will children receive the instruction and reinforcement that is necessary to attain mastery of phonic analysis. Certainly, it is true that more phonic elements and phonic generalizations are presented in a formal phonic approach than in any other reading method.

The proponents of some formal phonic programs state that all children can learn to read successfully by the use of such a program. The statement definitely has not been supported by objective research studies. It is a certainty that some children fail to learn to read successfully by the use of any one single method, especially if that method is not well suited to their individual strengths and weaknesses.

The use of a formal phonic program also may help the average, and particularly the above-average, student improve spelling and composition ability. For example, a student with a good knowledge of phonic elements and rules then has a systematic way of spelling unknown words that are not contained in his or her visual memory. These phonic spellings sometimes are incorrect, but still are useful in helping the child attain independence in the creative writing of prose and poetry. Usually the child then later attains competency in accurate spelling as he or she is exposed more and more to conventional spelling in his or her reading.

THE LIMITATIONS OF FORMAL PHONIC PROGRAMS

Those who oppose the use of total or supplementary phonic programs in the primary grades usually give a number of reasons for their opposition of which you should be aware. Most of these reading specialists, however, do not oppose the teaching and reinforcement of phonic analysis skills. Instead, they simply believe that the typical formal phonic program presents too many phonic elements and generalizations and presents them too early in the reading program of most children.

Perhaps the major limitation of the extensive use of a formal phonic program is that it can cause a few children to become "word-callers," children who can pronounce words very effectively but have little or no comprehension of what they read. This author, for example, has seen some children in the classroom and the reading clinic who were laborious word-by-word readers and stopped to analyze each word phonically even if it was a word that they should recognize by sight. Apparently, these children thought that each word always should be analyzed phonically even if they had done so many times before. Because such students are so concerned about using their phonic analysis skills, they often have little time to think about what they are reading. They then do not attain the fluency required for successful comprehension. However, you must remember that this certainly does not occur with all children who are taught by a formal phonic approach. This disadvantage usually applies only to a limited number of students.

Another major limitation of the use of a formal phonic approach is that readers who are taught by such a method never are made aware of the advantages of using the other word identification techniques. Because the typical formal phonic program usually emphasizes phonic analysis to the virtual exclusion of the other word identification techniques, these children never become aware of the values of sight word recognition, of structural analysis, of contextual analysis, and of using the dictionary or glossary. As will be explained in Chapter 13, contextual analysis is an extremely useful word identification technique that the typical reader should use as often as possible for truly efficient reading.

Another limitation, not inherent in an actual formal phonic approach, is the way in which such an approach can be used in an entire kindergarten or first-grade class. When such a formal phonic approach is chosen, it is usually used with the entire class. However, you must remember that a few children in such a class do not have sufficient auditory discrimination ability to be successful in such a program. Then, too, some children do not have the requisite mental age to be successful in such a program. If a child is exposed to a formal phonic program with inadequate auditory discrimination ability or too low a mental age, this virtually makes certain that the child will not be successful in the program and may indeed develop a dislike for all types of reading activities. The author was once told of a little girl in kindergarten who simply could not succeed in the formal phonic program that was presented to her there. She subsequently developed a dislike for school and actually became ill when it was time for her to attend kindergarten each day. It seems a shame that a child in kindergarten had already learned to dislike school at that early age.

A number of formal phonic programs require children to memorize a myriad of phonic generalizations or rules. Although some children can recite these rules quite adequately, they seem unable to apply them while actually reading. Sometimes children are even adept at applying these phonic generalizations to words in isolated word lists such as those found on workbook pages or activity sheets. However, they are less adept at applying them to the words that are found in actual reading.

Then, too, formal phonic programs sometimes require children to analyze phonically words that are not in their speaking or oral language vocabulary. If a child does not know what a decoded word is supposed to be, how can he or she know that it has been sounded out correctly as there is no "click of recognition" when this has occurred. For example, a second-grade child may be able to sound out the word *correspondent*. However, if this word is not in his or her speaking vocabulary and he or she does not know its meaning, how can the child know if it was analyzed correctly?

It is possible that English is not phonetically regular enough to warrant teaching reading by a formal phonic method. Perhaps a language such as Finnish, which is completely phonetically regular, could be better taught by a formal phonic approach. However, as was briefly stated earlier, even in a country that has a phonetically-regular language, there are also disabled readers just as there are disabled readers in countries that do not have a phonetically-regular language.

As any experienced teacher of beginning reading can state, phonic analysis is very difficult to teach effectively. There are too many sounds that are spelled alike and too many sounds that have a variety of spellings. There also are many, many phonic generalizations or rules. In addition, as will be explained in detail later in this chapter, most of these have infinite exceptions that render the rules almost useless in many instances.

Certainly, a formal phonic approach never should be used with a child who is hard of hearing or deaf because he or she obviously cannot differentiate between the various sounds. In fact, a deaf or hard-of-hearing child can learn to read quite adequately without any competence at all in phonic analysis.

In some ways, the most significant limitation of a formal phonic program may be that it can stifle a child's innate interest in learning to read. Because the typical formal phonic approach emphasizes decoding or word pronunciation at the outset, the use of drills is greatly emphasized. Many of these drills are not very interesting and may not motivate some children to want to learn to read. These children also may equate such phonic drills with reading when indeed they should not. As has been mentioned earlier in this book, reading is, of course, comprehension.

ABOUT PHONIC ANALYSIS

As we defined the term earlier in this chapter, phonic analysis is using the phonic elements found in a word to determine its pronunciation and meaning. A number of reading teachers apparently believe that competency in phonic analysis is absolutely necessary for subsequent reading efficiency. This probably is the major reason why phonic analysis often receives more stress than do the other word identification techniques at the beginning stages of reading instruction.

Just how necessary do you believe competency in phonic analysis really is to the reading success of the average person? For example, how many times do you as an efficient adult reader stop to analyze the words phonetically that you find on the typical printed page? If you are typical, your answer to this question probably is, "Very seldom." This indicates that most adults do not use phonic analysis as a technique of word identification very often.

Most of the commonly used phonic elements and phonic generalizations are presented to the typical child by the end of the third-grade reading level. Thus, phonic analysis is most useful as a word identification technique in the primary grades. It becomes less effective at the middle-upper reading level, when students employ other word identification techniques such as contextual analysis and structural analysis much more often. In fact, the typical student in the intermediate grades or secondary school would find it very difficult to state or perhaps even apply some of the phonic generalizations that he or she was taught in the upper primary grades. Thus, one wonders if a number of the less useful phonic elements and generalizations that are taught are really worthwhile because they are retained and used by students for such a short period of time.

It also is important to remember that phonic analysis usually is most effective when it is used along with contextual analysis. For example, notice how the addition of the initial consonant in the following example helps you to determine the omitted word:

Susie would like to have a red b_____.

coat
bicycle
umbrella

As was briefly stated earlier, it is perfectly possible for a person to be a competent reader with little or no ability in phonic analysis. For example, a deaf person must learn reading by a predominantly sight method, for he or she obviously cannot hear the various phonic elements. However, even some students with adequate auditory acuity (hearing ability) and adequate auditory discrimination ability simply do not seem to be able to learn phonic analysis skills very well. After a number of failures in teaching this word identification technique to a child, the teacher probably should abandon much further instruction in phonic analysis and simply stress sight word recognition and contextual analysis. This is not to say that competency in phonic analysis is not important to the reading success of most students. It is very important for the typical student to attain some degree of ability in phonic analysis. But if a student experiences extreme difficulty in learning to use phonic elements and rules, it is better to stress other word identification techniques.

A student normally should have good auditory discrimination ability before being taught phonic elements and generalizations. Chapters 2 and 3 provided many different ways of improving a child's auditory discrimination ability at the initial stages of reading instruction. Variations of these activities also are appropriate for the older severely disabled reader or older nonreader.

As was briefly mentioned earlier, a number of reading specialists believe that a mental age of approximately seven years may be necessary before a child can learn many of the phonic elements and generalizations. Only the very bright child attains a mental age of seven in kindergarten. A child normally has to be brighter than average to attain a mental age of seven even in first grade. Thus, you can see that presenting phonic elements and generalizations to all children in a kindergarten or first-grade class can be disastrous for those children without the requisite mental age to succeed in such a program.

Again, as was mentioned briefly earlier, there are two main types of phonic analysis that can be presented to students. *Analytic phonic analysis* is that type of phonic analysis that is used in the basal reader approach and in a few formal phonic programs. It is the more useful type of phonic analysis in the opinion of this author for several reasons. In analytic phonic analysis the reader begins with an entire word that he or she first inspects visually. In this visual inspection the reader mentally breaks any polysyllabic word into its syllables or other parts that may not be actual syllables. The reader next sounds each syllable or part separately at first and then blends the various syllables or parts together in what is hoped will be a recognizable word that is in his or her speaking vocabulary. As an example, if a child met the unknown word *tiger,* here is what his or her thought processes might look like if analytic phonic analysis were being used:

I think that this word has two syllables.
The first one probably is *ti,* and the last one must be *ger.*

I think that the *i* would have a long sound because it ends the syllable so it would be pronounced *tī*.

The second part would be pronounced *ger* because that *e* is called *r*-controlled. I put both parts together, and the word is *tiger*. I've seen a lot of tigers at the zoo.

Because initial consonants are not sounded in isolation in analytic phonic analysis, they are not distorted as is done in synthetic phonic analysis. In addition, the child deals with larger units in analytic phonic analysis than in synthetic phonic analysis, which deals with individual sounds. As we mentioned earlier, these word parts can be chunks of words as well as actual syllables as defined by the dictionary. On the other hand, *synthetic phonic analysis* involves the blending of individual sounds or phonemes to form recognizable words, which, it is hoped, are then in the reader's speaking vocabulary. For example, a child may blend the individual phonemes "buh/a/tuh" into the word *bat*. Because it is virtually impossible to pronounce many of the consonants in isolation without adding a vowel sound, the consonant sound becomes somewhat distorted, and the child has difficulty in determining a recognizable word from the blended series of sounds. As was discussed earlier, various kinds of word families in which a final consonant is added to the beginning of words or in which an initial consonant is added to phonograms or word endings are other examples of synthetic phonic analysis.

Several variations of synthetic phonic analysis are found in different formal phonic programs. In the opinion of this author, those involving word families are preferable to true synthetic phonic analysis because they contain fewer distortions.

APPRAISING ABILITY IN PHONIC ANALYSIS

There are a number of standardized and informal ways of appraising a student's competency in the various phonic elements, phonic generalizations, and auditory blending ability.

Normally, the most effective way of doing this is simply to observe informally a student's ability to analyze a word phonetically when he or she is reading orally. You also can ask the child to explain his or her thought processes while analyzing a word phonetically. Obviously, the ultimate test of a student's ability to use phonic analysis as a word identification technique is in actual reading instead of some simulated situation such as a standardized or informal testing device.

However, there are a number of standardized devices that can be used to assess a student's competency in the various phonic analysis subskills. Although these standardized devices are described in detail in Chapter 17, they also are briefly mentioned here. Standardized group and individual diagnostic reading tests evaluate a student's understanding of the various phonic analysis subskills along with the other word identification techniques and comprehension subskills. They are norm-referenced, which means that you can compare a student's attainment in the various elements of phonic analysis with that of other similar students. However, the main value of such a test is to pinpoint a student's exact weaknesses in phonic analysis so that they can be corrected. The various levels of the *Stanford Diagnostic Reading Test* are an excellent example of a standardized group diagnostic reading test. On the other hand, here are some examples of individual diagnostic reading tests that assess competency in the various phonic analysis subskills: *Diagnostic Reading Scales, Durrell Analysis of Reading Difficulty,* and the *Gates-McKillop Reading Diagnostic Tests.*

There are also several standardized word identification tests that assess a student's ability in the various word identification techniques. However, the majority of these tests mainly stress the evaluation of the various phonic analysis subskills. These tests can be given on either an individual or a group basis. Several examples of word identification tests are the *Doren Diagnostic Reading Test of Word Recognition Skills,* the *McCullough Word-Analysis Test,* and the *Sipay Word Analysis Test.*

Criterion-referenced tests are also useful in evaluating a student's mastery of the various phonic analysis elements and generalizations. Criterion-referenced tests can also be called mastery tests because they specify the point at which a student has achieved mastery of one or more subskills. They are designed to help the teacher ascertain the reading skills in which a student is competent and those in which he or she needs additional instruction and/or reinforcement. They are particularly well suited to ascertain ability in phonic analysis because the various phonic elements and rules can be isolated very well on a test. Although criterion-referenced tests are described in more detail in Chapter 17, here are the names of several tests that are useful for assessing ability in the various elements of phonic analysis: *Fountain Valley Teacher Support System in Reading, Individual Pupil Monitoring System—Reading,* and *Wisconsin Design for Reading Skill Improvement.*

A teacher can also use a new approach to the assessment of phonic skills that was formulated by Dale D. Johnson and others at the University of Wisconsin. Johnson and his associates have been working for some time on a complete new word identification test battery. They have stated that their approach to evaluating competency in phonic analysis emphasizes decoding and still can be given to a group of children at one time. Their measure also uses synthetic or nonsense words rather than real words to ensure that a child cannot recognize any of the words on the test by sight instead of by using phonic analysis.[5]

You can also design your own individual or group inventory in phonic analysis to assess ability in the various aspects of this word identification technique. Usually, an individual inventory in phonic analysis is more valid than is a group inventory. A group inventory in phonic analysis often requires sound-symbol association whereas reading requires symbol-sound association, a much more difficult task because there are so many more options to select from. A phonic analysis inventory often uses nonsense or synthetic words to ensure that the student does not recognize some or all the words on the test by sight.

ABOUT THE PHONIC ELEMENTS

It should be understood at the outset that the study of phonic elements can be very complicated and comprehensive. In fact, a study of phonic elements could comprise an entire reading course very easily. Therefore, the discussion about the elements presented here certainly must constitute only a brief introduction to the study. However, each reading teacher in an elementary school should become very knowledgeable about the common phonic elements and generalizations in order to teach phonic analysis as effectively as possible.

According to a research study by George D. Spache and Mary E. Baggett, in the early 1960s a group of experienced teachers earned average scores at about the 50 percent to 60 percent competency level on phonic tests.[6] Therefore, for additional information on phonic elements or phonic generalizations, you are encouraged to consult one or more of the following sources:

Dolores Durkin. *Strategies for Identifying Words*. Boston: Allyn and Bacon, Inc., 1981.

Patrick Groff. *Phonics: Why & How*. Morristown, New Jersey: General Learning Press, 1977.

Marion A. Hull. *Phonics for the Teacher of Reading*. Columbus, Ohio: Charles E. Merrill Publishing Co., 1981.

---

[5]Dale D. Johnson, Susan D. Pittelman, Linda K. Shriberg, Judy Schwenker, and Sandra S. Dahl, *The Word Identification Test Battery: A New Approach to Mastery and the Assessment of Word Identification Skills* (Madison, Wisconsin: Wisconsin Research and Development Center for Individualized Schooling, 1980).

[6]George D. Spache and Mary E. Baggett, "What Do Teachers Know About Phonics and Syllabication?" *The Reading Teacher, 19* (November 1965): 96–99.

Consonants

A *consonant* is caused when the outgoing breath stream is blocked by an organ of speech. The organs of speech are the hard palate, the larynx, the soft palate, the tongue, and the vocal cords. When the obstruction is complete, the resulting sounds are known as *plosives* or *stops*. Those in which the obstruction is partial are called *continuants*. Consonants also are classified as voiceless or voiced, depending on whether or not the vocal cords vibrate while producing the sound. These are examples of plosives:

p̲ pen   b̲ baby
t̲ ten   d̲ dog
k̲ kite   g̲ get
c̲ can   x̲ expect

These nasal sounds are one type of continuants:

m̲ my   n̲ nice

Fricatives are continuants made when the outgoing breath stream escapes with audible friction.

f̲ fence   v̲ vine
s̲ sun   c̲ city
z̲ zebra   y̲ yes
r̲ red   w̲ win
h̲ hand   l̲ let

Consonant Blends

A *consonant blend* or consonant cluster consists of two or, less often, three consonant letters that appear together. Each consonant contains some element of its own sound while blending with that of the others. Although most consonant blends occur at the beginning of words, they also can be found at the end.

bl̲ black   br̲ brown   cl̲ cloud
cr̲ crow   dr̲ dress   fl̲ flower
fr̲ friend   gl̲ glass   gr̲ growl
pl̲ play   pr̲ pretty   sc̲ scowl
sk̲ sky   sm̲ small   sn̲ snow
sp̲ spin   spl̲ splash   spr̲ spray
st̲ stop   str̲ string   sw̲ swim
tr̲ trip   tw̲ twin

Consonant Digraphs

A *consonant digraph* is composed of two consonants that record a single sound that is different from the sound that either one would normally record separately. Here are some examples of consonant digraphs:

th thin (voiceless)   th then (voiced)
sh ship   ch chin
wh when   ph phase
ng sing   gh rough

Vowels

Vowels result when the organs of speech modify the resonance chamber without impeding the flow of the outgoing breath. All vowels are voiced, and there are no nasal vowels in the English language. One vowel is distinguished from another by the quality of its sound.

a cake   a apple   a along
a tall   a arm   a air
a father

e me   e bed   e earn
e herd   e wear   e sergeant
i ice   i sit   i bird
o rope   o top   o often
o or   o worm
u use   u juice   u nut
u fur
y fly   y baby   y myth
w how (diphthong)

The Schwa Sound

The *schwa sound* is the vowel sound in an unaccented syllable in a word of more than one syllable. Any one of the five major vowel sounds can be the schwa sound if it is found in an unaccented syllable. The schwa sound has a sound very much like that of the short /u/. Here are some words that illustrate the schwa sound:

a comma   e label   i pencil
o button   u minus

Diphthongs

A *diphthong* is composed of two vowel sounds that together record one sound that is different from the sound either of the vowels would have recorded alone. Here are some examples of words containing a diphthong:

<u>oi</u> b<u>oi</u>l   oy t<u>oy</u>   <u>ou</u> h<u>ou</u>se
<u>ow</u> c<u>ow</u>   ew f<u>ew</u>   ey th<u>ey</u> (not everyone considers this a diphthong)

Vowel Digraphs

A *vowel digraph* occurs when two vowels next to each other record only one sound. Here are some examples of words that contain a vowel digraph:

<u>ai</u> r<u>ai</u>n   <u>ay</u> d<u>ay</u>
<u>ee</u> b<u>ee</u>t   <u>ea</u> m<u>ea</u>t
<u>ie</u> p<u>ie</u>
<u>oa</u> g<u>oa</u>t   <u>oe</u> t<u>oe</u>
<u>oo</u> b<u>oo</u>k   <u>oo</u> g<u>oo</u>se
<u>ow</u> cr<u>ow</u>
<u>ui</u> j<u>ui</u>ce

Phonograms

Phonograms or *graphemic bases* are groups of vowels and consonants that are often learned and pronounced as a unit. Here are some examples:

<u>all</u> f<u>all</u>   <u>ill</u> w<u>ill</u>
<u>ick</u> p<u>ick</u>   <u>igh</u> h<u>igh</u>
<u>ight</u> n<u>ight</u>   <u>ank</u> b<u>ank</u>
<u>ink</u> p<u>ink</u>   <u>ate</u> pl<u>ate</u>

Homophones (Homonyms)

A *homophone* is a word that is pronounced the same as another word but has a different spelling and meaning. Here are some examples:

bear   bare
pear   pair   pare
here   hear
roll   role
whole   hole

Homographs

Homographs are words that have the same pronunciation and spelling but have different meanings.

I *can* ride to school on my bicycle.
My mother is going to *can* some peaches.
The farmer put his milk in a *can.*

SEQUENCE OF PRESENTATION OF THE IMPORTANT PHONIC ELEMENTS

It should be stated at the outset that research has not established one best sequence for the teaching of the phonic elements and phonic generalizations. As was pointed out earlier, there is quite a variation among the different basal reader series and among the formal phonic programs as to the sequence that is used when presenting the various phonic elements and phonic generalizations.

Generally, it is believed that phonemes or sounds are the easiest to distinguish when found at the beginnings of words. They are generally somewhat more difficult to distinguish at the ends of words, and they are usually the most difficult to distinguish in the medial or middle positions of words. In the medial position of a word, the sound or phoneme often has a tendency to lose its own identity and, therefore, be more difficult to distinguish than when it is found in the initial or final position.

Initial consonant phonemes are often presented at the beginning stages of reading instruction in many basal reader series and a few formal phonic programs because a sound in the initial position is the easiest to distinguish and also because consonant phonemes are more stable than are the vowel phonemes. Long vowel sounds or short vowel sounds are presented first in various other formal phonic programs. This, however, may not always be the most expedient, for vowel sounds are much less stable than are consonant sounds. In addition, there are not as many words that begin with a vowel phoneme as words that begin with a consonant phoneme.

Certainly not all reading specialists would agree, but here is one sequence of presentation of the major phonic elements that I have found to be useful. It is best represented by the basal reader approach: initial consonant sounds, short vowel sounds, final consonant sounds, long vowel sounds, common phonograms, consonant blends, vowel digraphs, consonant digraphs, diphthongs, r-controlled vowels, the schwa sound, and the circumflex ô (any vowel sound like /âw/).

RESEARCH ABOUT FORMAL PHONIC PROGRAMS AND PHONIC GENERALIZATIONS

Countless research studies have been conducted on the potential values of using various formal phonic programs, especially at the early primary-grade level. It is certain that phonic analysis and phonic generalizations have been greatly overresearched in comparison with other aspects of reading such as interpretive comprehension, critical reading, and creative reading. There are several reasons for this. Phonic instruction has always been the subject of much controversy. In addition, it is a fairly easy area to research in comparison to other areas in reading. For these two main reasons, it has been studied extensively for many years.

Generally, the results of many of the research studies have been difficult to interpret objectively. For example, some publishers of formal phonic programs have commissioned researchers to conduct studies on the use of their programs. Because some of these studies did not use a control group for comparison, the excellent gains in reading achievement that were discovered cannot be accepted as very valid.

In the mid-1960s, Jeanne Chall of Harvard University and a number of associates reviewed most of the research studies that were conducted on the use of formal phonic approaches between 1910 and 1965. However, she and her associates did not review any of the federally financed studies that are mentioned later in this section.

Chall reported the results of examining the research studies in a scholarly, but very controversial, book entitled *Learning to Read—The Great Debate*.[7] From examining the research studies, Chall and her associates concluded that a reading approach that emphasized a *code-emphasis method* generally resulted in superior reading achievement at the beginning stages of reading. A code-emphasis method stresses decoding or cracking the code at the beginning stages of reading instead of comprehension of what is read. The Chall conclusions have been criticized because the federally financed first-grade studies that to an extent contradicted some of the findings presented were not included in the review of research studies. In addition, the findings reported in the book were taken out of context and used as an endorsement of formal phonic programs, especially by some administrators and by the publishers of some formal phonic programs.

One well-known research study in the area of phonic instruction that is considered a classic was conducted by Donald Agnew in 1939.[8] Agnew discovered that an intensive emphasis on phonic analysis in the primary grades resulted in superior scores on tests of phonic ability, word pronunciation, accuracy of oral reading, eye-voice span, vocabulary, and some aspects of reading comprehension. However, Agnew also learned that intensive phonic training did not improve accuracy or speed of silent reading. Because a child who has been taught by a formal phonic program sometimes is inclined to be a word-by-word

---

[7]Jeanne S. Chall, *Learning to Read—The Great Debate* (New York: McGraw-Hill, Inc., 1967).

[8]Donald D. Agnew, "The Effectiveness of Varied Amounts of Phonetic Training on Primary Reading" (unpublished doctoral dissertation, Duke University, Durham, North Carolina, 1939).

reader, it follows that use of a formal phonic program would be likely not to result in rapid reading.

The federally sponsored U.S. Office of Education first-grade studies included evaluations of formal phonic programs in comparison with other approaches such as the basal reader approach, the basal reader approach supplemented by a phonic approach, and the initial teaching alphabet. Very briefly, the results of a number of these studies found that the *Lippincott Basic Reading Program* (called a formal phonic program in this textbook) appears to result in superior achievement in tests of word identification and in phonic tests, particularly among average and above-average children. However, in first grade the Lippincott program was not found to be clearly superior in all respects to the other approaches. In any case, when some of the studies were continued into second grade, the Lippincott program led to better achievement on phonic tests, on spelling tests, and in word identification, especially for average and above-average children. It also resulted in higher scores in comprehension only for the above-average children, probably because they possessed a very good meaning vocabulary.[9]

Duane R. Tovey recently conducted an interesting study to determine if students had a working understanding of the phonic terms that they had been taught at one time. This study was conducted with individual students in grades two through six. Tovey found that most children did not appear to grasp the meaning of phonic terms to any great extent and were unable to define such terms as consonant, consonant blend, consonant digraph, the final *e* rule, and the *r*-controlled vowel. However, interestingly enough, Tovey discovered that these same children were much better able to use sound-symbol relationships for decoding on a test than they were able to define the phonic terms. He concluded by recommending that sound-symbol relationships be emphasized while avoiding the use of the terms.[10]

Theodore Clymer, formerly of the University of Minnesota, conducted a classic research study in 1963 that attempted to determine the stability or consistency of forty-five commonly taught phonic generalizations. Clymer used four sets of basal readers to determine the phonic generalizations that were presented in the primary grades at that time. Then he arbitrarily decided that a phonic generalization

---

[9]Guy L. Bond and Robert Dykstra, "The Cooperative Research Program in First-Grade Reading Instruction," *Reading Research Quarterly*, 2 (Summer 1967): 5–141.

[10]Duane R. Tovey, "Children's Grasp of Phonics Terms vs. Sound-Symbol Relationships," *The Reading Teacher*, 33 (January 1980): 431–437.

should be 75 percent consistent or stable to be presented to children. Out of the forty-five generalizations, Clymer found only eighteen generalizations that were 75 percent consistent and, therefore, should be presented to primary-grade children.[11]

The eighteen phonic generalizations that Clymer believed should be presented to children in the primary grades were as follows:

The r gives the preceding vowel a sound that is neither long nor short.

Words having double e usually have the long e sound.

In ay the y is silent and gives a its long sound.

When y is the final letter in a word, it usually has a vowel sound.

When c and h are next to each other, they make only one sound.

Ch is usually pronounced as it is in *kitchen, catch,* and *chair,* not like sh.

When c is followed by e or i, the sound of s is likely to be heard.

When the letter c is followed by o or a, the sound of k is likely to be heard.

When ght is seen in a word, gh is silent.

When two of the same consonants are side by side, only one is heard.

When a word ends in ck, it has the same last sound as in *look.*

In most two-syllable words, the first syllable is accented.

If a, in, he, ex, de, or be is the first syllable in a word, it usually is unaccented.

In most two-syllable words that end in a consonant followed by y, the first syllable is accented and the last is unaccented.

If the last syllable of a word ends in le, the consonant preceding the le usually begins the last syllable.

When the first vowel element in a word is followed by th, ch, or sh, these symbols are not broken when the word is divided into syllables and may go with either the first or second syllable.

When there is one e in a word that ends with a consonant, the e usually has a short sound.

When the last syllable is the sound r, it is unaccented.

After Clymer's study on the utility of phonic generalizations, other researchers investigated the same aspect of phonics. For example, Mildred Hart Bailey of Northwestern Louisiana State College reexamined Clymer's forty-five phonic generalizations. She found that

---

[11]Theodore Clymer, "The Utility of Phonic Generalizations in the Primary Grades," *The Reading Teacher, 12* (January 1963): 252–258.

twenty-seven of the generalizations that she studied reached Clymer's 75 percent utility level.[12]

Robert Emans of Ohio State University also reexamined Clymer's forty-five phonic generalizations, but included words beyond the primary-grade level. Emans discovered that twenty-seven of the phonic generalizations reached Clymer's 75 percent utility level.[13]

In a recent study, Ivo P. Greif researched the pronunciation of words that end in a vowel-consonant-final e pattern. This rule, which states that the vowel is long and the final e is silent, is often presented to students. Greif found that only 53 percent of the 7,687 words that he studied exemplified this rule. Therefore, Greif concluded that this rule is so unpredictable that it should not be taught again to children.[14]

THE PSYCHOLINGUISTIC VIEW OF PHONIC ANALYSIS

As is explained in detail in Chapter 8, some psycholinguists view phonic instruction and phonic analysis somewhat differently from the way other reading specialists view them.

Some psycholinguists correctly believe that comprehension is the ultimate goal and that decoding is only a means to achieving that goal and is not an end in itself. They believe that graphophonic clues always should be used along with semantic and syntactic clues. Stated very simply, this indicates that phonic analysis should be used along with word meaning and word order clues as a person is reading. A reader, they feel, should use only enough graphophonic clues to be able to obtain the overall meaning of the material. Some of these scholars state that if a reader possesses a good background in the reading material, he or she will not need to rely so extensively on the graphophonic clues to obtain the meaning of the material.

Very briefly, some psycholinguists are not very concerned if a child "miscues" or makes an error on a word if it does not interfere with the child's general comprehension of the material. These scholars obviously feel this way because their overall goal is comprehension of what is read, not completely accurate word pronunciation.

---

[12]Mildred Hart Bailey, "The Utility of Phonic Generalizations, in Grades One Through Six," *The Reading Teacher, 20* (February 1967): 413–418.

[13]Robert Emans, "The Usefulness of Phonic Generalizations Above the Primary Grades," *The Reading Teacher, 20* (February 1967): 419–425.

[14]Ivo P. Greif, "A Study of the Pronunciation of Words Ending in a Vowel-Consonant-Final E Pattern," *The Reading Teacher, 34* (December 1980): 290–292.

PHONIC ANALYSIS AS PRESENTED IN THE BASAL READER LESSON

As was explained in detail in Chapter 5, the traditional basal reader lesson has a number of parts, one of which is the presentation and reinforcement of the various word identification and comprehension skills.

We stated earlier that the basal reader approach now presents more phonic elements and phonic generalizations and presents them earlier than was done in the past. Many of these phonic elements and rules are carefully presented and reinforced by the time the typical child has completed the third-grade reading level. The basal reader manuals very carefully outline a scope and sequence for presenting the various phonic elements and rules. The teacher is also given numerous strategies for teaching and reinforcing phonic analysis.

The phonic analysis skills that are presented in the basal reader approach are viewed as integrated phonic analysis instead of as the isolated phonic analysis more typically found in a formal phonic program. The basal reader approach views phonic analysis as one important word identification technique that should be used along with other word identification techniques such as contextual analysis, structural analysis, and sight word recognition. Phonic analysis is never viewed as an end in itself, but rather as a means to an end, which is effective comprehension of what is read.

PHONIC ANALYSIS AS PRESENTED IN THE LANGUAGE EXPERIENCE APPROACH AND IN INDIVIDUALIZED READING

As was explained in Chapters 4 and 6, phonic analysis skills are taught in a somewhat incidental way in the typical language experience approach or individualized reading plan. In these two approaches, ability in phonic analysis is viewed as a means to an end, which is effective comprehension.

In the initial stages of the language experience approach, letter-sound relationships are mainly presented from group-dictated experience charts and individually dictated language experience stories. However, they also may be presented or reinforced in short-term needs groups. In addition, phonic analysis skills can be reinforced in reading stations on an individual basis. (See Chapter 6.)

Phonic analysis skills are also presented and reinforced in a somewhat incidental manner when the pure or true individualized reading plan is used. As was explained in detail in Chapter 6, phonic analysis skills normally are taught on an individual basis as a result of diagnostic-prescriptive reading instruction in individual reading conferences. In addition, the teacher forms short-term flexible needs or skills groups when he or she has determined that a group of children need instruction and/or reinforcement in some elements of phonic analysis. A child also can practice phonic analysis subskills on an independent basis at a reading station or at his or her desk when pure or true individualized reading is used. In relation to phonic analysis skills, a child normally should learn and practice only those elements of phonic analysis in which he or she has been found to lack competence.

Interestingly enough, some above-average children develop their own phonic analysis strategies for decoding unknown words. This may be particularly true when they are using the language experience approach or individualized reading. However, it also is true to some extent when the basal reader approach is used. These strategies often involve "chunking" an unknown word into pronounceable parts and then blending these parts into a recognizable word. These informal phonic analysis strategies often serve the above-average children who use them very well indeed.

EXAMPLES OF TEACHING STRATEGIES FOR PHONIC ANALYSIS

There are countless strategies and materials that a teacher can use to improve a child's competence in the various phonic analysis subskills. The strategies that are given here are only designed to serve as illustrations. As was stated previously, the basal reader manuals contain many suggestions also.

There are countless materials and devices that you can use to improve ability in phonic analysis in addition to those found in basal reader series or formal phonic programs. There are commercial activity sheets placed on duplicating masters, transparencies, letter people, special phonic workbooks, and many commercial games. There also are various devices such as teaching machines or computers, which can be used to present elements of phonic analysis.

Here are only a few teaching strategies that can be used to present and/or reinforce aspects of phonic analysis. As you may remember, ideas for improving ability in auditory discrimination were included in Chapter 3 so they are not included here again.

> Have the child make up sentences. Each sentence should have as many words as possible that begin with the same sound. For example: *Betty's ball bounced into the bathroom.*

Construct a word wheel by cutting out two circles of tagboard, one of ⌐¹ which is slightly smaller than the other. Fasten the two disks with a brass fastener. Print phonograms on the larger disk, and print initial consonants or consonant clusters on the smaller disk. Have the child spin the smaller disk and pronounce each newly formed word.

Make eight cards out of tagboard, each of which contains a phonogram. Make a number of small cards of tagboard, each one of which has a consonant or consonant blend printed on it. Have the child choose a small card from the deck of cards and place it in front of a phonogram to form a word. The first child to pronounce the eight words formed on the cards correctly wins.

Type a short story omitting all the vowels. Have the child try to read the ⌐⁴ story silently or orally mentally adding the vowels that were omitted. You also can have the child print in each omitted vowel.

Print two columns of words on the chalkboard or on a transparency. One ⌐² word in each column should contain the same vowel sound as a word in the other column although the spellings can be different. Have the child draw a line between the two words that contain the same vowel sound.

Print a single consonant, a consonant blend, or a consonant digraph on ⌐³ small tagboard cards. Place all the cards in a grab bag. Have the child choose a card and give a word beginning with the correct phonic element. If the child is correct, he or she can keep the card. If not, it is put back into the bag. The child with the most cards is the winner.

Tape-record this activity. Pronounce some words, each of which contains the hard or soft sound of *c* or *g*. If a word contains the hard sound of *c*, have the child write a *k;* but if the word contains a soft sound, have the child write an *s*. If the word contains the hard sound of *g,* have the child write a *g;* but if it contains the soft sound, have the child write a *j*.

Print some letters on the chalkboard, including both consonants and vowels. Have each student form as many words as possible by using combinations of these letters. Each student writes the words that he or she has formed on a sheet of paper. The student who forms the greatest amount of words wins the game.

Write on the chalkboard or a transparency a number of words that have been spelled phonetically. Have the student pronounce each of these words by interpreting the phonetic spellings.

Write on the chalkboard or a transparency some words that contain the schwa sound (diamənd). Have the student write each word on a sheet of paper using the correct spelling.

SELECTED REFERENCES

Carnine, Douglas W. "Phonics Versus Look-Say Transfer to New Words." *The Reading Teacher, 30* (March 1977): 636–640.

Cronnell, Bruce. "Phonics for Reading Vs. Phonics for Spelling." *The Reading Teacher, 32* (December 1978): 337–340.

Dallmann, Martha, Roger L. Rouch, Lynette Y. C. Char, and John J. DeBoer. *The Teaching of Reading.* New York: Holt, Rinehart and Winston, 1982.

Durrell, Donald D., and Helen A. Murphy. "A Prereading Phonics Inventory." *The Reading Teacher, 31* (January 1978): 385–390.

Farr, Roger, and Nancy Roser. *Teaching a Child to Read.* New York: Harcourt Brace Jovanovich, Inc., 1979, pp. 205–225.

Groff, Patrick. "Teaching Reading by Syllables." *The Reading Teacher, 34* (March 1981): 659–664.

Haddock, Maryann. "Teaching Blending in Beginning Reading Instruction *Is* Important." *The Reading Teacher, 31* (March 1978): 654–659.

Heilman, Arthur W. *Phonics in Proper Perspective.* Columbus, Ohio: Charles E. Merrill Publishing Co., 1981.

Lapp, Diane, and James Flood. *Teaching Reading to Every Child.* New York: Macmillan Publishing Company, Inc., 1983.

Mason, Jana M. "Refining Phonics for Teaching Beginning Reading." *The Reading Teacher, 31* (November 1977): 179–184.

Miller, Wilma H. *Reading Correction Kit.* West Nyack, New York: Center for Applied Research in Education, 1981, Section 3.

———. *The Reading Activities Handbook.* New York: Holt, Rinehart and Winston, 1980, Section 3.

Otto, Wayne, Robert Rude, and Dixie Lee Spiegel. *How to Teach Reading.* Reading, Massachusetts: Addison-Wesley Publishing Company, Inc., 1979, pp. 113–130.

Speckels, Judith. " 'Poor' Readers Can Learn Phonics." *The Reading Teacher, 34* (October 1980): 22–26.

SUGGESTED ACTIVITIES

1. If you can, examine a contemporary formal phonic program and a formal phonic program dating from the early twentieth century. In what ways are these programs alike, and in what ways are they different?

2. Read the following books: *Why Johnny Can't Read and What You Can Do About It* and *Learning to Read—The Great Debate.* Discuss the ways in which the two books are alike and are different.

3. Contrast the scope and sequence of phonic elements and phonic generalizations as they are presented in a basal reader series and a formal phonic program.

4. Examine one of the standardized norm-referenced or criterion-referenced word identification tests mentioned in the chapter.

5. Visit a primary-grade classroom in which a total formal phonic program is being used. What was your impression of this program?
6. Construct a game for phonic analysis. You can find some ideas for making games in this article: Sandra McCormick and Betty M. Collins, "A Potpourri of Game-Making Ideas for the Reading Teacher," *The Reading Teacher, 34* (March 1981): 692–696.

The contributions of psycholinguistics

Do You Think That This Should Have Happened?

Ms. Chambers was a beginning second-grade teacher in a small town in the Southeast. She began her first week of teaching reading by randomly dividing the children in her second-grade class into three groups. When she asked the children in one of the groups to read orally, she especially noticed the oral reading of a girl named Elena.

Although it appeared to Ms. Chambers that Elena was a fairly adequate reader, the girl seemed inordinately afraid of making errors while she was reading orally and appeared to hesitate on many of the difficult words instead of attempting to predict what they might be by guessing at them. Elena also found it rather difficult to answer comprehension questions about the reading material because she apparently focused too extensively on the individual words instead of trying to grasp the meaning of the reading material.

Ms. Chambers had taken several reading courses at the university from which she had graduated the previous May. In one of these reading courses she had acquired a limited amount of information about the contributions that psycholinguistics can make to reading instruction and had been quite impressed with them. She was able to determine that none of these insights probably had been applied to Elena's reading instruction in first grade. For example, Elena undoubtedly had not been encouraged to take chances on word identification while reading, but clearly had been cautioned to pronounce each word in the reading material correctly. There probably had been an overemphasis on phonic analysis as a word identification strategy in her reading program. In addition, Elena might not have been encouraged to use prediction strategies such as posing questions that she was to read to answer. Perhaps she had not been encouraged to use her background of experiences or nonvisual information while reading to lessen her need for visual information or the reading material on the printed page.

Ms. Chambers knew that she could not totally erase Elena's past experiences with reading. However, she encouraged her to predict unknown words rather than not even to attempt them. Thus, she tried to get Elena to use semantic (word meaning or context) and syntactic (word order) clues as much as possible in word identification. Ms. Chambers also helped Elena to set purposes for reading to aid her comprehension and to use her own nonvisual information as much as possible. After several months in second grade, Elena was somewhat more willing to use prediction strategies in word identification and also comprehended what she read somewhat better. However, Ms. Chambers knew that Elena still had considerable progress to make.

After you have read this chapter, you will understand a little more the contributions that insights from psycholinguistics can make to reading instruction, and, one hopes, you may be able to employ some of these insights in your own teaching of reading because they seem to reflect a good deal of common sense.

ONE VARIATION OF THE PSYCHOLINGUISTIC DEFINITION OF READING

It should be recognized at the outset that the information presented in this chapter is a somewhat simplistic account of the psycholinguistic view of reading. It is offered in this manner mainly to facilitate the understanding of this theory by the reader. Therefore, it may be helpful at the beginning to provide a definition of reading that may be held by some of those who subscribe to the psycholinguistic theory of reading. Some psycholinguists apparently believe that reading is not extracting sounds from print or simply decoding words, but rather that it is bringing meaning to print. Comprehension of what is read, not word pronunciation, is the most important goal of reading instruction. Thus, it is believed that reading always must be an active process in which the reader should be highly involved and should bring his or her own experiences (schemata) to bear on the reading.

Some psycholinguists think that reading consists of using visual and nonvisual information. The visual information is the material on the printed page, and the nonvisual information is the experiential background that the reader brings to the reading. It is correctly stated that the more nonvisual information the reader has, the less visual information will be required for effective comprehension. As an example, the serious student of history ordinarily can comprehend a history textbook much more easily and effectively than a person with little background in history because the serious student brings much more experiential background or nonvisual information to the reading. Fluent reading requires redundancy to reduce the need for visual information. This redundancy often can take the form of prior experiences or related reading.

One strongly held concept is that reading always requires risk taking on the reader's part, implying that the child should not be afraid of making mistakes in oral or silent reading if these errors or miscues do not interfere significantly with comprehension. A reader should use prediction strategies such as graphophonic (letter-sound) clues, semantic (word meaning) clues, and syntactic (word order) clues to arrive at comprehension. It is evident that some beginning readers have been required to strive for perfection in word pronunciation at the expense of effective comprehension.

Psycholinguists believe that children always should strive for comprehension when they are learning to read. Such effective comprehension requires that they seek answers to questions that they have posed about their own reading. Thus, reading becomes an active, meaning-gathering process.

CHARACTERISTICS OF GOOD READING ACCORDING TO ONE BRANCH OF PSYCHOLINGUISTICS

According to some of the psycholinguists, fluent reading possesses a number of characteristics. Reading should be fairly rapid and the reader should not place undue emphasis on details while it is being done. Slow, word-by-word reading gives too much attention to word pronunciation and not enough attention to comprehension of what is read. Indeed, many reading specialists believe that fairly rapid reading is related to good comprehension. Quite often the slow, word-by-word reader does not comprehend very effectively. He or she may have forgotten what was read previously. However, you must understand that in some instances rapid reading may be superficial.

Some psycholinguists also state that reading must be selective in that the reader only samples the text. This suggests that reading always should be purposeful and should be done only in terms of the questions that the reader has posed for himself or herself to answer. Not every word—perhaps not even every sentence—must be read in order for the reader to satisfy his or her purposes for comprehension. This, of course, depends on the degree of detail that the reader wants to gain from the reading material, and it would vary according to the reader's purposes.

As was mentioned earlier, some psycholinguists feel that a reader should use nonvisual information as much as possible while reading. The use of nonvisual information reduces the reader's dependence on visual information or the printed material. Nonvisual information can consist of the reader's direct or secondhand experiences with the topic found in the reading material or any previous reading that the reader has done in the area. Nonvisual information can also be developed for a child by the teacher as he or she improves the child's experiential background in the topic by class discussion, demonstrations, experiments, films, filmstrips, cassette recordings, records, or other means.

In addition, it is believed that prediction by the reader is of great importance in comprehension. This prediction can greatly reduce the reader's dependence on graphophonic (letter-sound) clues as a result of his or her greater use of semantic (word meaning) and syntactic (word order) clues.

THE ROLE OF VARIOUS TYPES OF CLUES

There are three main types of clues that the reader uses in determining unknown words that are met while reading. One type of clue is called a *graphophonic* or *orthographic clue.* Such clues involve the visual appearance of a word, the letter order found in words, or the letter-sound relationship found in words. As an example, when a child substitutes the word *house* for *horse,* he or she is overrelying on graphophonic clues and not attending to semantic or word meaning clues. The same also can be said when the child substitutes the word *watch* for *catch.* Although graphophonic clues are recommended as an aid to word identification, an overreliance on them is not recommended.

There perhaps can be more dependence on *semantic* or *word meaning clues* than on graphophonic clues. For example, a child may be able to guess accurately at the meaning of an unknown word in a sentence if he or she knows the meaning of most of the rest of the words in that sentence. In fact, the child sometimes may be able to skip one or several unknown words in a sentence and still be able to grasp the meaning of that sentence. This would be acceptable if comprehension of the passage were retained. The use of semantic clues is an example of using contextual analysis for word identification. As is explained in Chapter 13, contextual analysis can be defined as obtaining the meaning, and less often the pronunciation, of an unknown word by examining the context in which it is located. The context may be the same sentence, a nearby sentence, or the paragraph.

Syntactic or *word order clues* are also useful in reducing a reader's dependence on graphophonic clues. English has a prescribed word order that helps the reader predict unknown words found in the reading material. For example, when an article (*a, an,* or *the*) is found in a sentence, it is a certainty that a noun will follow it. Again, when the words *have been* are found in a sentence, the reader can be sure that a verb will follow them. Thus, the use of word order can help a reader predict some of the unknown words found in the reading material.

In summary, effective reading may involve the extensive use of semantic and syntactic clues and the less extensive use of graphophonic clues.

LETTER AND WORD IDENTIFICATION IN A BRANCH OF PSYCHOLINGUISTIC THEORY

The child can use feature analysis, or the visual clues contained in the letters, to learn to identify the various letters of the alphabet. This means that a child can contrast alphabet letters to determine the differences in their features or characteristics. For example, a child can learn letters such as *a* and *o* or *m* and *n* by contrasting their unique features. Feature analysis is supposedly more effective than having the teacher place a single letter on the chalkboard and say, "This is an *a*." Apparently then the child has no basis for comparison.

In some branches of psycholinguistic theory, word identification in reading can be immediate, in which case the child recognizes a word by sight. In such an instance, the reader probably does not really notice the individual letters in a word but rather recognizes it immediately. Word identification by analogy, in which the reader looks for clues to a word from words that are similar in appearance, may be recommended. In what is called mediated word identification, contextual analysis normally is highly recommended, but phonic analysis usually is *not* highly recommended.

COMPREHENSION IN A BRANCH OF PSYCHOLINGUISTIC THEORY

Differentiation can be made between two aspects of language that are called *surface structure* and *deep structure*. Surface structure is considered to be the observable characteristics of language such as the marks on the printed page. On the other hand, deep structure is considered to be the meaning of language. Obviously, deep structure goes beyond surface structure and is the true language. The following two sentences may help to illustrate the differences between surface structure and deep structure. Notice that these sentences are very similar in surface structure (appearance) and yet differ greatly in deep structure (meaning).

> John is easy to please.
> John is eager to please.

Another interesting example of this same concept is the following sentence:

> Flying planes can be dangerous.

Notice how the preceding sentence can be interpreted in two different ways.

Comprehension in reading is of primary importance, and word identification is of secondary importance. Therefore, each and every word need not be identified while reading, especially if the unidentified words do not carry a significant meaning to the sentence.

The meaning of a sentence is not totally equivalent to the meaning of each of the words in a sentence. For example, the meaning of an entire sentence is greater than the combined meanings of the individual words found in that sentence. In other words, we have here an example of the statement "The sum is greater than the total of its parts."

THE ROLE OF THE TEACHER

Some psycholinguists also have a view about the role of the teacher in reading instruction. The teacher should be more of a facilitator of reading instruction than its direct initiator. The role of the teacher in beginning reading instruction then probably would be to read aloud to children on a regular basis to add to their experiential background as well as to motivate them to want to learn to read. The teacher also can provide a reading model for the children by showing them that he or she also values reading.

Reading instruction probably should be rather indirect. The teacher can provide appropriate reading materials that the children can read. They are then to learn to read by reading.

Another primary role of the teacher is to add to each child's non-visual information or experiential background so that he or she can comprehend the reading material more effectively. This improvement of nonvisual information can take the form of discussions, experiments, demonstrations, and the use of various kinds of multimedia aids as was mentioned earlier.

SEVERAL RECOMMENDED READING APPROACHES

Although most psycholinguists generally are reluctant to recommend any particular reading program, most of them probably favor the use of aspects of several different types of approaches and plans.

Children first should learn to recognize by sight words that are found in their everyday environment. These could be words on signs, television, and can labels. Such informal exposure to print would take place at the preschool level and could occur in the home or in some type of informal school setting. (See Chapters 2 and 3.)

The language experience approach is a very good way to introduce reading instruction in kindergarten or first grade. It is beneficial because it uses each child's own background of experiences or nonvisual information. It also emphasizes the comprehension of what is read and teaches decoding skills such as phonic analysis and structural analysis in an incidental, informal way instead of in a structured, drill-like way (see Chapter 4).

Individualized reading as a major method of class organization may be recommended because comprehension of what is read is always stressed in the individual reading conferences that are the major components of this reading plan. In addition, as you remember from Chapter 6, the reading skills are presented in a predominantly diagnostic-prescriptive manner in individualized reading instead of in a structured, drill-like way.

A READING APPROACH NOT RECOMMENDED BY MANY PSYCHOLINGUISTS

Certainly the one single reading approach that most psycholinguists never would recommend would be a formal phonic program. (See Chapter 7.) They believe that a formal phonic program focuses far too much on word identification or decoding and stresses comprehension of what is read far too little.

Phonic rules are believed to have too many exceptions to be valid. In addition, an overreliance on phonic analysis as a word identification technique is disapproved of highly because it stresses decoding too much. As has been stated before, the use of contextual analysis is much preferred because it is more closely related to meaning.

Phonic analysis does not reflect the various dialects found in the English language. For example, some vowel sounds do not sound exactly the same in various parts of the country like the Northeast, Midwest, or South.

In summary, most psycholinguists generally remain inalterably opposed to formal phonic programs or the extensive use of phonic analysis in any type of reading program.

MISCUE ANALYSIS

Some psycholinguists have developed a rather complicated means of analyzing a student's oral reading errors. As has been stated earlier, psycholinguists call oral reading errors *oral reading miscues* to avoid the connotation that they are somehow bad. For example, if the student reads "The king went to his *palace*" for "The king went to his *place*," the substitution of *palace* for *place* is a relatively unimportant miscue. In the preceding substitution the reader has utilized his or her experiential background (schemata) quite effectively.

Kenneth S. Goodman and Yetta Goodman, among others, have played a most prominent role in the linguistic analysis of oral reading miscues. A very complex system for analyzing oral reading miscues was simplified in a device that is called the *Reading Miscue Inventory*.[1] In this inventory, oral reading miscues are evaluated in terms of graphic similarity, sound similarity, grammatical function, syntactic acceptability, semantic acceptability, meaning change, and correction and semantic acceptability. In addition, the reader's comprehension is evaluated by having him or her retell as much of the material as he or she can recall. The recall can be aided by open-ended questions.

---

[1]Yetta Goodman and Carolyn Burke, *Reading Miscue Inventory* (New York: Macmillan Publishing Company, Inc., 1972).

AN ASSESSMENT OF THE BRANCHES OF PSYCHOLINGUISTIC THEORY

Psycholinguistic theory has some unique characteristics that can be considered by the elementary teacher of reading. This does not indicate that all aspects of it are necessarily practical, but rather that some of its aspects may be useful in presenting a good elementary reading program.

It is a certainty that schemata or a good background of experiences always aids reading comprehension. Thus, it certainly is helpful for the teacher to attempt to improve a student's experiential background before the student reads a selection. As you remember from Chapter 5, this is done in the typical basal reader lesson. However, it probably is even more important when a student is to read a difficult passage from a content textbook.

Certainly, comprehension of what is read always must be considered of primary importance in reading instruction. It is true that absolutely accurate oral reading or silent reading is not always necessary if comprehension of the material is achieved. The child may be able to omit or substitute words occasionally if they are not meaning-carrying words that interfere with comprehension. Certainly, a few children in the early primary grades develop a dislike for oral reading if they are so afraid of making an oral reading error that they will not take any risks. The teachers of such children probably should encourage them to be a little less cautious.

It is also a certainty that phonic analysis can receive far too much stress as a word identification technique. Although phonic analysis skill often is important to effective reading, contextual analysis usually is of more importance in successful comprehension. Contextual analysis should receive great stress as it does in psycholinguistic theory.

However, I believe that some children need much more direct instruction than is recommended by many psycholinguists. A number of children do need the direct instruction of the word identification and comprehension skills that is provided by the basal reader approach. (See Chapter 5.) For example, how can children learn to read by reading if they do not possess any word identification skills?

In addition, if the philosophy of skipping unknown words *is carried to an excess,* comprehension must certainly be damaged. It is a concept that must be kept in perspective if children are not to abuse it and continually skip all words that appear difficult to them.

In summary, the contributions of psycholinguistic theory are important and useful, but I believe that it always must be evaluated carefully and used with some discretion and judgment on the part of teachers of reading.

SELECTED REFERENCES

Canady, Robert J. "Psycholinguistics in a Real-Life Classroom." *The Reading Teacher, 34* (November 1980): 156–159.

D'Angelo, Karen, and Robert L. Wilson. "How Helpful Is Insertion and Omission Miscue Analysis?" *The Reading Teacher, 32* (February 1979): 519–520.

Goodman, Kenneth S., ed. *The Psycholinguistic Nature of the Reading Process.* Detroit: Wayne State University Press, 1968.

Newman, Harold. "Oral Reading Miscue Analysis Is Good but Not Complete." *The Reading Teacher, 31* (May 1978): 883–886.

Smith, Frank. *Psycholinguistics in Reading.* New York: Holt, Rinehart and Winston, 1973.

———. *Understanding Reading.* New York: Holt, Rinehart and Winston, 1982.

Spache, George D. *Diagnosing and Correcting Reading Disabilities.* Boston: Allyn and Bacon, Inc., 1981, pp. 135–142.

Spiegel, Dixie Lee. "Meaning-Seeking Strategies for the Beginning Reader." *The Reading Teacher, 31* (April 1978): 772–776.

SUGGESTED ACTIVITIES

1. Tape-record the oral reading of an elementary-school student. Then later listen to the reading. Does the student appear to be an overly cautious reader, or does he or she take chances that probably would lead to effective comprehension?

2. If possible, select a small group of students who are to read a difficult passage from a content textbook. Help add to their schemata or experiential background by the use of a motivated class discussion, an experiment, a demonstration, a film, a filmstrip, or a recording. Do you believe that this increased schemata added to each student's comprehension of the passage?

3. Examine the *Reading Miscue Inventory* that was discussed in the chapter. Do you believe that this is a valid means for analyzing a student's oral reading miscues?

Diagnostic-prescriptive reading programs and reading management systems

Why Did She Feel This Way?

Mr. Wong had been teaching second grade at Coolidge School in a large city in the Far West for two years. He used the basal reader approach predominantly although he supplemented this approach to some extent by a formal phonic approach. He had always considered himself to be a good teacher of reading; however, that was before he met a little girl named Mavis at the beginning of his third year of teaching.

After only about two weeks of school, Mavis began to complain rather heatedly to Mr. Wong about the reading lessons that were being presented to her reading achievement group, which was the above-average group. She told him that she already knew all of the phonic elements and phonic generalizations that he was presenting to the children in her group. Then she asked Mr. Wong why she should have to learn all of these phonic elements and phonic rules when she knew them already. Mavis also said that it was a waste of her time to complete workbook pages and activity sheets that provided practice in phonic elements and rules that she already knew.

Indeed, Mr. Wong could not think of any logical answers to Mavis's questions about why she should have to learn and practice various reading skills in which she already was compe-tent. After thinking about it, Mr. Wong decided that it probably was a waste of time for Mavis.

Because Mr. Wong was taking a graduate reading course at a local university, he decided to ask his instructor how to help Mavis so that she would not have to learn and practice reading skills of which she already had mastery. The college reading instructor explained diagnostic-prescriptive reading instruction and reading management systems to Mr. Wong. He suggested that Mr. Wong examine a reading management system and do reading on diagnostic-prescriptive reading programs.

After some reading, Mr. Wong attempted to present reading instruction to his above-average reading achievement group in a diagnostic-prescriptive manner. Later he hoped to do the same with his two other reading achievement groups as much as possible. From that time on, Mavis mainly learned and practiced only those reading skills in which she did not have competence, and she then was a more satisfied child.

After reading this chapter, you will know the major characteristics of diagnostic-prescriptive reading instruction and reading management systems. You then will be better able to teach reading in a diagnostic-prescriptive way in the future.

CHARACTERISTICS OF DIAGNOSTIC-PRESCRIPTIVE TEACHING OF READING

The diagnostic-prescriptive teaching of reading consists of a number of different elements. True diagnostic-prescriptive reading instruction should be employed in any reading program as is explained later in this chapter. This type of reading instruction enables a student to read on his or her appropriate level and to learn and practice only those reading skills in which he or she lacks competence. Such a program is in contrast to a more traditional reading program in which all reading skills are presented to all students whether or not they already have mastery of these skills. In addition, a diagnostic-prescriptive reading program also should always attempt to build upon a student's present reading competencies.

In a more traditional reading program all the prescribed reading skills in that program are presented to all students even if they already have mastery of these skills before the presentation. As an example, all the students in a reading achievement group were taught the diphthongs at a predetermined time even if some of the students in the group already were competent in them. Usually, all the students in this group were given a comparable amount of practice in all the reading skills in the form of workbook pages, activity sheets, or other means. This procedure did not provide enough reinforcement for mastery to be achieved by some of the students in the group whereas it was a waste of time for other students.

In the past, many students at a grade level were required to read the same level of material whether or not they could do so. This was true in the case of basal readers, content textbooks, and supplementary reading materials. Such a practice was especially harmful for below-average readers because they spent their entire school career reading materials that were too difficult for them. However, it also was harmful for above-average readers because they were not given the opportunity to read materials that challenged them.

Diagnostic-prescriptive reading instruction is designed to change these traditional practices. In such instruction, a student normally does not have to learn or practice those reading skills of which he or she already has mastery. This practice certainly is an inefficient use of teacher and student time and may result in lowered student motivation. In addition, a student should read on his or her instructional or independent reading level. A student usually should not read material that is very difficult for him or her unless he or she has a great motivation to do so for some reason.

However, diagnostic-prescriptive reading instruction also can be presented in a formal way in what typically is called a *reading management system*. There are a number of such management systems, most of which originated less than twenty years ago. Such a system can be purchased from a publisher. As is explained in detail later in this chapter, the typical reading management system consists of some type of preassessment device that enables the teacher to place the student in the system. It also consists of a number of behavioral or performance objectives that the student is supposed to accomplish. In addition, the reading management system consists of many criterion-referenced tests that the student is to complete to determine if he or she has mastery of the various reading skills in the system. The typical reading management system does not contain any instructional reading materials. Instead, it provides numerous references to specific pages in basal reader teachers' manuals, phonic programs, basal reader workbooks, phonic workbooks, and commercial activity sheets placed on duplicating masters.

The typical reading management system subdivides the reading process into small units that can be easily tested and subsequently presented and reinforced if necessary. Because it is easier to subdivide the lower levels of reading than the higher levels, much attention is given to phonic analysis and structural analysis in a typical reading management system. However, a reading management system normally does attempt to assess competency in such reading skills as these: aspects of reading readiness, sight word recognition, phonic elements, structural analysis, contextual analysis, literal comprehension, interpretive comprehension, critical reading, and the various study skills.

Record keeping is of vital importance to the success of a reading management system. Normally the record keeping system includes a list of the reading skills in that program and a notation system of some type to indicate whether or not each of the reading skills has been mastered. Normally, the point of mastery of a reading skill varies from 60 percent to 100 percent, with 80 percent competency level being the most typical.

Record keeping can take several forms, one of which is the use of a key-sort filing system. In such a system there is a card for each student in the classroom. The skills in the program are written around the edge of the card next to the corresponding holes. When a student has mastered a skill, the hole that represents the skill is clipped open with a special notcher. When the teacher is ready to group children for reading skill instruction, he or she stacks all the cards and runs a skewer through the hole representing that skill. When the skewer is lifted, the cards with the notched hole will fall, and the unnotched cards will remain. The cards remaining on the skewer represent students who have not yet learned that reading skill.

Because the record keeping involved in a reading management system is quite time-consuming, a computer bank is sometimes used now for this purpose. Teachers in schools having computer terminals can have the computer identify children who need instruction and/or reinforcement in a specific reading skill. I believe that computers will play an important part in reading instruction in the future. Therefore, computers may well become practical in the future as tools to do the record keeping in reading management systems. Because computers are very motivating for many children, they also can be quite useful in reinforcing the various reading skills. Of course, computers are not as expensive as they were even in the recent past.

There are simpler ways to keep records in such a system also. For example, the teacher can maintain separate record sheets in a file folder for each student. A few teachers use a wall chart to manage the record keeping in a reading management system. One axis of the chart lists the names of the students, and the other axis lists the skills taught in that program. As a student indicates mastery of a reading skill, the cell marking the intersection of the student's name and the skill is coded in some way, as by a check mark.

Diagnostic-prescriptive reading instruction sometimes has a slightly different connotation in special education. In this area a diagnostic-prescriptive teacher assesses each special child in terms of his or her reading strengths and weaknesses and reading expectancy level. The teacher then writes a prescriptive educational program for each child that includes long-range goals, short-range goals, the methods for teaching reading skills, and the materials for teaching reading skills. Then this teacher proceeds to teach the special child on a predominantly individualized basis.

THE IMPORTANCE OF TEACHING READING IN A DIAGNOSTIC-PRESCRIPTIVE MANNER

Although it is very important to present reading instruction in a diagnostic-prescriptive manner as much as is possible to all students, it may be particularly important in the case of disabled readers, reluctant readers, slow learners, learning disabled children, and children with perceptual handicaps.

There are a number of reasons why it is important to present reading skills in as diagnostic-prescriptive a manner as is possible. For one thing, all children are unique individuals with their own reading competencies, reading deficiencies, and learning styles. In addition, the children in any reading achievement group possess different reading skill strengths and weaknesses. Thus, one type of prescribed reading instruction and/or reinforcement is not really necessary for all the students in any reading achievement group.

Each child also probably has his or her own learnable moment in which he or she can most efficiently learn a reading skill. In addition, it is obvious that normally no two children can learn the same reading skills in the same amount of time with the same amount of practice. Some children must have additional instruction and/or reinforcement to attain mastery of a reading skill. Finally, each reading skill that a child learns usually must be reviewed on a periodic basis, or it may be forgotten.

However, as was stated earlier, diagnostic-prescriptive reading instruction usually is of even more importance to children with reading difficulties or learning disabilities. For example, most children with reading problems experience little reading success at school. Such children often must read material that is too difficult for them and causes them to dislike reading. In addition, important reading skills such as sight word recognition and phonic elements are often presented at too fast a pace with insufficient motivated practice. Because some of these important reading skills were not thoroughly learned before additional reading skills were presented, the student became confused and began to have reading problems. After a time a number of such students may develop mild or major emotional problems as a result of the reading problems. These emotional difficulties can, in turn, compound the reading problems.

Thus, it is very important to teach reading in a diagnostic-prescriptive manner to children who have even minor reading problems. Such instruction can prevent their minor reading difficulties from becoming major reading difficulties.

Therefore, you should teach reading in a diagnostic-prescriptive manner to all students to ensure that they experience the optimum amount of reading success possible. However, it is even more important to teach reading diagnostically and prescriptively to students with unique problems. All students should be allowed to read materials with which they are comfortable, and they should learn and practice only those reading skills in which they do not have competence.

USING CRITERION-REFERENCED TESTS IN DIAGNOSTIC-PRESCRIPTIVE READING INSTRUCTION AND IN READING MANAGEMENT SYSTEMS

Criterion-referenced tests are an integral part of commercial reading management systems. However, as will be explained briefly later, they also can be used in diagnostic-prescriptive reading instruction outside of reading management systems.

Criterion-referenced tests are considered to be standardized tests because they have been carefully formulated, field-tested, and revised in the light of the testing. They also can be called *mastery tests* because they are used to determine whether a student has mastered specific reading skills. They are not norm-referenced as are most standardized reading tests because they do not compare a student's reading performance with the reading performance of similar students at the same grade level. Instead, they merely seek to determine in which reading skills a student has achieved competence and in which reading skills he or she needs additional instruction and/or reinforcement.

As was stated earlier, the typical reading management system contains a preassessment test that is used as a child's entry level into the program. It also contains numerous criterion-referenced tests. For example, one reading management system that is described later contains seventy-seven criterion-referenced tests and assesses competency in 277 different reading skills. Thus, you can see that the typical reading management system subdivides the various elements of the reading process into small segments and assesses a child's competency in each of these reading skills. This probably is particularly true in the case of the phonic elements.

The major purpose of using criterion-referenced tests in a reading management system is to help a teacher determine the specific reading skills in which a student already is competent and those in which additional instruction and/or reinforcement are needed. The teacher then directs the child to attain mastery of a reading skill in which he or she has been diagnosed to be weak by providing instruction in a short-term group or reinforcement by the use of some type of material. After a period of instruction and reinforcement in a reading skill, the student takes another criterion-referenced test to determine if he or she now has attained mastery of that reading skill. If mastery now has been attained, the student moves on to another reading skill in which he or she has been found to lack competency. However, if the student still has not attained competency in that reading skill, further instruction and/or reinforcement are provided. This cycle continues until the student finally has demonstrated mastery of the selected reading skill on a criterion-referenced test.

More detail is provided on criterion-referenced tests in Chapter 17 of this book. However, here is a very brief listing of some criterion-referenced tests:

Individual Pupil Monitoring System—Reading
Prescriptive Reading Inventory
SRA Diagnosis

As is explained in more detail later, a teacher can use his or her own criterion-referenced test in any traditional reading program, such as the basal reader approach. Sometimes several teachers at the same grade level can work together on this type of project. The teachers can create their own criterion-referenced tests, which are then used to determine if a student has mastery of a reading skill that has been presented and reinforced. As an example, criterion-referenced tests may be used to evaluate a child's competence in such phonic analysis subskills as short vowel sounds, consonant blends, consonant digraphs, vowel digraphs, diphthongs, *r*-controlled vowels, or phonic generalizations. Although any teacher can set any criterion of competency on any mastery test, most often the *80* percent level is used for this purpose. A teacher also may be able to adapt the tests that accompany a basal reader series into criterion-referenced tests.

EXAMPLES OF READING MANAGEMENT SYSTEMS

The characteristics of commercial reading management systems have been explained in detail earlier in this chapter. As was described, a typical reading management system contains a preassessment test, many criterion-referenced tests, and a prescription guide in which the teacher is referred to many different types of commercial materials for suggestions on presentation and reinforcement of any specific reading skill.

Reading management systems have been in existence for about twenty years. In the recent past a great number of reading management systems have appeared on the market. Therefore, one must conclude that publishers apparently believe that they are an educational innovation that will sell very well.

One of the first of the reading management systems was *The Wisconsin Design for Reading Skill Development*. The Wisconsin Design was developed by Wayne Otto and some of his associates at the University of Wisconsin through a funded grant from the government. It was first used in the Madison, Wisconsin, public schools in 1964.

The Wisconsin Design evolved over the next ten years to include criterion-referenced tests, sophisticated record keeping, carefully developed skill assessment procedures, and lists of commercially published lessons from many sources. Today the Wisconsin Design is published by the National Computer Systems of Minneapolis, Minnesota. Although it is considerably more sophisticated than when it was first published, it still is quite representative of all reading management systems. It is also probably the most commonly used reading management system in the country.

Here are some of the other reading management systems that currently are available:

Criterion Reading. Random House, Inc., 201 East 50 Street, New York, New York 10022.
This reading program determines competency in 450 different reading skills. It also provides references to published materials.

E. P. I. Retrieval System. Educational Patterns, Rego Park, New York 11374.

This reading program allows the teacher to identify aspects of each student's reading such as specific skills, grade level, and interest level. The system is custom-designed for each school district and can be used with any diagnostic reading test.

Fountain Valley Teacher Support System in Reading. Richard L. Zweig Associates, Huntington Beach, California 92647.

This reading program contains seventy-seven tests on cassette tapes and assesses competency in 277 reading skills.

Harper & Row Classroom Management System. Harper & Row, Publishers, 10 East 53 Street, New York, New York 10022.

This reading program contains assessment tests for word identification and comprehension skills, a prescriptive reference chart, pupil performance record cards, and a control file.

Individualized Reading Skills Program. Houghton Mifflin Company, 2 Park Street, Boston, Massachusetts 02107.

This reading program consists of preassessment and postassessment tests, self-teaching and self-scoring reading skill booklets providing instruction and practice in thirty reading skills, and class and individual record cards.

Individual Pupil Monitoring System—Reading. Houghton Mifflin Company, 2 Park Street, Boston, Massachusetts 02107.

This reading program is designed for grades one through six. It contains criterion-referenced tests based on behavioral objectives in the areas of discrimination, decoding, comprehension, and study skills. It also contains references to published materials.

Right-to-Read Management System. Winston Press, 430 Oak Grove, Suite 203, Minneapolis, Minnesota 55403.

This reading program can be used in the primary grades, the intermediate grades, or the secondary school. It contains assessment devices and provisions for record keeping.

SMS: Skills Monitoring System—Reading. The Psychological Corporation, 757 Third Avenue, New York, New York 10017.

This reading skills management system is designed for grades three through five and can be used with any reading program. It contains criterion-referenced tests in the various word identification and comprehension skills.

SRA Diagnosis. Science Research Associates, North Wacker Drive, Chicago, Illinois 60606.

This reading program contains criterion-referenced tests and a prescription guide.

Wisconsin Design for Reading Skill Improvement. National Computer Systems, 4401 West 76 Street, Minneapolis, Minnesota 55435. This reading program contains a rationale, a set of guidelines, teachers' planning guides, resource files, and tests for reading skills assessment. (See Figure 9-1.)

ADVANTAGES OF READING MANAGEMENT SYSTEMS

The use of a commercial reading management system does have several unique advantages. As it is a certainty that achieving the maximum individual reading success is extremely important, the major advantage of using a reading management system is that a student receives instruction and reinforcement in only those reading skills in which he or she has been diagnosed to be weak. A student then does not have to waste time learning or practicing reading skills in which he or she already has competence. Instead, the teacher can teach a child to correct carefully diagnosed weaknesses, and that theoretically should be a more efficient use of time and effort.

The reading management system also provides the teacher with a convenient means of assessing a student's competencies in the various word identification and comprehension techniques. The preassessment device helps the teacher place the student in the system. The criterion-referenced tests help the teacher determine whether or not a student has achieved mastery of any specific reading skill. Because all the criterion-referenced tests are commercially prepared, the teacher does not have to use his or her valuable time in formulating them.

Another advantage to the use of a reading management system is that a student receives enough instruction and reinforcement to attain competency in each reading skill. In the past in a traditional reading program, such as the basal reader approach or a formal phonic approach, a student was sometimes expected to attempt to learn a reading skill before he or she had mastered a previously presented reading skill. Therefore, a student could become confused and sometimes experience subsequent reading problems. This may not be so likely to occur when a reading management system is used because each skill must be mastered before a subsequent skill is presented. This mastery, of course, is demonstrated by the student's performance on the criterion-referenced test.

It also is a certainty that the typical reading management system provides sufficient structure so that it can be implemented fairly successfully even by an inexperienced teacher of reading. The preassessment test provides the teacher with information about where to begin the system. The criterion-referenced test enables the teacher to determine whether or not a student has mastered a specific reading skill.

Test 2—Consonants and Their Variant Sounds

| Examples | x. ca<u>k</u>e—<u>ci</u>der | ○ same ○ different | y. ca<u>k</u>e—<u>c</u>ar | ○ same ○ different |

1. a<u>s</u>k—<u>s</u>ing   ○ same ○ different
2. <u>c</u>ir<u>c</u>le—pen<u>c</u>il   ○ same ○ different
3. wi<u>s</u>e—<u>s</u>it   ○ same ○ different
4. <u>c</u>ir<u>c</u>le—<u>c</u>art   ○ same ○ different
5. a<u>s</u>k—i<u>s</u>   ○ same ○ different
6. on<u>c</u>e—<u>c</u>andy   ○ same ○ different
7. musi<u>c</u>—<u>c</u>old   ○ same ○ different
8. ha<u>s</u>—<u>s</u>ee   ○ same ○ different
9. a<u>s</u>k—mus<u>t</u>   ○ same ○ different
10. di<u>g</u>—<u>g</u>ave   ○ same ○ different
11. wi<u>s</u>e—no<u>s</u>e   ○ same ○ different
12. <u>g</u>eneral—en<u>g</u>ine   ○ same ○ different

13. <u>c</u>ould—<u>c</u>ar   ○ same ○ different
14. <u>g</u>eneral—plu<u>g</u>   ○ same ○ different
15. <u>c</u>ould—mi<u>c</u>e   ○ same ○ different
16. <u>g</u>ot—<u>g</u>iant   ○ same ○ different
17. a<u>g</u>e—<u>g</u>o   ○ same ○ different
18. <u>c</u>ent—<u>c</u>ure   ○ same ○ different
19. <u>g</u>ym—<u>g</u>ood   ○ same ○ different
20. pa<u>g</u>e—lar<u>g</u>e   ○ same ○ different
21. brid<u>g</u>e—bi<u>g</u>   ○ same ○ different
22. a<u>g</u>ain—ru<u>g</u>   ○ same ○ different
23. sa<u>ck</u>—look<u>s</u>   ○ same ○ different
24. pay<u>s</u>—day<u>s</u>   ○ same ○ different

STOP

Raw Score	1	2	3	4	5	6	7	8	9	10	11	12	13	14	15	16	17	18	19	20	21	22	23	24
% Correct	4	8	13	17	21	25	29	33	38	42	46	50	54	58	63	67	71	75	79	83	88	92	96	100

FIGURE 9-1

The prescription guide directs the teacher to numerous commercial materials that are designed to provide strategies for teaching and reinforcing the various reading skills. The typical reading management system probably contains almost as much structure and direction as does the typical basal reader series.

Perhaps the use of a reading management system can help some teachers to individualize reading instruction more effectively than might be possible with the use of a true or pure individualized reading program that is less skill-oriented.

LIMITATIONS OF READING MANAGEMENT SYSTEMS

Many teachers to whom I have talked believe that the major limitation of a reading management system is the extreme amount of teacher time required for effective record keeping, especially in a class of twenty or more students. The record keeping that is required in a typical reading management system can be extremely unpleasant for a number of teachers.

A reading management system can be less burdensome if the record keeping can be made less time-consuming. Computers can be used to keep classroom records for a reading management system. As was stated earlier, I believe that this practice may become much more common than is the case at present. Computers are considerably less expensive than they were even in the recent past. Therefore, they probably will be much more commonly purchased by school districts in the future. Then the preassessment test can be scored by the computer, which can print out the appropriate reading program for each student. As the student completes different parts of his or her own prescribed reading program, the computer can be used to keep performance records. If a student attains a competency with the initial instruction and reinforcement, the computer can direct him or her to another reading skill. On the other hand, if the student does not attain a competency at the first attempt, the computer then can direct him or her to additional practice in that reading skill. In addition, the computer probably can be used to evaluate much of a student's work.

Many reading specialists believe that a reading management system neglects the affective aspects of reading or those aspects of reading that deal with the emotional reaction to reading. The affective aspects of reading appeal to a student's emotions and interests, such as wanting to read for pleasure, being influenced by one's reading, and using the knowledge and attitudes gained from reading for problem solving. It is a certainty that a reading management system overemphasizes some of the lower-level reading skills at the expense of the more important aspects of reading. Such skills lend themselves much more easily to the format of the reading management system than do higher-level reading skills such as critical reading and creative reading. This is why the phonic elements are stressed so heavily in the typical reading management system.

Another limitation of the reading management system is that it divides the reading skills into minute segments and then tries to present them in sequence. For example, one reading management system presents 450 different reading skills, although research has not determined a specific sequence that is the most effective for presenting the reading skills. In addition, some reading specialists (for example, some of the psycholinguists—see Chapter 8) view reading in a more global sense and do not think that it is comprised of a great number of separate reading skills.

After careful consideration, this author believes that a more traditional reading program, such as the basal reader approach, the language experience approach, or individualized reading, probably fits the needs of most students better than a commercial reading management system if the program is presented in a diagnostic-prescriptive manner. Guidelines for doing this are provided later in this chapter. The typical commercial reading management system seems to be too likely to overemphasize the lower-level reading skills at the expense of the more important higher-level reading skills. Then, too, the record keeping involved in such a system can at its worst turn the teacher into a secretary rather than a true teacher.

TEACHING READING DIAGNOSTICALLY AND PRESCRIPTIVELY IN THE BASAL READER APPROACH

Although the basal reader approach is a traditional, structured reading approach, as was explained in Chapter 5, it can be adapted somewhat and presented in a diagnostic-prescriptive manner in some ways similar to a typical reading management system.

Very briefly, to do so the teacher should consult the manuals of basal readers, and select the reading skills for an individual child or a group of children to learn during a specified period of time such as a quarter, a semester, or an entire school year. Then write objectives that will put these selected reading skills in a form that can be evaluated in behavioral terms. (See the next section of this chapter.) Formulate simple criterion-referenced tests for each behavioral objective, recognizing that it is more difficult to evaluate competency in the higher-level reading skills than in the lower-level reading skills.

When a student attains mastery of the reading skill assessed by one criterion-referenced test, he or she can continue on to a subsequent reading skill. If the student does not master the reading skill included in a criterion-referenced test, additional instruction, reinforcement, and assessment can be provided.

When reading is taught diagnostically and prescriptively in the basal reader approach, needs or skills groups similar to those found in the individualized reading plan can be used. (See Chapter 6.) These short-term needs or skills groups can sometimes take the place of the traditional reading achievement groups that are found in the basal reader approach. In such a group the teacher can present the reading skill in which a small group of children have been diagnosed to lack competence. After the instruction and reinforcement, each child in the group can take the appropriate criterion-referenced test to see if he or she has attained mastery of that reading skill.

Chapter 6 also explained the use of diagnostic individual reading conferences to determine a student's present instructional reading level and specific reading skill strengths and weaknesses. Such diagnostic individual reading conferences probably can be used to supplement or supplant criterion-referenced tests when the basal reader approach is presented in a diagnostic-prescriptive manner.

USING BEHAVIORAL OBJECTIVES

Behavioral objectives are an innovation of the past thirty years and have received great attention among American educators. *Behavioral objectives* are also called *instructional objectives* or *performance objectives*. Behavioral objectives differ considerably from *teaching objectives*. Reading management systems make use of behavioral objectives.

The concept of using behavioral objectives in education is the work of Benjamin S. Bloom and his associates, among others. Bloom and his associates classified the knowledges, skills, and attitudes that can be developed into three different areas or domains: the *cognitive domain,* the *psychomotor domain,* and the *affective domain.* The cognitive domain is concerned with intellectual processes; the psychomotor domain, with physical processes; and the affective domain, with the processes that appeal to the emotions and attitudes.[1,2]

Within each of these domains, the knowledges, skills, and attitudes that can be included in that domain have been classified from the

---

[1]Benjamin S. Bloom, M. D. Engelhart, E. J. Furst, W. H. Hill, and D. R. Krathwohl, *Taxonomy of Educational Objectives,* Handbook I: *Cognitive Domain* (New York: David McKay Co., Inc., 1956).

[2]David R. Krathwohl, B. S. Bloom, and B. B. Masia, *Taxonomy of Educational Objectives,* Handbook II: *Affective Domain* (New York: David McKay Co., Inc., 1964).

concrete level to the more abstract level. The various elements of reading comprehension can be related to elements in the cognitive domain. (See Chapters 1 and 14.)

Bloom and his associates have recommended that the knowledges, skills, and attitudes contained in the different levels of the domain be presented in terms of behavioral objectives. Learning should be specified in precise terms so that each teacher will know if and when a student attains competency in a specific objective.

Perhaps this concept can be clarified if you examine the following behavioral objective in the area of phonic analysis:

> Given the opportunity, the student will be able to identify all the words on a criterion-referenced test that contain the CVC (consonant, vowel, consonant) spelling pattern at an *80* percent level of competency.

Contrast the preceding behavioral objective with the following teaching objective for the same concept:

> My objective for this lesson is to present the CVC spelling pattern to the students in the above-average reading achievement group.

Although the teaching objective indicates the concept that the teacher is going to present, it does not ensure that each student in the group will attain mastery of the concept at the time it is presented or later. However, the use of a behavioral objective is designed to ensure that this concept will be presented and then sufficiently reinforced for mastery by each student. Thus, the use of behavioral objectives enables the teacher to be very specific about the knowledges, skills, and attitudes to be presented. In addition, the teacher supposedly can objectively determine whether or not a student has mastery of the knowledges, skills, and attitudes presented or reinforced in that particular behavioral objective.

A behavioral objective contains three elements. First, it indicates specifically what knowledges, skills, attitudes, or performances the student should be able to do or have as a result of completing the objective. Second, it indicates the condition under which the student must demonstrate the competency, such as an oral evaluation, a written test, the completion of an activity sheet, a demonstration, a written paper, or a construction. Lastly, the behavioral objective specifies the level at which the student must demonstrate the competency. In a written evaluation, the criterion level often is about the 80 percent level of competency. In some other forms of evaluation, it is much more difficult to specify the level of competency required with that much precision.

If a teacher does not feel that he or she has the time or expertise to write his or her own behavioral objectives, there are several sources for behavioral objectives. One such source is the Instructional Objectives Exchange, Box 24095, Los Angeles, California 90024. This source has collections of behavioral objectives entitled *Decoding Skills K-12, Structural Analysis K-12,* and *Comprehension Skills K-12.*

USING BEHAVIORAL OBJECTIVES IN A READING PROGRAM

As was briefly stated earlier, behavioral objectives can be used in any reading program such as the basal reader approach, a combination reading approach, the language experience approach, or individualized reading.

The use of behavioral objectives in any reading program can provide the teacher with specific knowledge of what each student is supposed to accomplish in a specified period of time. The teacher then can determine objectively when the reading skills have been mastered or when a student needs additional instruction and/or reinforcement in a reading skill. Thus, the use of behavioral objectives can make the teaching of reading more precise and measurable.

However, you must remember that behavioral objectives are easier to apply to the lower levels of reading such as phonic analysis and structural analysis than they are to the higher levels such as critical reading and creative reading. Therefore, they must be used judiciously.

SELECTED REFERENCES

Farr, Roger, and Nancy Roser. *Teaching a Child to Read.* New York: Harcourt Brace Jovanovich, Inc., 1979, pp. 481–487.

Fry, Edward. *Elementary Reading Instruction.* New York: McGraw-Hill Inc., 1977, pp. 254–264.

Good, Cecil G. "Organizing Reading Management Systems in Urban Districts." *The Reading Teacher, 33* (April 1980): 816–818.

Lapp, Diane, and James Flood. *Teaching Reading to Every Child.* New York: Macmillan Publishing Company, Inc., 1983.

Mason, George E., and Jay S. Blanchard. *Computer Applications to Reading.* Newark, Delaware: International Reading Association, 1979.

Moore, Julia Thompson. "A Systems Approach to Individualized Reading." *The Reading Teacher, 32* (May 1979): 951–955.

O'Donnell, Holly. "ERIC/RCS: Computer Literacy, Part I: An Overview." *The Reading Teacher, 35* (January 1982): 490–493.

———. "ERIC/RCS: Computer Literacy, Part II, Classroom Applications." *The Reading Teacher, 35* (February 1982): 614–617.

Otto, Wayne, Robert Rude, and Dixie Lee Spiegel. *How to Teach Reading.* Reading, Massachusetts: Addison-Wesley Publishing Company, Inc., 1979, Chapter 4.

Peterson, Gordon, and Patrick Groff. "Behavioral Objectives for Children's Literature? YES! NO!" *The Reading Teacher, 30* (March 1977): 652–663.

Shenkman, Harriet. "Beyond Behavioral Objectives: Behavioral Processes." *Journal of Reading, 32* (November 1978): 113–116.

Strange, Michael, and Richard L. Allington. "Use the Diagnostic Prescriptive Model Knowledgeably." *The Reading Teacher, 31* (December 1977): 290–293.

SUGGESTED ACTIVITIES

1. Examine one of the reading management systems described in the chapter. Does it illustrate the guidelines stated in the chapter?
2. If possible, visit a classroom that uses a reading management system. Does it seem like an effective method of teaching reading to you? Why or why not?
3. Select five phonic elements or phonic generalizations from Chapter 7. Formulate one behavioral objective and one teaching objective for each of these phonic elements or phonic generalizations. Notice how they are different.
4. Select one reading skill, and try to formulate a criterion-referenced test to assess mastery in that reading skill.
5. Select a specific grade level, and then try to outline the reading skills that you would cover at that grade level for a specified period of time such as one week. Then try to write behavioral objectives for those reading skills. You may want to work with a partner on this activity.

A recommended primary-grade reading program

Why Was This Better?

Mrs. Hayes had been teaching third grade at Jefferson Davis School in the South for a number of years. She always had used the basal reader approach to teach reading to the children in her class, and she had always been fairly well satisfied with it. Her class was divided into three reading achievement groups, which always seemed to remain fairly rigid even though she knew that this was not very desirable, especially for the children in the below-average group.

However, Mrs. Hayes was not really satisfied with the sole use of the basal reader approach. Her children seemed to get rather bored with meeting in the reading group every day and following the steps of the traditional basal reader lesson—development of an experiential background, presentation of new vocabulary terms, guided silent reading, purposeful oral reading, extending skill development, and enriching experiences. Therefore, Mrs. Hayes decided to ask the reading specialist at Jefferson Davis School how to improve her reading program so that it would be more motivating and challenging for her students.

Mr. Baker, the reading specialist, suggested that Mrs. Hayes try to incorporate individualized reading into her reading program. Such a program of individualized reading involves self-selection of reading materials and periodic individual reading conferences. Mr. Baker told Mrs. Hayes that it was possible to combine effectively both the basal reader approach and individualized reading at the third-grade level to utilize best the features of both programs.

However, Mrs. Hayes was rather reluctant to begin using any program of individualized reading with her entire class of twenty-eight third-graders all at once. Mr. Baker understood her misgivings and explained how it was possible, and even desirable, to begin combining the basal reader approach and individualized reading only in her above-average group at first. He told her that later, when she felt more at ease with the concept, she could begin following similar procedures in her two other reading achievement groups. Mr. Baker then outlined a sample weekly schedule for Mrs. Hayes, showing her how to organize this recommended reading program.

After about four months, Mrs. Hayes was very effectively combining the basal reader approach and individualized reading in all three reading achievement groups. She was amazed at how much more motivated her students were about their reading period each day and how they still were able to master all the word identification and comprehension skills as well as they did when the basal reader approach had been used alone. Therefore, Mrs. Hayes determined that she would use this combination reading approach in the future.

After you have read this chapter, you, too, will know how to combine the language experience approach, the basal reader approach, and individualized reading to use all of the programs with the greatest effectiveness. This chapter also contains several sample weekly schedules for implementing variations of a combination reading approach that are similar to the schedule that Mr. Baker gave Mrs. Hayes to use as a model.

A RECOMMENDED READING PROGRAM FOR FIRST GRADE

The language experience approach can be used at the initial stages of reading instruction either in kindergarten or first grade depending upon the mental maturity and the linguistic aptitude of each child. It contains certain features that in this author's opinion seem to make it an ideal way of improving reading readiness as well as introducing reading instruction.

As was discussed in detail in Chapter 4, the language experience approach shows children that reading is a meaningful process. It also makes use of each child's schemata or experiential background very effectively. It can be very useful in teaching sight words and rudimentary letter-sound relationships and structural analysis. Because the language experience approach also uses each child's language, it is easy for the child to comprehend. Language experience charts and stories can be structured to teach many of the words that are found in the preprimers of the basal reader series that the children are going to use later. Thus, when the child attempts to read a preprimer, he or she can experience instant success because the majority of the words contained in that preprimer already are known by sight.

As was explained in detail in Chapter 4, when the language experience approach is used, individual children dictate language experience stories, which are transcribed and typed to be read back later. Each language experience story also can be illustrated by the child. After a time, the typed language experience stories can be bound into a booklet with a colorful cover. Group-dictated experience charts also are transcribed and rewritten to be read back later. Sight word recognition, beginning phonic analysis, and rudimentary structural analysis are very well presented by the use of experience stories and experience charts.

However, the language experience approach should not constitute the entire reading readiness and beginning reading program. As was explained in Chapter 3, kindergarten and first-grade teachers should supplement it with activities in visual discrimination, auditory discrimination, left-to-right progression, picture interpretation, letter-name knowledge, letter-sound knowledge, and additional sight words.

This author believes that the basic word identification and comprehension skills can best be presented to most children in kindergarten or first grade by the use of the basal reader approach. As was explained in Chapter 5, this approach presents and reinforces all the word identification techniques and stresses reading comprehension from the beginning. Thus, it seems to be the most beneficial approach for most students if it is used in a flexible, judicious manner as is outlined in detail later in this chapter. This author does not recommend the use of a formal phonic approach for most children in kindergarten or first grade. As was discussed in Chapter 7, a formal phonic program appears to emphasize decoding too much at the expense of comprehension, in the opinion of this author. In addition, it appears to present too many phonic elements and generalizations to be very practical for most children.

It is obvious that the basal reader approach with its structured skill development should be presented to a group of children only when they are ready for it. In a first-grade class that is divided into three reading achievement groups, it is obvious that the basal reader approach first is presented to the above-average group; next it is begun with the average group; and only later is it started with the below-average group. This initiation into a structured reading program may take place in late kindergarten, in beginning first grade, or in later first grade depending upon the readiness attainment of the children in any reading achievement group and/or the philosophy of the school district.

When the basal reader approach is used in the *above-average group* in first grade, normally one story and its accompanying materials are covered a day. Basal reader stories, skill development, and workbook pages should be skipped when they are inappropriate. It is absolutely not necessary to cover an entire basal reader or basal reader workbook with the children in the above-average group. This author recommends that the basal reader approach be used about two or three days per week with this group in first grade.

Individualized reading can be introduced almost immediately in first grade to the children in the above-average group. Individual reading conferences can be held two or three days a week with the children in this group, who always should be encouraged to read on their own level. Diagnostic individual reading conferences can be used very effectively with the children in this group for basal reader placement. (See Chapter 6.)

Moreover, the children in this group usually can write their own language experience stories and read the experience stories of other children quite effectively. Oral reading should receive some degree of emphasis in first grade in this group; however, it is very important that round-robin reading not receive much stress.

Most children in the above-average group very much enjoy working independently or with a partner at reading stations to receive reinforcement of the various reading skills. Such children usually are very well able to complete challenging tasks of various types that interest them on an independent basis. They also function extremely well as leaders or group members in research or interest groups in which they explore topics on their own reading level from various sources. (See Chapter 15.) Children in the above-average group also do very well in peer tutoring situations in which they help children who are less able in reading than themselves.

First-grade children who are members of the above-average reading group often should receive rudimentary instruction in how to read in the various content areas such as social studies, science, and arithmetic. Chapter 16 provides detailed directions about this.

The basal reader approach can be used an average of three times per week in the *average reading achievement group*. Normally, the children in this group should be using a different basal reader series from the children in the two other groups. Most, but not all, of the basal reader stories and workbook pages can usually be used in this group. The children may or may not be able to cover one basal reader lesson a day.

Individualized reading can be used about two days a week with periodic individual reading conferences. The children should read easy, predictable, self-selected material. Diagnostic individual reading conferences can be used to some extent in this group for basal reader placement.

The children in the average group often still may want to dictate language experience stories and read the experience stories of other children. They usually also enjoy reinforcing reading skills at reading stations. In addition, they can serve as members of research or interest groups in which they are given the opportunity to read about the chosen topic on their own level.

Often the children in the *below-average reading achievement group* should continue reading readiness development for quite some time in first grade with the use of the language experience approach and other reading readiness strategies and materials. This period of time can be anywhere from several months to an entire semester depending upon the reading readiness attainment of the children.

When they have attained sufficient reading readiness, the basal reader approach can be introduced. It probably should be used about four days a week in this group. Normally, it takes about two days to cover one basal reader lesson thoroughly. Each important word identification and comprehension skill should be learned by the children in this group to the point of mastery. It may be necessary to provide considerable meaningful, drill-like reinforcement of some of the reading skills, especially the important phonic analysis skills.

One day a week individualized reading and individual conferences should be used with the children in this group because they enjoy the undivided, one-to-one teacher attention. In addition, they usually find individualized reading very motivating.

It is very important for children in the below-average reading group in first grade to participate as members of research and interest groups. They should read material on the selected topic on their own level, if possible, or in some other way participate in the group. This group membership enables them to work with above-average and average readers and thus to avoid the stigma of always belonging only to the below-average group. Such children also can receive help from above-average and average readers in a peer tutoring setting. They also can work at reading stations to reinforce previously presented important reading skills. However, children in the below-average reading achievement group often need considerable direction and guidance before being able to work independently in a reading station setting. Without such careful guidance this type of activity may become time-wasting and meaningless.

A SAMPLE WEEKLY SCHEDULE FOR A FIRST-GRADE READING PROGRAM

Figure 10-1 shows a sample schedule for a recommended first-grade, second semester reading program. Based on the use of three flexible reading achievement groups, it is merely designed to be illustrative of how one week in such a reading program might be organized. It should be modified in terms of the needs of a first-grade classroom.

A RECOMMENDED READING PROGRAM FOR SECOND GRADE

The *above-average reading achievement group* can use a predominantly individualized reading program in second grade. The children in this group can meet in the basal reader achievement group an average of one day a week. Certainly, many stories and many workbook pages can be skipped by the children in this group. The group should always read a basal reader that is on their instructional reading level, very often a third reader. The children in this group should receive much practice in responding to interpretive comprehension questions and critical questions. They also should have many opportunities to engage in such elements of creative reading as creative writing, creative dramatics, role playing, art activities, rhythm activities, and construction activities.

The children in the above-average group should read self-selected reading materials on their own level an average of four days a week. Phonic analysis skills and structural analysis skills should be presented and reinforced to the children in this group in a mainly diagnostic-prescriptive manner. They will not need the structured, sequential presentation of these skills in the way in which children in the average and below-average groups do. Many diagnostic individual reading conferences can be held with the children in this group to help to determine their basal reader placement. The children in the above-average

Sample Weekly Schedule—First Grade
Reading Period 9:00–10:30 A.M.

	Monday	Tuesday	Wednesday	Thursday	Friday
Above-average Group	Individualized Reading Four Individual Reading Conferences Informal Sharing of Reading Material with One or Two Classmates	Basal Reader Lesson with Most of Its Traditional Steps	Basal Reader Lesson with Most of Its Traditional Steps	Individualized Reading Four Individual Reading Conferences Research Group from Science on Topic "Baby Animals"	Individualized Reading Three Individual Reading Conferences Research Group from Science on Topic "Baby Animals"
Average Group	Basal Reader Lesson with Most of Its Traditional Steps	Individualized Reading Five Individual Reading Conferences Informal Sharing of Reading Material with One or Two Classmates	Basal Reader Lesson Presentation of New Vocabulary Guided Silent Reading	Basal Reader Lesson Purposeful Oral Reading Skill Development Enriching Experiences Workbook	Individualized Reading Five Individual Reading Conferences Research Group from Science on Topic "Baby Animals"
Below-average Group	Basal Reader Lesson Development of Experiential Background Presentation of New Vocabulary Guided Silent Reading	Basal Reader Lesson Oral Reading Skill Development Workbook	Basal Reader Lesson Development of Experiential Background Presentation of New Vocabulary Oral Reading	Basal Reader Lesson Skill Development Enriching Experiences Workbook	Individualized Reading Four Individual Reading Conferences Research Group from Science on Topic "Baby Animals"

FIGURE 10-1

group very much enjoy and benefit from challenging activities at reading stations in which they can participate on an independent basis or with one or several partners.

Children in this group also can receive some instruction in how to read in the content areas of social studies, science, and arithmetic. (See Chapter 16.) This instruction will serve them well as they participate in research or interest groups as group leaders or group members. In these groups the children read on their own level about the selected topic from a variety of sources such as content textbooks, trade books, reference books, or children's magazines or newspapers.

Normally, the children in the *average reading achievement group* use a different basal reader in second grade from the ones the children in the above-average group and in the below-average group use. They normally use the basal approach an average of two or three days a week and should receive an introduction to interpretive comprehension and critical reading at their own level. They can skip some inappropriate basal reader stories and workbook pages. However, normally the teacher should present the phonic analysis elements and generalizations and the structural analysis skills contained in the basal reader to the children in this group in a fairly structured way. Some oral reading can be used with the children in this group, but not to the extent that it is used with the children in the below-average group.

Children in the average group in second grade can do individualized reading an average of two or three days a week. This reading should use self-selected reading materials on the child's own level and employ periodic individual reading conferences. Some diagnostic individual reading conferences also can be used in this group for basal reader placement. Children in the average group also very much enjoy motivating reinforcement of reading skills at reading stations on an independent basis or with a partner.

Usually, children in the average group in second grade can have some limited introduction to the special skills needed for reading in the content areas. (See Chapter 16.) This introduction also can help them to be effective members or leaders of research or interest groups in which they explore a topic on their own instructional or independent reading level.

The children in the *below-average reading achievement group* normally can use the basal reader approach on an average of four days a week in second grade. The basal reader that the children in this group use should not be the same as that which was used by the children in the two other groups so that the stories are new to them. Normally, it takes approximately two days to cover most of the steps of one basal reader lesson in this group. Normally, too, the children in this group should use most, but not all, of the basal reader stories and workbook pages.

The phonic analysis skills, structural analysis skills, and contextual analysis skills that are included in each basal reader lesson usually should be presented to and carefully mastered by the children in this group. They need deliberate, careful teaching of the important word identification and comprehension skills. Literal comprehension should be the main stress in this group, but some emphasis also should be placed upon interpretive comprehension, critical reading, and creative reading. Oral reading should receive considerable stress in this group as well because below-average readers seem to enjoy it, and oral reading apparently adds a kinesthetic reinforcement to word identification. I believe that oral reading does not always have to be preceded by silent reading for the children in this group.

Children in the below-average group usually enjoy individualized reading and individual reading conferences about one day each week. This individual reading should be from self-selected easy reading material that normally is on the first-grade level. These children should have one conference a week if possible, but at the minimum one conference every two weeks. They also enjoy working at reading stations if they have had sufficient guidance in using reading stations and in working independently there.

Children in the below-average group in second grade also should participate in interest groups and research groups so that they will have a chance to work with above-average and average readers sometimes. They also often benefit from peer tutoring very much.

A RECOMMENDED READING PROGRAM FOR THIRD GRADE

I recommend that *above-average readers* in third grade have a mainly individualized reading program that takes place on an average of four days per week. In this individualized program, each child should be on his or her own level, which often may be the intermediate-grade level. These challenging materials sometimes should be self-selected or can relate to social studies topics, science topics, research groups, or interest groups. Children in this group usually very much enjoy the creative writing of prose and poetry and many other types of creative activities. (See Chapter 14.) They also enjoy work at reading stations if it is challenging to them.

Children in the above-average group in third grade usually can meet in the basal reader achievement group an average of one day a week. The basal reader stories and workbook pages should be used in a very selective way instead of in a routine way in which all the stories and workbook pages are covered. These children need little instruction in phonic analysis and structural analysis at the third-grade level. Many of the elements of these word identification techniques can be presented in a diagnostic-prescriptive manner in short-term needs or skills groups instead of in the basal reader achievement group. (See Chapter 15.) Children in the above-average group need considerable exposure to responding at the interpretive and critical levels and many opportunities to do all types of creative activities. They should do little oral reading unless it is in an audience situation as is explained later in this chapter. They also can participate in peer tutoring in which they help the average and below-average readers in their class.

The children in the *average reading achievement group* in third grade can do individualized reading an average of three days a week from predominantly self-selected reading materials on their level. Diagnostic individual reading conferences can be used with these children for basal reader placement.

The children in the average group in third grade can participate in a basal reader achievement group an average of two days a week. The basal reader stories and workbook pages should be chosen in a selective way. The children in the average group need a somewhat structured, but not rigid, program of development of the phonic analysis and structural analysis skills. Interpretive comprehension, critical reading, and creative reading should receive some emphasis in this group, but oral reading should receive limited stress. The children in this group very much enjoy independent work that is appropriate at reading stations.

Children in the average group in third grade need direct instruction in how to read successfully in the various content areas. (See Chapter 16.) This instruction should help them participate effectively as leaders or members of research and interest groups in which they read on their own level from a wide variety of content textbooks, trade books, and reference books.

The students in the *below-average reading achievement group* in third grade can use the basal reader approach an average of three days a week. This should be a basal reader that is on their instructional reading level (often the second reader level) and a basal reader that was not used by any other group in this class so that the material remains fresh. Many, but not all, of the stories and workbook pages can be used with the children in this group. They usually need a fairly structured development and reinforcement of the phonic analysis skills, structural analysis skills, and contextual analysis skills. Normally, it takes about two days to cover one basal reader lesson as carefully as should be done in this group. Children in the below-average group are best able to respond at the literal level of comprehension but also should be given as many opportunities as possible to respond at the interpretive, critical, and creative levels within the limits of their ability. Below-average readers enjoy oral reading at this level if it is not overemphasized.

Children in this group can do individualized reading an average of two days a week in mainly self-selected reading materials on their own level. They also enjoy peer tutoring in which they receive help from better readers, if this activity is used carefully.

Children in the below-average group in third grade can begin to receive some practical instruction in how to read successfully in the content areas of social studies, science, and arithmetic. Below-average readers often have great difficulty in reading content materials at both the intermediate-grade and secondary school levels. Therefore, it is important for them to be exposed to many useful strategies for learning how to read in the content areas as early as possible. This instruction also should enable them to be more effective members of research and interest groups in which they read on their own level from a wide variety of materials.

A SAMPLE WEEKLY SCHEDULE FOR A THIRD-GRADE READING PROGRAM

Figure 10-2 provides a sample schedule for a recommended third-grade reading program. It is based upon the use of three flexible reading achievement groups. This schedule is only designed to be illustrative of how one week in such a reading program could be organized. This schedule always should be modified in terms of the needs of a third-grade classroom.

ABOUT ORAL READING

Oral reading was the only type of reading in American elementary reading instruction until about 1920, when silent reading also began to receive emphasis. Today, of course, both oral and silent reading are stressed in American elementary schools. It is obvious that oral reading receives the highest degree of stress in the early primary grades, and silent reading receives by far the greatest amount of stress in the upper primary grades.

There are basic differences in the eye movements between oral and silent reading. As each word must be pronounced separately in oral reading, there are obviously many more fixations or pauses in oral reading than in silent reading. In silent reading a proficient reader may be able to move from print to meaning without pronouncing individual words. The span of recognition also is much shorter in oral reading than in silent reading. (See Chapter 1.)

You should consider the differences in eye movements between oral and silent reading when evaluating a very common procedure in the

Sample Weekly Schedule—Third Grade
Reading Period 9:00—10:30 A.M.

	Monday	Tuesday	Wednesday	Thursday	Friday
Above-average Group	Individualized Reading Three Individual Reading Conferences Interest Group on "Space Flight"	Individualized Reading Three Individual Reading Conferences Interest Group on "Space Flight"	Basal Reader Lesson Emphasis Placed on Critical Analysis of the Story and on Creative Follow-up Activities	Individualized Reading Three Individual Reading Conferences Research Group from Social Studies Unit Entitled "Indian Children"	Individualized Reading Three Optional Individual Reading Conferences Research Group from Social Studies Unit Entitled "Indian Children"
Average Group	Basal Reader Lesson Emphasis Placed on Structural Analysis and Interpretive Comprehension	Individualized Reading Four Individual Reading Conferences Interest Group on "Space Flight"	Individualized Reading Four Individual Reading Conferences Work at Reading Stations and Informal Sharing	Basal Reader Lesson Emphasis Placed on Critical Analysis of Story and Creative Follow-up Activities	Individualized Reading Three Individual Reading Conferences Research Group from Social Studies Unit Entitled "Indian Children"
Below-average Group	Basal Reader Lesson Experiential Background Presentation of New Vocabulary Guided Silent Reading	Basal Reader Lesson Oral Reading Skill Development— Phonic Analysis Workbook Reading Stations	Basal Reader Lesson Experiential Background Presentation of New Vocabulary Oral Reading	Basal Reader Lesson Skill Development— Interpretive Comprehension Workbook Reading Stations	Individualized Reading Six Individual Reading Conferences Research Group from Social Studies Unit Entitled "Indian Children"

FIGURE 10-2

primary grades called *round-robin reading*. This procedure also some-times is called "reading around the circle" or "barbershop reading." In this procedure each child in a reading achievement group reads a por-tion of the basal reader story aloud, for example, a sentence, a para-graph, or a page. While this oral reading takes place, the other children in the group are supposed to follow along in their copy of the reader. In practice this rarely happens because the children usually already have read the material silently. Instead of following along, they often engage in many different types of poor behavior. Indeed if they did follow along conscientiously, it probably would harm the eye move-ments of their silent reading.

Round-robin reading is essentially meaningless also for the oral reader himself or herself because he or she is too concerned with cor-rect word pronunciation to be very concerned with effective compre-hension. For example, there is a well-known incident in which Johnny was asked to read a paragraph of a basal reader story aloud. After he read very well, his teacher asked, "Now, Johnny, tell us what your paragraph was about." Johnny replied: "I don't know. I wasn't listen-ing." Thus you can see why round-robin reading should be used only infrequently in the primary grades. It continues to be overused in many primary-grade classrooms primarily because of tradition and the fact that some children are inclined to think that they are not reading at all unless they are reading aloud.

Oral reading does have some value in the primary grades. It is very useful in first grade, when children are learning to read, to show them that they are reading. It is also useful in the upper primary grades with below-average readers because it seems to provide them with a kinesthetic reinforcement that aids their word identification. There-fore, as mentioned earlier, I do not believe that oral reading always must be preceded by silent reading with below-average readers as is recommended in the basal reader manuals.

Oral reading also is valuable in the diagnosis of oral reading mis-cues and oral reading patterns such as omissions, substitutions, mis-pronunciations, and additions. It also is useful in determining a student's independent, instructional, and frustration reading levels. (See Chap-ter 17.) Lastly, oral reading is useful in an audience situation. This occurs when a student has carefully prepared a portion of reading material to read aloud. The child then reads it orally to a group of peers or to the entire class. The children in the audience should not have a copy of the reading material so that they will not follow along but can focus on the reader.

If you consider how often the typical adult reads aloud, you will know why I recommend predominantly silent reading in the elemen-tary school after the beginning stages of reading instruction. Silent reading is used so much more extensively in adult life than is oral reading that it should receive much more stress in elementary reading programs.

SELECTED REFERENCES

Barnard, Douglas P., and James DeGracie. "Vocabulary Analysis of New Primary Reading Series." *The Reading Teacher, 30* (November 1976): 177–180.

Dallmann, Martha, Roger L. Rouch, Lynette Y. C. Char, and John J. DeBoer. *The Teaching of Reading.* New York: Holt, Rinehart and Winston, 1982.

Heilman, Arthur W. *Principles and Practices of Teaching Reading.* Columbus, Ohio: Charles E. Merrill Publishing Co., 1977, Chapter 12.

Karlin, Robert. *Teaching Elementary Reading.* New York: Harcourt Brace Jovanovich, Inc., 1980, pp. 203–226.

Rosecky, Marion. "Are Teachers Selective when Using Basal Guidebooks?" *The Reading Teacher, 31* (January 1978): 381–384.

Spache, George D., and Evelyn B. Spache. *Reading in the Elementary School.* Boston: Allyn and Bacon, Inc., 1977, Chapter 8.

SUGGESTED ACTIVITIES

1. If possible, visit a primary-grade classroom that uses some version of a combination or eclectic approach.
2. Outline a sample weekly schedule for a second grade that uses the basal reader approach and individualized reading in three reading achievement groups similar to the ones contained in the chapter for first grade and third grade.
3. Observe round-robin reading in a basal reader achievement group. Is it essentially a meaningless procedure, or did you see some value in it?

A recommended middle-school reading program

Why Was This Better?

Ms. Connors was in her first year of teaching fifth grade at Lakeland School in a rural area in the upper Midwest. She was told to use the fifth reader of a certain basal reader series with all the children in her class even though she was going to divide them into three reading groups—the above-average group, the average group, and the below-average group.

However, Ms. Connors had learned in several reading courses at the university from which she had graduated the previous May that it was not possible to use only one basal reader with all the students in any class. It was obvious that this reader would be too easy for the above-average readers and too difficult for the below-average readers. However, she decided to do what she was told to for at least a while because she was a new teacher, and she considered herself lucky to have gotten a teaching job.

Ms. Connors soon discovered that it was not going to be possible to use the fifth reader with all the students in her class. She found it especially difficult with the below-average group because the children simply could not comprehend the material in that reader and were constantly frustrated by attempting to read the material. She then decided to attempt to formulate some tentative plans for working with the children in this reading group that she could present to her principal, Mrs. Barnett.

Ms. Connors decided to place two of the boys in her below-average group,

Tony and Mike, into a separate group and use the language experience approach with them because they were virtual nonreaders in the fifth grade. She wanted to use their own North-woods experiences—such as fishing, hiking in the woods, and canoeing—as the basis for their language experience stories. She decided to use a third reader with the four other students in her below-average group. She found a third reader in one basal reader series to be fairly interesting, and it had not been used by these children before. However, she also wanted to use some high interest, low vocabulary materials with these children to make sure that their reading materials were not too juvenile for them.

Ms. Connors also decided to present some important phonic analysis skills and structural analysis skills to the children in this group. These skills would be presented to Tony and Mike from language experience stories and to the other children in this group from the basal reader teachers' manual. She also formulated some additional plans for working with the children in the below-average reading achievement group that are included later in this chapter.

After a good deal of persuasion on her part, Ms. Connors was able to convince Mrs. Barnett of the importance of helping her slow readers to succeed. She was then able to implement her plans. She was relatively successful with the modifications she made as she went along. After completing her first year of teaching, Ms. Connors felt that she had been fairly successful, but she was sure that she could do an even better job of teaching reading the next year.

After reading this chapter, you will know how to organize a middle-school reading program that seems very practical and usable in this author's opinion. It is my recommended middle-school reading program.

GENERAL CONSIDERATIONS ABOUT A MIDDLE-SCHOOL READING PROGRAM

This part of the chapter will briefly summarize in general some important considerations about a good middle-school reading program. Although some of these considerations are again mentioned later in this chapter, they are considered to be of enough importance to be discussed here also.

One major issue in the middle-school reading program concerns how many reading achievement groups to use. As was stated earlier, the typical primary-grade classroom has three reading achievement groups. Because the reading range in the intermediate grades can be ten years or more, it seems logical that at least four reading achievement groups be used. However, in practice, two reading achievement groups are more typical. This is mainly because the intermediate-grade teacher has so many other subjects to teach in a very limited time that he or she simply cannot find the time to use more than two groups. In any case, it must be realized that two reading groups cannot provide for the wide variety in reading achievement that is found in the typical intermediate-grade classroom. That is why I recommend the use of three reading achievement groups in the intermediate grades if it is at all possible.

I recommend the use of mainly individualized reading in the intermediate grades. In such an individualized reading program, each student is given the opportunity to read extensively on his or her own instructional or independent reading level from a wide variety of predominantly self-selected materials.

Most of the basic word identification and comprehension skills have been mastered by many students by the time they reach the intermediate grades. That is why I recommend the extensive use of diagnostic-prescriptive teaching of these skills with the extensive use of short-term flexible needs or skills groups. The reinforcement of these reading skills can take place independently by using teacher-made or commercially available materials.

I recommend the limited use of the basal reader approach in the intermediate grades. I think it is of most value to the students in the below-average reading group, who still need a somewhat more sequential presentation of the word identification and comprehension skills.

Most students in the intermediate grades need additional practice in responding at the interpretive and critical levels of comprehension. They have to learn how to locate implied main ideas, how to compare materials from different sources, and how to analyze the various propaganda techniques. Some of them need additional instruction in the meanings of prefixes and suffixes, in syllabication, and in studying word origins. All this instruction usually can take place in the small-group setting and the teacher can employ content materials as well as basal readers.

Effective content area instruction should be of major importance for many students in the intermediate grades. These students need to know how to comprehend materials effectively in the areas of social studies, science, and mathematics. They should learn important specialized vocabulary terms in these areas. The use of the unit plan, in which a student reads about a selected topic from a wide variety of content material at his or her own level, is of value also. Intermediate-grade reading instruction can employ research and interest groups extensively.

Study strategies and skills also should receive considerable emphasis for most students in the intermediate grades. Many such students can benefit from such study skills as selection and evaluation, organization, following directions, locating information, and using graphic aids. They can further benefit from learning a study strategy such as Survey Q3R.

Various types of mediated instruction can be used with students in the intermediate grades. Some students benefit from the use of the tachistoscope or a controlled reading device to improve their visual perception skills and rate of reading. Others may benefit from the use of various types of teaching machines. Reading stations also have a place in the intermediate-grade classroom.

Some intermediate-grade students may benefit from contract learning in which they proceed through prescribed reading skills at their own rate of speed. They thus are responsible for their own learning in contract teaching and may also benefit from various types of peer tutoring. For example, a below-average intermediate-grade reader may work with a primary-grade child in reinforcing one or several reading skills. This reinforcement then benefits both the tutor and the tutee. As another example, an above-average reader in the intermediate grades may work with a below-average reader in reinforcing a skill in which the latter lacks competence.

Oral reading generally receives little emphasis in the intermediate-grade reading program. Its major purpose probably is in the diagnosis of oral reading miscues and in the determination of a student's independent, instructional, and frustration reading levels. In addition, audience reading and choral reading have a place in the intermediate-grade reading program for most students.

A RECOMMENDED READING PROGRAM FOR ABOVE-AVERAGE READERS IN THE INTERMEDIATE GRADES

It should be stated at the outset that there are differences between the reading activities of above-average readers in the fourth, fifth, and sixth grades. However, it was decided not to attempt to differentiate the reading activities in each of these grades to avoid undue repetition.

I recommend a mainly individualized reading program an average of four days a week for above-average readers in the intermediate grades. They should read predominantly self-selected materials on their own level. Such students often are interested in pursuing a topic in depth on an individual or group basis from a variety of reading materials, many of which may be at the junior high school or secondary school level for some above-average readers.

A basal reader at the appropriate level may be used an average of one day a week. Reading skills are taught in a mainly diagnostic-prescriptive manner in a basal reader group or a needs or skills group for above-average readers. Virtually no phonic analysis need be presented to intermediate-grade above-average readers. Such students may want to learn the meanings of some useful prefixes and suffixes in the area of structural analysis and may also enjoy exploring word origins. In addition, they need to learn syllabication and accent skills. Students at this level often benefit greatly from the use of contextual analysis in determining the meaning of unknown words, especially in content materials. Above-average readers often enjoy completing variations of the cloze procedure to improve ability in contextual analysis. (See Chapter 13.)

Interpretive comprehension obviously should receive much stress with above-average readers. Such students also are able to respond at the critical level of comprehension very effectively. They do exceptionally well in a small-group setting in which they challenge each other's opinions on controversial issues in a tactful way. They also are very good in comparing materials from different sources. Above-average readers at this level usually very much enjoy analyzing television and newspaper advertisements in terms of such propaganda techniques as the halo effect, testimonials, the bandwagon technique, and glittering generalities. Above-average readers also very much benefit from the use of various parts of the newspaper such as the news section, editorials, and letters to the editor.

Above-average readers in the intermediate grades often are able to exhibit great creativity if they are given the opportunity to do so. For example, they often are very capable in the creative writing of both prose and poetry. They also may be adept at such dramatic activities as simple play production. They also may be able to relate art and music very well to reading. (See Chapter 14.) In addition, above-average readers at this level often may enjoy reading materials that deal with such issues as divorce, death, drugs, or physical handicaps.

Above-average readers at this level often can profit from the introduction of such study strategies as Survey Q3R. (See Chapter 16.) In this study technique the student is taught to survey, question, read, recite, and review to aid in comprehension and retention of reading materials. Such students also can be taught how to organize their study time and how to take different types of examinations such as objective examinations and essay examinations.

Above-average readers in the intermediate grades also can learn how to use various study skills, especially in reading and studying content materials such as textbooks, trade books, and reference books. They can profit from learning how to locate implied main ideas, how to locate significant details, how to summarize, the techniques of outlining, the techniques of note-taking, how to follow directions, how to use reference materials, how to use the library card catalog, and how to interpret maps, charts, diagrams, and graphs. Such students also function very well as leaders or members of research and interest groups.

Above-average readers often enjoy independent work with such devices as a tachistoscope or a controlled reader. They may be able to improve their rate of reading in some materials by the use of such a device. Above-average readers also can learn and practice the concept of reading flexibility—the ability to vary one's reading rate depending upon his or her purposes for reading and the difficulty of the reading material. This is possible because such students have good basic word identification and comprehension skills. Such students also may enjoy helping less able readers in a peer tutoring situation.

Oral reading should receive little stress with above-average readers. However, they may enjoy participating in audience oral reading or choral reading on occasion. (See Chapter 10.)

A RECOMMENDED READING PROGRAM FOR AVERAGE READERS IN THE INTERMEDIATE GRADES

I recommend using an individualized reading program about three or four days a week with average readers in the fourth, fifth, and sixth grades. Such students should read mainly self-selected reading materials from a wide variety of sources at their instructional or independent reading level.

Such students can use a basal reader at the appropriate level an average of one or two days each week. These should be different basal readers from those used by students in the above-average and the below-average groups in the same grade. The basal reader stories and workbook pages should be selected only when they are appropriate and should not be used in a routine way. I do not recommend presenting new vocabulary terms to average students at the intermediate-grade level because they should be able to use their own word identification techniques to determine many unknown words that are met in the reading material.

Phonic analysis skills should receive very little stress with average readers at this level. Such students, however, can profit from direct instruction in the meanings and use of prefixes and suffixes. They also need instruction and practice in syllabication, accent, and dictionary usage.

Average readers in the intermediate grades should have numerous opportunities to respond at the interpretive level of comprehension. Such students also can answer critical questions and compare reading material from several sources at their own level. The newspaper is a useful tool with average readers at about the sixth-grade level. Some average readers in the intermediate grades enjoy the creative writing of prose and poetry, and some of them enjoy reading material that appeals to their attitudes and emotions. Average readers at this level may also enjoy following up their reading by various kinds of art and construction activities such as murals, collages, dioramas, puppets, posters, or book jackets.

It may be appropriate to present the Survey Q3R study technique to some average readers in the intermediate grades. They also can learn how to apply some of the easier study skills to their content reading. Some of these easier study skills may be locating directly stated main ideas, finding significant details, and locating irrelevant details. Some average readers at the fifth-grade or sixth-grade level also may learn how to use the study skills of summarization, locating implied main ideas, outlining, note-taking, following directions, using reference materials, using a library card catalog, and interpreting simple maps, charts, diagrams, and graphs.

Average readers in the intermediate grades need to learn how to read successfully in the content areas of social studies, science, and mathematics. They always should read content materials that are on or near their instructional reading level. Such students may well profit from instruction and practice in how to read and solve verbal problems in mathematics. Such students also can function effectively as leaders or members of research and interest groups in which they read materials on their own level.

Average readers in the intermediate grades should do fairly little oral reading. However, oral reading miscues can be used to determine their typical reading patterns and to determine their independent, instructional, and frustration reading levels. Some such students also may profit from participating in audience oral reading and in choral reading.

A RECOMMENDED READING PROGRAM FOR BELOW-AVERAGE READERS IN THE INTERMEDIATE GRADES

At the outset it should be understood that it is difficult to propose one single recommended reading program for all below-average readers in the intermediate grades because their reading achievement can vary from the nonreader level to just under the reading level in the grade in which they are placed. I recommend the language experience approach as a major reading approach for the most severely disabled readers in the intermediate grades. These are the students who are virtual nonreaders or reading at the early primary-grade level. As is explained in detail in Chapter 4, the language experience approach is especially useful with older disabled readers because it employs their own unique experiences and language patterns. Therefore, the reading material seems relevant to them and is not juvenile or boring. Very important letter-sound relationships, sight words, and structural analysis skills can be presented to such severely disabled readers at the intermediate-grade level directly from their own individually dictated language experience stories. Often it may be necessary to have a special group for the most severely disabled readers in an intermediate-grade classroom, in which the language experience approach can be used.

The basal reader approach can be used as a major approach for the remainder of the students in the below-average reading achievement group in the intermediate-grade classroom. I recommend that it be used an average of three days a week. It is important for such students to use a basal reader on their own instructional reading level. For example, a fourth reader may be appropriate for use with the below-average reading group in sixth grade. If such a reader seems too juvenile, it is possible to use high interest, low vocabulary books in addition to, or in place of, a traditional basal reader. I recommend that many, but not all, of the basal reader stories and workbook pages be used with below-average readers.

I believe that below-average readers in the intermediate grades need a fairly structured presentation and reinforcement of the most important phonic analysis and structural analysis skills. However, such skills should be taught only if they seem to be truly necessary for effective word identification. Many disabled readers in the inter-mediate grades already have been exposed to far too many phonic elements and phonic generalizations and have come to dislike them very much. Because it is important not to require a student to learn many reading skills at which he or she already has failed, I recommend the very judicious presentation of phonic analysis skills. Such students also can learn the value of contextual analysis as a very important word identification strategy.

It is obvious that a below-average reader in the intermediate grades must first learn to respond at the literal level of comprehension. How-ever, it is important for such students to learn to respond at the in-terpretive and critical levels of comprehension as much as possible. They also should read materials that appeal to their attitudes and emotions at their instructional or independent reading levels. Below-average readers also can engage in creative dramatics, role playing, and construction and art activities that relate to their reading.

Individualized reading can be used with below-average readers in the intermediate grades an average of two days a week. They should read predominantly self-selected reading materials on their own level. *High interest, low vocabulary materials* may be very useful in such an individualized reading program. These are reading materials that have a reading level that is usually several grades below their interest level. Such students also may enjoy independent reinforcement of the var-ious word identification and comprehension skills at reading stations on an individual basis or with one or several peers. Oral reading has some place in the intermediate-grade reading program for below-av-erage readers. However, it should be used carefully and not be merely the round-robin oral reading that was described in detail in Chapter 10.

It is very important to use practical reading materials with below-average readers in the intermediate grades. They can benefit greatly from learning how to use the dictionary. A mail order catalog and a telephone directory also may be very useful as reading materials. Older below-average readers may find it useful to learn how to read various parts of the newspaper such as the want ads and to learn how to complete job applications.

Students in the below-average reading achievement group in the intermediate grades always should read content textbooks on their own instructional reading level. There is little value in placing such a student in a basal reader on the appropriate reading level and then placing him or her in a content textbook that is too difficult. It may be helpful to use the unit plan in social studies and science with such students. In the unit plan the student reads about the selected topic from appropriate content textbooks, reference books, trade books, and children's magazines and newspapers. Such students also can participate as members of research or interest groups.

Rudimentary study skills can be presented to below-average readers in the intermediate grades. Two important study skills that such students can learn to use from appropriate reading material are locating directly stated main ideas and locating significant details. Such students also may benefit very much from peer tutoring.

ONE MORE IMPORTANT POINT

The point should be made again that at the intermediate-grade level a student must develop a lifelong interest in reading and the desire to read for pleasure. In the past, American elementary schools have done a fairly good job of teaching reading but a rather unsatisfactory job of teaching students to value reading for pleasure. For example, about one-half of the students who graduate from college never again read books for pleasure. If a student does not learn to value reading in the intermediate grades, it is unlikely that he or she ever will learn to do so. Most students who do read for pleasure, for example, read the most at about the age of twelve.

Students in the intermediate grades can share their reading in many creative and interesting ways. (See Chapter 6.) They might enjoy informal book clubs. Several commercial methods for recording a student's reading are available, perhaps the most commonly known being *My Reading Design.*[1] (See Figure 11-1.)

A SAMPLE RECOMMENDED INTERMEDIATE-GRADE READING PROGRAM

Figure 11-2 is a sample recommended reading program for a fifth grade. It only is illustrative of a recommended intermediate-grade reading program, and it should be revised in terms of the needs of your own students.

---

[1]G. O. Simpson, *My Reading Design* (Defiance, Ohio: The Hubbard Company, 1962).

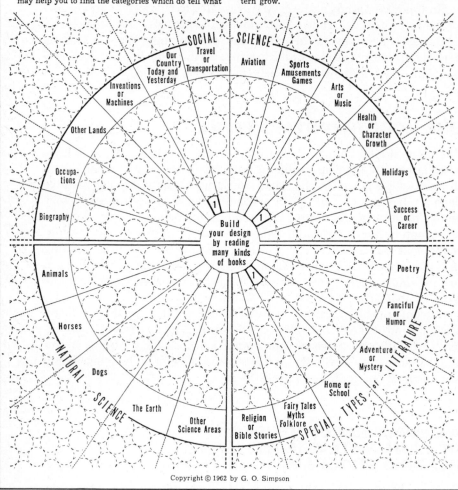

MY READING DESIGN

TO THE READER:—Here is an unfinished design. You may make it yours, if you complete it, as you read and enjoy the books which you like to read. First, find the book which you wish to read. Read it and write the title on the opposite page. Recall the things which you enjoyed in the book. Then, note the categories around the circle, and select those which tell what you enjoyed in the book. Check the subareas on the back page. They may help you to find the categories which do tell what you enjoyed in the book. Put the number of the book in the small circles nearest the center of the design, under the categories which tell what you enjoyed in the book. Then trace the small circles with your pencil. See Sample, opposite page. Very few books belong in more than three categories. Some books belong in one category only. If you read many books and record each book as you read, it will be fun to watch your pattern grow.

Copyright © 1962 by G. O. Simpson

FIGURE 11-1

Sample Weekly Schedule—Fifth Grade
Reading Period 9:00-10:30 A.M.

	Monday	Tuesday	Wednesday	Thursday	Friday
Above-average Group	Individualized Reading Three Individual Reading Conferences Writing Advertisements Demonstrating Propaganda Techniques in Small Groups	Basal Reader Lesson Emphasis on Learning Implied Main Ideas in Skill Development	Individualized Reading Three Individual Reading Conferences Sharing Advertisements Written on Monday with Entire Above-Average Group	Individualized Reading Two Individual Reading Conferences Independent Reading for Social Studies Unit on Westward Movement	Individualized Reading Two Individual Reading Conferences Introduction to Survey Q3R Study Technique
Average Group	Individualized Reading Four Individual Reading Conferences Complete Cloze Procedure for Contextual Analysis	Individualized Reading Three Individual Reading Conferences Independent Reading for Social Studies Unit on Westward Movement	Basal Reader Lesson Emphasis on Preparation of Tape-recorded Radio Broadcast from This Story	Individualized Reading Three Individual Reading Conferences Tape-record the Radio Broadcast	Individualized Reading Three Individual Reading Conferences Independent Reading for Social Studies Unit on Westward Movement
Below-average Group	Basal Reader Lesson Experiential Background Silent Reading of Story / Two Students—Dictate Experience Stories	Basal Reader Lesson Skill Development of Syllabication Workbook Page on Syllabication / Two Students—Phonic Analysis from Experience Stories	Individualized Reading Three Individual Reading Conferences Independent Reading for Social Studies Unit on Westward Movement	Basal Reader Lesson Silent Reading of Story Skill Development of Syllabication / Two Students Read Experience Stories from Past Two Weeks	Individualized Reading Three Individual Reading Conferences Independent Reading for Social Studies Unit on Westward Movement

FIGURE 11-2

SELECTED REFERENCES

Bessai, Frederick, and Con Cozac. "Gains of Fifth and Sixth Grade Readers from In-School Tutoring." *The Reading Teacher, 33* (February 1980): 567–570.

Heilman, Arthur W. *Principles and Practices of Teaching Reading.* Columbus, Ohio: Charles E. Merrill Publishing Co., 1977, Chapter 14.

Johns, Jerry L., and Lawrence P. McNamara. "The Superiority of Survey Q3R Has Not Yet Been Demonstrated Empirically." *Journal of Reading, 23* (May 1980): 705–708.

Mason, George E. "High Interest—Low Vocabulary Books: Their Past and Future." *Journal of Reading, 34* (April 1981): 603–607.

Moray, Geraldine. "What Does Research Say About the Reading Interests of Children in the Intermediate Grades?" *The Reading Teacher, 31* (April 1978): 763–768.

Spache, George D., and Evelyn B. Spache. *Reading in the Elementary School.* Boston: Allyn and Bacon, Inc., 1977, Chapter 9.

Tadlock, Dolores Fadness. "Survey Q3R—Why it Works, Based on an Information Processing Theory of Learning." *Journal of Reading, 22* (November 1978): 110–112.

Zintz, Miles V. *The Reading Process.* Dubuque, Iowa: William C. Brown Company, Publishers, 1980, Chapter 14.

SUGGESTED ACTIVITIES

1. If possible, visit an intermediate-grade classroom that uses some variation of a combination approach as discussed in this chapter.
2. Formulate a sample weekly schedule for either a fourth-grade or a sixth-grade classroom that tries to combine several approaches as described in the chapter. You may want to work with a partner on this activity.
3. Formulate ten different types of reading activities that can be done in the intermediate grades by using a newspaper. Why do you think that the newspaper is such a versatile tool to use for reading instruction and reinforcement at this level?

Developing sight and meaning vocabularies

What Should She Do?

Mrs. Rodriguez had been teaching second grade at Washington School in a large city in the Northeast for several years. Although she had always considered herself to be a good teacher of reading, she had never before encountered a child quite like Danny. It did not take her long to discover that Danny just could not retain sight words. He apparently possessed fairly good phonic analysis skills, but he could not remember any words by sight. Mrs. Rodriguez knew that he could not become a proficient reader if he had to stop and sound out each word that he met while reading. Because she knew that only a few hundred sight words make up the majority of common reading material, she knew how important it was for Danny to master the words on the Dolch Basic Sight Word List by the time that he had completed third grade.

Mrs. Rodriguez first tried a number of strategies for helping Danny to retain sight words that had worked fairly well before with other students. Two of these were using flash cards with a partner and writing a sight word in a sentence in a different color from the words in the rest of the sentence. However, as none of these commonly used strategies were successful with Danny, Mrs. Rodriguez knew that she undoubtedly would have to use some more unusual strategies if he were to learn the important sight words.

Because Mrs. Rodriguez did not know any other strategies for improving a child's sight word recognition ability, she decided to purchase a reading aid at the local bookstore. She found one that contained numerous ideas for helping improve the sight word recognition ability of students like Danny, and she subsequently purchased it.

She then tried some of the strategies contained in this instructional aid with Danny and found them to be quite successful. He especially liked tracing over words with salt letters that were glued on cardboard. He also liked tracing sight words made of Christmas glitter letters that were glued on cardboard. However, Mrs. Rodriguez was careful to put the sight words that Danny learned by tracing into phrase context or sentence context as soon as he had learned them, for she knew that sight words usually are retained better in context than in isolation.

After several months, Danny had learned a number of the common sight words. At this point he did not have to trace the majority of the new sight words that he was trying to remember. Instead, he was able to print each sight word several times, visualizing it in his mind and saying it to himself as he visualized it. By the end of second grade, Danny was able to recognize immediately about 150 of the words on the Dolch Basic Sight Word List of 220 words. Mrs. Rodriguez felt that he undoubtedly would be able to recognize most of the words on this list by the time that he completed third grade. She also felt that the perceptive ideas contained in the instructional aid that she had purchased had been extremely helpful to Danny in learning to retain sight words.

After you have finished reading this chapter, you will know numerous practical strategies for improving sight word recognition at the primary-grade level and for improving meaning vocabulary at both the primary-grade and intermediate-grade levels. These strategies should prove very helpful to you in your teaching of elementary reading.

A DESCRIPTION OF SIGHT WORD RECOGNITION

Sight words are usually described in several different ways. They can be designated as those words that a reader recognizes immediately upon seeing them. They then are the words that a reader does not have to stop and analyze by the use of another word identification technique such as phonic analysis or structural analysis. In addition, sight words can be described as words that do not have a regular sound-symbol relationship. Therefore, such words cannot be analyzed effectively but are most efficiently learned as a total unit. Several examples of sight words are *where, should, one, does,* and *of.*

Most often, a sight word is recognized as a total unit instead of by its individual letters or word parts. Sight word recognition is said to consist of such subskills as recognizing a word by its total shape, its first few letters, its distinctive characteristics such as double letters, its ascending letters such as *h, f,* and *b,* and its descending letters such as *g, q,* and *p. Configuration,* or drawing a frame around a word, is another subskill of sight word recognition. Here is an example of configuration:

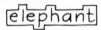

It is important to remember that some subskills of sight word recognition provide fairly irrelevant cues to word identification. One such *fairly irrelevant cue* is configuration. In the past, configuration was presented as a cue to word identification fairly often at the beginning stages of reading. However, it is not presented very much at the present time because words such as *man, son, run,* and *can* have an identical configuration. Another irrelevant cue is the double *o* in the word *look,* which is supposed to look like two eyes. A number of other words such as *hook, book, cook,* and *shook* also have a double *o* in the same position. One other irrelevant cue that sometimes was presented in the past was the practice of having the child find small words in larger words. You can see that the technique of having a child find the words *fat* and *her* is not applicable in decoding the word *father.*

To be an efficient reader, a student must have a large stock of words that he or she is able to recognize at sight. Often these are the words found on a sight word list as is described later in this section. Therefore, many words that are first decoded by the use of another word identification technique such as phonic analysis or structural analysis eventually should become part of a student's sight word bank through continued meaningful exposure in a variety of settings.

The most commonly used sight words are found in a number of different sight word lists. There is considerable overlap among all the lists although the words contained on the lists do vary somewhat depending on the sources from which they were taken.

The most commonly used sight word list certainly is the *Dolch Basic Sight Word List,* which was formulated by the late Edward Dolch of the University of Illinois in 1941. Although it may appear to you from the date that this sight word list must be dated, this is not true because the words contained in it are very comparable to those included on the newer sight word lists. This list of 220 words is said to make up about 70 percent of the words found in most first readers and about 65 percent of the words found in most second and third readers. You can obtain the Dolch Basic Sight Word List at a nominal cost from the Garrard Press, 1607 North Market Street, Champaign, Illinois 61820.

Edward Fry of Rutgers University has compiled a new version of the *Instant Word List,* which he first compiled in 1957. This list is composed of 300 words that probably should be mastered by the end of the third grade. According to Fry, these 300 words and their common variants make up about 65 percent of all the words in any textbook, any newspaper, or any writing sample in English. Fry further stated that half of all the written material in English is composed of just the first hundred Instant Words and their common variants.[1] A copy of the 300 words included in this sight word list is found in Appendix I.

Another valuable sight word list is the *Kucera-Francis Corpus,* which is composed of 220 words. This sight word list is based upon the work of Henry Kucera and W. Nelson Francis and was included in the book *Computational Analysis of Present-Day American English.*[2] For this sight word list, Kucera and Francis processed 1,014,232 running words by computer and then placed these words in rank order of their use. Eighty-two (37 percent) of the words found on the Kucera-Francis Corpus are not contained on the Dolch List. Thus, you can see that the words contained on the two lists are at least somewhat comparable.

Another valuable sight word list is *Hillerich's 240 Starter Words,* which was compiled by Robert L. Hillerich. Hillerich formulated this

---

[1]Edward Fry, "The New Instant Word List," *The Reading Teacher,* *34* (December 1980): 284–289.

[2]Henry Kucera and W. Nelson Francis, *Computational Analysis of Present-Day American English* (Providence, Rhode Island: Brown University Press, 1967).

list from old and new word lists, juvenile and adult writing, and juvenile and adult printed materials.[3] A copy of this sight word list is included in Appendix II. One other sight word list that is rather unique is the *Van Allen List of 300 High-Frequency Words.* Roach Van Allen compiled this list from the language children used while dictating and writing experience stories.[4] Another sight word list is unique in that it extends into the intermediate grades. This is the *Harris-Jacobson Core List,* and it covers materials from grades one through six.[5]

HOW TO DIAGNOSE A STUDENT'S ABILITY IN SIGHT WORD RECOGNITION

There are several different means that can be used to determine a student's competency in sight word recognition. One of the most obvious is simply to observe a student while he or she is reading aloud in a setting such as a reading achievement group, some other type of group, or the entire class. If you see that a student habitually stops to analyze commonly used words that he or she should recognize by sight, the student may have an insignificant stock of sight words. Usually, this is more typical of a student who is reading at the third reader level or below, no matter what grade he or she is attending.

If you want to assess the probable sight word bank of a student, you can easily construct a simple inventory in sight word recognition by using the words contained on any of the basic sight word lists that have been previously described in this chapter. Such an inventory can be given on either an individual or a group basis.

When you want to give a sight word test to an individual child, type two copies of the word list that you have chosen. If the student who is to take this test is in the primary grades, you may wish to type the student's list on a primary typewriter. In any case, give the student his or her copy, and have him or her try to pronounce each of the words on the list aloud. Mark the student's responses on your copy of the list with a plus sign (+) for a word that he or she pronounces correctly and a minus sign (−) for a word that the student does not pronounce almost immediately.

If you want to give a sight word recognition inventory on a group basis, type each of the words on a line along with several options. Then

---

[3]Robert L. Hillerich, "Word Lists—Getting It Altogether," *The Reading Teacher,* 27 (January 1974): 367.

[4] Roach Van Allen, *Language Experiences in Communication* (Boston: Houghton Mifflin Company, 1976), pp. 218–219.

[5]Albert J. Harris and Milton D. Jacobson, *Basic Elementary Reading Vocabularies* (New York: Macmillan Publishing Company, Inc., 1972).

pronounce the one sight word per line that you want the students to recognize, and have each student underline or circle this pronounced word.

It is fairly easy to evaluate a student's performance on a sight word test. For example, the following may be used to determine a student's approximate instructional reading level by using his or her performance on the Dolch Basic Sight Word List:

Words Recognized	Reading Level
0–75	Preprimer
76–120	Primer
121–170	First reader
171–210	Second reader
Above 210	Third reader or above[6]

As the Kucera-Francis Corpus also contains 220 sight words, you probably can use these same figures for it. Probably about the same percentages can be used on the other sight word lists to determine a student's approximate reading levels. You should remember that all the percentages must be considered tentative and that a student normally should have instant recognition of the vast majority of the words on a basic sight word list before he or she progresses into the intermediate grades.

STRATEGIES AND MATERIALS FOR IMPROVING COMPETENCY IN SIGHT WORD RECOGNITION

There are many different strategies and materials that can be used to improve a student's competency in sight word recognition. Most of these are the most applicable with students in the primary grades. However, they may also be useful with students in the intermediate grades who have not mastered the basic sight words. Often these are the disabled readers in the intermediate grades. Normally, the teacher can select one of the sight word lists discussed earlier in this chapter and concentrate on presenting and reinforcing the words contained in that list. It can be stated at the outset that, as much as possible, sight words should be presented and reinforced in *phrase context* or *sentence context*. Most of the words on a sight word list are *function* or *structure words*, which means that they have no referent. Some examples of function or structure words are *of, the, once,* and *so.* On the other hand,

---

[6]Miles V. Zintz, *The Reading Process* (Dubuque, Iowa: William C. Brown Company, Publishers, 1975), p. 82.

a *content word* such as *mother* has a referent. Therefore, a child usually finds it easier to learn structure or function words in context than in isolation. For example, it normally is easier for the child to learn the word *on* in a phrase such as *on the table* instead of in isolation. However, it is acceptable to isolate sight words occasionally for student mastery.

There are a variety of tracing techniques that can be used to help a child retain difficult-to-remember sight words. Have the child form the sight word on a piece of cardboard or tagboard by placing glue on it. Then the child can sprinkle over the glue letters of the sight word with sugar, salt, or Christmas glitter. The child then traces over the completed word with his or her index finger, saying the word aloud as he or she does so. You also can form a sight word by cutting sandpaper or felt letters and gluing them to a cardboard or simply placing them on a desk. The child can then trace over these sandpaper or felt letters, saying the sight word aloud as he or she traces it.

In another variation of tracing, the child can print or write sight words in a salt tray or a sandbox. In this case, the child uses a model to copy the sight word and says it aloud as he or she forms it with the index finger. Some teachers print a series of dots on the chalkboard or on an activity sheet in the form of a sight word. The child then is to trace over this series of dots pronouncing the word aloud or silently as he or she does so. Below is an example of a word formed by the use of this technique:

would   (would)

The *Fernald Tracing Method* is another type of tracing technique that can be very useful in improving competency in both sight word recognition and in the syllabication aspect of structural analysis. In this remedial technique, the student chooses a word that he or she wants to learn to recognize. The teacher then writes this word on a strip of tagboard or poster board with a dark crayon. If the child can read cursive handwriting, it is more acceptable to use this form. However, manuscript handwriting is acceptable if necessary. In any case, the student traces the word with his or her index finger while saying it aloud in syllables. The student then writes the word from memory. If he or she cannot do so, the student retraces it pronouncing it in syllables. This retracing and writing continue until the student can write the word from memory. The student also is to use the newly learned word in a sentence as soon as possible. Usually he or she also writes it on a small card and places it in a variation of the word bank that was mentioned in Chapter 4 in connection with the language experience approach. For more detail on this method, you can consult the footnote below. However, as this method is very time-consuming, it should be used only with students who have great difficulty in learning sight words. These normally are older disabled readers in the intermediate grades.[7]

✔ A very interesting activity is to have the child locate and cut out sight words from magazines or newspapers. Have the child then paste these sight words on a large sheet of construction paper in the form of a design. Several children can work together in identifying all the sight words found on several designs. As another interesting activity that can be used in the primary grades, you can have the child pantomime sight words that do not lend themselves to illustrations. Verbs and prepositions are especially useful in pantomiming. Here are some sight words that can be pantomimed: *between, over, under, up,* and *down.*

You can construct a word puzzle with a number of pairs of look-alike sight words. Divide a long piece of tagboard into sections, and cut each section apart in a different puzzle pattern. Print a sight word on each section of the puzzle as is illustrated. Then the child pairs the look-alike sight words in order to complete the puzzle.

yes	goes	where	one	mother
eyes	does	were	once	other

✔ Another interesting technique that can be used to improve competency in sight word recognition is the grab bag technique. Print difficult sight words on tagboard expressing any type of seasonal theme such as autumn leaves, Christmas trees, or snowmen. Place the sight words in a bag, and have each child select a word card from the bag and try to pronounce it. If he or she can do so correctly, the child keeps the word. If not, it is placed back in the bag. At the end of the game, the child with the most word cards wins.

One of the best ways of improving sight word recognition is for the student to read independently from very interesting, easy materials on his or her independent reading level. Today there are countless relevant reading materials that greatly appeal to the interests of all students in the elementary school, such as trade books, supplementary reading materials, and children's magazines and newspapers. Wide reading of easy material helps to improve sight word recognition because the students are motivated and find few unknown words. They then can practice instant word identification.

---

[7]Grace M. Fernald, *Remedial Techniques in Basic School Subjects* (New York: McGraw-Hill, Inc., 1943).

As another activity to improve sight word recognition, write a number of phrases on the chalkboard or on a transparency, leaving off the structure or function words. Have a small group of children suggest as many different structure or function words as possible that can be included at the beginning of each phrase. Here are some phrases that can be used in this activity:

　　——— new bicycle
　　——— little puppy
　　——— old house

Game boards that use sports, especially track games, are very popular for improving ability in sight word recognition. There are many different types of commercial and homemade board games that can be modified for these purposes. Some of them are baseball, football, the turtle race, an auto race, or a tunnel race.

The typewriter is a very useful kinesthetic aid for older students in learning to remember difficult sight words. A typewriter often is effective for teaching sight word recognition because it emphasizes left-to-right progression and adds a tactile reinforcement to sight word recognition. Another technique for improving ability in this word identification skill is to use a variation of the cloze procedure. (See Chapter 13.) For this variation, which emphasizes function or structure words, type a passage on the appropriate reading level that was taken from a basal reader story, supplementary reading material, or a content textbook. Type the first and last sentence of the passage intact, and delete every eighth structure or function word in the remainder of the passage. Have the student complete the cloze procedure by writing in a structure or function word that makes sense in each blank. Any structure or function word that the student writes in the blank that makes sense should be considered correct.

A *tachistoscope* may be useful in improving immediacy of sight word recognition in phrase context and in isolation. A tachistoscope is a device that uses filmstrips and flashes words, phrases, or patterns on a screen at rates of speed that vary from one second to one-hundredth of a second. A tachistoscope is available from such manufacturers as Psychotechnics, Educational Developmental Laboratories, Keystone View Company, and the Society for Visual Education.

There are several other commercially available machines that can be used to present or review sight words. Several are *The Language Master* (Bell and Howell Company), *efi Audio Flashcard System* (Educational Futures), and *TTC Magnetic Card Reader* (The Teaching Technology Corporation). Each of these machines uses large cards with strips of magnetic tape placed on them. The student can look at the card, try to identify the word, place the card in the machine, and listen through earphones as the machine says the word.

My dog is black and white.

FIGURE 12-1

As another method for stressing sight words, the teacher can print a sentence containing the sight word written in red and the remainder of the sentence written in black. (See Figure 12-1.) Sight words also can be stressed by using window cards with the language experience approach. As was explained in Chapter 4, the language experience approach is one of the better ways of presenting sight word recognition in meaningful context, especially at the beginning reading level. A window card can also be used with beginning basal reader stories if the print is large enough in them.

Flash cards are probably the most traditional way to reinforce the knowledge of various sight words. The teacher can make the flash cards, or a child can make them depending upon his or her age. In any case, each sight word is printed on one side of the card with a magic marker or crayon, and a picture of the word is placed on the other side if it is possible to illustrate the word. Usually, a student works with a partner while using flash cards if it is possible.

Charles H. Hargis and Edward E. Gickling recently developed a strategy using imagery to help children retain difficult-to-remember sight words. Very briefly, this procedure consists of the following steps: have the child look at a word printed on a card while the teacher pronounces it; have the child repeat the word; have the teacher use the word in a sentence; have the child repeat the word and use it in his or her own sentence; have the child look at the word again and pronounce it; present the word to the next child, repeating the preceding five steps; present a second word, and review the first word, and so on until four words are covered in each training session; shuffle the cards and have the students take turns identifying and pronouncing all of the sight words.[8]

Computer-assisted instruction (CAI) undoubtedly can be used effectively in the presentation and/or reinforcement of sight words. According to an article by Jay S. Blanchard, this type of instruction occurs when a student and computer meet for a specified instructional goal. CAI is very effective in a drill-and-practice situation that is based on the stimulus-response learning theory. (See Chapter 6.) In this type of instruction, the student does not see a video presentation but instead interacts with the computer through a keyboard that prints out both the student's and the computer's responses on a continuous roll of

[8]Charles H. Hargis, and Edward E. Gickling, "The Function of Imagery in Word Recognition Development," *The Reading Teacher, 31* (May 1978): 870–874.

paper. According to Blanchard, computers never will replace teachers. However, they can help teachers to individualize reading instruction. Blanchard further states that there may be more computers in the classroom in the future as their cost declines and the overall quality of educational programs improves. As has been stated earlier in this book, I believe that computers will be used extensively in elementary reading instruction in the future. They most certainly are the educational innovation of the future, and every prospective elementary reading teacher should know how to utilize microcomputers in his or her reading program. For more detail on using computers in reading instruction, consult this footnote[9] or one of the references found in Chapter 9.

There are several strategies that can be used with older students to learn sight words that sometimes are called "target words." To use one of these strategies, write a target word at the top of a duplicating master. Have the remainder of the sheet contain the target word at random intervals along with many other words of similar appearance. Then have the student trace from left to right as rapidly as possible, circling or underlining the target word each time that it appears. In another strategy, the student writes sentences, paragraphs, television commercials, comic strips, jingles, or anecdotes, using the target terms that you have selected.

It is always important, as is explained in detail in Chapter 16, to present the new, important vocabulary terms found in content reading assignments. Such vocabulary presentations can use media aids. As a variation, you can have a group of students survey a textbook chapter to identify the special vocabulary terms that should be presented before another group of students reads the material.

In addition, many other strategies and materials for improving ability in sight word recognition can be found in other professional books, in instructional aids, and in basal reader manuals. One aid that teachers have found useful is the following:

Miller, Wilma H. *Reading Activities Handbook.* New York: Holt, Rinehart and Winston, 1980.

A DESCRIPTION OF MEANING VOCABULARY KNOWLEDGE

Reading specialists agree that if a child is to be able to comprehend effectively what he or she reads, the child must have a good meaning

[9]Jay S. Blanchard, "Computer-Assisted Instruction in Today's Reading Classrooms," *Journal of Reading, 23* (February 1980): 430–434.

vocabulary. Effective understanding of what is read always depends first on the reader's possession of many word meanings. If a student is to have truly effective comprehension, he or she must know all the shades of meaning that are found in many words. If a student is to read effectively, he or she must be able to give the approximate same shade of meaning to the terms found in the reading material that the writer of the material gave them.

A number of words in English have a number of different meanings. This is especially true of abstract terms. For example, according to one dictionary, the word *run* has fifteen different meanings when it is used as a verb and eleven different meanings when it is used as a noun. Examine the following sentences:

> Jimmy can *run* faster than any other boy in our class.
>
> File drawers always *run* on ball bearings.
>
> Nancy has a long *run* in her stocking.
>
> Water always *runs* downhill.
>
> That play has had a *run* of seven months.
>
> My father will *run* a splinter into his finger if he is not careful.

In each of the preceding examples, the student must have the correct meaning for the word *run* if he or she is to comprehend the sentence effectively.

On the other hand, more precise terms such as *photosynthesis* and *osmosis* generally only have one or a very few different meanings.

There are a number of different kinds of meaning vocabularies that a person can possess. These are the listening vocabulary, the speaking vocabulary, the reading vocabulary, the writing vocabulary, and the potential or marginal vocabulary.

The child first learns the *listening vocabulary*. A young child learns to associate the sounds that are used by his or her parents, other family members, or other people with the objects and concepts that they represent. For example, a child learns to associate the sounds that are heard in the word *baby* with the babies that the word represents. That is why a child normally uses about the same vocabulary terms and dialects that are used by his or her family and the other older people with whom he or she comes into contact. In the elementary school, a child's listening vocabulary usually is surpassed by his or her reading vocabulary by the time the child is in the lower intermediate grades unless he or she is a disabled reader. The listening vocabulary sometimes is used to determine a disabled reader's potential for reading improvement as is explained in detail in Chapter 17.

The preschool child next acquires the *speaking vocabulary*. Because the child learns to speak by imitating the oral language of the adults with whom he or she comes into contact, the child uses the same kind of vocabulary and dialect that they use. For example, a young black child from the inner-city often uses the black dialect when speaking.

The child next acquires the *reading vocabulary*. As was explained in Chapter 2, some early readers begin to acquire this vocabulary in the home. However, the reading vocabulary usually is acquired mainly in the school setting. A student usually should not be taught to identify a word unless it is in his or her speaking vocabulary. For example, if a student analyzes a word by the use of phonic analysis, he or she will not know if this has been done correctly if the word is not familiar to him or her. (See Chapter 7.) Unless a student is disabled in reading, the reading vocabulary usually is larger than both the listening and speaking vocabularies.

The *writing vocabulary* is the next one that the child typically learns. This type of vocabulary often is developed along with the reading vocabulary. The writing vocabulary usually is the smallest type of vocabulary because a person usually can read and understand words that he or she does not use in writing. A person normally also uses words in the speaking vocabulary that he or she does not use in writing.

The *potential* or *marginal vocabulary* is the fifth type of meaning vocabulary. It contains the words for which a reader can determine meaning by using context clues, prefixes, suffixes, or derivatives. It is difficult to determine the size of a student's potential or marginal vocabulary because the circumstances in which he or she encounters an unknown word may determine whether or not he or she can deduce its meaning.

In a recent article, Gary A. Negin and Dee Krugler have formulated another type of vocabulary. These are the terms that apparently were required for functional literacy in the urban community of Milwaukee, Wisconsin. In order to obtain these vocabulary terms, 461 adults were surveyed in relation to their reading needs. This article by Negin and Krugler contains an interesting master list of vocabulary and skills needed for functional literacy. It deals with such items as bank statements, directions for preparing food, job applications, directions on products for housecleaning or home improvement, street and traffic signs, directions on medicine bottles, applications for loans from banks, health and safety pamphlets, state and federal income tax forms, bills for good or services, insurance policies, and size, weight, and price information needed while shopping.[10]

---

[10]Gary A. Negin and Dee Krugler, "Essential Literacy Skills for Functioning in an Urban Community," *Journal of Reading, 24* (November 1980): 109–115.

HOW TO DIAGNOSE A STUDENT'S ABILITY IN MEANING VOCABULARY

There are several ways of making a diagnosis of competency in meaning vocabulary knowledge. One of the simpler ways is to listen to a student carefully while he or she is speaking or to examine his or her creative writing carefully. While making a diagnosis of a student's meaning vocabulary knowledge from his or her oral language, normally you should focus on the use of vocabulary, not on the content of the speech. This type of focus can help you to determine if the student may have a limited meaning vocabulary, uses vocabulary terms in an imprecise way, or overuses common vocabulary terms. In addition, you can examine a student's creative writing to gain an insight into the quality and extent of his or her meaning vocabulary.

Some teachers use a type of informal inventory to assess a student's competency in meaning vocabulary knowledge. In such an inventory, the student usually marks the one of several options that is a synonym for the selected word in each case. An inventory in meaning vocabulary knowledge can be given either on an individual or a group basis. It often has the same limitations as do the word-meaning subtests on standardized reading tests, which will be discussed shortly.

As an alternative, you can determine a student's probable ability in aspects of meaning vocabulary by examining the vocabulary (word-meaning) subtest on a standardized survey reading or achievement test on the appropriate reading level. This type of subtest usually requires a student to choose the meaning of a word correctly from context. As many words have different meanings, depending upon their context, this kind of subtest has a limitation in that the student may know only one meaning of a word that has multiple meanings, and this meaning may not be one of the options on the subtest. In addition, because a student must be able to read all the words on a word-meaning subtest, he or she may be penalized for a lack of word identification ability even if he or she may know the meaning of the word. Also, such a subtest needs to be given orally to a disabled reader who cannot identify the words.

Chapter 17 contains a detailed description of the survey reading or achievement tests that contain word-meaning subtests. However, here is a brief list of this type of test:

California Achievement Test: Reading
Gates-MacGinitie Reading Tests
Iowa Silent Reading Tests
Metropolitan Achievement Tests: Reading
Stanford Achievement Tests: Reading

STRATEGIES AND MATERIALS FOR IMPROVING COMPETENCY IN MEANING VOCABULARY

In general, *firsthand* or *direct experiences* are always the most valuable in improving meaning vocabulary knowledge. Good examples of direct experiences are school trips to such interesting places as the police station, fire station, museum, zoo, dairy, post office, farm, bakery, or planetarium. To maximize vocabulary improvement, the teacher should carefully discuss examples of vocabulary terms that may be encountered on the trip prior to the trip. They then should be pointed out during the trip and subsequently discussed again upon return to the classroom. If it is appropriate, each vocabulary term also can be written on the chalkboard.

A somewhat less valuable, but still important, means for vocabulary development is through the use of *secondhand* or *vicarious experiences*. As it is recognized that not all things can be experienced directly, secondhand experiences are a fairly good substitute for firsthand experiences when necessary. For example, although a child cannot travel to the moon, he or she can view a film about a trip to the moon. Examples of secondhand or vicarious experiences are the use of films, filmstrips, slides, cassette tape recordings, records, models, experiments, construction activities, dioramas, and pictures.

Another important point to be made at this time is the value of a teacher who is interested in vocabulary improvement. His or her attitude toward vocabulary improvement can be a significant factor in the amount of success he or she has in building the vocabulary of students. The typical school day offers many opportunities for vocabulary improvement in both an incidental and a structured way. For example, if a child brings in a photograph of a fish that he recently caught, there may be opportunities to learn such vocabulary terms as *gills, scales, fins,* or *hooks.* However, it should be remembered that vocabulary improvement should be planned as well as incidental. The strategies that are contained in this chapter may serve as planned or structured means for vocabulary improvement, but they always should be supplemented by incidental means as was previously mentioned.

There are many specialized strategies that can be used in the primary grades for vocabulary improvement in addition to the direct and vicarious experiences that were mentioned previously. For example, have a group of children stand near a cassette tape recorder. Have one child make up a story and talk for several minutes. The next child is to continue the story, and the procedure continues until each child has had a turn. Then the entire story can be replayed, with the children listening and subsequently discussing the interesting vocabulary in it. As another example, make a synonym tree out of tagboard or poster board for a bulletin board. Cut a slot in the trunk so that a word card can be attached. Then make appropriate fruit patterns such as apples, pears, or cherries out of tagboard or poster board. Have children write synonyms for the word card on the trunk on the fruit patterns and attach them to the tree as shown below. Change the word card on the trunk periodically.

As another upper-primary-grade activity for vocabulary improvement, write a number of words that have antonyms in color on one side of index cards. Write one or several antonyms for each word in black on the other side. Have two children play this game. One child holds up each word card while the other child gives an antonym. If he or she is correct, the card can be kept; otherwise, it is discarded. The child keeps a record of how many antonyms he or she named and then tries to do better the next time. An additional activity is to have a group of children sit on the floor in a circle. Spin a 78-rpm phonograph record on its side in the center of the circle, and call out a word that has an antonym. Call on a student to give an antonym and to catch the record before it falls flat.

There are a myriad of activities that can be used in the intermediate grades for vocabulary improvement. One of them is to divide the class into small groups and give each group manila paper. Then provide each group with a number of figurative expressions, and have each group illustrate both the literal and figurative meaning. Here are several examples:

mad as a wet hen
bury the hatchet
hungry as a bear
chip off the old block

One activity for vocabulary improvement that students have liked very much is to have the student write some terms on a sheet of paper as though these terms could be heard as well as seen. The student should think of how a word might sound. Here are several examples:

big

little

fast

s l o w

MEAN

Barbara Crist has discussed interesting vocabulary activities based on students' names in a classroom. The teacher can help each child find out what his or her name means and what country it came from originally. For example, the name *George* comes from the Greek word *georgos,* meaning "farmer." *Irene* is the Greek word for "peace," and *Gertrude* comes from two Teutonic words meaning "spear maiden." Here are several references that Crist provided in her article that you may find useful:

Dunkling, Leslie A. *First Names First*. New York: Universe Books, 1977.

Lambert, Eloise, and Mario Pei. *Our Names*. New York: Lothrop, Lee and Shepard, 1961.

Smith, Elsdon. *New Dictionary of American Family Names*. New York: Harper & Row, Publishers, 1973.

Stewart, George R. *American Given Names: Their Origin and History in the Context of the English Language*. New York: Oxford University Press, 1979.[11]

Another interesting activity for vocabulary improvement at the intermediate-grade level is to place a thermometer of terms on the chalkboard or a transparency. Then help the students to see how these terms relate to each other.

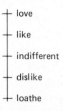

love

like

indifferent

dislike

loathe

The student at the intermediate-grade reading level may find it useful to learn how to use a thesaurus. After the student has learned

---

[11]Barbara Crist, "Tim's Time: Vocabulary Activities from Names," *The Reading Teacher, 34* (December 1980): 309–312.

how to use it, give each student a copy of the thesaurus for this activity. Then have a group of students engage in a gamelike activity that involves the thesaurus. Here are some possible questions for this activity:

What are some synonyms for the word *happy?*

What are some synonyms for the word *large?*

What are some synonyms for the overworked word *swell?*

The study of etymology or the history of words is a very good way to improve vocabulary at the upper-intermediate-grade reading level. However, the study of word origins is only beneficial to above-average readers at this level who are interested in it. Analyzing the vocabulary of well-known nursery rhymes is an interesting activity for students at this reading level. In any case, there are several good sources that give the history of words in a very interesting way. Here are several of them:

Funk, Wilfred. *Word Origins and Their Romantic Stories.* New York: Funk & Wagnalls, Inc., 1968.

Francis, W. Nelson. *The History of English.* New York: W. W. Norton & Company, Inc., 1963.

As another interesting activity for vocabulary development at the intermediate-grade level, have a group of students place a large outline map of the United States on a bulletin board. Then have the students do research reading on the type of dialect that is spoken in various parts of the country. Have the students write examples of this dialect on word cards, and attach the cards to the proper places on the map to indicate where this kind of dialect is used.

As a way of having students review important vocabulary terms, you can place them in a crossword puzzle, an acrostic, or an anagram. Such a word puzzle can be placed on a duplicating master. The student then can complete it individually or with one or several partners.

Many students in the intermediate grades do not know how to use the specialized aids found in content textbooks to add to their meaning vocabulary. These specialized aids should be presented to students at this level, and then practice should be given in using them. Such specialized aids are boldface type, capitalization of important terms, italics, the textbook glossary, maps, tables, charts, diagrams, and the use of color.

There are several types of activity sheets that can be placed on duplicating masters and used with some students at the upper-intermediate-grade reading level. As one example, formulate an alternate-association activity sheet. This activity sheet should contain pairs of words that are either synonyms, antonyms, or homonyms. Then have the student mark each pair correctly. Here are several examples that can be placed on such an activity sheet:

    _____ ordinary—commonplace

    _____ proud—modest

    _____ stationery—stationary

You also can formulate a multiple discrimination activity sheet. Each line of five words on this sheet should contain four synonyms and one unrelated word. You then have the student cross out the unrelated term in each line. Here is one line that can be found on such an activity sheet:

    decide determine exchange resolve settle

A few students in the upper intermediate grades may find it beneficial to keep a word file or a vocabulary notebook to help them master important vocabulary terms from the content areas. If word cards are used, have the student print the vocabulary terms on one side of the card and use the back of the card for the phonetic pronunciation, the meaning or meanings, synonyms, or antonyms.

In a recent brief article, Shirley Koeller and Samina Kahn provided some suggestions for vocabulary expansion that may be useful with some above-average readers at the upper-intermediate-grade level. They suggested that students watch television newscasts and read current periodicals and newspapers to look for new words and meanings. They also recommended that students compile dictionaries of words and meanings so recent that they are not found in actual dictionaries. They also recommended that students compare and contrast various unabridged and abridged dictionaries to trace derivations and histories of words. Finally, they suggested that students explore and experiment with words, even coining their own new words.[12]

In another recent article, Elaine M. Kaplan and Anita Tuchman recommended several strategies for vocabulary improvement that may be applicable with some students in the upper primary grades. They stated that students should look at the chapter titles and headings in a content textbook before reading a new selection and should then predict words that will be included in that selection. Later the students can note if the words really were in the selection. In addition, they suggested that the teacher select an appropriate concept word found

[12]Shirley Koeller and Samina Kahn, "Going Beyond the Dictionary with the English Vocabulary Explosion," *Journal of Reading, 24* (April 1981): 628–629.

in a unit of study. The students then have two minutes to write down as many words as possible that relate to the subject word. The students later can write a paragraph using that word.[13]

SELECTED REFERENCES

Culyer, Richard C., III. "Guidelines for Skill Development: Vocabulary." *The Reading Teacher, 32* (December 1978): 316–322.

Cunningham, Patricia M. "Teaching *Were, With, What* and Other 'Four-Letter' Words." *The Reading Teacher, 34* (November 1980): 160–163.

Duffelmeyer, Frederick A., and Barbara Blakely Duffelmeyer. "Developing Vocabulary Through Dramatization." *Journal of Reading, 23* (November 1979): 141–143.

Floriani, Bernard P. "Word Expansions for Multiplying Sight Vocabulary." *The Reading Teacher, 33* (November 1979): 155–157.

Harris, Albert J., and Edward R. Sipay. *How to Increase Reading Ability*. New York: Longman, Inc., 1980, pp. 448–468.

Hood, Joyce. "Sight Words Are Not Going Out of Style." *The Reading Teacher, 30* (January 1977): 379–382.

Ignoffo, Matthew F. "The Thread of Thought: Analogies as a Vocabulary Building Method." *Journal of Reading, 23* (March 1980): 519–521.

Johnson, Dale D., and P. David Pearson. *Teaching Reading Vocabulary*. New York: Holt, Rinehart and Winston, 1978.

Karstadt, Roberta. "Tracing and Writing Activities for Teaching Reading." *The Reading Teacher, 30* (December 1976): 297–298.

McCabe, Don. "220 Sight Words Are Too Many for Students with Memories Like Mine." *The Reading Teacher, 31* (April 1978): 791–793.

Mangieri, John N., and Michael S. Kahn. "Is the Dolch List of 220 Basic Sight Words Irrelevant?" *The Reading Teacher, 30* (March 1977): 649–651.

Otto, Wayne, Robert Rude, and Dixie Lee Spiegel. *How to Teach Reading*. Reading, Massachusetts: Addison-Wesley Publishing Company, Inc., 1979, pp. 133–136.

Pachtman, Andrew B., and James D. Riley. "Teaching the Vocabulary of Mathematics Through Interaction, Exposure, and Structure." *Journal of Reading, 22* (December 1978): 240–244.

Spache, George D., and Evelyn B. Spache. *Reading in the Elementary School*. Boston: Allyn and Bacon, Inc., 1977, Chapter 12.

[13]Elaine M. Kaplan and Anita Tuchman, "Vocabulary Strategies Belong in the Hands of Learners," *Journal of Reading, 24* (October 1980): 32–34.

SUGGESTED ACTIVITIES

1. Obtain a copy of one of the sight word lists that were mentioned in the chapter. Then give this sight word list on an individual basis to a student who is reading at about the second-grade or third-grade level.
2. If possible, try using one of the tracing techniques suggested in the chapter to help a child learn a difficult-to-remember sight word. Was it successful with the child?
3. If your university has a reading clinic, learn to use a tachistoscope.
4. Select a common abstract term, and look it up in a dictionary. How many different meanings did you find that it has?
5. Locate a number of figurative expressions that were not included in the chapter, and have one or several children illustrate both the literal and figurative meanings of each expression.
6. Locate information about your own first name from one of the references included in the chapter.

Improving ability in structural analysis and contextual analysis

Why Was This Better?

Mr. Cohen was in his first year of teaching sixth grade at Golda Meir Academy in a suburban city in the Midwest. After he had been teaching for several months, he noticed that a number of the students in his class were not very adept at using context clues to deduce the meaning of unknown words. He tried using some traditional activity sheets for improving ability in contextual analysis, but he was still rather dissatisfied. He wanted a more interesting way to help his students improve their ability in this very important word identification technique.

After some thought, Mr. Cohen remembered that his college reading instructor had recommended the use of the cloze procedure for improving contextual analysis ability. He also remembered that when the cloze procedure was used for this purpose, a synonym to the deleted word in each case was considered to be acceptable. He then constructed a cloze procedure from a basal reader story at the sixth-grade reading level that his students had not read. This traditional cloze procedure consisted of 250 words with the deletion of every fifth word for a total of fifty deletions. However, Mr. Cohen was careful to keep the first and last sentences of the cloze procedure intact. He then decided to give this procedure only to the students in his above-average reading achievement group.

Mr. Cohen provided his students with the appropriate directions for completing the cloze procedure. He also gave them sufficient time to complete the procedure. However, he was shocked at the reaction of his students to this activity. They found it extremely frustrating and complained loudly about how difficult it was to do. It was not an exaggeration to say that the experiment with the cloze procedure was a complete failure. Because Mr. Cohen wondered what had gone wrong, he decided to telephone his former college reading instructor, Dr. Young, and explain the situation to her.

After listening to Mr. Cohen's problem, Dr. Young suggested that he try a modified variation of the traditional cloze procedure to serve as an introduction before trying to have his students complete the traditional cloze procedure. She suggested that he place all the deleted words in random order at the bottom of the cloze procedure so that the students could select the correct option for each blank space. After several experiences with this version of the cloze procedure, Dr. Young suggested that Mr. Cohen add an initial consonant, consonant blend, or vowel at the beginning of each deletion to provide some clue as to the omitted word. Only then did she feel that the students would be truly ready for the more difficult traditional cloze procedure.

Mr. Cohen tried these suggestions and found them to be very successful. By the end of the school year, a number of the students in his class did enjoy and benefit from completing the many different variations of the cloze procedure if they were on the appropriate reading level.

After reading this chapter, you also will know how to use many different variations of the useful cloze procedure to improve ability in contextual analysis. Some of these variations certainly should be appropriate for the students with whom you may work now and in the future.

A DESCRIPTION OF STRUCTURAL OR MORPHEMIC ANALYSIS

Structural or morphemic analysis may be defined as the use of word structure or word parts to determine the pronunciation and meaning of unknown words encountered during reading. This word identification technique can be very useful in adding words to a student's meaning vocabulary, especially if it is used along with contextual analysis and phonic analysis.

Structural or morphemic analysis is composed of a number of different subskills. One such subskill is attaching a *prefix* or *suffix (affix)* to a *base* or *root word* to form a *derivative.* This word identification technique also deals with *inflections,* which are changes in a word that are made for grammatical reasons. As an example, an inflection occurs when the singular form of the word *ball* is made into the plural form *balls* by the adding of the suffix *s.*

Structural or morphemic analysis also deals with the term *morpheme,* which is the smallest unit of meaning in the English language and may be either free or bound. A *free morpheme* is a group of letters that make up any meaningful word, such as these: *house, play,* or *happy.* On the other hand, a *bound morpheme* is composed of one or several letters that have a meaning but are not able to function in isolation as do words. Some examples of bound morphemes are the *ed* in the word *landed,* the *un* in the word *untie,* and the *s* in the word *trees.*

Some other subskills of structural or morphemic analysis are the understanding of the use of *compound words, syllabication, accent,* and *word origins.* Even though *contractions* are supposed to be one other element of structural analysis, they normally should be learned as sight words, especially at the beginning stages of reading instruction.

The study of useful prefixes, suffixes, word roots, or word origins may be a valuable aspect of structural analysis because this type of study may make it possible to add a number of words to a student's meaning vocabulary. Here is a list of the more common prefixes and their meanings:

Prefix	Meaning	Example
ab	from, away	abnormal
ante	before	antedate

Prefix	Meaning	Example
be	by	bedazzle
com	with, together	composition
de	down, with	dehumidify
dis	apart	disconnect
en	in	enclose
ex	out	export
in	in	inject
in	not	insincere
pre	before	prepaid
post	after	posthumous
pro	before, for	promote
re	again, back	remake
sub	under	submarine
un	not	unhappy

Here is a list of the most common suffixes and their meanings:

Suffix	Meaning	Example
able	indicating a quality	lovable
al	dealing with something	mechanical
ant	having a quality of	conversant
en	made of	wooden
er	one who does	teacher
ful	full of	joyful
hood	state of being	childhood
ion	the act or condition of	perfection
less	without	penniless
ly	in what manner	slowly

You might also be interested to know that the following suffixes are among the most commonly presented ones in the elementary school:

-s	-es
-ed	-ing
-ly	-en
-er	-less
-hood	-ness
-est	-ful

Here is a list of the most common word roots and their meanings:

Root	Meaning	Example
fac, fact, fic	to make or do	factory
mis, mit	to send	missile
mot, mov	to move	motion
par	to get ready	prepare

Root	Meaning	Example
port	to carry	portable
pos, pon	to place, put	position
spect, spic	to look, see	spectator
ven, vent	to come	convention
vid, vis	to see	vision

Structural or morphemic analysis usually is the most useful when it is used in conjunction with contextual analysis and/or phonic analysis. For example, if a student attacks a polysyllabic word structurally, he or she first must be able to decode each of the syllables phonetically and then blend them into a recognizable word that is in his or her meaning vocabulary. After the word has been analyzed both phonetically and structurally, the student then must employ contextual analysis to determine if it makes sense in sentence context.

Some contemporary reading specialists do not think that traditional syllabication is very useful in word identification. One prime example of such a reading specialist is Patrick M. Groff. Groff, for example, believes it generally to be more useful to divide a word into "chunks" of meaning instead of into syllables that exactly match those found in a dictionary. He believes that traditional syllabication probably is more useful in writing than in reading. This author tends to agree with Groff although she would place some emphasis on traditional syllabication, especially as an aid to writing.

Some elements of structural or morphemic analysis can be taught and reinforced near the beginning stages of reading instruction. As an example, such simple suffixes as -s, -ed, and -ing can be added to regular base or root words at the beginning reading level. At this level children also can learn to recognize and syllabicate true simple compound words in which the meaning of the compound word is derived from the combined meanings of the two words of which it is composed. Here are several examples of such true simple compound words: *playhouse, doghouse, cowboy, blueberry,* and *blackbird.*

Some reading specialists recommend that children at the primary-grade level learn the words of which the common contractions are composed. However, I believe that it is generally more useful for children to learn such common contractions as *can't, didn't, don't,* and *I'm* by sight at the beginning reading level. It is very difficult for many students in the primary grades to determine what the omitted letters are in a contraction, and it probably is not worthwhile for most of them. However, a few above-average students in the upper primary grades may enjoy an activity sheet or a game in which they have to match contractions with the words of which they are composed.

Readiness for syllabication also is presented at the first-grade reading level by having the child clap out or tap out the number of syllables in simple polysyllabic words of two or three syllables.

Simple prefixes such as *un-* and *re-* are presented and practiced at the upper-primary-grade reading level. Other useful prefixes are presented and reinforced at the intermediate-grade reading level. Many of the suffixes that were included in this chapter are presented and reinforced at the intermediate-grade reading level.

Syllabication and accent are presented at the upper-primary-grade reading level and refined at the intermediate-grade reading level. Syllabication generalizations usually should be presented by using known words and should be practiced on unknown words. Consistent structural analysis and accent generalizations often are presented and refined at the same levels. Both types of generalizations usually are presented in an inductive manner in which the teacher structures situations to enable the student to discover each of the generalizations in a meaningful way, as is illustrated later in this chapter.

There are a myriad of structural and accent generalizations that can be presented to children. However, I believe the following are perhaps the most useful ones. The accent generalizations included in this list were taken from the following source: *Carol Winkley, "Which Accent Generalizations Are Worth Teaching?"* The Reading Teacher, *20 (December 1966): 219–224, 253.*

1. Each syllable must contain at least one vowel, and the syllable is the unit of pronunciation.
2. When two consonants are located between two vowels, the word is divided between the two consonants (VCCV pattern *mon/key*).
3. When one consonant is located between two vowels, the first syllable usually ends with the vowel, and the second syllable usually begins with the consonant. This makes the vowel in the first syllable long, and that syllable is said to be open (VCV pattern *ta/ble*).
4. A compound word is divided between the two small words that comprise it (*cow/boy*).
5. When a word contains two vowels together, the word is divided between the two vowels unless they form a diphthong (CVVC pattern *cru/el*).
6. Suffixes that begin with a vowel usually form a separate syllable. However, this is not true of *-ed* except when it is preceded by *t* or *d* (*jump/ing*).
7. Prefixes usually form a separate syllable when they are added to a word (*re/make*).
8. Certain letter combinations at the end of words form a final syllable. Some examples are *-ble, -cle, -dle, -gle, -kle, -ple, -tle,* and *-zle* (*tur/tle*).
9. When the first vowel in a word is followed by *ch, sh,* or *th,* these consonant digraphs are never divided when the word is divided into syllables (*dish/es*).

10. When there is no other clue in a two-syllable word, the accent is usually placed on the first syllable (*hap'/py*).
11. In inflected or derived forms of words, the primary accent usually falls on or within the root word (*re/place'*).
12. If *a-, be-, de-, ex-, in-,* or *re-* is the first syllable in a word, it usually is unaccented (*a/long'*).
13. Two vowel letters together in the last syllable of a word may be a clue to the accented final syllable (*im/peach'*).
14. When there are two of the same consonant letters within a word, the syllable before the double consonants usually is accented (*lad'/der*).
15. The primary accent usually occurs on the syllable before the suffixes *-ion, -ity, -ic, -ical, -ian, -ial,* or *-ious,* and on the second syllable before the suffix *-ate* (*tu/i'/tion*).
16. In words of three or more syllables, one of the first two syllables usually is accented (*per/cep'/ti/ble*).

Structural analysis skills can be taught in an inductive or a deductive manner as can phonic analysis skills also. (See Chapter 7.) In the inductive teaching of structural analysis, the teacher may place several examples of a base word on the chalkboard, on chart paper, or on a transparency; and the group of children attempt to discover for themselves how the base word should be altered before the suffix is added. The children then are helped to state the structural analysis generalization in their own words. The most common structural generalizations taught in the upper primary grades are those dealing with dropping the final silent *e* before adding a suffix beginning with a vowel (changing *bake* to *baking*), doubling the final consonant when the base word is a short word containing one vowel before adding the suffix (changing *hop* to *hopping*), and changing *y* to *i* when adding a suffix beginning with a vowel (changing *lady* to *ladies*).

An illustration of the inductive teaching of structural analysis can be this actual classroom incident. Mrs. LaPorte is a second-grade teacher using the basal reader approach who wants to have her above-average reading achievement group derive an important structural generalization in an inductive manner. The structural generalization states that when a word that ends with *y* is preceded by a consonant, the *y* is changed to *i* before adding *-es*.

Before beginning the actual lesson, Mrs. LaPorte wrote the following words on the chalkboard:

baby	babies
pony	ponies
lady	ladies
party	parties
penny	pennies

Mrs. LaPorte then discussed the words with the children in the reading group.

Mrs. LaPorte:	Can one of you read both of these lists of words?
Kathy:	I can. The words are *baby, babies, pony, ponies, lady, ladies, party, parties, penny, pennies.*
Mrs. LaPorte:	That's exactly right. Now look at all of the words in the column on the right. Do any of you see how all of these words are different from the words in the other list?
Jackson:	All of the words in the list on the right side end with *ies.* But all of the words in the other list end with *y.*
Mrs. LaPorte:	What do you suppose happened to all of the words when the suffix *es* was added to them?
Maria:	I think that the *y* was changed to *i* before the *es* was put on.
Mrs. LaPorte:	Do you think that the *y* is changed to *i* in all words before a suffix is added? Look at these words. (Mrs. LaPorte printed the words *turkey, monkey,* and *donkey* on the chalkboard.)
Dave:	No, to those words you just put an *s* after the *y.*
Mrs. LaPorte:	Now look at all of the words. What is the difference between the words in the first list and these three words?
Marcia:	I know. You only change the *y* to *i* when there is a consonant in front of the *y* instead of a vowel.
Mrs. LaPorte:	That's very good, Marcia. Do all of you understand the rule?
Reading Group:	Yes.

HOW TO DIAGNOSE A STUDENT'S COMPETENCY IN STRUCTURAL OR MORPHEMIC ANALYSIS

There are a number of ways that can be used to diagnose a student's competency in the various elements of structural analysis. You can do so by the use of careful teacher observation, structural analysis inventories, diagnostic reading tests, word identification tests, or criterion-referenced tests.

The simplest way of ascertaining a student's strengths and weaknesses in the various elements of structural analysis is by the use of teacher observation with or without a structured checklist. For such an observation, you notice the student's competency in the various elements of structural analysis when he or she is reading aloud, participating in a lesson that stresses structural analysis, or completing a workbook page or an activity sheet that is devoted to structural analysis.

As a supplement or an alternative to teacher observation, you can use a group-administered or an individually administered inventory in structural analysis to attempt to determine a student's strengths and weaknesses in this skill. However, you should regard such an inventory only as an indicator of a student's competency in structural analysis, for it obviously cannot determine the effectiveness with which a student employs structural analysis in an actual reading situation. In any case, such an inventory should be constructed on the appropriate reading level and can be used to evaluate a student's competency in such elements of structural analysis as the following: locating a base or root word in a derivative; locating a prefix or suffix in a derivative; adding a prefix to a base word; adding a suffix to a regular or irregular base word; syllabicating a word; forming a compound word; marking the primary or secondary accent in a word; determining the meaning of an unknown word by using the meaning of a prefix, suffix, or word root; or applying the appropriate structural analysis generalization.

In addition, you can ascertain a student's weaknesses in the structural analysis subskills by using an individually administered or group-administered standardized diagnostic reading test. As such a test also ascertains competency in a number of other reading skills, you should give the student only those subtests that evaluate elements of structural analysis. Although Chapter 17 provides more detail on such tests, here are several diagnostic reading tests that can be used for this purpose:

Durrell Analysis of Reading Difficulty, new ed.
Gates-McKillop Reading Diagnostic Tests
Stanford Diagnostic Reading Tests

In addition, there are a few standardized diagnostic reading tests that are solely devoted to determining ability in the various word identification techniques. A few of these tests evaluate a student's ability in the various elements of structural analysis. Here are two tests that can be used for this purpose:

McCullough Word-Analysis Tests
Sipay Word Analysis Tests

As is explained in more detail in Chapter 17, criterion-referenced or mastery tests also may be useful in trying to determine a student's specific strengths and weaknesses in the various elements of structural analysis. A criterion-referenced test indicates whether or not a student has achieved mastery of a specific reading skill. Although Chapter 17 provides more detail on criterion-referenced tests, here are several of them that can be used to ascertain mastery of the various structural analysis subskills:

Harper & Row Classroom Management System
Individual Pupil Monitoring System—Reading
SRA Diagnosis
Wisconsin Design for Reading Skill Improvement

STRATEGIES AND MATERIALS FOR IMPROVING COMPETENCY IN STRUCTURAL ANALYSIS

There are many interesting strategies and materials that can be used to improve ability in the various structural analysis subskills at both the primary-grade and intermediate-grade levels. As you may imagine, the various basal reader manuals present many suggestions that can be used for presenting and reinforcing structural analysis skills. However, this chapter also contains many additional strategies that can be used for this purpose.

As one example of a strategy that can be used in the early primary grades, have the child discriminate between comparatives by the use of concrete objects. Place sets of objects of three different sizes on a desk or table, and have the child determine which object in each set is *big, bigger,* or *biggest* or which object in each set is *little, littler,* or *littlest.* As another example, you can have the child differentiate between any set of comparisons that can be pictured. Select three pictures that illustrate the concept of *tall, taller,* and *tallest.* Give the child each of these words printed on a separate piece of tagboard or poster board, and have him or her then match the proper label with the proper picture.

Cut pieces of tagboard, and then print a compound word on each one with a marking pen. Then cut each piece apart between the two words that form a compound word with a different pattern, as is shown in Figure 13-1. Place all the puzzle parts in a large brown envelope, and have the child try to reassemble the puzzle and pronounce each compound word either alone or with a partner. Another similar activity that also can be used in the early primary grades is to print a compound word on an object made of tagboard or poster board, representing it as is shown in Figure 13-2. Then cut each piece in half between the two words that form the compound word. Have the child reassemble each puzzle and pronounce the word. Here are some compound words that can be used in this activity: *snowman, doghouse, pancake, birdhouse, airplane, snowflake, cowboy,* or *fireman.*

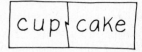

FIGURE 13-1

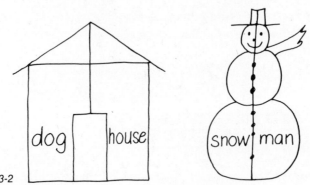

FIGURE 13-2

The following are several activities involving compound words that can be used at about the second-grade reading level. Place a number of words that can form compound words at the top of a duplicating master. Write other words near the bottom, and have the child form the compound words. Here is an example of this type of activity:

black	fire
bed	motor
dog	cow

_____ house
_____ room
_____ berry
_____ boat
_____ girl
_____ man

In another related activity, write some true compound words and some words written together that do not form a compound word on the chalkboard, a transparency, or a duplicating master. Then have the child indicate which words do not form a compound word. Here are several examples that can be used in this activity:

strawberry	treeleaf
sailboat	policeman
cartire	football
hamburgerbun	catfur

As another activity that can be used in the primary grades, tape-record the speech of several students as they are talking. Then transcribe their speech, writing out each of the contractions found on the tape. Have the children follow along on copies of the transcript as the tape is being replayed. Some better readers at this level may want to write in each contraction in the correct place on the transcript. Another interesting activity involving contractions that can be used at about the third-grade reading level is to construct a crossword puzzle for contractions and place it on the chalkboard or a duplicating master.

The words for the crossword puzzle are the two or three words from which the contractions are formed. The answers to the crossword puzzle are the contractions.

Here is another activity that can be used at about the third-grade reading level. Have the child make a number of appropriate base word cards from pieces of tagboard or poster board. Then construct a spinner with suffixes written near the edge. Have each child engaging in this activity spin and attempt to pronounce a derivative by adding the suffix to one of his or her base word cards. If the child can do so, he or she gets a point. After one base word card is used, it cannot be used again in the game. The game ends when one of the players runs out of base word cards.

Word wheels are valuable in the upper primary and lower intermediate grades in reinforcing elements of structural analysis. A word wheel can be made from a circular disk of tagboard or poster board with a smaller disk made from the same material. In one type of word wheel, a prefix is written on the center disk with various base words written on the larger disk. The student then pronounces the different words formed by adding the prefix to each base word as is shown in the accompanying illustration.

A fold-in card also may be used to improve competency in structural analysis. In a fold-in card, a prefix is printed on the left-hand fold of a piece of tagboard, poster board, or construction paper. Then the base word is printed on the right-hand side. If it is possible, an illustration of the word is drawn on the middle part of the piece of tagboard, poster board, or construction paper. The student then places the two folds together and pronounces the new word as is shown in the accompanying illustration.

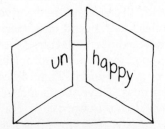

In another activity that is appropriate for the third-grade reading level, have each child in a reading achievement group make cards of tagboard on which the numbers 1, 2, 3, and 4 are printed. Pronounce a number of words, and have the child hold up the correct number card depending upon the number of syllables in each word. As one more activity for this reading level, place base or root words in groups of four on the chalkboard, a transparency, or a duplicating master. Write appropriate suffixes in random order in a column on the right. Then have the child draw a line from each base word to the suffix to make a derivative.

wood	ly
slow	hood
talk	en
child	ing

There are a myriad of strategies that can be used for teaching and reinforcing the various structural analysis subskills in the intermediate grades. The strategies included in the first part of this section are the most appropriate for the lower intermediate grades, whereas those included in the latter part of the section are generally more suited for the upper intermediate grades.

As one activity, print a derivative on each word card in a stack of word cards made from tagboard or poster board. Print the base or root word on the back of each word card. Have several students take part in this activity. The first student takes a card, reads the derivative, and says the base word without looking at the back. If the student is accurate, he or she may keep the card. However, if the student is not accurate, the card must be put at the bottom of the stack. When all of the cards have been used, the student having the most cards is the winner. As one more activity, select three shoe boxes, and label them PREFIXES, BASE WORDS, and SUFFIXES. Make word cards of tagboard or poster board each of which contains a prefix, a base word, or a suffix. Have the student select a card from each shoe box and make a word from the three word parts. The student then should pronounce the word if it is a derivative.

In another activity that is appropriate for the lower-intermediate-grade level, make a spinner with the numerals 1, 2, 3, 4, and 5 on it. Have the students in a group take turns spinning the spinner. When the spinner stops on a numeral, the student must give a word containing that number of syllables. At the end of a specified period of time, the student with the most points is declared the winner. For another activity write base or root words and appropriate prefixes on word cards made of tagboard or poster board. Then place both piles of cards in the center of a table or desk. Have the first student turn over the top prefix card and the top base or root word card. Have the student pronounce the formed derivative and use it in a sentence. If he or she can do so, one point is earned. If he or she cannot do so, another student has a turn. The game is completed when all the prefix cards are used.

In an activity that is appropriate for the fifth- and sixth-grade reading level, have the student write a humorous paragraph or story containing words that have different pronunciations depending on the placement of the accent. These words are called *homographs*. Then have the student read the material aloud, using the wrong pronunciation. Here are some homographs that the student may wish to use: *convict, present, protest, perfect, produce, conduct, rebel, address,* and *subject.* In another fairly similar activity, you can write a number of sentences containing homographs on the chalkboard or on a duplicating master. Then have the student place the accent mark in the proper place in each sentence.

In an activity that may be appropriate for the upper-intermediate-grade level, write prefixes, word roots, and suffixes on a duplicating master. Have the student form as many words as possible using each word part. The student also should define each newly formed word. The student can use the dictionary for this activity. As was stated in Chapter 12, it is very important to present new, crucial vocabulary terms prior to the student's reading of content materials. This presentation may be especially beneficial when the meaning of prefixes and word roots is helpful in determining the meaning of specialized vocabulary terms in such content areas as science and social studies.

A DESCRIPTION OF CONTEXTUAL ANALYSIS

Contextual analysis or context clue usage is a word identification technique in which the reader determines the meaning, and less often the pronunciation, of unknown words by examining the context in which they are found. The context may be that sentence, the adjacent sentences, the paragraph, or even the entire passage. Contextual analysis can also be called the use of semantic or meaning clues as was explained in some detail in Chapter 8.

Several reading specialists have determined that there are several different kinds of context clues. Although their categories of context clues differ to some extent, here is one classification that I have found to be useful:

> *Experience clues.* The reader uses his or her own background of experiences to determine the meaning of the unknown word.
> *Association clues.* The reader tries to associate the unknown word with a known word. As an example, the man was as *ravenous* as a lion.

Synonym clues. There is a synonym to the unknown word in the sentence to explain it. For example, the *ancient* house was so old that it looked as if it were going to fall down.

Summary clues. Several sentences are used that summarize the meaning of the unknown word.

Comparison or contrast clues. There is a comparison or contrast to the unknown word in the sentence or paragraph that gives its meaning.

Previous contact clues. Readers can determine the meaning of the unknown word from a previous contact with a similar word.[1]

Contextual analysis should be presented as early as the kindergarten level, when the teacher orally gives a sentence with an omitted word. The teacher then asks the children to supply a word orally that makes sense in that sentence. At the primary-grade reading level, children read sentences and underline the word that makes sense in each sentence. The following two sentences are examples of this activity. In the first sentence, you can notice how the initial consonant is used in combination with context to determine the unknown word.

Maria would like to go to the z _____ with her family next week.

      lake
      zoo
      museum

I would like to buy my mother a _____ for her birthday.

      ring
      road
      ride

Students should be taught in the elementary school that contextual analysis is not merely guessing at the meaning of unknown words. Instead, it is a calculated estimation of the meaning of unknown words that demands inferential thinking on the reader's part. In the opinion of most reading specialists, it is an extremely valuable word identification technique, especially when it is used in combination with an initial consonant, consonant blend, or consonant digraph. Indeed, it well may be the most useful word identification technique.

It is important to remember that a very few students make too much use of contextual analysis and, therefore, can be described as *context readers.* This type of student usually uses no other word identification technique effectively but simply guesses wildly at the meaning of unknown words from context. Such a student undoubtedly needs instruction and reinforcement in the other word identification techniques—such as sight word recognition, phonic analysis, and structural analysis—and in reading carefully for details.

---

[1]Harold L. Herber, *Teaching Reading in Content Areas* (Englewood Cliffs, New Jersey: Prentice-Hall, Inc., 1967), p. 163.

In addition, it is important to remember that contextual analysis is not a very effective word identification technique if the reading material contains too many unknown words. When the student is being taught to use contextual analysis, you must provide him or her with reading materials on the independent reading level. Usually, such reading material should not contain more than two or three unknown words in each one hundred running words.

A DESCRIPTION OF PICTURE CLUES

For the sake of convenience, picture clues are also described in this chapter. *Picture clues* are used when readers determine the pronunciation and meaning of an unknown word by examining a picture found near the materials that they are reading. Picture clues are used quite often at the beginning stages of reading, especially in the basal reader approach.

The typical beginning basal reader contains many, many pictures. The teacher must be careful that the beginning reader does not rely too heavily on picture clues for word identification. It is very important that the child learn to identify the words and not just rely on the pictures for word identification. If this is done, the use of picture clues can do the child a disservice.

Although picture clues receive less emphasis as the child progresses through the elementary school, they may be of value even to secondary school students and adults. For example, picture clues may be especially helpful in such content areas as science, home economics, and industrial technology. They may enable the reader to follow the directions for doing or making something.

HOW TO DIAGNOSE A STUDENT'S COMPETENCY IN CONTEXTUAL ANALYSIS

There are a number of means that can be used to diagnose a student's competency in contextual analysis. Undoubtedly, the simplest way is to determine a student's oral reading in a reading achievement group, an individual reading conference, or the total-class setting. If you determine from careful observation that a student usually substitutes words for unknown words that make sense in sentence context, he or she probably has a good understanding of the usefulness of context clues. As an example, if a student substitutes the word *house* for *home,* he or she has made good use of sentence context. However, if the student substitutes the word *horse* for *house,* he or she has not considered context but instead has substituted a word with a similar visual appearance.

You can construct a contextual analysis inventory to determine a student's competency in this word identification technique. Often a contextual analysis inventory is a written test that requires a student to underline one of several options that make sense in sentence context.

It is possible to diagnose competency in contextual analysis by determining if a student can recognize words in sentence context more effectively than in a word list. The majority of students are able to do this. To make this determination, present a list of words that the student can pronounce. Take note of how many of these words the student was able to recognize at sight. Later, present each of these same words in sentences, and ask the student to read each of the sentences aloud. Then take note of how many of the same words he or she was able to pronounce correctly in sentence context. If the student can pronounce more of the words correctly in sentence context, he or she undoubtedly has a fairly good competency in contextual analysis.

You can use variations of the *cloze procedure* to ascertain a student's probable competency in contextual analysis. The variations of the cloze procedure are a useful kind of diagnostic device that can be used in an attempt to determine a student's comprehension ability and contextual analysis ability. The different variations of the cloze procedure will be explained in detail later in this chapter. However, in brief, to formulate a cloze procedure, you delete every *n*th word from a written passage of about 250 words. The *n*th can be every fifth word, eighth word, or tenth word. You do not omit proper nouns from the cloze procedure, and you type the first and last sentences of the passage with no deletions. Have the student read the passage silently and fill in each blank space with a word that makes sense. When using the cloze procedure to determine probable ability in contextual analysis, encourage the student to complete each blank with a word that makes sense in the passage. Although no objective data exist in this area, if a student completes about 80 percent or more of the omitted words in a cloze procedure with words that make sense, you can conclude that he or she probably has competency in contextual analysis.

There are few standardized diagnostic reading tests that can be used to ascertain a student's competency in contextual analysis. However, here is one such test:

Stanford Diagnostic Reading Tests

As is explained in more detail in Chapter 17, criterion-referenced or mastery tests often are useful in ascertaining a student's competency in contextual analysis. Although Chapter 17 contains a more comprehensive list, here are a few examples of criterion-referenced tests:

Criterion Reading
Fountain Valley Teacher Support System in Reading
Prescriptive Reading Inventory
SRA Diagnosis
Wisconsin Design for Reading Skill Improvement

STRATEGIES AND MATERIALS FOR IMPROVING COMPETENCY IN CONTEXTUAL ANALYSIS

There are a myriad of useful strategies and materials that can be used to improve ability in contextual analysis and in picture clue usage at both the primary-grade and intermediate-grade levels. The basal reader manuals provide many valuable suggestions that can be used for presenting and reinforcing these two word identification skills. However, this chapter provides many additional useful strategies that can be used for this purpose.

There are a number of strategies that can be used for improving ability in contextual analysis at the beginning reading level. As one example, provide the child with some pictures from magazines or catalogs. Read some sentences aloud, or record them on tape, omitting one word in each sentence that can be completed by one of the pictures. Have the child show the picture from the group of pictures that takes the place of the omitted word. In another interesting activity for the beginning reading level, have a group of children dictate a language experience chart (see Chapter 4) and use rebuses (pictures) in place of some of the difficult, but interesting, vocabulary terms. This activity can be varied by providing rebuses in recipes for cooking or baking that are placed on chart paper. Such cooking or baking activities as baking cookies, frosting cupcakes, making peanut brittle, making deviled eggs, making cocoa, or making a gingerbread man lend themselves to this activity.

In several other activities that can be used at about the first-grade reading level, you can select sentences from dictated language experience stories and print each sentence on a strip of tagboard or poster board, omitting one word. Then print each omitted word on a word card. Have the child place the proper word card in each sentence strip. You can make slits in each sentence strip if you wish. In another activity, you can print a short passage on the appropriate reading level on a transparency and place masking tape over the words that are to be omitted. You should not omit more than one word out of every ten words. Then have a small group of children guess each deleted word. After the guess is made, remove the masking tape, and have the children compare the actual word with their guesses.

In an interesting activity for use at about the second-grade reading level, place each word in a sentence on a large card, and give each child in the group a card. Have the children stand in a line so that the sentence demonstrates syntax. Have a child from the large group read the formed sentence aloud. If the sentence can have another syntax, have the children change places, and have another child read the newly formed sentence. In another activity at about the same reading level, select a trade book at the child's independent reading level, and tape small paper flaps over some of the words in the book in a random order. Then have the child read the trade book, guess at each of the covered words, and lift each flap to see the actual covered word.

The tape recorder is a very interesting device to indicate to a student at almost any reading level if he or she is using context effectively. To do this, have the child read a passage orally that you tape-record. Even though the passage should contain several unknown words, it should not contain more than one unknown word in forty running words. Later the tape recording should be played back, and the child should be helped to determine if he or she used sentence context effectively or merely substituted words that made no sense in sentence context.

To illustrate the effectiveness of using only context for children at the upper-primary-grade level, write a number of sentences on the chalkboard, a transparency, or a duplicating master in which only context indicates the omitted word. Here are several sentences that can illustrate this type of activity:

> On a nice, sunny day the sky is always _____. (blue)
> In June the color of grass is _____. (green)

Variations of the *cloze procedure* are an excellent way of improving competency in contextual analysis from about the second-grade level on. The basic cloze procedure that was developed by Wilson L. Taylor in 1953 is based upon the principle of *closure,* which is the desire of a person to complete a blank space in a larger pattern.[2] There are many variations of the cloze procedure that will be explained and illustrated later in this section.

Undoubtedly, the most common variation is what can be called the *traditional cloze procedure.* To construct a traditional cloze procedure, select a passage of about 250 words from a basal reader, supplementary reading material, a trade book, or a content textbook on the appropriate reading level. Then type the passage on a stencil or duplicating master, omitting every *n*th word unless that word is a proper noun. Every tenth word usually is deleted at the primary-grade reading level, every eighth word usually is deleted at the intermediate-grade reading level, and every fifth word usually is deleted at the upper-grade reading level. The first and last sentences of the passage are typed without deletion. In the traditional cloze procedure, the length of each blank space should be about fifteen spaces long so that the length of the blank is not a clue to the length of the deleted word. Each student then is given as much time as is needed to complete the cloze procedure independently or with a partner or partners. When any variation of the cloze procedure is used to improve ability in contextual analysis, any synonym to a deleted word that makes sense in sentence context should be considered correct.

A number of students in the elementary school have found the traditional cloze procedure rather difficult to complete if they have had no introduction to this type of technique previously. Therefore, I recommend that the traditional cloze procedure be used only at the intermediate-grade reading level and above and only with students who have completed other, easier variations of cloze as are described later. In any case, here is a brief illustration of what a traditional cloze procedure may look like at the eighth-grade reading level:

Ike

Dwight David Eisenhower, nicknamed Ike, was one of the exceptionally outstanding military geniuses of American history as well as a popular President. He was born in Dennison Texas, _____ 1890 but grew up _____ Abilene, Kansas, with a _____ mother and father and five _____.[3]

A very useful variation of the cloze procedure combines practice in contextual analysis and phonic analysis. In this variation the initial letter or the first two letters of each omitted word are placed at the beginning of each blank space. These phonic analysis elements then give the reader a clue to the omitted word, which is helpful in deducing the omitted word. Here is a brief excerpt from this type of cloze procedure:

A Walk for Mankind

The people in our city Walk for Mankind every spring. Each year many children and a few gr_____-_____ participate in this walk. Everyone has a v_____ good time, and they also are able t_____ raise a large amount of money to h_____ poor children in all parts of the w_____.[4]

---

[3]Wilma H. Miller, *Reading Diagnosis Kit* (West Nyack, New York: Center for Applied Research in Education, 1978), p. 274.

[4]Wilma H. Miller, *The Reading Activities Handbook* (New York: Holt, Rinehart and Winston, 1980), p. 205.

In another variation that is suitable for use when the cloze procedure is first being introduced, all the deleted words in the procedure are placed in columns in random order at the bottom of the sheet containing the passage. The student then selects the proper words for each blank space from these words. Another variation combines meaning clues and word length clues because each omitted word is replaced by a typewritten space as long as the omitted word. It is a fairly difficult version.

There are several other versions of the cloze procedure that are fairly difficult and are most useful at the intermediate-grade reading level and above. In four of these versions, deleted nouns, deleted verbs, deleted adjectives, or deleted adverbs can be used. In each of these cases the deletions are made in a random manner. The following cloze procedure with random deletions of nouns may illustrate how these four variations can be used:

The Life of Coretta King

The life of Coretta King should serve as an inspiration to all people because her life clearly illustrates how a sense of purpose can overcome all hardships and fears. Although Coretta is the widow of the slain civil rights leader Martin Luther King, Jr., she also is an admirable _____ in her own right.

Coretta King grew up in Perry County, Alabama, long before the _____ for black equality had even begun. She knew racial prejudice in her early life in many ways. As an example, once her family's rented _____ was burned to the ground because her hardworking father was trying to compete with some white truck owners.[5]

Florence G. Schoenfeld suggested some rather unique instructional uses of the cloze procedure in a recent article. As an introduction to the cloze procedure if the students are very young, Schoenfeld recommended that sensorimotor experiences first be used such as a picture puzzle with one piece removed. She next suggested that visual representations of whole structures from which a part has been deleted be used such as a picture with one feature of the face left blank or a familiar word with one letter erased. Only later should oral cloze and written cloze exercises be used, according to Schoenfeld.[6]

In another recent article, Donald D. Neville and Rudolph R. Hoffman studied the effect of personalized cloze passages. These stories were written to include the name of the reader and names of people and places familiar to the reader. Such personalization improved the

[5]Miller, *The Reading Activities Handbook*, p. 217.

[6]Florence G. Schoenfeld, "Instructional Uses of the Cloze Procedure," *The Reading Teacher, 34* (November 1980): 147–151.

comprehension of the cloze procedure and probably would improve contextual analysis ability as well.[7]

In any case, any variation of the cloze procedure may lend itself to the instructional procedure recommended by Robert Bortnick and Genevieve S. Lopardo. They suggested that these steps be used:

1. The student should read the entire cloze passage silently.
2. The student should then reread the cloze passage, trying to complete each blank space.
3. During a subsequent class discussion, the students can give their reasons for choosing the words they used to fill in the blanks. Each word that makes sense in the sentence should be considered correct.
4. The students then should compare the words they selected with the original passage.
5. During a class discussion, all the students should compare both passages. The teacher can direct the discussion to focus on whether the meaning of the passage was changed by certain responses.[8]

Another variation of the cloze procedure that is valuable and has been developed recently is called *clozentropy*. This procedure was described in a recent article by Daniel R. Hittleman. Clozentropy is a variation of the cloze procedure that does not compare the reader's responses to the original material. Rather, the responses are compared against all the responses written in the blanks by a criterion group of students. This procedure states that a word in a blank is correct to the degree that the members of the criterion group agree that it is correct.[9]

There are several additional strategies that can be used to improve competency in contextual analysis at the intermediate-grade level. As one example, place a number of familiar proverbs or sayings on a duplicating master, omitting one word in each proverb. Then have the child complete each proverb in writing. Here are several examples that can be used on such an activity sheet:

The grass is always _____ on the other side of the fence.

An _____ a day keeps the doctor away.

The early _____ catches the worm.

---

[7]Donald D. Neville and Rudolph R. Hoffman, "The Effect of Personalized Stories on the Cloze Comprehension of Seventh Grade Retarded Readers," *Journal of Reading, 24* (March 1981): 475–478.

[8]Robert Bortnick and Genevieve S. Lopardo, "An Instructional Application of the Cloze Procedure," *Journal of Reading, 16* (January 1973): 296–300.

[9]Daniel R. Hittleman, "Readability, Readability Formulas, and Cloze: Selecting Instructional Materials," *Journal of Reading, 22* (November 1978): 117–122.

Analogies are another valuable way of improving ability in contextual analysis. Incomplete analogies can be placed on the chalkboard, a transparency, or a duplicating master. There are several different variations that analogies can take. Here are two of them:

> flock: geese—school: (fish)
>
> Shoes are to feet as gloves are to _____. (hands)

In an activity that is undoubtedly appropriate only for good readers in the upper intermediate grades, write a number of sentences on the chalkboard or on a transparency, each of which contains the same unknown word. You then can help the students in a group try to deduce this word's meaning from its use in the various contexts. Here is an example of such an activity:

> That man has always been kind, *magnanimous,* and giving.
>
> Even though she was hurt badly, Mrs. James was *magnanimous* toward her attacker and refused to press charges.
>
> I am neither *magnanimous* nor forgiving.

STRATEGIES FOR IMPROVING COMPETENCY IN PICTURE CLUE USAGE

There are a few ways in which picture clue usage can be improved. For example, the picture interpretation activity included in Chapter 3 can be used to enable children to use picture clues effectively. Children can learn to interpret the pictures found in trade books and beginning basal readers critically and creatively. At the beginning stages of reading instruction, the basal reader teachers' manuals can be followed to help children make effective use of picture (context) clues.

When a content textbook is being used by students in the upper primary or intermediate grades, the teacher should help the students recognize the potential usefulness of the illustrations contained in such textbooks. As was stated earlier, picture clues may be especially valuable in such content areas as science, home economics, and industrial technology.

SELECTED REFERENCES

Blachowicz, Camille L. Z. "Cloze Activities for Primary Readers." *The Reading Teacher, 31* (December 1977): 300–302.

Burns, Paul C., and Betty D. Roe. *Reading Activities for Today's Elementary School.* Chicago: Rand McNally College Publishing Company, 1979, pp. 64–65, 71–76.

Farr, Roger, and Nancy Roser. *Teaching a Child to Read.* New York: Harcourt Brace Jovanovich, Inc., 1979, Chapter 5 and pp. 225–236.

Frank, Richard. "Context and Reading Acquisition." *Journal of Reading, 24* (October 1980): 11–15.

Gipe, Joan P. "Use of a Relevant Context Helps Kids Learn New Word Meanings." *The Reading Teacher, 33* (January 1980): 398–402.

Grant, Patricia L. "The Cloze Procedure as an Instructional Device." *Journal of Reading, 22* (May 1979): 699–705.

Greathouse, Larry J., and Barbara J. Neal. "Letter Cloze Will Conquer Contractions." *The Reading Teacher, 30* (November 1976): 173–176.

Karlin, Robert. *Teaching Elementary Reading.* New York: Harcourt Brace Jovanovich, Inc., 1980, pp. 249–253, 269–278.

Lapp, Diane, and James Flood. *Teaching Reading to Every Child.* New York: Macmillan Publishing Company, Inc., 1983.

Lee, Joyce W. "Increasing Comprehension Through Use of Context Clue Categories." *Journal of Reading, 22* (December 1978): 259–262.

McCabe, Patrick P. "Give Readers a B. O. P. P." *Journal of Reading, 23* (December 1979): 199.

Marino, Jacqueline L. "Cloze Passages: Guidelines for Selection." *Journal of Reading, 24* (March 1981): 479–483.

Miller, Wilma H. *The Reading Activities Handbook.* New York: Holt, Rinehart and Winston, 1980, Chapters 4, 5.

Propst, Ivan K., Jr., and Richard B. Baldauf, Jr. "Use Matching Cloze Tests for Elementary ESL Students." *The Reading Teacher, 32* (March 1979): 683–690.

SUGGESTED ACTIVITIES

1. Examine several sets of contemporary basal readers. How many differences in the presentation sequence of the structural analysis skills did you notice in the various basal readers at the same grade level?
2. Construct several compound word puzzles as illustrated in the chapter.
3. Construct a word wheel as described in the chapter.
4. If possible, visit an elementary classroom, and observe the teaching of a lesson in structural analysis or contextual analysis.
5. Construct one of the variations of the cloze procedure that were described in the chapter. If possible, administer it to an elementary-school child at the appropriate reading level, and evaluate his or her competency in contextual analysis as determined by this device.

Developing ability
in comprehension

What Did She Learn?

Janey was a student in Sister Mary Benedict's sixth-grade class at Holy Trinity School in a large city in the Midwest. She had been given the assignment of reading a trade book (library book) of her own choice and preparing some type of creative oral book report about it. Because she liked studying history very much, Janey chose a popular trade book about Mary Todd Lincoln. She enjoyed reading the book a great deal and was especially interested in the part about how Abraham Lincoln had loved a young woman named Ann Rutledge in New Salem, Illinois, and how he had grieved very much when she died. Janey also was interested to learn that the book stated that Lincoln had never really loved his wife, Mary Todd Lincoln, and that she had always been very difficult to live with.

Janey prepared an interesting book report for her class in which she pretended to be the character of Ann Rutledge. In her report she told about how much Abraham Lincoln cared for her. The sixth-grade class enjoyed the report so much that they clapped when it was finished.

However, later Sister Benedict talked informally with Janey about her book report. She told her that some historians do not believe that Lincoln ever really loved Ann Rutledge but rather thought of her as a very close friend and grieved when she died because of that. She also told her that Ann Rutledge had been engaged at that time to another man. She further said that some historians believed that Lincoln did indeed love his wife, Mary,

although it was true that she sometimes was rather difficult. Sister Benedict then suggested to Janey that she consult some other sources about Lincoln, Mary Todd Lincoln, and Ann Rutledge to see if she could locate the facts about this incident. Janey then decided to read several other trade books about this period of history, portions of some history textbooks, and several encyclopedia articles about Lincoln and his wife.

After about a week, Janey told Sister Benedict that she had indeed found out that Ann Rutledge probably was only a very close friend of Lincoln's. She also said that the story about his loving her probably was a myth begun by a man named William Herndon after Lincoln's death because Herndon never had liked Mary Todd Lincoln. Janey also said that most historians believed that Lincoln had indeed loved his wife.

Janey then asked Sister Benedict for the opportunity to report her new findings to the class, and she did so very well. She concluded her report by saying how surprised she was that a person cannot always believe what is found in a book. Before that time, she said that she always thought everything found in books was true.

After reading this chapter, you will understand why it is so very important to teach students in the elementary school to evaluate what they read critically. Even many adults believe that everything found in books is completely accurate. This is why it is very crucial that critical reading skills be taught effectively in contemporary elementary schools.

A DESCRIPTION OF
LITERAL COMPREHENSION

Comprehension or understanding of what is read is the most important aspect of the reading process. The vast majority of reading specialists consider reading without comprehension to be not really reading but instead "verbalism" or "word-calling." Comprehension of what is read should receive much stress from the beginning stages of reading instruction.

Different reading specialists have classified comprehension in different ways. Although these systems of classification vary somewhat, there also is some overlap between them. As was explained briefly in Chapter 1, I classify comprehension into the following four levels: literal, interpretive, critical, and creative. Other reading specialists call these levels literal, interpretive, and applied. The authors of a recent article classified reading comprehension into the following five levels: association, categorization, seriation, integration, and extension.[1] One of the purposes of classifying comprehension questions probably is to help teachers be sure that they are giving sufficient emphasis to all the various levels of comprehension in their teaching of reading.

It also is important to note at the outset that comprehension of what is read at any level requires that the student possess a good meaning vocabulary and adequate competency in the word identification techniques of sight word recognition, contextual analysis, structural analysis, and phonic analysis. If this is the case, many aspects of literal comprehension are quite easy for most students to master.

The lowest level of reading comprehension is called either *literal* or *factual comprehension* or *recall*. Literal comprehension is the level of understanding upon which interpretive comprehension, critical reading, and creative reading are based. It is the level of comprehension at which the reader uses no analysis while responding. Literal comprehension can be related to the knowledge or translation level of the *Taxonomy of Educational Objectives,* a way in which intellectual processes are categorized in education today.[2]

There are two different levels of literal comprehension. The lower level of the two sometimes is called *reproduction*. At the reproduction level the reader simply reproduces or parrots the words of the author while making a response to the material. However, the higher level

---

[1]Doris C. Crowell and Katheryn Hu-pei Au, "A Scale of Questions to Guide Comprehension Instruction," *The Reading Teacher, 34* (January 1981): 389–393.

[2]Benjamin S. Bloom and David R. Krathwohl, *Taxonomy of Educational Objectives,* Handbook I: *Cognitive Domain* (New York: David McKay Co., Inc., 1956).

of literal comprehension may be called *translation*. At this level the reader paraphrases the writer's words while responding, but no true analysis is involved with the response.

As an attempt to clarify literal comprehension, you should find it helpful to examine the following literal comprehension questions. They were constructed from a story called "A Special Day" from a basal reader at the third reader level. Very briefly, this story concerns several children in Texas who celebrate the Mexican Independence Day. In this celebration, the children are trying to retain their Mexican heritage although they live in the United States. Here are the questions at the literal level:

What were the names of the two girls in the story?

How long was Texas a free country?

What did Anita like best about the Mexican Independence Day?

How old was Rosa in this story?

From whom had Rosa received the costume that she wore?[3]

Literal comprehension is composed of a number of subskills in addition to the subskill of responding to questions at the reproduction and translation levels. One such subskill is placing a number of steps in correct sequential order. Another important subskill is that of reading and following directions. Reading to follow directions is a fairly difficult skill for some students in the elementary school to master, and indeed it also is difficult for a number of adults. However, it is a very important and practical reading skill.

Another element of literal comprehension is that of locating a directly stated main idea in a paragraph. Many, but not all, paragraphs contain one central idea or thought, and this thought sometimes is in the form of a topic sentence located at the beginning of the paragraph, the end of the paragraph, or near the mdidle of the paragraph. A related subskill is that of finding the significant details in a paragraph. These important details often clarify or contrast the directly stated main idea in that paragraph. The location of irrelevant or unimportant details in the paragraph is one more subskill of literal comprehension. Such irrelevant details do not add in any way to the information found in the paragraph.

All types of *who, what, when, where,* and *how* questions also are considered to be at the literal level of comprehension. One other subskill of literal comprehension is the understanding of sentence structure and sentence parts.

---

[3]Carol Childress and Kathleen Much, "A Very Special Day," *Secrets and Surprises* (New York: Macmillan Publishing Company, Inc., 1980), pp. 74–79.

Literal comprehension should be stressed from the earliest stages of reading instruction, when the teacher asks the child questions about the material that he or she has heard or that he or she has read. Literal comprehension questions should receive decreasing stress as the student progresses through the elementary school into the secondary school. Quite often, elementary teachers ask too many literal questions at the expense of interpretive and critical questions. For example, Frank J. Guszak recorded about 2,000 questions in second-grade, fourth-grade, and sixth-grade classrooms. Guszak found that teachers mainly asked literal comprehension questions, although the percentage of such questions decreased from about *67* percent in second grade to about *48* percent in both fourth and sixth grades. He found that even the critical questions that were asked often required only a *yes* or *no* response instead of a rationale for the response.[4] However, it is important to remember that the higher levels of comprehension always are based upon comprehending at the literal level. In addition, students sometimes must respond at the literal level in such content areas as science, home economics, industrial technology, and physical education.

You also should remember that literal comprehension questions are easy for a teacher both to construct and to evaluate. This is one reason why they are used so often. Answering a literal comprehension question is an example of a *convergent-type activity* because there usually is only one correct answer for each question.

Children in the primary grades can receive rudimentary instruction in placing a number of steps in correct sequential order. For example, a child can retell a story in correct sequence that has been told or read or can place a number of cut-apart comic strip frames in correct sequence. Children at this level also can receive some instruction in learning to read and follow directions. For example, oral directions that must be carried out can first be given to the child whereas later the child can read and carry out one-step directions or directions with several steps. However, both of these elements of literal comprehension should be refined and extended at the intermediate-grade reading level.

Locating directly stated main ideas, locating significant details, and noting irrelevant details can be first introduced at the upper-primary-grade reading level. However, most of the instruction and reinforcement of these elements of literal comprehension should take place at the intermediate-grade reading level. There are many strategies that can be used to improve ability in these elements of literal comprehension as are suggested later in this chapter.

---

[4]Frank J. Guszak, "Teacher Questioning and Reading," *The Reading Teacher, 21* (December 1967): 227–234.

A DESCRIPTION OF INTERPRETIVE COMPREHENSION

A higher level of comprehension is *interpretive* or *inferential comprehension*. This is a level of understanding in which analysis is required on the reader's part while responding. Interpretive comprehension corresponds to the interpretation or extrapolation levels of the *Taxonomy of Educational Objectives,* a manner in which intellectual processes are classified in contemporary education.[5]

In an attempt to clarify interpretive comprehension, it may be helpful if you examine the following interpretive comprehension questions that were constructed from the third-grade basal reader story that was discussed earlier in this chapter. Here are the questions at the interpretive level:

Why would it be a good idea to have dancers from Mexico City come for the celebration of the Mexican Independence Day in Texas?

Why do you think that Texas wanted to join the United States and not be a free country?

Why do you think that Anita had to be nine years old to wear her grandmother's dress?

Why do you think that more than one prize had to be given at the celebration?

Why do you think it was important for Rosa and Anita to remember the country that their family came from?[6]

One important aspect of interpretive comprehension is responding to questions at the analysis level. Such responses include interpreting what is read, inferring from what is read, reading between the lines, and drawing conclusions and generalizations. Additional subskills of interpretive comprehension are summarizing what is read, predicting the outcome, sensing the author's mood and purpose, and understanding such patterns of writing as cause-effect and comparison-contrast.

Interpretive comprehension also includes the subskill of determining the implied main idea of a paragraph. A number of paragraphs do not contain a single, directly stated main idea that the reader can easily find. Instead, the implied main idea must be determined by synthesizing much of the information that is found in the paragraph. Determining an implied main idea in a paragraph is much more difficult for most students than is locating a directly stated main idea. In fact, a number of adult readers are not able to infer the implied main idea in a paragraph.

---

[5]Bloom and Krathwohl, *Taxonomy.*

[6]Childress and Much, "A Very Special Day."

Another subskill of interpretive comprehension is determining the main idea in a longer selection that consists of many paragraphs. An additional subskill of interpretive comprehension is understanding the literal meaning of figurative language such as similes and metaphors.

Most children who have good word identification techniques and a good meaning vocabulary can become quite competent in responding at the interpretive level. However, it is somewhat more difficult for slow-learning students to do this because interpretive comprehension does require some degree of abstract intellectual ability.

Interpretive comprehension can be stressed to some extent at the beginning stages of reading instruction when children respond to interpretive questions within the limits of their experiential background to do so. However, it should receive increased emphasis as the student progresses through the primary grades into the intermediate grades. Many of the comprehension questions that are used at the intermediate-grade reading level should be of the interpretive type. You will find that interpretive questions are fairly easy to construct. They often are questions of the "why" type. However, interpretive comprehension questions are not always easy to evaluate because there may be more than one correct, logical answer to a question. Any response that the student can justify in a logical manner should be considered correct. Responding at the interpretive level is often a *divergent activity*.

Children in the primary grades can learn to predict the outcome by an activity such as predicting the story content from reading the title. They also are able to sense the author's moods when writing a short selection, a story, or an entire book. Children at this level also can briefly summarize a reading selection in either an oral or a written form. However, much of the refinement of these skills must be made at the intermediate-grade reading level. The skill of locating the implied main idea and the skill of noting organizational patterns must be presented and reinforced at the intermediate-grade reading level. The determination of the main idea of a longer selection normally also is presented at this level. You will find many strategies to improve ability in all the elements of interpretive comprehension later in this chapter.

SOME CONCLUDING REMARKS ABOUT BOTH LITERAL AND INTERPRETIVE COMPREHENSION

As was stated earlier, comprehension most certainly is the most important aspect of the reading process. However, it also is a very complex aspect of the reading process. Therefore, it has not been studied as extensively in the past as have other less complex aspects of reading such as phonic analysis. Today, however, researchers are beginning to study comprehension more extensively than was the case in the past.

In any event, in 1944, Frederick B. Davis conducted a pioneer research study in which he attempted to ascertain the major components of reading comprehension. Davis discovered that comprehension is composed of the ability to select the appropriate meaning for a word or phrase in context, the ability to select the main idea of a passage, the ability to follow the organization of a passage, the ability to answer questions that are specifically answered in the passage, the ability to paraphrase answers from a passage, the ability to draw inferences from a passage, and the ability to recognize literary devices.[7]

Contemporary research in comprehension now includes the study of the comprehension of story structure, the drawing of inferences, the attempt to relate background knowledge to the reading, the integration of sentences, the testing of hypotheses, and reading as a process of searching for information. Many of the contemporary researchers in reading comprehension are not reading specialists, but rather psychologists who have chosen to study reading comprehension. It is also interesting to note that a research center devoted entirely to reading was established by the National Institute of Education in the 1970s, and its major focus was to be comprehension in the middle grades. Undoubtedly, comprehension as a complex aspect of the reading process will continue to be studied quite extensively in the future.[8]

Another interesting finding about reading comprehension has recently been reported by Dolores Durkin of the University of Illinois. She studied the teaching of comprehension quite extensively by observation in elementary classrooms. She discovered that teachers apparently do very little in the way of teaching comprehension. Instead, they spend much of the time dealing with comprehension by testing competency in it. Durkin recommended that teachers spend considerably less time in testing comprehension and much more time in teaching it. She considered that the effective teaching of comprehension should be of primary concern in the teaching of reading in the future.[9]

---

[7]Frederick B. Davis, "Fundamental Factors in Comprehension in Reading," *Psychometrika, 21* (September 1944): 185–197.

[8]John T. Guthrie, "The 1970s' Comprehension Research," *The Reading Teacher, 33* (April 1980): 880–882.

[9]Dolores Durkin, "What Classroom Observation Reveals about Reading Comprehension," *Reading Research Quarterly, 14* (Summer 1978–79): 481–533.

HOW TO DIAGNOSE COMPETENCY IN LITERAL COMPREHENSION AND INTERPRETIVE COMPREHENSION

There are a number of ways of diagnosing a student's competency in both literal comprehension and interpretive comprehension. As is explained in more detail later, this can be done by using teacher observation, several types of standardized reading tests, criterion-referenced devices, and informal inventories.

As is true of most other reading skills, the easiest way to diagnose a student's ability in either literal comprehension or interpretive comprehension is by the use of teacher observation. Teacher observation can occur during a reading achievement group, during an individual or group reading conference, or after a student has read a content assignment. Some teachers prefer to aid their observation by the use of a checklist. In any case, when you are observing a student's competency in literal comprehension, you should focus on his or her ability to respond to factual questions, to distinguish sequential order, to read and follow directions, and to lcoate directly stated main ideas and significant details. When you are observing the student's ability in interpretive comprehension, you note his or her ability to respond to questions that require inferencing, to predict outcomes, to summarize, to sense the author's mood and purpose, and to locate implied main ideas.

You can also use various subtest scores on standardized survey reading tests or achievement tests in an attempt to ascertain a student's literal and/or interpretive comprehension ability. Although it varies somewhat on different tests, normally you examine a student's score on a sentence comprehension or paragraph comprehension subtest to make this type of determination. You must note if the questions on any subtest mainly assess literal comprehension ability or also assess interpretive comprehension ability. In the past, a number of the questions on such standardized reading tests were of the literal type although now there are more interpretive comprehension questions on such tests. Chapter 17 describes many such tests in more detail. However, here is a brief list of standardized survey reading and achievement tests:

Gates-MacGinitie Reading Tests
Iowa Silent Reading Tests
Metropolitan Achievement Tests: Reading
Stanford Achievement Tests: Reading

As is explained in Chapter 17, there are several diagnostic reading tests that also can be used to ascertain a student's ability in literal comprehension. Two good examples are the following:

Diagnostic Reading Scales, rev. ed.
Durrell Analysis of Reading Difficulty, new ed.

There is one very good group of standardized diagnostic reading tests that can be useful in assessing ability in both literal and interpretive comprehension:

Stanford Diagnostic Reading Tests

As is also discussed in Chapter 17, an oral reading test can be used to determine literal comprehension ability because the questions included on such a test always are at the literal level. Here are the two most commonly used oral reading tests:

Gilmore Oral Reading Test
Gray Oral Reading Tests

As is explained in Chapter 17, criterion-referenced or mastery tests are very commonly used to determine a student's competency in the many elements of both literal and interpretive comprehension. You often must examine the questions on such a test to determine at what level they are. Here are several such tests:

Fountain Valley Teacher Support System in Reading
Harper & Row Classroom Management System
Individual Pupil Monitoring System—Reading
Right-to-Read Management System

An informal inventory also can be used to determine a student's competency in the various subskills of literal comprehension and interpretive comprehension that were described earlier. As one example, such an inventory can consist of some passages at the appropriate reading level that the student can read either orally or silently. The student then answers a number of questions at either or both levels of comprehension. It is important that such questions not evaluate a student's previous experiences and knowledge but rather evaluate his or her ability to comprehend effectively. Informal inventories also can be designed from the student's own textbooks to ascertain competency in all the other elements of literal and interpretive comprehension. More detail is provided about constructing such types of inventories in Chapter 16.

STRATEGIES AND MATERIALS FOR IMPROVING COMPETENCY IN LITERAL COMPREHENSION

There are many, many strategies and materials that can be used to improve ability in all the elements of literal comprehension that were mentioned previously in this chapter at both the primary-grade and intermediate-grade levels. The basal reader manuals contain numerous useful strategies that can be used for this purpose. The references included at the end of this chapter also can prove very useful for this purpose. However, this chapter also provides you with many practical ideas for improving ability in the various subskills of literal comprehension.

At the beginning stages of reading instruction, read a simple trade book with several discrete parts to the child to improve sequential ability. Have the child then try to retell the story in correct sequence. Usually, the material should not contain more than three or four major parts at this level. To provide practice in simple sentence comprehension, read a trade book aloud to a small group of children. Have them dictate an account of the material and print the sentences on chart paper. Then have the children point to and count the sentences. Next cut apart the words of several sentences, and have the children count the words in the sentences.

A very good activity for improving literal comprehension ability at the beginning reading level is to formulate some direction cards that the child can read and carry out. Print each direction on a strip of tagboard with a marking pen, and then have the child read and follow it. Here are several examples:

Walk to the door and open it.

Jump up and down four times.

Get a game from the game corner to play with another child.

Draw a circle on the chalkboard.

There are a number of every-pupil response techniques that can be used to improve ability in literal comprehension because each child has many chances to respond with these techniques. As one variation, have the child make two small cards of tagboard or poster board and then print the word *yes* on one card and the word *no* on the other card. Ask literal comprehension questions about a story the group of children have read, and have the child then answer each question by holding up the *yes* or *no* card. Other variations of every-pupil response techniques may consist of cards with faces, stick figures, numbers, homonyms, letters, or sight words printed on them. After the teacher asks a question, each student selects the most appropriate answer and holds up the correct response card for the teacher to see. By looking at the raised cards, the teacher can quickly determine which students have mastered the skill and which have not. Such techniques enable all students to become active participants in the lesson and help the reluctant students to respond. For more detail on using such techniques, you can consult an article by Carol J. Hopkins.[10]

In an activity to develop sequence ability, have the child listen to a story with several different parts. Then have the child draw three pictures about the story on small sheets of paper or cards and label each sheet or card *First, Middle,* or *Last.* Next have the child draw something that happened first in the story, that happened in the middle of the story, and that happened last in the story. Ask the child then to tape the cards together and share them with other children.

In a recent article, Lea M. McGee and Gail E. Tompkins have suggested the use of videotaping as an aid to comprehension. This article stated that children remembered more from viewing a teacher read a story by videotape than by listening to the same teacher read the story live. Viewing a videotape also is something that children can do independently. In this article it is stated that videotaping of stories and follow-up activities is a very innovative and effective way of improving reading comprehension, especially at the prereading level, for children who have little experience in listening to and in retelling stories.[11]

To improve sequential ability at the second-grade and third-grade levels, you can locate a comic strip that indicates sequence and cut it apart in frames. If you wish, you can laminate the frames. Then have the child place all of the comic strip frames in correct sequence. In an activity at the same reading level for improving ability in reading and following directions, have the child find a hidden object by giving him or her a series of simple written clues that he or she is to follow exactly to locate the object. Place all the clues all around, or write them all on one sheet of paper so that they can be followed in exact order.

Joan Mary Macey has suggested an interesting exercise in sequencing that probably can be used effectively in the upper primary or lower intermediate grades. She suggested that the teacher list the events of a routine school day in jumbled order and then have the children number these events in the order of their occurrence. If the children have difficulty in numbering the sentences, the sentences can be cut apart so that each sentence is on a separate strip of paper. The

[10]Carol J. Hopkins, "Using Every-Pupil Response Techniques in Reading Instruction," *The Reading Teacher, 33* (November 1979): 173–175.

[11]Lea M. McGee and Gail E. Tompkins, "The Videotape Answer to Independent Reading Comprehension Activities," *The Reading Teacher, 34* (January 1981): 427–433.

children then can rearrange the strips and place them in the correct order.[12] In another activity to improve sequential ability, you can make a peg from the core of a roll of paper. Print a story that lends itself to sequence on rings of tagboard or poster board. Each ring should contain one important event from the story. Then have the child place the rings on the peg in correct sequential order.

In an interesting activity at the upper-primary-grade reading level designed to improve competency in recognizing important details, have the child keep a detailed record of an important classroom event. To improve ability in stating the main idea, select a trade book that the child is going to read, and tape a paper cover over the title of the book, or cover it in some other way. After the child has read the book, have him or her write a title on the paper cover and then compare that title with the actual title.

There are a number of strategies that can be used to improve ability in the various elements of literal comprehension at the intermediate-grade reading level also. One of these is *repeated readings,* which consists of having the student reread a fairly short, meaningful passage several times until a satisfactory level of fluency is reached. Then the procedure is repeated with a new passage. This procedure gives the student the opportunity to master materials before progressing to other materials. However, repeated readings should be used cautiously in order that the student understand that reading is always much more than word-calling. He or she should never be allowed to lose sight of the fact that reading without comprehension is not really reading. If this concept is kept in mind, this technique may be of some value if it is not overused.

In an activity for improving ability in locating main ideas and significant details, select a paragraph at the appropriate reading level with the directly stated main idea in the form of a topic sentence at the beginning. Print the sentences in the paragraph on separate strips of tagboard or poster board. Have the student then reassemble the paragraph. In another activity relating to the main idea, write a paragraph on the appropriate reading level on the chalkboard or on a transparency. Have each student in a group read the paragraph silently and write a title for it on a sheet of paper. Have the students compare their titles to decide which title probably is the best.

In an activity for use at about the fifth-grade or sixth-grade reading level, select several newspaper advertisements, and glue them to a sheet of paper. Then on a sheet of paper write questions that can be answered by reading the advertisements. Have the student write the answers to these questions.

---

[12]Joan Mary Macey, "Exercise in Sequencing," *The Reading Teacher,* *34* (October 1980): 67.

The *maze technique* is an innovative way to improve a student's comprehension ability. It also can be used as a diagnostic device. In any case, a maze technique can be constructed from basal reader material, other graded reading materials, a trade book, or a content textbook. It is constructed from a passage of about 120 words, which is typed in sentences with approximately every fifth word being replaced with alternatives. One alternative is the correct word, another is an incorrect word that is the same part of speech, and the third word is incorrect and another part of speech. The student then circles the correct word in each set of choices.

Here is an example of a maze technique that was constructed from material on the fifth-grade reading level:

Sarah Bush Lincoln

Bush

Abraham Lincoln's stepmother Sarah Brush Lincoln was a remarkable

Break

influence

woman who had a great infection on his life.

quickly

loudly

Sarah was a widow by   three children when she married Abe's

with

pretty

father and moved at   Indiana.[13]

to

In a recent article, Michael C. McKenna adapted the maze technique to the teaching of poetry. His modified maze format, which involves one or more distractors of similar meaning, may be useful in teaching any principle of poetry and thus adding to the comprehension of poetry.[14]

STRATEGIES AND MATERIALS FOR IMPROVING COMPETENCY IN INTERPRETIVE COMPREHENSION

There are numerous strategies and materials that can be used to improve competency in all the subskills of interpretive comprehension

---

[13]Wilma H. Miller, *Reading Diagnosis Kit* (West Nyack, New York: Center for Applied Research in Education, 1978), p. 277.

[14]Michael C. McKenna, "A Modified Maze Approach to Teaching Poetry," *Journal of Reading, 24* (February 1981): 391–395.

that were discussed previously in this chapter at both the primary-grade and intermediate-grade levels. The contemporary basal reader manuals include many useful ideas that can be employed to improve ability in interpretive comprehension. The references included at the end of this chapter also are helpful for this purpose. In addition, this chapter contains many ideas for improving ability in the various sub-skills of interpretive comprehension.

At the prereading level, you can construct a classification board of tagboard or construction paper. Place a picture at the top of the board, indicating a specific category. Obtain other pictures, some of which belong in the same category and others of which do not. Have the child place the proper pictures on the classification board. In another type of classification activity, have children sort objects into predetermined categories. For one example of a category, use large objects, medium-sized objects, and small objects.

In an activity that is appropriate for the beginning reading level, place two very simple paragraphs on an activity sheet on a duplicating master. Each paragraph should reflect either a happy or an unhappy mood. Then have the child read each paragraph and draw a face to illustrate the mood of the child or adult in that paragraph. In an

activity that is appropriate at about the second-grade reading level, write a short paragraph that describes something on the chalkboard or on a duplicating master. Have the child then read the description carefully and draw what was described.

As an activity that is appropriate for the second-grade and third-grade reading levels, have a group of children read a suitable basal reader story. After they have finished, divide the group into two teams. Ask questions about the basal reader story that require interpretive responses. Alternate from team to team and from child to child. Give each team one point for a correct answer, and subtract three points for an incorrect answer. If you wish, you can use this activity instead after a group of children has completed an entire basal reader.

An interesting technique that can be used to improve ability in interpretive comprehension at both the upper-primary-grade level and lower-intermediate-grade level is called "slicing" or recasting to obtain a better response. For example, you can ask for a smaller part of a larger issue. You can also give the child some alternatives to select from in what then becomes a multiple-choice format. Another interesting technique that can be used at about the same reading level is encouraging students to make brain pictures in their minds as they read. Have them make mental images while they are reading. They can begin by visualizing specific things and later sharing their brain pictures or mental images. As the children are reading, you can stop them to ask questions that are not to be answered but are simply to help children improve their visual imagery.

Russell G. Stauffer developed the Directed Reading-Thinking Activity (DRTA) a number of years ago. Stauffer remains the chief proponent of this very valuable technique for improving ability in some aspects of interpretive comprehension. This technique normally is most useful in a basal reader achievement group although it also can be used on an individual basis in individualized reading or in the language experience approach. This technique helps children to learn to predict outcomes, set purposes for reading, and analyze their reading. Have a group of children or an individual child set purposes for reading by reading the title and then skimming the material. Next, questions are posed about the material, and hypotheses are formulated to test. The children or the child confirms or rejects the hypotheses. After the material is read, each child then proves his or her prediction to the rest of the group.[15] Jane L. Davidson studied the DRTA technique a number of years ago and found that teachers who used it asked more interpretive comprehension questions than teachers who did not follow this procedure.[16]

At the intermediate-grade reading level, *glossing* can be used to improve interpretive comprehension ability. To do so, read aloud a portion of narrative or content material that ordinarily would be rather difficult for your students to comprehend at the interpretive level. Then explain this portion of the material to them by discussing the hidden meanings found in the material. This procedure can help them to later read their own simpler material interpretively.

Select a large piece of tagboard or poster board, write phrases on one half that are causes, and write phrases on the other half that are effects. Place the correct heading on each half. Punch holes along the side of each cause and each effect, and attach a piece of yarn to each hole on the cause half. Then have the student thread the yarn into the proper effect hole so that each cause and each effect match. In another interesting activity at the intermediate-grade level, have the student construct a message that he or she would like to send to someone. The student then should condense the message so that it can be sent by telegram. Western Union may be able to give you telegram blanks that the students can use. If this is not possible, you can make your own telegram blanks on a duplicating master.

---

[15]Russell G. Stauffer, *The Language-Experience Approach to the Teaching of Reading* (New York: Harper & Row, Publishers, 1980).

[16]Jane L. Davidson, "The Quantity, Quality, and Variety of Teachers' Questions and Pupils' Responses During an Open-Communication Structured Group Directed Reading-Thinking Activity and a Closed-Communication Structured Group Directed Reading Activity," unpublished doctoral dissertation, University of Michigan, 1970.

In an activity that is appropriate for use on the intermediate-grade reading level, locate two stories that seem quite different on the surface but provide about the same information. Have the student read both stories and decide on only one title that he or she thinks is equally appropriate for both of the stories. In another activity on about the same reading level, write words describing character traits near the top of a duplicating master. Have the student read a story with a number of characters. Then the student is to write the names of each character in the story who displayed the various character traits. Some examples of character traits that can be included are as follows: happy, shy, curious, bold, miserly, sensitive, and patient. It also may be helpful in improving a student's ability in interpretive comprehension if he or she is taught the usefulness of such words as *therefore, furthermore, however, consequently, on the other hand,* or *moreover.* Each word should be taught in sentence context.

At the intermediate-grade reading level an interesting activity to improve ability in drawing conclusions and generalizations is to read material such as a fable and state in writing or orally the lesson that it illustrates.

A DESCRIPTION OF CRITICAL READING

The next higher level of the reading process is called *critical reading* or *evaluative reading.* Some reading specialists think of critical reading as a high level of interpretive comprehension whereas others think of it as a separate entity that is at a higher level than interpretive comprehension. I consider it to be a separate entity although it often is difficult to differentiate between interpretive comprehension and critical reading.

In any case, critical reading can be defined as evaluating or judging the truthfulness or accuracy of the reading material in terms of some criteria that the reader has formulated by prior experiences or previous reading. Critical reading consists of such subskills as distinguishing between fact and fantasy, evaluating the truthfulness and accuracy of the reading material, comparing reading material from several sources, sensing an author's biases, interpreting figurative language, and recognizing such propaganda techniques as the bandwagon effect, testimonials, cardstacking, the halo effect, sheer repetition, emotionally toned words, and glittering generalities. Critical reading corresponds to the evaluation level of the *Taxonomy of Educational Objectives* by Bloom and Krathwohl.

In an attempt to illustrate critical reading, it may be helpful if you examine the following critical questions that were constructed from the third-grade basal reader story that was discussed earlier in this chapter. Here are the questions at the critical level:

Why do you believe that it is important for a country to be free?

Do you think that the people of Texas are now glad that they are a part of the United States? Why or why not?

Which Independence Day probably is the most important to Rosa's and Anita's family? Why do you think so?

Were the two volcanoes on the stage real or make-believe? Why do you think as you do?

Why do you feel that it was important for the Hernandez family to learn about their heritage?[18]

The vast majority of students in the elementary school can achieve at least some degree of competency in the various elements of critical reading within the boundaries of their background of experiences and intelligence. Although it is true that critical reading requires some abstract intellectual ability, even slow-learning students can learn to read critically to some extent.

Elements of critical reading can begin to receive stress as early as the prereading level in kindergarten or first grade, when the teacher asks the children to decide if a story that has been read or told to them is real or make-believe. However, the elements of critical reading should receive increasing emphasis as the child progresses into the primary grades and the intermediate grades. It is absolutely essential that citizens in our contemporary democratic society be able to think and read critically if that society is to survive and prosper. Critical reading skills are perhaps more important now than they ever have been in the past.

Critical reading probably has not received as much stress in a number of elementary classrooms in the past as it should have. This resulted in part because some teachers did not want divergent responses that differed from their own views. Then, too, some teachers were justifiably cautious about discussing controversial issues in their classroom. However, it is encouraging to note that many contemporary elementary-school teachers in America are encouraging critical, divergent responses more than was done in the past.

There are numerous strategies that can be used to improve ability in the various subskills of critical reading. Several of them are as follows: deciding if a story is fact or fantasy, answering critical questions, participating in small-group discussions, comparing materials from different sources, and analyzing newspaper advertisements. This chapter contains many useful ideas for improving ability in critical reading.

[18]Childress and Much, "A Very Special Day."

HOW TO DIAGNOSE COMPETENCY IN CRITICAL READING

There are several means that can be used to try to ascertain a student's probable competency in the various elements of critical reading. As is explained later, you can use teacher observation, a few standardized reading tests, criterion-referenced tests, and informal inventories for this purpose.

As in the case of most other reading skills, normally the easiest way to assess ability in the various critical analysis subskills is by teacher observation. Teacher observation can take place during a reading achievement group when all the students have read a story or book that can be analyzed critically. By observing at this time, the teacher can note a student's ability to respond to critical questions and to interact critically with the statements made by the other children in the group. Teacher observation of critical reading ability often can take place during an individual or a group reading conference when you ask critical questions about a trade book that has been read independently. In addition, observation of critical reading ability can be done very effectively after a student has read a content assignment, perhaps especially in English and social studies because these areas lend themselves very well to critical analysis.

It is fairly difficult to use a standardized survey reading or achievement test or a standardized diagnostic reading test to attempt to determine a student's competency in critical reading. Most standardized tests of this type do not contain questions that call for critical responses. However, the newer tests of this type perhaps are better in this way than are the older ones. In any case, you can examine some of the tests that are described in detail in Chapter 17 to see if the comprehension subtests contain many critical questions.

Some criterion-referenced or mastery tests can be used to ascertain a student's ability in critical reading. In this case also, you must examine the questions to determine if they indeed require evaluative responses. A list of some criterion-referenced tests was included earlier in this chapter.

An informal inventory also can be used to determine a student's competency in the various subskills of critical reading. Such an inventory normally would be given mainly in the intermediate grades and would be given either on an individual or a group basis. It often uses material in such content areas as social studies or English. To formulate such an inventory, select a reading passage at the appropriate level. The student then responds to a number of critical questions, which should evaluate the student's ability to critically analyze what he or she has read, to judge the truthfulness and accuracy of the reading material, or to locate propaganda techniques.

STRATEGIES AND MATERIALS FOR IMPROVING COMPETENCY IN CRITICAL READING

There are many strategies and materials that can be used to improve competency in all the subskills of critical reading that were mentioned previously in this chapter. You will find that the basal reader manuals contain many ideas that can be used for this purpose. The references contained at the end of this chapter also can be very helpful for this purpose. In addition, this chapter gives you many useful suggestions for improving ability in the various elements of critical reading.

At the beginning reading level, you can read a factual or make-believe story to a group of children or have a child read such a story independently. Then have the child or children decide if the story is real or make-believe and state the reasons for that decision. However, you should realize that only a beginning can be made at this level, and true discrimination between fact and fantasy probably cannot be done with complete accuracy until about the third-grade reading level. As another related activity, formulate or find two paragraphs on one topic. One of them should be factual whereas the other should be fanciful. Have the child determine which paragraph is factual and which paragraph is fanciful. The two paragraphs can be placed on the chalkboard or on a duplicating master. In a somewhat more difficult, but related, activity, write on the chalkboard or on a transparency a series of expressions that may indicate that a story is fantasy or make-believe, and have a group of children then analyze these expressions. Here are some examples of such expressions:

An ugly fairy
Once upon a time
In a kingdom long ago
A wicked witch

At the upper-primary-grade or the intermediate-grade level, children can begin to evaluate an author's qualifications to write certain material. As an example, students in the intermediate grades can determine if the author Isaac Asimov is qualified to write science-fiction books.

There are numerous strategies that can be used with students who are reading at the intermediate-grade level. As one activity, make a gameboard of tagboard or poster board with a start and finish. You probably can adapt an existing gameboard for this activity. Place many statements on a sheet of paper, some of which are fact and some of which are opinion, and label the statements. The monitor for this game reads a statement and asks if it is a fact or an opinion. If the answer is correct, the student spins the spinner and moves the token the number of spaces indicated. The first player to reach the finish line wins the game. In another interesting activity, make a number of cards of tagboard or poster board, and print the word *fact* on half of them and the word *fantasy* on the other half of them. Have two students take turns drawing a card. Each student then gives a sentence that is fact or fantasy depending upon the card drawn. Have the other student guess what word was on the card. The student scores one point for each correct answer.

Students at the intermediate-grade reading level should learn to compare information found in several sources to note the differences and similarities of the material. This is an extremely important aspect of critical reading ability, as was illustrated in the introduction to this chapter. Several such sources that can be compared are the following: two or more biographies of the same person, the account of an event in a newspaper and a news magazine, a book and a filmstrip of the same book, two or more content textbooks, and a trade book and an encyclopedia article. In another related activity, select two books that contain information about a certain topic. One book should contain current information, and the other should contain outdated information. Some topics that could be used for this activity are an illness that now is obsolete or space travel. Read the information to the class, and help them determine why the information is so different. Through guided discussion the students should conclude that the copyright dates of the two books mean that one is current and one is outdated.

In a recent article, Anthony V. Manzo suggested using proverbs to teach aspects of interpretive comprehension and critical reading. He stated that the ability to comprehend proverbs was a critical variable in overall progress toward reading maturity. Manzo stated that proverbs are so useful in this regard because they are the abstracted essence of many of the everyday experiences of many people. Manzo further believed that proverbs were especially valuable to students who speak English as a second language. In this article, Manzo provides many suggestions for using proverbs to improve critical reading and also provides sources for locating proverbs.[19]

In a recent article, John P. Lunstrum explained how to increase a student's motivation and thus improve reading comprehension through the planned use of controversy. He stated that because controversial issues in which alternatives are present are so much a common part of our society, students should learn to deal with controversial issues. Teachers in many areas today are able to deal effectively with contro-

---

[19]Anthony V. Manzo, "Using Proverbs to Teach Reading and Thinking; or, Come faceva mia nonna (The way my grandmother did it)," *The Reading Teacher, 34* (January 1981): 411–416.

versial topics in a way that could not be done in the past. This article describes how to use controversy in an upper-level classroom.[20]

To conclude, you must remember that at every reading level the teacher's attitudes and the classroom environment are always very important in encouraging critical analysis. To encourage the greatest amount of evaluative thinking, the teacher must really value divergent responses and show it in concrete ways to his or her students.

A DESCRIPTION OF CREATIVE READING

To be competent in creative reading, a student first must have a good command of the various word identification techniques and possess a good meaning vocabulary. *Creative reading* can be defined as applying the knowledge, concepts, attitudes, and insights gained from reading to the reader's own life. Creative reading also can be called *applied reading, assimilative reading,* or *integrative reading. Bibliotherapy,* which is problem solving through reading, is one aspect of creative reading. When a reader applies what is read in some meaningful way, the highest level of comprehension has taken place.

Creative reading apparently corresponds to the application or synthesis level of Bloom and Krathwohl's *Taxonomy of Educational Objectives.* Creative reading also is a part of the affective domain, that area of the learning process that is related to a student's attitudes and emotions.[21]

It may be helpful in clarifying creative reading if you examine the following statements that were constructed from the same third-grade basal reader story that was mentioned earlier in this chapter:

> Plan a celebration that you could put on with several other children to celebrate the United States' Independence Day on July 4.
>
> Draw a picture of the costume that you would like to wear during this celebration.
>
> Write a short story about the prize that you believe that Rosa Hernandez won for having the most beautiful costume in the parade.
>
> Select several friends, and pretend that you are the dancers from Mexico City. Do the dance the way in which you think the dancers did it in the celebration for the Mexican Independence Day.
>
> Draw a picture about your favorite part of this story.[22]

---

[20]John P. Lunstrum, "Building Motivation Through the Use of Controversy," *Journal of Reading, 24* (May 1981): 687–691.

[21]David R. Krathwohl and others, *Taxonomy of Educational Objectives,* Handbook II: *Affective Domain* (New York: David McKay Co., Inc., 1965).

[22]Childress and Much, "A Very Special Day."

All the ways in which reading can be followed up are examples of creative reading. All creative reading activities are *divergent activities*. There are many examples of creative reading activities that can be used in the elementary school. A student reads creatively, for example, when his or her life is altered in some way as a result of the reading. A student also reads creatively when he or she constructs or formulates something new as a direct result of the reading.

Creative reading should begin to receive stress from the earliest stages of reading instruction within the limits of the student's background of experiences. It should receive emphasis at a more sophisticated level as the student progresses through the primary grades into the intermediate grades.

Here are some examples of creative reading activities that may be appropriate for use either in the primary or intermediate grades with some variation: cooking and baking activities, art activities, rhythm activities, construction activities, creative dramatics, dramatic play, role playing, sociodrama, creative writing of prose and poetry, demonstrations, scientific experiments, various types of oral and written book reports, problem solving in mathematics, and reading materials that specifically appeal to the student's attitudes and emotions.

HOW TO DIAGNOSE COMPETENCY IN CREATIVE READING

It is very difficult to diagnose a student's competency in creative reading effectively. Teacher observation probably is the most effective way of doing this, but teacher observation is also difficult to use because a student's attitude changes or behavior changes as a result of reading may not be observable until long after he or she has left your classroom. However, you may be able to notice elements of a student's creative ability in a number of different settings. As an example, you can observe the student's desire and ability to follow up reading through such activities as additional relevant reading, creative writing, dramatization, role playing, art activities, and construction activities.

Apparently, there are no contemporary standardized tests that really evaluate a student's creative reading ability. Although it is not very easy to use any type of informal inventory to assess a student's creative reading ability, it is possible to use several different types of informal inventories and devices to make at least some assessment of ability in this very important reading skill.

There are several different kinds of informal attitude inventories. You can easily formulate your own attitude inventory to which a student can respond. Questions such as the following can be used on this kind of attitude inventory:

Do you believe that reading is very important? Why or why not?

What kind of things have you learned from reading that have helped your life in some way?

What kind of characters do you most like to find in the books that you read?

In what ways do these characters influence your life?

You can use various other kinds of informal devices to gain an insight into a student's creative reading ability. Some examples of these devices are as follows: the Incomplete Sentences Test, the Wish Test, the reading autobiography, and the open-ended story. You can find information on all these devices in the following source:

Miller, Wilma H. *Reading Diagnosis Kit*. West Nyack, New York: Center for Applied Research in Education, 1978.

STRATEGIES FOR IMPROVING COMPETENCY IN CREATIVE READING

There are numerous strategies that can be used to improve ability in all the elements of creative reading. The basal reader manuals contain countless valuable suggestions that you can use for this purpose. In addition, the references contained at the end of this chapter also are very helpful for this purpose. Moreover, this chapter also provides you with some suggestions for improving ability in creative reading.

There are a number of activities that can be used to improve competency in creative reading at the prereading and beginning reading levels. For example, write the recipe for a simple cooking or baking activity on a piece of tagboard or construction paper with a marking pen. Use very simple terms and rebuses (pictures) for the ingredients. Then help the child read the recipe and follow it. Here are some things that children in kindergarten and beginning first grade have made successfully with some help: frosted cupcakes, deviled eggs, sugar cookies, instant pudding, gingerbread men, pretzel dough letters, and baked pumpkin seeds.

There are a number of dramatization activities that can be used in various levels of the primary grades. For example, have a small group of children dramatize a trade book, story, or nursery rhyme that has been read or told to them. The dramatization can involve puppets at times. A good type of puppet can be a body of construction paper glued to a tongue depressor or popsicle stick, which is held by the child. Additional puppets that can be used are the paper-bag puppet, the paper-towel-roll puppet, the vegetable puppet, and the papier-mâché puppet with a head made out of a balloon or a light bulb. A packing box with a large hole cut in the top can be a very good puppet stage.

Another interesting dramatization technique is the self-directive dramatization, which was developed by the late Lessie Carlton and Robert H. Moore. As was explained in detail in Chapter 6, several children can engage in a self-directive dramatization after they have read the same trade book. Carlton and Moore described the self-directive dramatization as "Each child's original, imaginative, spontaneous interpretation of a character of his choosing in a story which he selects and reads cooperatively with other children in his group, which is formed for the time being and for a particular story only."[23]

A recent article by Jeannette L. Miccinati and Stephen Phelps described how to use synchronized movement and pantomime for the improvement of creative reading. They stated that drama was a natural companion to reading instruction because a child who acts out a story must be able to comprehend it very effectively. These authors described synchronized movement as the whole class moving around the room at the same time in some type of pretend situation, for example, how Little Red Riding Hood walked when she left home or when she entered the woods. They described the mirror game as a pantomime activity that required concentration and observation. For instance, one person performs the actions while his or her partner tries to act as the mirror reflection. This article contained many other interesting strategies that you may wish to explore.[24]

There are countless art and construction activities that can be used to follow up reading in the primary grades. For example, trade books by Leo Lionni and Ezra Jack Keats have illustrations that are done in collage. After the child has read such a trade book, have him or her construct his or her own collage pictures. The child then can describe the collage picture orally for the rest of the class. As another activity, after one or several children have read a trade book, have the child or children display the title and its major characters by using mobiles made from clothes hangers. As one more activity, after the child has read a trade book, have him or her make a collage about the book, using pictures and words from magazines, and glue them on a piece of tagboard. If some other child in the classroom has read the same trade book, it may be possible to have him or her explain the collage.

One interesting activity for the primary grades that relates music and reading is to have a group of children read a trade book, a story,

---

[23]Lessie Carlton and Robert H. Moore, *Reading, Self-Directive and Self-Concept* (Columbus, Ohio: Charles E. Merrill Publishing Co., 1968), p. 13.

[24]Jeannette L. Miccinati and Stephen Phelps, "Classroom Drama from Children's Reading: From the Page to the Stage," *The Reading Teacher, 34* (December 1980): 269–272.

or a poem. The children then can interpret the reading material creatively through the medium of dance. Their dance can be accompanied by a record or original music at the piano.

There also are numerous strategies that can be used to improve creative reading ability at the intermediate-grade reading level. For example, Chapter 6 contained numerous creative ways for sharing trade books that the children have read. One other idea is to have the student select and read a fictional trade book in which he or she is very interested. The student then can write another episode for this book, using the original characters and settings. If the student wishes, he or she then can share this episode with a group or the class.

In an attempt to relate music and reading at the intermediate-grade level, have one student or several students listen to a record of some type. Then have the student write a paragraph about his or her feelings or reactions to the music. In another attempt to relate music and reading, have a group of students put a story into ballads. The students can pretend that they are singing the story as minstrels did long ago. The story can be retold in free or rhyming verse. Guitar music can add to the atmosphere.

Another interesting activity is to have a group of students read the local newspaper for a few days with the purpose of finding stories for which a dialogue can be created. This dialogue should be between several living persons without giving away the names of the persons. Then have the students work in groups of two to formulate the "guess-who" dialogue. You can have the rest of the group or class guess the identity of the two people. Another interesting activity is to encourage several students to work together to create a story with some make-believe words. Each student should have a glossary for the make-believe words. Have groups of students exchange stories and use the glossaries to help them read the stories.

You can also have a student at the intermediate-grade reading level write to a living author or poet. A number of the writers of children's prose and poetry usually respond to letters from students. Some schools are also able to arrange the visit of an author or a poet. In another activity, read one or several stories of a particular type to the students such as a certain kind of myth, tall tales, or the *Just So Stories*. Have other stories of the same kind available so that the students can read them for themselves. Then have the students attempt to write a story of the same type. Later they can share the story with the rest of the class.

Some good readers in the upper intermediate grades may enjoy this activity. After such a student has read a book with a main character, have the student write a statement that projects this character five or ten years into the future. This statement can indicate what he or she may be doing at that time in a number of different ways.

Have the student choose a book that he or she has recently read and enjoyed. The student then can try to relate this book to music by selecting a record that he or she thinks represents it. Have the student make a presentation to the class or to a group by briefly summarizing the book and then playing the record or a part of it. After playing the record, the student should tell why he or she thinks that this record represents the book very well.

SELECTED REFERENCES

Bellows, Barbara Plotkin. "Running Shoes Are to Jogging as Analogies Are to Creative/Critical Thinking." *Journal of Reading, 23* (March 1980): 507–511.

Clary, Linda Mixon. "How Well Do You Teach Critical Reading?" *The Reading Teacher, 31* (November 1977): 142–146.

Dallmann, Martha, Roger L. Rouch, Lynette Y. C. Char, and John J. DeBoer. *The Teaching of Reading.* New York: Holt, Rinehart and Winston, 1982.

Eeds, Maryann. "What to Do When They Don't Understand What They Read—Research-Based Strategies for Teaching Reading Comprehension." *The Reading Teacher, 34* (February 1981): 565–571.

Hansen, Jane. "An Inferential Comprehension Strategy for Use with Primary Grade Children." *The Reading Teacher, 34* (March 1981): 665–669.

Harris, Albert J., and Edward R. Sipay. *How to Increase Reading Ability.* New York: Longman, Inc., 1980, Chapters 16, 17.

Lapp, Diane, and James Flood. *Teaching Reading to Every Child.* New York: Macmillan Publishing Company, Inc., 1983.

Maya, Antonia Y. "Write to Read: Improving Reading Through Creative Writing." *The Reading Teacher, 32* (April 1979): 813–817.

Pearson, P. David, and Dale D. Johnson. *Teaching Reading Comprehension.* New York: Holt, Rinehart and Winston, 1978.

Smith, Charlotte T. "Evaluating Answers to Comprehension Questions." *The Reading Teacher, 31* (May 1978): 896–900.

Strange, Michael. "Instructional Implications of a Conceptual Theory of Reading Comprehension." *The Reading Teacher, 33* (January 1980): 391–397.

Tatham, Susan Masland. "Comprehension Taxonomies: Their Uses and Abuses." *The Reading Teacher, 32* (November 1978): 190–193.

Taylor, Marilyn J. "Using Photos to Teach Comprehension Skills." *Journal of Reading, 21* (March 1978): 514–517.

Tovey, Duane R. "Improving Children's Comprehension Abilities." *The Reading Teacher, 30* (December 1976): 288–292.

Vawter, Jacquelyn M., and Marybelle Vancil. "Helping Children Discover Reading Through Self-Directed Dramatization." *The Reading Teacher, 34* (December 1980): 320–323.

SUGGESTED ACTIVITIES

1. Select a basal reader story at the primary-grade or intermediate-grade level. Read the story silently, and formulate four literal comprehension questions, four interpretive comprehension questions, four critical questions, and four creative statements or questions from this story. Use the comprehension questions included in the chapter as a model.
2. Visit a primary-grade or intermediate-grade classroom. Try to categorize the comprehension questions that the teacher asks. Were they of all the types mentioned in the chapter?
3. Locate a comic strip, cut it into frames, and laminate it as suggested in the chapter. Use this comic strip to improve a primary-grade child's sequential ability.
4. Construct a maze technique as was explained in the chapter. Do you prefer the maze technique or a variation of the cloze procedure?
5. If possible, use the Directed Reading-Thinking Activity as described in this chapter with one child or a group of children.
6. Construct a puppet that can be used in the dramatization of a story or a trade book.

Ways of organizing elementary reading instruction

Why Was This Wrong?

Many years ago a six-year-old boy named Kenny was eagerly looking forward to going to first grade at Beverly School in a very large Midwestern city. Kenny came from a typical middle-class family in which reading was valued. However, no one in his family had made a concerted effort to improve his reading readiness or to teach him beginning reading skills, principally because the climate of the times was to leave the teaching of reading entirely to the schools. However, Kenny's parents encouraged him to learn to read well in first grade, and he was sure that he would do so.

Thus, Kenny entered Miss Mason's first-grade classroom one September. Although he liked first grade, he did have some difficulty in learning sight words as quickly as did most of the rest of the children in the class. Then after several weeks Miss Mason divided the children in her class into three reading achievement groups—the above-average group, whom she called the Bluebirds; the average group, whom she called the Redbirds; and the below-average group, whom she called the Sparrows. Unfortunately, Kenny was placed in the Sparrow group. He quickly decided that he must not be as good a reader, or perhaps not even as good a child, as the other children in the first-grade class. For a while he tried to learn how to read as hard as he could, but he later decided that it wasn't worth the effort because he probably never would learn to read as well as the other children in the first-grade class anyhow. That is when he

stopped trying to learn to read.

As Kenny progressed through the elementary school, he always remained in the below-average reading achievement group as indeed do most children who are placed in that group in first grade. He continued to have great difficulty with both reading and spelling although he was quite competent in arithmetic. Although Kenny was a disabled reader and speller in high school, he was able to graduate by listening carefully to the presentations of his teachers and by relying as little as possible on reading. Although Kenny wanted to go to college very much, he thought he would be unsuccessful because of his low reading ability. That is the reason why he enrolled in a special reading and spelling class at a local university right after high school graduation. However, this class did not help him. Therefore, Kenny took a job driving a large truck in the city, an honorable although very difficult job. However, one is forced to wonder what other kind of life Kenny might have had as an adult if he had not been a member of the Sparrows reading achievement group in first grade. That is perhaps the most important message of this chapter.

This chapter explains why it is extremely important to use reading achievement groups very judiciously in the elementary school. It also discusses why it is crucial to avoid stigmatizing below-average readers by encouraging them to participate in all kinds of reading groups. If you understand these concepts, perhaps the plight of future Kennys will be avoided.

AN INTRODUCTION TO GROUPING

There are a number of reasons why elementary teachers of reading have grouped students in the past and continue to do so in the present. Theoretically, groups should make for more efficient teaching of reading. Therefore, they ought to make the teaching of reading easier for the typical classroom teacher. Because having a number of different types of reading groups reduces the range of teaching that is needed, they should make for more effective teaching of reading.

In addition, some types of reading groups enable students to learn and reinforce only those reading skills in which they have been found to be weak. Other types of reading groups give students the opportunity to interact with each other in various ways. Some of these students may be of the same reading ability whereas others may be of varying abilities.

However, at the outset you should realize that no one method of grouping results entirely in accurately formed groups. As an example, if the children are grouped into three reading achievement groups, considerable differences in the reading ability of the children within any one of the groups will still always exist. In the above-average group, for example, two or three of the children may be at a much higher reading level than the rest of the group. Or in the below-average group one or two children may read well below the level of the rest. As reading is a complex process, any child may be considerably weaker in one or several subskills of reading than in the rest of the subskills. That is why children of the same approximate reading level may still vary greatly in their reading abilities.

When a class is grouped by intellectual ability, problems may result from the differences within the class. Because all intelligence tests have an error of measurement, a child may not even be placed in the proper classroom. In addition, a child may be intellectually superior but may not have achieved well in a subject area such as reading or arithmetic and, therefore, is below the rest of the class in this area. When students are grouped for the Joplin Plan on the basis of reading achievement, they may be placed in the wrong reading level because of an error in the teacher's judgment or on the reading test. In this case also, a child may be weaker in one or more areas of reading than in the other areas.

There is a possibility that some forms of grouping such as a reading achievement group may, in fact, be unconstitutional. This is because such groups may well discriminate against the children in the below-average reading achievement group as is explained later in this chapter. This is an area that undoubtedly will be the subject of much controversy in the near future.

READING ACHIEVEMENT GROUPS

Certainly, by far the most commonly used reading groups in contemporary elementary classrooms are those in which the children are grouped on the basis of their reading achievement or ability. Usually, this grouping is made on the basis of a child's total or overall reading achievement rather than on competency in specific reading skills, for any child can possess a good overall reading ability and still be weak in one or several of the reading subskills. On the other hand, a student may possess a rather weak overall reading ability but still have strengths in some specific reading subskills.

In an elementary classroom, students are usually grouped on the basis of reading and/or achievement test scores and teacher judgment. In early first grade, children are often grouped on the basis of a reading readiness and/or group intelligence test and the kindergarten teacher's rating. In the later primary and intermediate grades, the students usually are placed into a reading achievement group on the basis of survey reading and/or achievement test scores and the teacher's evaluation. If the results of an achievement test are used for forming reading achievement groups, the vocabulary (word meaning) and paragraph comprehension subtests usually are used as the criteria. You should remember that no test is an infallible indicator of a child's reading readiness or reading achievement. That is why it is so very important always to use teacher judgment in forming reading achievement groups and also to regard the placement of a child in any reading achievement group as only a *tentative, and not a fixed,* placement.

As was alluded to earlier, when the children have been placed in one of the three or four reading achievement groups, their actual reading achievement may still vary widely for several reasons. Standardized survey reading or achievement tests are not completely accurate measures of reading achievement and do not always evaluate all facets of the complex reading process effectively. In addition, most students have one or more reading skills in which they are weak, and these weaknesses normally are not considered when the reading achievement groups are formed. Although there usually is a fairly wide range between the best and the poorest reader in both the above-average and the below-average reading achievement groups, reading achievement of the children in the average group usually is fairly similar.

Most primary-grade classrooms contain three reading achievement groups—the above-average group, the average group, and the below-average group. In a typical primary-grade classroom, the average group contains the most children, the above-average group contains the next greatest number of children, and the below-average group usually is the smallest. In a primary-grade classroom with twenty-five children, the average group may contain eleven children, the above-average group may contain eight children, and the below-average group may contain six children.

Reading achievement grouping is most commonly used in the basal reader approach. However, it is also used in formal phonic approaches. The basal reader teachers' manuals recommend that all reading achievement groups should be *flexible,* meaning that students should be able to move easily from one group to another as their reading skills change. Although flexible grouping is always recommended, this does not occur in practice in most elementary classrooms. Because the reading skills are presented developmentally, it becomes especially difficult for a student in the below-average group to move up to the average or above-average group. It is also difficult for a student in the average group to be placed into the above-average group. As was demonstrated in the introduction to this chapter, fixed grouping almost guarantees that children in the below-average group will feel stigmatized and will give up trying to improve their reading skills because they feel that it is hopeless.

Some intermediate-grade classrooms contain three reading achievement groups. However, other intermediate-grade classrooms contain two reading achievement groups, and a few classrooms at this level use a single reading achievement group. Unfortunately, fewer groups sometimes are used in the intermediate grades, where the reading ability range may be eight or ten reading grade levels. However, as intermediate-grade students must study many different subject matter areas, the time for developmental reading instruction often is more limited than it is in the primary grades.

NEEDS OR SKILLS GROUPS

A needs or skills group can also be called a diagnostic-prescriptive reading group. As was explained in Chapter 6, a needs or skills group is used fairly often in both primary-grade and intermediate-grade reading instruction. It is a short-term flexible group that the teacher forms when he or she has decided by some type of formal or informal diagnosis that some students need instruction or reinforcement in a word identification or comprehension skill.

A needs or skills group is rarely used in the basal reader approach or a formal phonic approach, although it often would be helpful to make such a structured reading program more prescriptive and better able to meet the reading needs of students. A needs or skills group is more commonly used when the children are using individualized reading, the language experience approach, or a diagnostic-prescriptive reading program. This is the case because such methods of reading instruction do not employ long-term structured achievement grouping.

As an example, a needs or skills group may be formed to present and reinforce the short vowel sounds of /e/ and /i/ if several children in the classroom have been found by the teacher to lack competency in this phonic analysis subskill. Sometimes the needs or skills group is composed of above-average and below-average students if they show the same reading skill weaknesses. A needs or skills group is disbanded when the children have become proficient in the word identification subskill or comprehension subskill for which it was formed.

RESEARCH GROUPS

A research group usually is used in the later primary or intermediate grades. In this kind of group, the teacher assigns a topic to be researched by some children. The topics usually are connected with a unit in such content areas as social studies or science. The students in the group then read about the topic individually or with a partner, on their instructional or independent reading level, from content textbooks, trade books, reference books, newspapers, or magazines. All the students in the research group then make oral or written reports to the class when the research is finished. A research group normally is disbanded when the problem that it was formed to research is solved.

A research group is very useful in the elementary school, especially when the basal reader approach is the major method of reading instruction, because it enables below-average readers to avoid the stigma of always reading only with other below-average readers. Instead, it provides them with the opportunity to read on their own level but be able to work on the project with average and above-average readers.

INTEREST GROUPS

An interest group is quite similar to a research group. However, in an interest group the children themselves decide that they want to learn more about a particular topic. An interest group may consist of above-average, average, and below-average readers and is thus useful because it enables below-average readers to work with other children. An interest group is disbanded when the members have researched the topic to their own satisfaction. The following classroom incident may clarify how an interest group can be created and used:

Mr. Marks teaches in a second-grade classroom in a small city. One late winter day, Joel was very excited when he came to school in the morning. He couldn't wait to tell Mr. Marks about what he had found the afternoon before.

> Joel: Mr. Marks, look at what I found yesterday afternoon!
>
> Mr. Marks: What is it, Joel?
>
> Joel: I don't know what it is, but I found it hanging on the bottom of one of the bushes in front of my house.
>
> Mr. Marks: It's called a cocoon. What do you know about cocoons?
>
> Joel: I think butterflies come out of them.
>
> Mr. Marks: In fact, both butterflies and moths come out of cocoons. How could you find out something about this particular cocoon?
>
> Joel: I guess I could look it up in a library book.

Meanwhile Susie and Dave had joined Mr. Marks and Joel and also were interested in looking at the cocoon and finding out more about it.

> Susie: I'll help you look up something about the cocoon in our children's encyclopedia.
>
> Dave: I'll see what I can find in some library books.

The children then formed an interest group to study butterflies and moths. They read several trade books, items from science textbooks, and material from a children's encyclopedia on the subject, individually or as a group. They later reported their findings orally to the rest of the class. They also kept the cocoon in their classroom in a jar until it became a beautiful Cecropia moth in early March.

INDIVIDUAL AND GROUP
READING CONFERENCES

As was explained in detail in Chapter 6, individual reading conferences and group reading conferences are the cornerstone of the individualized reading plan. The individual reading conference is the one-to-one meeting between the teacher and the student in which they discuss a trade book or other reading material that the student has read. During an individual reading conference, the teacher also usually asks the student comprehension questions, and the student often reads aloud a portion of the material to the teacher. As was explained in more detail in Chapter 6, the teacher also attempts to diagnose the student's reading strengths and weaknesses during the individual reading conference.

As was also discussed in Chapter 6, group reading conferences can be used in the individualized reading plan as well. Such a conference can take place when several students have read fairly similar books. Normally, more general comprehension questions are asked in group reading conferences. Each student also can read orally from his or her own material if the teacher wishes.

VARIOUS TYPES OF INDEPENDENT INSTRUCTION

There are a number of ways of organizing elementary reading instruction that involve various types of independent activities. For example, the reading management systems that were described in detail in Chapter 9 often involve either individual or small-group instruction. As you may remember, when a reading management system is used, the student learns and practices those reading skills in which he or she has been found to be weak by diagnostic procedures.

Another type of predominantly individualized instruction in reading is the very commonly used reading laboratories. A reading laboratory consists of kits of materials at various elementary-school reading levels. Normally, a kit contains reading selections, answer keys, student's record books, test pads, and a teacher's handbook. A student normally progresses through these reading materials as rapidly as his or her ability allows. Science Research Associates has published the most commonly used reading laboratories, which are the *SRA Reading Laboratory* and the *SRA Reading for Understanding Laboratory*. The former emphasizes many different kinds of reading skills and is designed for use in grades one through thirteen. The latter mainly emphasizes the improvement of comprehension skills and is designed for use in grades three through twelve. Here are the names of several other reading laboratories:

Building Reading Power. Charles E. Merrill Publishing Co.

The Literature Sampler. Redgrave Publishing Company.

The Reading Practice Program. Harcourt Brace Jovanovich, Inc.

Another way of organizing reading instruction is by the use of learning contracts. A learning contract may be defined as a work agreement between a student and a teacher for the student to complete certain projects or activities. A learning contract is somewhat like a series of assignment sheets.

When the teacher has ascertained a child's reading level and reading needs, the teacher may formulate a contract that can be a piece of paper marked off in some way by days or by times, with the suggested learning activities placed in the proper slots. Obviously, learning contracts vary greatly depending upon the reading ability and age of the learners. If you wish to see good examples of learning contracts, you can consult the textbook referred to in the footnote.[1]

---

[1]Roger Farr and Nancy Roser, *Teaching a Child to Read* (New York: Harcourt Brace Jovanovich, Inc., 1979), pp. 391–394.

PEER TUTORING

Peer tutoring also can be called a tutorial group or the buddy system. Peer tutoring can be used effectively in both the primary and the intermediate grades. Peer tutoring usually is composed of a group of two children, a child-teacher and a child-student. Although this is not always the case, the child-teacher normally is a competent reader, and the child-student often is a below-average reader or a child who needs special help because he or she has been absent from school. The child-teacher can teach or more often review a word identification or comprehension skill with which the child-student needs help. Obviously, the child-teacher must thoroughly understand the selected reading skill and how to teach it or review it effectively.

Peer tutoring is probably being used more often now in elementary classrooms to improve reading instruction than was the case in the past. It may have advantages for both children. The tutor may learn tolerance and must be thoroughly knowledgeable about the chosen reading skill whereas the tutee may understand the other child's instruction better than he or she may understand the teacher's instruction. Although children can teach each other effectively, normally peer tutoring should be used mainly to review reading skills. Peer tutoring should not continue day after day, for both children will soon tire of it.

Amy Roseman Allen and Nancy Boraks explained a unique system of peer tutoring in a fairly recent article. They called their program Reciprocal Peer Tutoring (RPT). In this program children were taught to be tutors, and then they alternated the tutor and tutee roles for different reading lessons. They were of similar reading ability levels. Allen and Boraks found that peers of the same age and of comparable ability levels were able to tutor each other in various reading skills and profit from the experience. They found these results to be true both for urban and suburban children.[2]

CROSS-AGE TUTORING

Cross-age tutoring is a variation of peer tutoring that also has been used successfully in the improvement of reading instruction. However, it is somewhat more difficult to organize because of the logistics involved than is peer tutoring.

In cross-age tutoring, an older disabled reader normally is the tutor, and a younger average or below-average reader is the tutee. For example, a disabled reader in the intermediate grades may be the tutor

[2]Amy Roseman Allen and Nancy Boraks, "Peer Tutoring: Putting It to the Test," *The Reading Teacher, 32* (December 1978): 274–278.

for a child in the primary grades. In another variation, a high school disabled reader may be the tutor for a child in the intermediate grades. In either case, the teachers from the two grade levels must cooperate in planning the tutoring program.

The tutor should receive direct instruction and practice in how to present or reinforce a reading skill before actually doing it. He or she must also learn the reading skill very thoroughly so that it can be presented effectively. Often the tutor and the tutee should be matched in terms of personality characteristics as much as possible to avoid any potential conflict. The older disabled reader who is the tutor can receive much benefit from this type of program. He or she must learn the reading skill very well, and he or she gains a great deal in self-esteem by being placed in a position of respect and authority. Cross-age tutoring thus can be very beneficial in helping a disabled reader view himself or herself in a more positive way. The tutee often benefits also from cross-age tutoring by establishing a positive relationship with an older, caring student whom he or she can respect. It is certain that cross-age tutoring can be a very beneficial program if it is carefully planned and executed.

Nancy A. Mavrogenes and Nancy D. Galen explained cross-age tutoring very well in a recent article. In this article they first discussed how cross-age tutoring has resulted in both cognitive and affective gains in reading programs. They stated that almost all teachers who were involved in such a program were very enthusiastic about it. This article also very carefully described how to organize such a program, select and pair students, and train teachers for such an experience. The authors also described methods and materials that could be used in cross-age tutoring such as bookmaking, oral reading, and the use of games. Finally, the authors described how to evaluate such a program. This is an excellent article to consult before you engage in a program of cross-age tutoring.[3]

THE JOPLIN PLAN

The Joplin Plan is a form of modified homogeneous grouping in which students are shifted from classroom to classroom only during their reading period each day. This reading plan was begun in Joplin, Missouri, in 1952, and it was later publicized in the professional literature.[4]

---

[3]Nancy A. Mavrogenes and Nancy D. Galen, "Cross-Age Tutoring: Why and How," *Journal of Reading, 22* (January 1979): 344–353.

[4]Raul Tunley, "Why Johnny Can Read in Joplin," *Saturday Evening Post,* October 1967, pp. 108–110, 130.

When an elementary school uses the Joplin Plan, the children in the fourth, fifth, and sixth grades—and less often the first, second, and third grades—are given a survey reading or achievement test and evaluated by their teacher on the basis of their reading achievement. Using these criteria, the students are placed for reading instruction with a teacher who may or may not be their regular classroom teacher. The reading period then is scheduled for all participating classrooms at the same time each day. The children move from their own classroom into the classroom to join children on their own reading level. At the conclusion of the reading period, they move back into their own classroom.

As was stated earlier, the Joplin Plan usually is employed in the intermediate grades. It is best used in three classrooms of the same grade such as three fourth-grade classrooms, three fifth-grade classrooms, or three sixth-grade classrooms. It normally is not quite as effective when it is used across grade lines, as in one fourth-grade classroom, one fifth-grade classroom, and one sixth-grade classroom.

There are some advantages and limitations to the use of the Joplin Plan. For example, the wide range of reading achievement that is found in the typical upper-primary-grade or intermediate-grade classroom is reduced somewhat when this plan is used. Consequently, the teacher may have an easier task in presenting a reading program. However, standardized survey reading or achievement tests are not infallible in selecting children who have the same overall reading ability. In addition, there often is some difficulty in emotional adjustment for some students participating in this plan because a sixth-grade child may have to read with a fourth-grade child, which may be difficult for the older disabled reader. Teachers using the Joplin Plan may not know the children in their reading group very well if the students are not in their regular classroom. In addition, the children may become "readers" instead of children with unique reading needs and interests. Finally, some teachers do not very much enjoy working with the below-average reading group, and the students in the group may well be cognizant of this fact.

HOMOGENEOUS AND HETEROGENEOUS GROUPING

Homogeneous grouping is commonly referred to as tracking. Homogeneous classrooms are formed occasionally in contemporary elementary schools as an attempt to reduce the range of differences in ability that the teacher must cope with while teaching reading in the more common heterogeneous classroom. As an example, if all the first-grade classrooms in an elementary school are grouped in a homogeneous manner, one first-grade teacher teaches the intellectually superior children, another teacher works with the average class, and the third teacher teaches the children who are below-average in intellectual ability. Once in a while, homogeneous grouping is done in the primary grades on the basis of reading readiness test scores. However, most elementary schools use intelligence test scores. If children are homogeneously grouped on the basis of reading achievement, they often differ in their ability in arithmetic, social studies, science, and the other curricular areas. On the other hand, if children are grouped on the basis of their intellectual ability, they often may differ greatly in the various areas of the curriculum.

In the intermediate grades, students usually are grouped on the basis of intelligence test scores and, less commonly, on the basis of reading test scores. Potential differences in all of the areas of the curriculum are even greater in the intermediate grades than they are in the primary grades. Homogeneous grouping is very difficult to do effectively when all the differences that may exist in a so-called "homogeneous" group are considered. Most teachers who teach in a homogeneously grouped classroom discover enough differences in reading achievement to use several reading achievement groups. In addition, a good teacher who is teaching a homogeneously grouped classroom should end the year with a fairly heterogeneous classroom if each child's individual differences in style and pace of learning have been considered.

Both at the primary-grade and intermediate-grade levels, research has not found that one form of grouping is significantly superior to the other. In addition, some potentially detrimental effects can occur in a homogeneously grouped classroom. Sometimes students in the above-average classroom feel that they are intellectually superior to their peers in the other classrooms, and their parents may even feel superior to the parents of students in the other classrooms. Therefore, parents may pressure the school administration to place their child in the above-average classroom.

On the other hand, students in the below-average classroom usually think of themselves as being in the "dummy room," and their self-esteem often suffers. The students then receive no intellectual stimulation from the brighter children, as they would in a heterogeneous classroom. Teachers of the below-average classrooms sometimes feel that their job is virtually impossible. This author believes that most often a heterogeneous classroom can best serve the needs of most students in both the primary and intermediate grades.

DEPARTMENTALIZED READING

Departmentalization, which is another form of classroom organization rarely used in the primary grades and mainly used in the intermediate grades, is not actually a way of grouping for reading. Instead, it is a way of organizing for reading instruction. In departmentalization, students have one teacher for reading and language arts, another for social studies, another for science, another for mathematics, and other teachers for the special subjects.

For one period each day, the intermediate-grade students go to the reading and language arts teacher, who then organizes the period, often using other forms of grouping. Departmentalization utilizes the special skills and knowledges of the teachers very effectively. However, it often does not enable the teacher to learn to know the students very well. This may result in their reading achievement's being considered apart from their total development.

TEAM TEACHING

Team teaching is used occasionally in a primary-grade or intermediate-grade classroom to present instruction. When team teaching is used, two or more teachers work together to provide the instruction for the same group of students. This obviously is a greater number of students than would be assigned to one teacher. The members of the team must coordinate their planning and teaching very well for team teaching to be effective.

Team teaching may enable a teacher to utilize his or her areas of expertise effectively. For example, a team member with special training in reading would primarily be responsible for the teaching of reading to the group of students. However, there is apparently a lack of significant difference between team teaching and solitary-teacher teaching because there was no significant change in actual teaching practices when team teaching was used.[5]

SELECTED REFERENCES

Bessai, Frederick, and Con Cozac. "Gains of Fifth and Sixth Grade Readers from In-School Tutoring." *The Reading Teacher, 33* (February 1980): 567–570.

Boraks, Nancy, and Amy Roseman Allen. "A Program to Enhance Peer Tutoring." *The Reading Teacher, 30* (February 1977): 479–484.

Dallmann, Martha, Roger L. Rouch, Lynette Y. C. Char, and John J. DeBoer. *The Teaching of Reading.* New York: Holt, Rinehart and Winston, 1982.

[5]David G. Armstrong, "Team Teaching and Academic Achievement," *Review of Educational Research, 47* (Winter 1977): 65–86.

Hall, MaryAnne, Jerilyn K. Ribovich, and Christopher J. Ramig. *Reading and the Elementary School Child.* New York: D. Van Nostrand Company, 1979, pp. 314–320.

Harris, Albert J., and Edward R. Sipay. *How to Increase Reading Ability.* New York: Longman, Inc., 1980, Chapters 5, 6.

Heilman, Arthur W. *Principles and Practices of Teaching Reading.* Columbus, Ohio: Charles E. Merrill Publishing Co., 1977, Chapter 9.

Karlin, Robert. *Teaching Elementary Reading.* New York: Harcourt Brace Jovanovich, Inc., 1980, Chapter 3.

Spache, George D., and Evelyn B. Spache. *Reading in the Elementary School.* Boston: Allyn and Bacon, Inc., 1977, Chapter 14.

SUGGESTED ACTIVITIES

1. Examine the cumulative folders of some children in the below-average group in sixth grade. How many of them were first placed in the below-average group in first grade? What conclusions can you draw from this?
2. If possible, present a basal reader lesson to a reading achievement group at the grade level in which you are most interested.
3. If possible, observe a needs or skills group that a teacher has formed in the primary grades or in the intermediate grades.
4. If possible, arrange a peer tutoring session between an above-average reader and a below-average reader in the primary grades or intermediate grades.
5. Choose a disabled reader at the intermediate-grade level. Help this student to plan a short lesson to present to a child in the early primary grades. Then the disabled reader can present the brief lesson to the primary-grade child. Later discuss the lesson with the disabled reader for his or her reactions to it.

Teaching reading
in content areas

Why Was This Better?

Mr. Warren was in his first year of teaching sixth grade at Lincoln School in a small city in the South. After about one month of teaching, he was pleased to have determined that most of the students in his class were reading on or near grade level although a few of them were disabled in reading. Most of the children in his class seemed to be able to read the basal reader that he had selected for them fairly effectively, and the remainder of the students read from an easier basal reader.

However, Mr. Warren was absolutely appalled by the difficulty most of the students in his class had with reading their social studies and science textbooks. They seemed unable to cope with the vocabulary and concepts found in these textbooks. They also did not seem to be able to comprehend or retain what they read very effectively. However, Mr. Warren was especially disturbed by the degree of difficulty his students had in comprehending and solving verbal arithmetic problems. They did not know which data in the problems were relevant. They also seemed to have no definite strategy to use in trying to read and solve the problems. In fact, almost all the students in his sixth-grade class seemed to be disabled in comprehending verbal arithmetic problems.

Mr. Warren wondered for a time about what he should do regarding his students' lack of ability in reading effectively in the content areas of social studies, science, and arithmetic. He then decided that he would first concentrate on trying to improve their ability to comprehend and solve verbal arithmetic problems. He consulted a professional textbook on the teaching of reading and located a strategy for helping his students comprehend and solve verbal arithmetic problems effectively. Very briefly, here is the strategy:

1. Read or preview the problem for an overall understanding of it.
2. Read the problem again more slowly to determine the details and relationships.
3. Have the student restate the problem in his or her own words.
4. Have the student visualize or express the computation steps that he or she will take.
5. Have the student attempt to solve the problem.
6. If necessary, have the student reread the problem to determine if his or her answer seems reasonable.

After the students in Mr. Warren's class had practiced this strategy for several months, they were more efficient in comprehending and solving verbal arithmetic problems, although they still needed more practice in the area. Mr. Warren then concentrated on using some of the strategies contained in this chapter to help his students improve their ability to comprehend and study their social studies and science textbooks. This also was a task that took considerable time but proved to be fairly effective.

After reading this chapter, you will know about some of the strategies that Mr. Warren used with his sixth-grade class to help them read more effectively in the content areas. These strategies should prove very useful to your students in the present and the future because effective reading in the content areas is vitally necessary for academic success in the elementary school, the secondary school, and college.

THE IMPORTANCE OF TEACHING READING IN CONTENT AREAS

There are a number of reasons why it is crucial for teachers in the elementary school to teach reading-study skills in the content areas of social studies, science, and arithmetic. Most teachers in the primary and the intermediate grades use the basal reader as the major mode of presenting reading instruction. The typical basal reader contains predominantly narrative material although it is acknowledged that recently basal reader publishers have made a concerted effort to include material from the content areas of social studies, science, and arithmetic in their readers. However, students in both the primary and intermediate grades need to have much additional exposure to content reading and to the reading-study skills that are required for effective content reading. Success in content reading includes many demands that are not found in basal readers.

It is also important to understand at the outset that success in content reading is crucial to academic success in the intermediate grades, the secondary school, and college. The typical classroom at all these levels puts a premium on effective reading skills. Without effective reading skills, the student has a great handicap in most classrooms. He or she has to rely on obtaining the necessary information from teachers' lectures, tape recorded materials, other students, or other sources.

Content textbooks differ from basal readers in a number of ways. Normally, they are made up of informational or expository reading. They contain much more material in a small amount of space than do basal readers. A chapter in a content textbook usually is organized with a title, headings, and subheadings. Such textbooks often contain specialized vocabulary terms that may be difficult because they seldom are found in other kinds of reading. A number of these specialized vocabulary terms also are fairly difficult to decode either structurally or phonetically. In addition, content textbooks often contain some vocabulary terms that have a different meaning in that content area from their meaning in ordinary usage. Then, too, content textbooks contain concepts with which the student may not be familiar. The lack of conceptual ability often hinders the student's reading comprehension in the content areas very greatly.

In addition, a number of other reading skills that are discussed in the next section of this chapter are required for effective comprehension of content textbooks. Although many of these reading skills are taught in the basal reader approach, they may function somewhat differently in the reading of content textbooks. These reading skills do not transfer automatically from basal readers to content textbooks. A student also needs to remember what is read from content material in much more detail than is typical with the reading of narrative material. This often is difficult for a student because content material is packed so densely with important facts in comparison to basal reader material.

A number of content textbooks are above the reading level of the students who are to use them. For example, a science textbook designed for use in the sixth grade often may be written on the seventh- or eighth-grade reading level. This obviously makes the textbook difficult to read effectively for all but the best readers in the class. However, textbook publishers are now more aware of this and are applying readability formulas to their textbooks. Therefore, the problem is not as acute as it was in the past. However, there still are some content textbooks that are above the reading level of the students who are to use them. You can make a *rough* determination of the reading level of a content textbook by using a readability formula such as the Fry Readability Formula or the Dale-Chall Readability Formula. You are given detailed directions on how to apply the Fry Readability Formula in a later section of this chapter. You should then try to match a content textbook with the student's reading level. Therefore, it is obvious that multilevel textbooks can be useful in teaching reading in the content areas.

A number of teachers apparently believe that content reading instruction should begin in the intermediate grades and receive additional emphasis in the secondary school. In reality, however, the teaching of reading in the content fields should begin as early as the latter half of first grade and receive some emphasis in second and third grades. For such instruction the teacher should use the child's own social studies and science textbooks and simple verbal arithmetic problems. For content reading instruction in the intermediate grades the teacher also should mainly utilize the student's own textbooks. As is explained later in this chapter, there are special materials that can be used to develop reading-study skills. However, it generally is better to use the student's own textbooks as the medium of instruction, although these special materials sometimes may be a help.

Content reading instruction always should be presented by the teacher who teaches that content area. This obviously is not a consideration in a self-contained classroom, but it is a consideration if departmentalization is used in the intermediate grades. (See Chapter 15.) The social studies teacher should teach the reading-study skills required for effective reading in social studies, the science teacher should teach the reading-study skills that are required for effective comprehension in science, and the arithmetic teacher should teach the necessary reading-study skills in arithmetic.

Contemporary elementary teachers understand the importance of teaching the reading-study skills in the content fields considerably more than did teachers of the past. Therefore, they generally are placing more emphasis on the teaching of these skills than teachers did in the past. This indeed is very encouraging.

SPECIAL READING-STUDY SKILLS IN THE VARIOUS CONTENT AREAS

The various content areas require competence in different reading-study skills for effective reading in that area. Although there is similarity between the ways that these skills are used in the different content areas, there also are differences that should be considered.

Because basal reader materials are predominantly narrative materials, the reading-study skills that are required for effective comprehension of basal reader materials also are applicable to most English materials. However, the content area of social studies does require some fairly unique reading-study skills. Social studies materials contain a number of specialized vocabulary terms, many of which, however, are fairly common terms that have a different meaning in social studies materials. One good example of this type of term is the word *cabinet.* The student who reads social studies materials must be able to locate main ideas and details and draw generalizations from the materials. Critical reading is also very important in most social studies materials, perhaps especially those dealing with political science. The ability to follow a sequence of events is also very important, especially in history. The student of history should also be able to follow a time line of events for effective comprehension. Social studies textbooks often use the cause-effect, comparison-contrast, or enumeration patterns of organization. The student in the intermediate grades may be able to have some exposure to these patterns of organization. Effective comprehension of graphic aids such as maps, graphs, diagrams, tables, and pictures also is necessary for effective comprehension of social studies textbooks. Stanford E. Taylor and others have compiled a useful core vocabulary in social studies that you may want to consult. This same resource also contains core vocabularies in reading, mathematics, and science.[1]

There are also some reading-study skills that are required for effective comprehension of science materials. Science textbooks contain many, many difficult specialized vocabulary terms that the student must be able to decode and comprehend. Many of these vocabulary terms are polysyllabic words that can be analyzed through structural analysis. The student who knows the meaning of some prefixes may also be able to decode a number of the polysyllabic terms effectively. The student of science must be able to read and retain many important details. The skill of reading and following directions is very important in carrying out scientific experiments effectively. The creative reading skill of actually performing the scientific experiments also is very applicable in reading in science. Many science textbooks contain either an enumeration pattern of organization or a sequential pattern of organization. To recognize the enumeration pattern of organization, the student can be alerted to cue words or phrases that introduce the enumeration. Such cue words may be cardinal numbers, ordinal numbers, or words such as *some, a few, several,* and *many.*

There also are a number of reading-study skills that are required for effective reading in arithmetic. Many of these skills apply mostly to the reading of verbal problems. Arithmetic contains both a specialized vocabulary and a special symbol system. Some of the vocabulary terms are ordinary words that have a different meaning when used in a mathematical context. As was stated in the introduction to this chapter, verbal arithmetic problems are very difficult for most students to comprehend. They need to know how to read for details, interpret what they read, note relevant and irrelevant data, and read creatively to solve the problem correctly. Successful reading in arithmetic also requires effective comprehension of many different kinds of graphic and tabular materials.

William P. Dunlap and Martha Brown McKnight have written a very good recent article on how to help students conceptualize mathematical word problems. They state that one major problem that affects a student's ability to solve mathematical word problems is the three-level translation of the vocabulary found in the problem. They state that the student must be able to translate from the general to the technical to the symbolic vocabularies. They further state that the

---

[1]Stanford E. Taylor and others, *EDL Core Vocabularies in Reading, Mathematics, Science, and Social Studies* (New York: EDL/McGraw-Hill, 1979).

translation process among the vocabularies is essential to the conceptualization of the message contained in the word problem. The authors then provide concrete examples of these vocabulary translations.[2]

IMPROVING COMPETENCY IN DICTIONARY USAGE

Dictionary usage is given a separate section in this textbook from the rest of the general reading-study skills for several reasons. Dictionary usage is called a word identification technique by some reading specialists, and it is called a reading-study skill by other reading specialists. Although it could be placed in the next section of this chapter under "Location of Information," it is placed separately because of the lack of agreement about its true classification.

In any case, many reading specialists consider dictionary usage to be a last resort for a student to use in determining the pronunciation and meaning of unknown words. Because dictionary usage is a fairly difficult skill for many students to master, it often has not been taught effectively at the elementary-school level. Dictionary usage consists of the ability to use alphabetical sequence, the ability to use phonic analysis, the ability to understand the function of guide words, the ability to understand the parts of speech, and the ability to select the correct definition of the unknown words. As sometimes none of the dictionary definitions exactly fits the requirement of the unknown word, this may be the most difficult subskill of all.

Readiness for dictionary usage is begun in the early primary grades, when children construct their own picture dictionaries or learn to use a commercially available picture dictionary. Actual instruction in dictionary usage begins at the upper-primary-grade level when children usually have their own copy of a simplified dictionary. At the second-grade reading level, children can locate words in the dictionary that begin with two or three letter sequences. They learn to use guide words at about the third-grade reading level. Dictionary usage should be refined in the intermediate grades.

Often elementary-school students are required to look up the meanings of a list of words in the dictionary and then to write the definition of each word on a sheet of paper. Because the student has so little motivation to find out the meaning of the words on this type of list, such an activity well may become a meaningless procedure. In addition, as many words have more than one definition, depending upon

---

[2]William P. Dunlap and Martha Brown McKnight, "Vocabulary Translations for Conceptualizing Math Word Problems," *The Reading Teacher*, 32 (November 1978): 183–189.

their use in context, the student often has difficulty in deciding which meaning to choose. Although it is far better to have students locate the pronunciation and meaning of unknown words in the dictionary when they really need to do so in their own reading, it is quite difficult to motivate this procedure effectively. However, the teacher should encourage this type of effective and meaningful use of the dictionary as much as possible.

Students in the intermediate grades also should learn to use a thesaurus as an alternative to a dictionary. A thesaurus contains synonyms to given words. The thesaurus is especially useful in creative writing because it contains unusual synonyms to commonly used words.

A DESCRIPTION OF THE GENERAL READING-STUDY SKILLS

There are a number of general reading-study skills in which a student must be competent before he or she can experience success in content reading. Although there are some differences in the ways in which these reading-study skills are applied in the various content areas of social studies, science, and arithmetic, there probably also is enough overlap between them to be able to describe them in general terms. However, you always must remember that each of these reading-study skills must be taught and practiced somewhat differently in the various content areas. For the sake of convenience, the reading-study skills are divided into the general categories of "Selection of Information," "Organization of Information," "Location of Information," "Use of Graphic Aids," "Following Directions," and "Improving Reading Rate and Flexibility."

Selection of Information

The major reading-study skills under the category of "Selection of Information" are comprised of locating the directly stated main idea, locating significant details, finding irrelevant details, locating the implied main idea, and locating the main idea of a longer selection such as a chapter or a subsection of a chapter.

A number of paragraphs contain one central idea or thought. This central idea is the directly stated main idea, which often takes the form of a topic sentence. The topic sentence may be found at the beginning of the paragraph, the end of the paragraph, or in the middle of the paragraph. Students generally learn to identify directly stated main ideas at the upper-primary-grade reading level and then receive refinement of this skill in the intermediate grades. A student can underline the topic sentence in the paragraph or place a check mark in front of one of a number of sentences found below the paragraph that best expresses the main idea.

Here is a paragraph with another way of determining a directly stated main idea:

> Read this paragraph silently. After you have read it, underline the one title above the paragraph that would be the best title for the paragraph.

Icebergs Are Born in Spring
Icebergs Can Float
All About Icebergs

> Although icebergs can be very dangerous, they also are extremely interesting. Most of the dangerous icebergs are formed in Greenland by great amounts of snow. New snow packs down old snow so that it becomes ice that is as hard as a rock. The icebergs in Greenland are born in the spring as ice tongues break off from the ice cap. The iceberg finds its balance and begins traveling south. Most of the iceberg is below the surface of the water in the same way that an ice cube floats in a dish of water. A small iceberg is large enough to fill a football field, and a giant iceberg may be a mile long. Most icebergs have jagged peaks that rise hundreds of feet above the surface of the water. Some icebergs travel as far as 5,000 miles. However, all icebergs eventually melt.[3]

Most paragraphs that contain a directly stated main idea also contain a number of significant details. The significant details may clarify or contrast with the directly stated main idea in that paragraph. A somewhat related reading-study skill is the location of irrelevant or unimportant details in a paragraph. These unimportant details do not add in any way to the information found in that paragraph.

Another reading-study skill in the area of "Selection of Information" is that of locating the implied main idea in a paragraph. Some paragraphs do not contain a directly stated main idea that the reader can locate easily. Instead, the reader must infer an implied main idea by synthesizing most of the information that is found in that paragraph. The location of an implied main idea in a paragraph usually is first presented in the intermediate grades. However, because it is a difficult skill for most students to master, they must have considerable practice before gaining competence in it. Indeed, many students in the secondary school and in college still are not really competent in locating implied main ideas.

Here is one example of a paragraph that illustrates locating an implied main idea:

---

[3]Wilma H. Miller, *The Reading Activities Handbook* (New York: Holt, Rinehart and Winston, 1980), p. 256.

Read this paragraph silently. Then put an X in front of the sentence that contains the best statement of the *implied main idea*.

Unfortunately, some true heroes of the Revolutionary War are unknown to most people except serious historians. One such person was a Cherokee Indian woman named Nanye'hi or Nancy Ward. She was called "Beloved Woman" by the Cherokee nation. She was a member of the tribal council, an honor she received partly because she kept on fighting against Creek Indians in a battle after her husband was killed in that battle. She helped the Cherokee nation greatly by introducing the usefulness of cattle and dairy products to them. Nancy Ward also played an important part in the success of the American Revolution by opposing the Cherokee involvement in this conflict on the side of the English. She once also helped free some American traders from an Indian stockade. Nancy Ward once sent a herd of cattle to feed some starving American troops.

_____ Nancy Ward introduced cattle and dairy products to the Cherokee nation.

_____ Nancy Ward was unique in that she was a woman member of an Indian tribal council.

__X__ Nancy Ward made many unique contributions to both her people and to the Americans.[4]

Another reading-study skill of the "Selection of Information" category is that of locating the main idea in a longer selection. The student must be able to read a selection such as a subsection of a textbook chapter or an entire textbook chapter and determine the main idea of this longer selection. This statement of the main idea can be given in an oral or a written form. It can be one or several sentences for a section of the chapter or a paragraph for the entire chapter.

Organization of Information

The major reading-study skills under the category of "Organization of Information" are summarization, outlining, and note-taking. The major purpose of all of these organizational skills is helping students to see the relationships among the ideas found in content textbooks. The ability to see these relationships should help a student to retain the information gained from reading most effectively.

Summarization can be called either a study skill or an aspect of interpretive comprehension, as was described in Chapter 14. In any case, it is important for a student to summarize the main ideas and details from reading material as an aid to its retention. To summarize a paragraph, a student must be able to identify the main idea and

---

[4]Miller, *The Reading Activities Handbook*, p. 306.

locate the significant details in that paragraph. To summarize a longer selection, the student should be able to synthesize the important information found in that selection.

Summarization can be presented in a rudimentary form in the upper primary grades but should be refined and extended in the intermediate grades. A student can summarize a paragraph or a selection either in an oral or a written form. Normally, the child gives an oral summary in the beginning stages of reading instruction and a written summary later. The student can summarize a paragraph with one or several sentences and can summarize a longer selection with a paragraph.

Here is an example of a paragraph that can be summarized by one sentence. It is at the approximate third-grade reading level.

> Read this paragraph to yourself. Then write a *one-sentence summary* of it on the lines below.
>
> There are some interesting animals who live in trees in a faraway country called Australia. These animals are called koala bears or Australian Teddy bears. A koala bear has gray-brown thick fur, small eyes, and a snout that looks like the nose on a person. A baby koala bear is very tiny and lives in its mother's pouch for three months. A koala bear eats only the leaves of the gum trees that are found in Australia, and it doesn't drink any water. The koala bear sleeps in a tree during the day and eats leaves at night. Most people have seen pictures of koala bears and think that they are cute because of the babyish expression that they have on their faces.[5]
>
> _____
>
> _____

Outlining is another important reading-study skill under the category of "Selection of Information." Outlining should add to a student's understanding and retention of the important main ideas and details from content reading. However, outlining always should be presented and practiced as an aid to comprehension and retention instead of as a busywork activity.

Outlining requires that the student be able to differentiate between the main ideas and details in the chapter. It also may require that the student differentiate between the chapter topic and subtopics and details found in the chapter.

Readiness for outlining can begin in the upper primary grades, when the student places a number of objects into categories. However, actual outlining usually is presented and reinforced in the intermediate grades. Most students need considerable reinforcement of this reading-study skill before they attain competency in it. Outlining can be presented

---

[5]Miller, *The Reading Activities Handbook*, p. 414.

by having the student complete a partially incomplete outline. As another activity, the student can formulate his or her own outline of a short selection and then check it against the teacher's outline of the same material. Only later should the student be expected to complete an entire outline independently.

Here is an example of a partly completed traditional outline that is appropriate for use at about the fifth-grade reading level:

> You are going to make an outline about creatures that are found in different parts of the world. The list on this sheet contains three categories of creatures that are found in different places in the world and names of some of the creatures that can be placed in these three categories. Write the name of each category beside a Roman numeral and each type of animal beside the Arabic numerals.

Creatures of Australia
giraffe
roadrunner
koala bear
lion
Gila monster
Creatures of the Desert
kangaroo
wombat
elephant
tarantula

hippopotamus
Creatures of Africa
platypus
coyote
rhinoceros
scorpion
wallaby
rattlesnake
chimpanzee
Tasmanian devil

I. _____
  1. _____
  2. _____
  3. _____
  4. _____
  5. _____
  6. _____
II. _____
  1. _____
  2. _____
  3. _____
  4. _____
  5. _____
  6. _____
III. _____
  1. _____
  2. _____
  3. _____
  4. _____
  5. _____
  6. _____

[6]

---

[6]Miller, *The Reading Activities Handbook*, pp. 418–419.

Here is an example of a newer form of outlining that has gained considerable recognition lately:

A Scientific Weather Experiment

1.0 Ask the appropriate question
2.0 Formulate an hypothesis
3.0 Formulate a plan of attack
    3.1 The first step
    3.2 The second step
    3.3 The third step
4.0 The results are acted upon
    4.1 Observe the results
    4.2 Tabulate the results
    4.3 Interpret the results[7]

Another important skill in the category of "Organization of Information" is that of note-taking. Note-taking is basically made up of picking out the main ideas and their supporting details and writing them down. It normally is presented and practiced at the intermediate-grade reading level. It is helpful if the student learns a number of note-taking techniques. The student should not make notes until he or she has read the entire selection and then should select the most important concepts and facts to remember. Moreover, the student should make notes on only one part of the topic and only from one source on each note card if index cards are used for note-taking. He or she should label each note card as to the topic and write on only one side of the card. The student then should place all the note cards in alphabetical sequence, using the topic labels of each note card.

Robert A. Palmatier has formulated a note-taking system (NSL). In this method the student writes notes on one side of 8½-inch by 11-inch loose-leaf sheets. A margin three inches from the left side of the paper may be added to lined paper that has no margin. The student then writes notes from reading or lectures to the right of the margin. Numbers and letters can be used to identify the various parts of the material. In the left-hand margin, the student writes labels that correspond to the different parts of information in the original notes. When studying the material, the student spreads out the pages so that only the left-hand margin shows. The student then converts each label in the left-hand margin to a question and attempts to answer the question by checking his or her notes.[8]

---

[7]Miller, *The Reading Activities Handbook,* p. 406.

[8]Robert A. Palmatier, "A Notetaking System for Learning," *Journal of Reading, 17* (October 1973): 36–39.

Following Directions

Following directions is another of the important reading-study skills. As was explained in Chapter 14, it also is considered to be a subskill of literal comprehension. In addition, it is a reading-study skill that is a prerequisite for success in many school activities as well as in actual life situations. Unfortunately, it is a skill that many adults have failed to master.

Learning to follow directions should receive much practice in the elementary school. It can first be presented in the early primary grades and should then be extended in the intermediate grades. At the beginning stages of reading instruction, the teacher can present oral directions of first one step and later several steps. Subsequently, written directions can be presented containing one step at first and later several steps. These written directions can be made relevant by trying to apply them to some type of actual classroom situation. In the intermediate grades the student should learn to read and carry out directions containing a number of points. The performing of scientific experiments and the solving of verbal arithmetic problems are two good ways to help a student attain competency in reading and following directions.

An activity such as the following also can be adapted at different grade levels to give a student enjoyable practice in reading and following directions:

Read and follow each direction found on this sheet as quickly as you can.

1. If there are seven days in the week, circle the last word in this sentence.
2. Draw a circle around the shortest word in this sentence.
3. If the words *tiny* and *small* mean about the same thing, write the number 8 under this sentence.
4. Cross out the longest word in this sentence.
5. If the words *warm* and *cool* mean about the same thing, write the number 2 under the sentence.
6. Write the first letter of the first month in the year under this sentence.
7. If children go to school on Tuesdays, write the number 9 under this sentence.
8. Draw a circle around the word in this sentence that begins with a capital letter.
9. Draw a happy face under this sentence.
10. Write your first and last names under this sentence.[9]

---

[9]Miller, *The Reading Activities Handbook,* p. 415.

Location of Information

The major reading-study skills under the category of "Location of Information" are those of using a table of contents, an index, a glossary, an appendix, an encyclopedia, the library card catalog, and the *Readers' Guide to Periodical Literature*. All these reading-study skills are designed to help a student use various resources in the acquisition of knowledges and skills in the various content areas.

The locational skill of using the table of contents of a book can first be presented as early as the latter half of first grade. Children at this level should be taught to use the table of contents in simple material that they are using such as a basal reader. A group of children can be asked such questions as these:

How many stories are there in the first part of this book?

How many parts are there in this book?

How many stories are there in this book?

On what page does the story "_____" begin?

Students in the intermediate grades should receive considerably more practice in using the table of contents in their basal readers and content textbooks. They should learn that a table of contents indicates the basic organization of the book. It shows whether the book is divided into units or chapters and what kind of information the book contains. They should learn that it also lists the aids that the book contains such as maps, graphs, tables, and diagrams. Students also should learn that tables of contents differ in format. In addition, they should learn to determine from a table of contents if a book is likely to contain the information that they want.

Teachers at the intermediate-grade level can design informal devices to give students practice in using a table of contents. Here are some sample questions that could be included on such a device:

1. What is Unit Three in this textbook about?
2. How many different topics are covered in Unit One in this textbook?
3. On what pages are the maps in Chapter 7 found?
4. How many chapters does this textbook contain?
5. On what page of this textbook does the glossary begin?
6. What is the major theme of Chapter 10?
7. On what page does the index of this textbook begin?
8. Does this textbook contain any appendixes?
9. On what page is the diagram in Chapter 2 found?
10. On what page can you find an exercise for determining how much you have learned from studying Chapter 8?

Students in the intermediate grades also should learn how to use the index in their content textbooks. They should learn that the index contains a detailed listing of all the topics in that book and that it gives precise page references to the topics contained in the book. To use an index effectively, the student must be able to determine the probable entry words, use alphabetical sequence to locate the entry words, see the relationships between the topics and subtopics, and interpret the symbols that are used. The student also must learn that an index can be in several different forms.

The teacher should present a number of direct lessons on using an index. The examples in the beginning lessons should be structured so that there is no doubt as to the entry words, and the later lessons should require more inferencing on the part of the student as to the probable entry words. Practice in using an index always is more efficient if a student is attempting to locate the answers to his or her own questions about topics, once the initial instruction has been given and understood.

The glossary of a textbook is very useful in helping a student to obtain the pronunciation and meaning of the difficult terms that are included in that textbook. Glossary usage entails a number of the same subskills as does dictionary usage. However, it is usually much easier to motivate students to learn it than dictionary usage. Because a glossary contains few words in comparison to a dictionary, the student usually can locate the unknown word quite easily. In addition, the glossary definition usually exactly fits the requirement of the unknown word in the way it is used in the student's basal reader or content textbook. Therefore, students in the upper primary and intermediate grades should be encouraged to use the glossary of their textbook whenever feasible.

A number of the content textbooks at the intermediate-grade level may contain one appendix or several appendixes. The student should learn that an appendix contains valuable information that the author did not wish to place in the body of the book. However, the information contained in an appendix still can be useful if a student wishes additional information about a topic that was mentioned in a briefer form in the body of the book. A student may wish to use the appendix as an aid to answering some important questions that he or she has about the topic covered in that appendix.

Encyclopedias can be a useful tool for a number of students in the upper primary grades and for many students in the intermediate grades because they offer such a comprehensive source of important facts about people, places, things, and events. The best-known children's encyclopedias are *Childcraft, The World Book Encyclopedia, The New Book of Knowledge, Compton's Encyclopedia,* and *Britannica Junior.*

Children in the upper primary grades can learn a good deal about how an encyclopedia is organized and how to use it by having opportunities to browse through it and look at the pictures. Older students, however, need to have some direct instruction in using encyclopedias. They need to learn that an encyclopedia is arranged in alphabetical sequence by the main subject entry. The student also should be able to alphabetize to the third and fourth letter because many encyclopedia entries begin with the same letter sequences. In addition, a student should be able to locate entries using guidewords. Obviously, the encyclopedia must be on the student's instructional or independent reading level if he or she is to be able to comprehend the material contained in the entry.

Some children undoubtedly do not enjoy using encyclopedias because they have been assigned questions to be answered from the encyclopedia entry. Undoubtedly, they will have infinitely more motivation to use encyclopedias to locate the answers to questions in which they really have some interest. Although these questions obviously can be connected with units of work in content areas, they may also simply be questions about which the student is curious. It is the teacher's responsibility to show students that encyclopedias are not merely storehouses of dry facts, but rather are sources of fascinating, vital information.

The library card catalog can be introduced to some children in the upper primary grades and to other children in the intermediate grades. If an elementary school has a central library, the librarian may be the ideal person to introduce the library card catalog. If the elementary school does not have a library, the teacher may be able to help the class develop a very simple card catalog for the classroom library. This catalog may contain simplified title, author, and subject matter cards.

However, if the school library has a traditional card catalog, the author cards, title cards, and subject cards can be shown to the students, who also can be shown the process of locating a book in the library by its call number. Libraries today use either the Library of Congress system or the Dewey decimal system for classifying books. In either case, students in the intermediate grades can learn to locate books by their call number.

The majority of students are most motivated to use the library card catalog when they wish to locate books on a topic in which they are interested either for a school assignment or for their personal pleasure. Without this kind of motivation, the library card catalog simply becomes a rather boring academic exercise for a number of students.

The *Readers' Guide to Periodical Literature* is a reference tool that you may wish to introduce at the fifth-grade or sixth-grade reading level, depending upon the maturity and interests of the students. The *Readers' Guide* is a listing of the topics found in a myriad of periodicals and the authors of the articles contained therein. It is best used when a student has a real need to locate information on a topic in which he or she is interested that is best found in a periodical. As in the case of other reference sources, without this motivation the use of this reference tool also can be drudgery for a student.

Using Graphic Aids

The most important reading-study skills under the category of "Using Graphic Aids" are those of interpreting a diagram, interpreting a chart, interpreting a table, interpreting a map, and interpreting a graph. This category of reading-study skills deals with helping the student attain competency in the use of the graphic aids that are mainly found in content textbooks. Instruction and reinforcement in the use of these aids are usually given chiefly at the intermediate-grade reading level.

Diagrams and charts probably are most common in children's social studies and science textbooks, where they are designed to clarify new vocabulary terms or illustrate concepts. The typical diagram contains labels that are designed to help the student interpret the diagram. As an example, a science textbook may contain a picture of a flower, with its various parts labeled to clarify the vocabulary terms that are associated with it. Sometimes children are asked to do the labeling on the diagram.

The flowchart is very commonly used today in content textbooks. The flowchart is a graphic aid that very effectively shows the flow of organization. Here is an example of a flowchart from the content area of social studies:

Citizens

Executive Branch	Legislative Branch	Judicial Branch
President Cabinet	Senators Representatives	Supreme Court[10]

A table is a comprehensive but concise way to display related facts and information. Content area textbooks often contain tables so that the student can receive additional or clarified information. Students should learn that specific information can be found from tables and that this information can be used comparatively. They also should learn that they can interpret additional information from the information given by the table.

---

[10]Miller, *The Reading Activities Handbook,* p. 408.

SS 1(2) USING MAP SKILLS
AND FOLLOWING DIRECTIONS

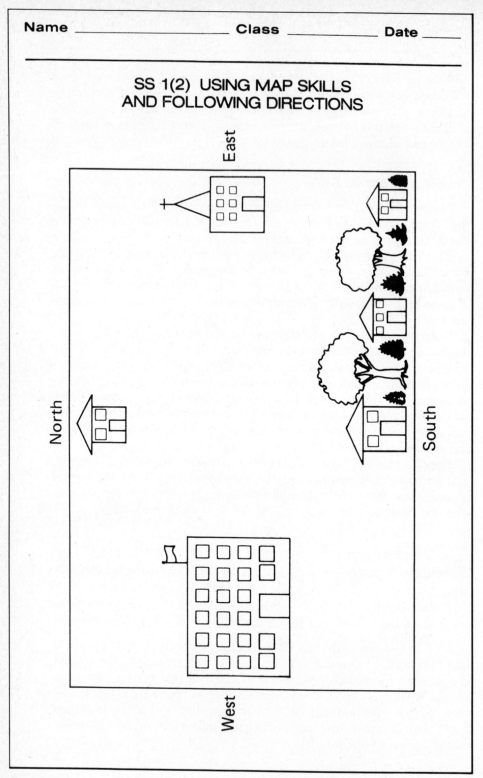

FIGURE 16-1

1. The school is located on the _____ side of the
   east/west
   map.

2. Draw an evergreen tree by the house on the north side of
   the map.

3. The church is located on the _____ side of the
   east/west
   map.

4. Draw two children standing by the door of the school.

5. Draw a large tree near the left side of the church.

Children in the early primary grades can be given the opportunity to make their own simple tables about tasks and events that are familiar to them. For example, a table entitled "Classroom Helpers," which contains the class jobs and the names of the children, is very common in primary-grade classrooms.

Intermediate-grade students can learn to interpret the tables found in content textbooks. Students at this level should learn to make comparisons from different sets of data and to draw conclusions from the data. Tables are used in social studies to present such information as average temperature, heights above sea level, and mileage between various cities. Tables in science generally are used to report the results of experiments, and tables in arithmetic show various kinds of relationships.

The student should always have valid reasons for trying to interpret a table. As in the case of the other reading-study skills, the interpretation of tables also has more motivation for the student who has a valid reason for obtaining the information contained in that table.

Map interpretation is perhaps one of the more commonly used reading-study skills in the category of "Using Graphic Aids." A map is a graphic representation of where things are located in relation to each other. Thus, maps can represent reality and also provide the student with a wealth of information.

Interpretation of maps may begin in the early primary grades, when children construct a map of their classroom or their neighborhood. They then learn to interpret this map. As is shown in Figure 16-1, such a simple map can be used for interpretation and for reading and following directions.

Students at the intermediate-grade level need to learn how to interpret other types of maps such as road maps; political maps showing different states or countries; and physical maps that show rainfall, temperature, or distances above sea level. In addition, content textbooks in the intermediate grades may contain special kinds of maps.

Map interpretation in the intermediate grades should be presented by using the maps found in content textbooks and other reference sources. Students should learn that a map uses symbols, is a scaled representation, and shows relative direction. Figure 16-2 illustrates a map that was reproduced from a sixth-grade social studies textbook.

A graph is a graphic aid that has been constructed to show some type of quantitative relationship. To interpret a graph, a student should determine what type of information can be learned from it and the unit of measurement that was used in reporting the information. Although graphs sometimes may be introduced in the upper primary grades, they are mainly used in the intermediate grades.

There are four main types of graphs. The circle or pie graph is constructed from a circle that is divided into percentages or fractions. It is a fairly difficult graph to understand because its interpretation depends upon a student's understanding of the parts of a whole. Here is an example of a circle or pie graph:

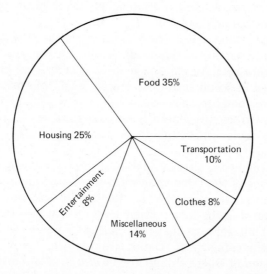

A picture graph or a photograph can be introduced in the primary grades. This is a simple graph that uses pictures to express information. A bar graph is another type of graph that can be introduced in

FIGURE 16-2

the upper primary grades and extended in the intermediate grades. Figure 16-3 shows a bar graph containing data about temperatures at which some things melt. It can be used at about the sixth-grade reading level.

A fourth type of graph is the line graph. Figure 16-4 shows a line graph about a student's percentile rank on nine weekly reading tests. It can be used at the upper-intermediate or junior-high-school reading level.

Edward Fry has written a very interesting recent article on graphical literacy. He stated that the use of graphs to communicate information has been around since before written verbal language. He further believes that reading teachers should present graphical literacy because they are the best equipped to do so. Fry presented an interesting taxonomy of graphs that any teacher who is interested in this subject should explore. He also provided some interesting suggestions for improving graphical literacy such as the following: ask reading comprehension questions about graphs, choose textbooks that have a good use of graphs, talk with students about the importance of graphs, grade graphs in student papers, and have a graphing contest.[11]

Improving Reading Rate and Flexibility

The improvement of reading rate and flexibility is also an aspect of the reading-study skills that can aid in a student's comprehension and

---

[11]Edward Fry, "Graphical Literacy," *Journal of Reading, 34* (February 1981): 383–390.

SS 11(6) INTERPRETING A BAR GRAPH

Read the bar graph below. Then place a ✓ in front of the correct answer to each question.

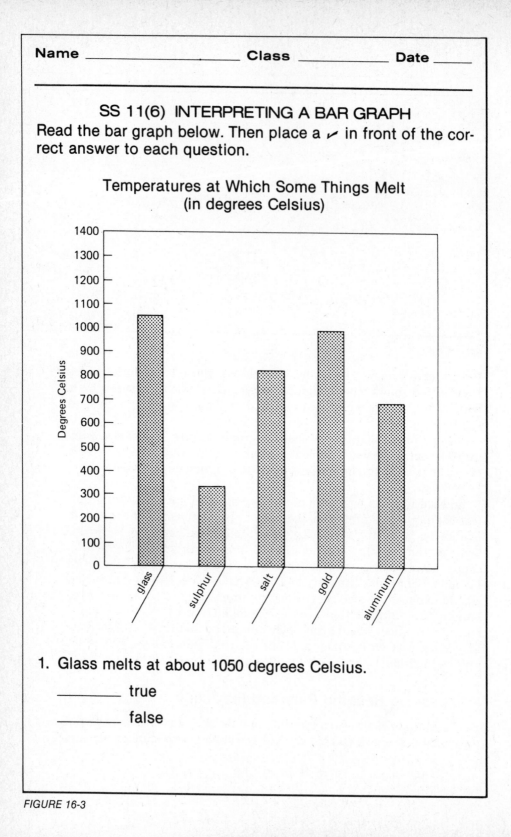

Temperatures at Which Some Things Melt
(in degrees Celsius)

1. Glass melts at about 1050 degrees Celsius.

_____ true

_____ false

FIGURE 16-3

2. Sulphur melts at about 300 degrees Celsius.

_____ true

_____ false

3. Salt melts at about 900 degrees Celsius.

_____ true

_____ false

4. Gold melts at about 963 degrees Celsius.

_____ true

_____ false

5. Aluminum melts at about 660 degrees Celsius.

_____ true

_____ false

retention of content materials. Reading rate improvement may generally be begun in the lower intermediate grades only for those students who have very good basic word identification and comprehension skills. It should never be stressed with students who are inadequate readers.

A student's rate of reading always should be dependent upon the difficulty of the reading material, the student's purpose for reading, and the student's background of experiences with the topic of the reading material. Thus, the student should vary his or her reading rate depending upon these factors. This concept is called _reading flexibility_. Most reading specialists have described the following reading rates:

> _Skimming._ Skimming is reading for a general impression of the reading material. It is a reading rate of over 1,000 words per minute.
>
> _Scanning._ Scanning is moving one's eyes rapidly to locate a specific detail such as a name, a place, or a date. As all the words are not perceived in scanning, it is impossible to estimate its rate.
>
> _Rapid reading._ Rapid reading is reading material such as a novel for main ideas. It often is at a rate of 400 to 600 words per minute.

SS 13(7–8) INTERPRETING A LINE GRAPH

Study this line graph, and answer each question below.

Mario's Percentile Ranks on Nine Weekly Reading Tests

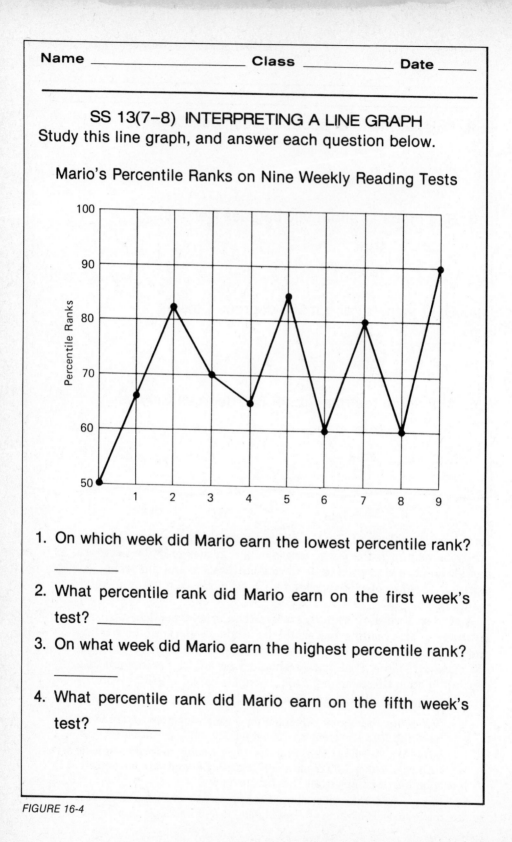

1. On which week did Mario earn the lowest percentile rank?

   _____

2. What percentile rank did Mario earn on the first week's test? _____

3. On what week did Mario earn the highest percentile rank?

   _____

4. What percentile rank did Mario earn on the fifth week's test? _____

FIGURE 16-4

5. What percentile rank did Mario earn on the seventh week's test? _____

6. Between which two weeks did Mario make the greatest improvement on the weekly reading test? _____

7. What percentile rank did Mario earn on the fourth week's test? _____

8. Between which two weeks did Mario decrease in reading performance the most on the weekly reading tests?

_____

Study-type reading. Study-type reading is reading mainly for facts and details in such content areas as social studies and science. It generally is at a rate of 250 to 350 words per minute.

Careful, analytical reading. Careful, analytical reading is reading and re-reading very carefully for details. It perhaps is best exemplified in reading and arithmetic verbal problems. It probably is at a rate of about 75 to 150 words per minute.

I have found that most college students and adults are inflexible, word-by-word readers who are unable to vary their reading rate. They generally read all materials in the same way at a rate of about 275 to 325 words per minute. Students in the intermediate grades who are adequate readers should begin to have opportunities to vary their reading speed depending upon the difficulty of the material, their purposes for reading it, and their background with it. They should not be cautioned to read all material carefully as a number of teachers have done in the past.

In beginning a program of reading rate improvement, the intermediate-grade teacher first should explain the concept of reading flexibility. Next the students should be given opportunities to learn to vary their reading rate. There are several different techniques and materials that are appropriate for this purpose in the intermediate grades. Students should select very easy, interesting reading material in which comprehension is no problem. They then should practice reading in thought units or groups of words instead of pausing or fixating on each individual word. For example, the following sentence is divided into thought units:

Every year/ my family/ has a/ big picnic/ in the summer/ as a/ family reunion.

After the student in the upper intermediate grades has developed proficiency in reading in thought units, he or she can use timed readings to improve reading rate. Have the student read easy material in thought units as rapidly as possible for three minutes. Then have the student determine his or her reading rate by using this simple formula:

$$\frac{\text{average number of words per line} \times \text{lines read}}{\text{minutes read}} = \text{words per minute}$$

The student should record his or her reading rate. On succeeding days have the student read five minutes, ten minutes, and three minutes from comparable material. Each day the student should determine and record his or her reading rate. The student should make considerable progress in the reading rate for easy material by the use of this method.

There are devices that can be used with good readers at the upper-primary-grade and intermediate-grade reading levels to improve reading rate. Although research has not discovered any relation between the use of such devices and improvement in reading rate, their use still can be very motivating.

One such device is called a *tachistoscope*. A tachistoscope is a device that projects letters, numbers, designs, words, or phrases on a screen at different rates of speed. The material found on a filmstrip appears on the screen at different rates of speed, varying from one second to one one-hundredth of a second. Generally, tachistoscopic training is begun at a slower speed and then gradually progresses to a higher speed. A tachistoscope is designed to improve a student's visual perception ability and, therefore, subsequently his or her rate of reading.

A *controlled reading device* uses filmstrips containing content to attempt to increase reading rate by improving left-to-right progression and eye span. Such filmstrips can be purchased from the companies manufacturing the devices with which they are designed to be used. In one variation, the entire screen is dark at the beginning, and a beam of light moving from left to right exposes the material a few words at a time at different rates of speed. In another variation, the material is exposed a line at a time. In either case, at the end of the passage, the student is supposed to answer some comprehension questions about the material that also appear on the screen.

An *accelerating device* or *pacer* uses actual reading material to improve the rate of reading. In such a device, a bar, shade, or beam of light moves down the page of the material that the reader places in the device. The student then reads below the bar or shade or within the beam of light. An accelerating device or pacer can be set at different rates of speed.

STRATEGIES AND MATERIALS FOR IMPROVING COMPETENCY IN CONTENT READING

There are many strategies and materials that can be used to improve a student's competency in reading in the various content fields. Many of the strategies operate most effectively if they are used within the context of the student's own content textbooks and other content materials. Although a few of these strategies can first be presented in the primary grades, many of them should be refined and extended in the intermediate grades.

As was stated earlier in this chapter, most content textbooks contain many difficult, specialized vocabulary terms. Before giving students an assignment from a content textbook, the teacher should read the material carefully and select some of the most crucial vocabulary terms from this assignment. These terms then should be presented before the students are asked to read the assignment. Place the terms on the chalkboard or on a transparency, and help the students to use their structural and phonic skills in decoding the words. It is often helpful to place each term in the same context in which it is used in the assignment so that contextual clues can also be used. In some content areas, the vocabulary presentation can be made more relevant by the use of a demonstration, an experiment, concrete objects, bottles, pictures, a film, a filmstrip, slides, or a recording.

Word wonder was described in a recent article as very useful when the students need help with the vocabulary terms and concepts that are contained in a story or content assignment. In a simple form, the students tell the teacher what words they expect to find in a certain story, and they then read to find out if they were right. In a more complex form, the teacher lists words, and the children determine whether each word is likely to appear in that story or assignment. The teacher should include some words that are likely to be chosen incorrectly. After the reading, the students can determine the accuracy of what they had decided earlier. Word wonder helps the teacher preteach only the vocabulary words that are necessary for effective comprehension of the material. In addition, the background of the students in relation to their ability to comprehend the material also is assessed prior to the reading.[12]

Another strategy for improving comprehension of content material is the *expectation outline*. In this strategy, students are asked to tell what they expect to learn from an assignment about a topic such as human digestion. As the students suggest questions such as "What

---

[12]Dixie Lee Spiegel, "Six Alternatives to the Directed Reading Activity," *The Reading Teacher, 34* (May 1981): 914–920.

organs are involved in digestion?" "What is the most important organ in digestion?" "How long does digestion take?" the teacher tries to group related questions on the chalkboard. The teacher then asks the students to make up a title for each category of questions. The students then read the story to find the answers to those questions. The expectation outline provides skills in prereading anticipation, categorizing, and identifying answers to specific questions.[13]

Another strategy for improving comprehension of content material is the prereading *guided reading procedure*. In this strategy students are asked to tell everything they know about the topic that they subsequently are going to read about. The teacher then records all the responses on the chalkboard, numbering each response. The students then are to search for inconsistencies in the information. They next suggest four or five categories and assign each piece of information to one of the categories. Then they read to find out if the information they have listed is correct. This procedure gives students practice in prereading anticipation, purpose setting, critical reading, and categorizing.[14]

There are a number of different study strategies that can be presented to students in the intermediate grades as an aid to the comprehension and retention of content materials. The best known of these study techniques is Survey Q3R—survey, question, read, recite, and review. Survey Q3R was developed by Francis P. Robinson. It is based on an information-processing theory of learning. Each part of Survey Q3R is designed to facilitate the processing of incoming print so that the student can deal with it most effectively.

Although Survey Q3R must be varied somewhat depending upon the content in which it is used, very briefly it contains the following steps:

> *Survey*. The student surveys the entire textbook chapter to gain an overall impression of what it is about. In this survey the student may read the introduction and summary of the chapter and the first sentence in each of the paragraphs and may examine the pictures, maps, diagrams, tables, and graphs found in the chapter.
>
> *Question*. The student poses questions that he or she wants to read to answer in this step of the procedure. The student can turn each subheading into a question and also formulate additional questions to read to answer.
>
> *Read*. The student reads the entire chapter selectively to try to answer the questions that he or she has posed. In this reading, the student tries to fill in the gaps in his or her own learning. This step of the procedure makes the student actively involved in the reading.

---

[13]Spiegel, "Six Alternatives."

[14]Spiegel, "Six Alternatives."

Recite. This step applies to only one section at a time. After the student has read a section at a time in a purposeful manner, he or she can recite the important information gained from that section in either an oral or a written form depending upon which is more efficient for the student.

Review. This step generally applies after the student has completed the chapter. He or she tries to review the important concepts, generalizations, and facts that were gained from the chapter. The student often can use the written notes he or she may have made in the fourth step of this procedure.[15]

There are a number of variations of the Survey Q3R technique that can be used as alternatives to it. Most of them use an overall survey of the reading selection, some type of self-questioning technique, setting purposes for reading, and a review step to fix the important information in mind.

Here is a listing of several of the other study techniques and one source for each where you can find information on how to use the techniques:

POINT—Walter R. Hill, *Secondary School Reading: Process, Program, Procedure.* Boston: Allyn and Bacon, Inc., 1979, pp. 155–160.

REAP—Lawrence E. Hafner, *Developmental Reading in Middle and Secondary Schools.* New York: Macmillan Publishing Company, Inc., 1977, pp. 179–180.

C2R—Mary A. Moore, "C2R: Concentrate, Read, Remember." *Journal of Reading, 24* (January 1981): 337–339.

Anthony V. Manzo has developed a very useful procedure called *ReQuest.* It is appropriate for students who need practice in comprehending at the interpretive level of comprehension from content textbooks. Very briefly, in this procedure both the teacher and students read just the title and first sentence of the selection. Then the students ask the teacher anything they want about the sentence. The teacher answers all the questions and praises students for asking questions above the literal level and answers the literal questions without comment. Then the teacher poses additional questions above the literal level. The following procedure can be followed for several additional sentences. The procedure can probably be varied to use one paragraph at a time instead of one sentence at a time.[16]

Another useful technique is the *C/T/Q Strategy,* which was also developed by Anthony V. Manzo. This strategy helps teachers to isolate key concepts, key vocabulary terms, and key questions and to

[15]Francis P. Robinson, *Effective Study* (New York: Harper & Row, Publishers, 1961).

[16]Anthony V. Manzo, "The ReQuest Procedure," *Journal of Reading, 13* (November 1969): 123–126.

present these in advance of a content reading assignment. Manzo suggested that students record these points in their notebooks to guide them through later lessons and home-school reading assignments.[17]

Harold L. Herber has suggested using reading guides with content textbooks to present subject matter content and the reading processes that help the student attain that content. Herber has called one type of reading guide the three levels of comprehension. He suggested giving all the students in the class the same content assignment and the same type of reading guide. However, he also suggested having below-average readers respond only to literal comprehension questions, average readers respond only to interpretive comprehension questions, and above-average readers respond only to creative questions. Each type of question would be marked in some way, as with one, two, or three asterisks. Herber also suggested other kinds of reading guides such as concept guides and pattern or organization guides.[18]

There are a number of vocabulary reinforcement exercises that can be used in the upper intermediate grades to help students review and remember the important specialized vocabulary terms that they have met in their content reading. These take the form of crossword puzzles, acrostics, word puzzles, categorization exercises, and matching vocabulary exercises. Here is an example of a word puzzle that can be used for vocabulary reinforcement in a social studies unit at about the sixth-grade level:

> Read each of these definitions of vocabulary terms found in a social studies unit on American Indians. Then complete each word puzzle by filling in the correct letters.
>
> 1. Give a three-syllable word for the name of a light ax that was used as a hand weapon by Indians.
>   t _ _ / _ / _ _ _ _
>
> 2. Give a two-syllable word for a punishment in early times in which a prisoner of the Indians had to run between two rows of Indians who hit him with sticks as he passed through.
>   g _ _ _ _ / _ _ _
>
> 3. Give a one-syllable word that describes one way the Indians had of killing the white enemies.
>   s _ _ _ _
>
> 4. Give a two-syllable word for a carved or painted figure placed on a pole.
>   t _ / _ _ _

---

[17]Anthony V. Manzo, "Three 'Universal' Strategies in Content Area Reading and Languaging," *Journal of Reading, 24* (November 1980): 146–149.

[18]Harold L. Herber, *Teaching Reading in Content Areas* (Englewood Cliffs, New Jersey: Prentice-Hall, Inc., 1978).

5. Give a three-syllable word for the name of the shoes that were worn by Indians.

m _ _ / _ _/ _ _ _ _ _

Answers: tomahawk, gauntlet, scalp, totem, moccasins

TEACHING CONTENT READING TO BELOW-AVERAGE READERS

As was stated earlier in this section, there are a number of below-average readers in the intermediate grades who have great difficulty in reading content area assignments, especially in social studies and science. Although there really is no perfect solution to their difficulties, there are several steps that an intermediate-grade teacher can take in the attempt to alleviate somewhat this difficult problem.

The language experience approach can be used with the most severely disabled readers in the intermediate grades. As you remember from Chapter 4, this approach involves the dictating and transcribing of materials. When the language experience approach is used to help disabled readers obtain social studies or science content, have a peer tutor, a teacher's aide, or a parent volunteer read the content assignment aloud to one or several severely disabled readers. The tutor and the students then discuss the material carefully, and the one or several disabled readers then dictate their account of the material to the tutor who transcribes it. If it is possible, the transcribed material later is typed for the below-average student or students, who then usually can read this account of the content material fairly successfully. All the transcribed materials can be kept in a loose-leaf notebook or folder so that the student can study them periodically.

As another alternative that is perhaps most useful for the mildly and moderately disabled readers in the intermediate grades, the teacher, a teacher's aide, or a parent volunteer can attempt to rewrite very difficult social studies or science materials. However, this is fairly difficult to do successfully because the specialized vocabulary often is essential to comprehension in these content areas. In any case, in rewriting the material, one can use simpler vocabulary whenever possible. Less complex sentence structure may help to increase comprehension although care must be taken that the sentences do not become so short as to be choppy and unnatural. The person who rewrites the material can attempt to explain vocabulary and concepts as much as possible. Topic sentences can be placed in paragraphs, and more headings and subheadings may be used. You should remember that such rewriting takes a great deal of time, and it may be helpful to have several teachers work together on such a project.

Another possible solution to the problem of students in the intermediate grades who cannot read the subject matter textbooks is to

select easier reading material for them. These may be content textbooks that are written on an easier reading level. For example, if a
fifth-grade class is studying weather, you may be able to locate science
textbooks written on an easier level that cover about the same material as the regular fifth-grade science textbook. In addition, you may
be able to use other materials such as pamphlets, brochures, and booklets. A recent book by Albert J. Harris and Edward R. Sipay also has
a number of easier reading materials for science, social studies, and
English.[19]

As was mentioned earlier in this chapter, the Fry Readability Formula can be used to determine the approximate reading level of basal
readers, content textbooks, supplementary reading materials, and trade
books. Here are the steps to follow in applying the Fry Readability
Formula:

1. Select the material to which you wish to apply the readability
   formula. Choose three 100-word passages. Usually one passage
   should be near the beginning, one should be near the middle,
   and one should be near the end of the material.
2. Count the 100-word passage for each selection, and put a slash
   mark after the hundredth word.
3. Count the number of syllables in each 100-word passage.
4. Determine the average number of sentences per 100 words. To
   do so, count the number of words in the sentence containing the
   hundredth word. Next count the number of words in this sentence that are contained in the 100-word sample. These are the
   words that appear before the slash mark. Then divide the total
   number of words in this sentence into the number of words in
   the sentence before the slash mark to find the average number
   of sentences per 100 words.
5. For each 100-word sample, the average number of sentences per
   100 words is the total number of sentences in the sample prior
   to the sentence containing the hundredth word or the part of the
   sentence containing the hundredth word.
6. After you have determined the average number of syllables per
   100 words and the average number of sentences per 100 words
   for each sample, average the figures for all three samples.
7. Then enter these figures on the graph (Figure 16-5) to determine
   the approximate reading level of the material. The average number of syllables per 100 words is located along the horizontal axis
   of the graph, and the average number of sentences per 100 words
   is located along the vertical axis of the graph. Put a dot on the

[19]Albert J. Harris and Edward R. Sipay, *How to Increase Reading
Ability* (New York: Longman, Inc., 1980), pp. 503–504.

graph where the two lines meet, and that is the *approximate* grade level of the textbook. If the dot falls into the gray area, the readability check was not valid.

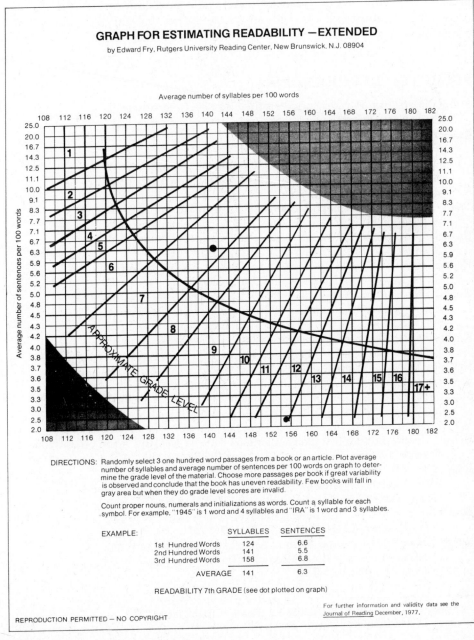

GRAPH FOR ESTIMATING READABILITY — EXTENDED
by Edward Fry, Rutgers University Reading Center, New Brunswick, N.J. 08904

DIRECTIONS: Randomly select 3 one hundred word passages from a book or an article. Plot average number of syllables and average number of sentences per 100 words on graph to determine the grade level of the material. Choose more passages per book if great variability is observed and conclude that the book has uneven readability. Few books will fall in gray area but when they do grade level scores are invalid.

Count proper nouns, numerals and initializations as words. Count a syllable for each symbol. For example, "1945" is 1 word and 4 syllables and "IRA" is 1 word and 3 syllables.

EXAMPLE:

	SYLLABLES	SENTENCES
1st Hundred Words	124	6.6
2nd Hundred Words	141	5.5
3rd Hundred Words	158	6.8
AVERAGE	141	6.3

READABILITY 7th GRADE (see dot plotted on graph)

For further information and validity data see the Journal of Reading December, 1977.

FIGURE 16-5

You also should know that readability determinations can be performed by microcomputers at this time. This, of course, would be a very timesaving way of determining the approximate reading grade level of content textbooks and other materials. In a recent article, Michael R. Schuyler has presented a complete program that can be used to determine textbook readability. He stated that this formula can be used by any reading specialist with access to a microcomputer.[20]

SELECTED REFERENCES

Ankney, Paul, and Pat McClurg. "Testing Manzo's Guided Reading Procedure." *The Reading Teacher, 34* (March 1981): 681–684.

Aulls, Mark W. *Developmental and Remedial Reading in the Middle Grades.* Boston: Allyn and Bacon, Inc., 1978, Chapters 3, 4.

Cunningham, James W., Patricia M. Cunningham, and Sharon V. Arthur, *Middle & Secondary School Reading.* New York: Longman, Inc., 1981, Chapters 5, 6, 7, 8.

Estes, Thomas H., and Joseph L. Vaughan, Jr. *Reading and Learning in the Content Classroom.* Boston: Allyn and Bacon, Inc., 1978.

Hansell, T. Stevenson. "Four Methods of Diagnosis for Content Area Reading." *Journal of Reading, 24* (May 1981): 696–700.

Herber, Harold L. *Teaching Reading in Content Areas.* Englewood Cliffs, New Jersey: Prentice-Hall, Inc., 1978.

Kaplan, Elaine M., and Anita Tuchman. "Vocabulary Strategies Belong in the Hands of Learners." *Journal of Reading, 24* (October 1980): 32–34.

Karlin, Robert. *Teaching Elementary Reading.* New York: Harcourt Brace Jovanovich, Inc., 1980, Chapter 8.

McClain, Leslie J. "Study Guides: Potential Assets in Content Classrooms." *Journal of Reading, 24* (January 1981): 321–325.

Macklin, Michael D. "Content Area of Reading Is a Process for Finding Personal Meaning." *Journal of Reading, 22* (December 1978): 212–215.

Nelson, Joan. "Readability: Some Cautions for the Content Area Teacher." *Journal of Reading, 21* (April 1978): 620–625.

Riley, James D., and Andrew B. Pachtman. "Reading Mathematical Word Problems: Telling Them What to Do Is Not Telling Them How to Do It." *Journal of Reading, 21* (March 1978): 531–534.

Schachter, Sumner W. "Developing Flexible Reading Habits." *Journal of Reading, 22* (November 1978): 149–152.

Wright, Jone Perryman, and Nann L. Andreasen. "Practice in Using Location Skills in a Content Area." *The Reading Teacher, 34* (November 1980): 184–186.

---

[20]Michael R. Schuyler, "A Readability Program for Use on Microcomputers," *Journal of Reading, 25* (March 1982): 560–591.

SUGGESTED ACTIVITIES

1. Select a content textbook that is designed for use in the intermediate grades. Apply the Fry Readability Formula as described in this chapter to this textbook. Does it match the grade level for which it is designed?
2. Examine a thesaurus. Why do you think it sometimes appeals more to students than does a dictionary?
3. Select a paragraph from another textbook on your own reading level. Try to determine if it has a directly stated main idea, an implied main idea, or no true main idea at all.
4. Which of the two forms of outlining described in the chapter do you prefer? Why do you feel as you do?
5. Analyze your own reading rate and flexibility either with a standardized test or informally. Are you a flexible reader or a word-by-word reader?
6. Try Survey Q3R on a chapter of this textbook or another textbook. After trying it, try to analyze how effective you think it is in improving your comprehension and retention of material.

Appraising progress
in reading

CHAPTER 17

Why Was This Wrong?

Ms. Richman was in her first year of teaching in an inner-city school in a medium-sized city in the Northeast. Because she had taken a number of reading courses at the university from which she had graduated the previous May, she felt quite well prepared to teach reading to her third-grade class at King School. She divided her class into three reading achievement groups and used the basal reader approach with the average and below-average groups and mainly individualized reading with the above-average group. Although her first year of teaching reading obviously was not perfect in all respects, she felt that she had done reasonably well with it. She was especially proud of the interest in reading for pleasure that a number of her students had evidenced.

Near the end of April, all the elementary teachers in the city in which Ms. Richman taught were required to give their students a standardized survey reading test. Ms. Richman did so and found that her students did not very much enjoy taking the test. However, she felt that they made a reasonable effort to do their best on a test in which they were not very interested and that did not reflect their experiential background very well. She sent the completed tests to the administrative office of the school district for scoring and evaluation.

When the scores were returned from the school administrative office, she saw that the mean grade equivalent score for her class was 3.6. She thought that this was a fairly good score for a test that her students had taken during the eighth month of third grade. She was very shocked when her principal talked with her several days later and told her that the mean grade equivalent score earned by her class was the lowest of any third-grade class in the city. He further stated that one third-grade class in the city had achieved a mean grade equivalent score of 5.3 on this test. Her principal told her that he hoped that she could achieve a somewhat higher mean grade equivalent score with her third-grade class the next year.

Because Ms. Richman was a first-year teacher and had encountered great difficulties in obtaining a teaching position, she did not tell her principal that she believed that it was unjust to expect her students to perform as well on a standardized survey reading test as did children from a more affluent neighborhood. She had learned in a reading course that a standardized reading test *never* should be used to evaluate a teacher's performance but rather to evaluate a student's reading strengths and weaknesses or to evaluate the reading performance of an entire school district.

After you have read this chapter, you will better understand the uses of all kinds of standardized reading tests. However, you also must always be aware of the limitations and misuses of such devices. They often are misused in a number of different ways in contemporary elementary schools.

AN INTRODUCTION TO TESTING

There are some general statements about appraising children's progress in reading that should be made at the outset. A teacher should evaluate a student's progress in reading mainly in order to take the appropriate instructional procedures with him or her. Improved prescriptive reading instruction that is geared toward the student's diagnosed reading weaknesses and is on his or her reading level should be the major reason for all types of standardized and informal testing in reading. However, this is not always the case.

A student's performance on any type of standardized reading test *never* should be thought of as an infallible indicator of his or her true reading strengths and weaknesses. The results of any type of testing always should be supplemented by continuous teacher observation over a period of time. Indeed, careful teacher observation often is a better indicator of a student's true reading competencies than are standardized reading test results. You should always remember that any student's performance on a reading test is only an indication of his or her performance on a specific day. The student's test score can be greatly influenced by his or her attitude toward the test, how he or she feels that day, and his or her familiarity with test-taking strategies.

A standardized reading test never should be used rigidly to place students in a specific reading achievement group, a homogeneous classroom, or a special education classroom. Neither should test scores ever be used to evaluate a teacher's performance. Far too often reading test scores are filed in the superintendent's office with little change in the instructional practice of the teachers. Instead reading test scores should be used to evaluate aspects of a student's reading progress or to evaluate the entire reading program of a school.

No standardized test score can be considered infallible. Any test score should be considered only as an indicator of a student's possession of the traits that the test is trying to measure. Each standardized test also has a standard error of measurement (SE_M), which is an indicator that a child's score can vary in either direction. Many standardized reading tests discriminate against culturally different students. Their actual reading achievement sometimes may be greatly underestimated because the test evaluates middle-class experiences to which the culturally different student has had little exposure.

No elementary reading program should contain so much testing that there is almost more testing than there is teaching. This may be a danger that is inherent in the use of criterion-referenced or mastery tests as is explained later in this chapter. Obviously, the reading program should contain infinitely more teaching than testing. Certainly, a teacher should not teach specifically for a test. Finally, most standardized reading tests do not assess a student's interest in reading or love of reading. These are the very important affective aspects of reading. Tests often tend to evaluate the more mechanical aspects of reading such as decoding and literal comprehension.

In summary, any standardized reading test is a useful tool for ascertaining knowledge about a student, but it *always* should be supplemented by informal testing and careful teacher observation.

INDIVIDUAL AND GROUP INTELLIGENCE TESTS

Because reading is a process in which symbols are manipulated, a degree of abstract intellectual ability usually is needed to succeed in reading. Therefore, the intelligence of most students in the elementary school is assessed so that their probable potential progress in reading can be estimated. This evaluation takes the form of an individual or a group intelligence test.

The *individual intelligence test* gives a fairly accurate estimate of the learning potential of any student in the elementary school. Therefore, it is especially useful with disabled readers because a group intelligence test normally requires some reading ability and may well underestimate the true learning potential of a disabled reader. However, an individual intelligence test normally must be given by a school psychologist or guidance counselor. Because the individual intelligence test obviously must be given on an individual basis, as desirable as this might be, it usually cannot be given to all students in the elementary school.

The *Weschler Intelligence Scale for Children,* revised edition (*WISC-R*), is an excellent individual intelligence test, which ascertains a student's intelligence quotient (IQ) in the three areas of verbal intelligence, performance, and total intelligence. Very often, a disabled reader in the elementary school scores the lowest on the subtests of digit span, information, and arithmetic.

In any case, here are the subtests on the *WISC-R* that evaluate the verbal IQ:

Information. This subtest evaluates the background of information that the student has gained.

Comprehension. This subtest evaluates a student's ability to use good judgment.

Arithmetic. This subtest evaluates a student's ability in the reasoning that is required for success in arithmetic.

Similarities. This subtest evaluates a student's ability in generalizing, abstracting, and conceptualizing.

Vocabulary. This subtest evaluates the mental processes that are used in vocabulary development.

Digit Span. This subtest evaluates a student's ability in auditory memory, attention span, and concentration.

Here are the subtests on the *WISC-R* that evaluate the performance IQ:

Picture Completion. This subtest evaluates a student's visual perception and ability to note details.

Picture Arrangement. This subtest evaluates a student's visual perception and ability to put a series of events in sequence.

Block Design. This subtest evaluates a student's hand-eye coordination, ability to copy a design, and visual perception.

Object Assembly. This subtest evaluates a student's visual perception, hand-eye coordination, and ability to analyze and synthesize.

Coding. This subtest evaluates a student's visual perception, hand-eye coordination, left-to-right progression, and ability to copy a number of symbols.

The *WISC-R* is available from the Psychological Corporation, 757 Third Avenue, New York, New York 10017.

The *Stanford-Binet Intelligence Scale* also can be used as an individual intelligence measure from the age of two years through the adult level. It gives a child's mental age (MA). The Stanford-Binet contains the subtests of Information and Past Learning, Verbal Ability, Memory Perception, and Reading Ability. This individual intelligence test can be obtained from Riverside Publishing Company, 1919 South Highland Avenue, Lombard, Illinois 60148.

Because the two previous individual intelligence tests must be given by a trained examiner, you will find the *Peabody Picture Vocabulary Test* of great value in ascertaining a student's probable intellectual level on an individual basis. This test can be used with children from two years of age through adults eighteen years of age. It contains a series of picture plates that become progressively more difficult. It is very easy to administer and evaluate, and it is quite valid also. You will find it especially useful for obtaining the intellectual ability of disabled readers in the elementary school. It is available from American Guidance Service, Publisher's Building, Circle Pines, Minnesota 55014.

Some students in the elementary school are given one or several group intelligence tests. As was stated earlier, most such tests also evaluate a student's reading ability and, therefore, do not give a very accurate intelligence quotient for a disabled reader. However, they are quite easy to administer and evaluate and, therefore, are quite useful with average and above-average readers in the elementary school.

Here is a brief description of several group intelligence tests that can be used with average and above-average readers in the elementary school:

California Short-Form Test of Mental Maturity. This test is available from California Test Bureau/McGraw-Hill, Del Monte Research Park, Monterey, California.

Hemmen-Nelson Tests of Mental Ability. Available from Riverside Publishing Company, 1919 South Highland Avenue, Lombard, Illinois 60148.

Kuhlmann-Anderson Measure of Academic Potential. Available from Scholastic Testing Service, 480 Meyer Road, Bensenville, Illinois 60106.

STANDARDIZED SURVEY READING OR ACHIEVEMENT TESTS

Nearly every elementary teacher gives standardized survey reading tests sometime during the school year. Although a *standardized survey reading test* can be given alone, most often it is given as part of an achievement test battery that includes tests in other curricular areas such as language usage, arithmetic, social studies, and science. Usually a survey reading test can be purchased separately from the rest of the entire achievement test battery.

In either case, both a standardized survey reading test and the reading subtests of an achievement test battery serve the same general purposes. Each attempts to evaluate a student's general or overall reading ability in the word identification skills (mainly at the primary-grade reading level), word meaning (vocabulary), sentence or paragraph comprehension, rate of reading, and comprehension of study skills in a specific content area such as social studies and science. Such a test is usually given to all students in an elementary classroom, and students who score below grade level on such a test subsequently should be given a standardized diagnostic reading test or an Individual Reading Inventory.

A standardized survey reading test is a group-administered, norm-referenced test that indicates that you can compare the results achieved by your group of students with the results achieved by a similar group of students in a standardization sample. Usually, these are students of the same grade level, sex, geographical location, or socioeconomic group. Norms on such a test can be reported in grade equivalent scores, percentile ranks, stanine scores, or standard scores. The grade equivalent score is the most commonly used and represents the grade level for which a raw score is the median score. As an example, if the median raw score for all students in the norm sample who were in the first month of third grade was 25, any student getting 25 correct answers has earned a grade equivalent score of 3.1. The percentile rank indicates how a student compares in performance with other students of his or her own age or grade. Stanines are normalized standard scores that range from a low of 1 through a high of 9, with 5 being the average performance. A standard score is a normalized score that enables the teacher to compare a student's performance on a number of different tests.

Any standardized reading test should be reliable and valid to be useful. *Reliability* refers to the degree to which a test provides consistent results. This means that if a student took the same test a number of times, he or she should earn about the same score each time. A reliability coefficient on the standardized reading test should be at least .80, whereas a coefficient of .90 is better. *Validity* indicates the degree of accuracy with which a test measures what it is supposed to measure.

A standardized survey reading test or the reading subtests of an achievement test have some *advantages* that make them useful in any elementary reading program. Perhaps the major advantage is the ease of administration and evaluation of such a test. For example, many such tests take about forty-five minutes to give and often can be scored and evaluated by computer. The teacher can receive a computer printout for his or her class that summarizes the test results very thoroughly.

Another advantage of a standardized survey reading test is that all such tests were formulated by experts in test construction. Therefore, most such tests are reliable. However, they may not all be entirely valid. Certainly, they have been subjected to field testing, item analysis, and revision. They generally reflect the curricula of most schools in the United States.

Any such test is very useful as a screening device to determine the overall effectiveness of reading instruction in an elementary school and to locate the students who need additional testing and diagnostic-prescriptive reading instruction. In too many elementary schools the scores on a survey reading test are simply filed in each student's cumulative folder. When the scores from such a test are merely filed with no substantial change in the reading program, a school system never can justify the time, effort, and expense of its testing program.

However, standardized survey reading tests have a number of *limitations* of which you should be aware. All such tests should be *passage dependent*. This indicates that a student should not be able to answer any of the multiple-choice questions that accompany a passage unless he or she has read and comprehended the passage. Some survey tests contain some questions on the paragraph comprehension subtest that are passage independent. This indicates that the student can answer these questions merely on the basis of his or her experiential background without having read the passage carefully.

The word meaning or vocabulary subtest in a standardized survey reading or achievement test may be subject to misinterpretation in several ways. For example, if the student cannot use his or her word identification skills to identify the vocabulary item, he or she obviously cannot determine its meaning even if the meaning is actually known. Then, too, the student may know one meaning of the vocabulary item, but perhaps not the meaning that is required on the test. A word meaning or vocabulary subtest is especially invalid if it evaluates vocabulary knowledge in isolation rather than in context.

On a number of survey reading tests literal comprehension is emphasized at the expense of interpretation and critical analysis. Such tests may have relatively few questions that require inferential thinking or critical analysis. The rate of reading score as determined from a standardized survey reading test often may be higher than the actual reading rate possessed by that student. For example, most students can read narrative or easy content material more rapidly for three or five minutes than they can for a longer time. Most such tests try to determine a student's reading rate from a short period of rapid reading, and this rate often is not the student's actual rate of reading in sustained silent reading.

One very significant limitation of most standardized tests is that they do not reflect a student's cultural or experiential background or use of a nonstandard English dialect. A culturally different student may perform less well on a survey reading test that is predominantly middle-class-oriented than he or she would on a test that reflected his or her experiential background. However, Walter H. MacGinitie does not apologize for the fact that such tests emphasize middle-class experiences and language. He has stated that a reading test should evaluate a student's ability in dealing with the same kind of material that he or she will encounter in school.[1]

Perhaps one of the more important limitations of a survey reading test or the subtests of an achievement test relating to reading is that such a test may *overestimate* a student's true instructional grade level by one or even several grade levels. The grade equivalent score on such a test may be a representation of the student's frustration reading level rather than his or her instructional reading level. As an example, a student who received a grade equivalent score of 4.4 on a survey reading test is likely to have a true instructional reading level of about

[1]Walter H. MacGinitie, "Testing Reading Achievement in Urban Schools," *The Reading Teacher, 27* (October 1973): 13–21.

3.4 as determined by an Individual Reading Inventory. This difference may be due to both the guessing factor on the test and the lack of passage dependency as was explained earlier.

As an illustration, Edward B. Fry of Rutgers University has cautioned against the "orangutan score" that can result from pure-chance guessing on a survey reading test. Here is an example of this concept:

> Suppose we took an orangutan and taught him to put a pawprint in one of four squares. He could choose any square he wished. Next we place a typical multiple-choice item in front of him with four choices. After he has read the item, he chooses one of the squares on which to place his pawprint. On the average, out of 100 items he will get 25 correct by pure chance; this raw score of 25 correct can then be translated into a grade level score.[2]

Fry computed the "orangutan score" for the California Reading Test, Junior High Level, at 5.2. This indicates that a nonreader could score at the fifth-grade reading level on this survey reading test because of pure-chance guessing. This author also once had a nonreader in second grade to whom she gave the Stanford Achievement Test, Primary II Battery. On this test the student scored 2.5 at the end of second grade although he actually could recognize fewer than five words. This is why a student's score on any standardized survey reading test always must be considered to be only an indicator of his or her actual instructional reading grade level.

You can find a description and reviews of most of the tests in reading by consulting the books *Reading Tests and Reviews*[3] and *Reading Tests and Reviews II*.[4]

Many reliable, valid, and useful survey reading tests are available. Those included here are presented as illustrations. Many other useful survey reading tests also could have been included.

California Achievement Tests: Reading. Available from California Test Bureau/McGraw-Hill, Del Monte Research Park, Monterey, California 93940.

This is a series of test batteries in Form C and D that evaluates reading achievement in terms of phonic analysis, vocabulary, structural analysis, comprehension, and reference skills depending upon the reading level.

---

[2]Edward B. Fry, *Reading Instruction for Classroom and Clinic* (New York: McGraw-Hill, Inc., 1972), p. 18.

[3]Oscar K. Buros, ed., *Reading Tests and Reviews* (Highland Park, New Jersey: Gryphon Press, 1968).

[4]Oscar K. Buros, ed., *Reading Tests and Reviews II* (Highland Park, New Jersey: Gryphon Press, 1975).

Gates-MacGinitie Reading Tests. Available from Houghton Mifflin Company, 2 Park Street, Boston, Massachusetts 02107.
This 1978 revision comes in six levels and evaluates reading competency in terms of letter sounds, letter recognition, vocabulary, and comprehension. There are two forms for all levels.

Iowa Silent Reading Tests. Available from Psychological Corporation, 757 Third Avenue, New York, New York 10017.
Level I of this test is designed for grades 6–9. It includes subtests of vocabulary, comprehension, study skills, and reading efficiency.

Metropolitan Reading Tests. Available from Psychological Corporation, 757 Third Avenue, New York, New York 10017.
This test evaluates word meaning in context and literal, inferential, and critical comprehension. It also yields a fairly accurate instructional reading level. It is both norm-referenced and criterion-referenced. (See Figure 17-1.)

Stanford Reading Tests. Available from Psychological Corporation, 757 Third Avenue, New York, New York 10017.
This measure evaluates vocabulary, comprehension, and word-study skills. It is available in Forms A and B at all levels.

STANDARDIZED CRITERION-REFERENCED TESTS

Criterion-referenced or *mastery tests* are considered to be standardized tests because they have been carefully formulated, field tested, and revised in the light of the testing. Such a test deals with one or several of the reading subskills and specifies the point at which the student has achieved mastery of that subskill or those subskills. They differ from norm-referenced tests, which compare a student's performance with the performance of other students who possess similar characteristics. Criterion-referenced tests do not compare a student's performance with students in a norm group, but rather attempt to determine if a student has achieved mastery of a certain reading skill or of several reading skills.

Criterion-referenced tests can be constructed to assess competency in many different reading skills. As an example, such a test can assess a student's competency in the word identification techniques of phonic analysis, structural analysis, contextual analysis, and dictionary usage. As phonic analysis contains so many subskills, many criterion-referenced tests deal with it. For example, tests in phonic analysis can assess knowledge of consonant sounds, consonant blends, long or glided

E1/JS

Reading

What To Do

Read each story. *Then* read each question about the story. *Pick* the best answer to the question. *Mark* the letter for that answer in your booklet or on your answer sheet if you have one. *Now* look at the sample.

Sample

One day, Sally came to my house to play. We played all day. Then we had some cake. I asked her to come back soon.

A Where did we play?
- Ⓐ At Sally's house
- Ⓑ In a tree
- Ⓒ On the train
- ● At my house

B After we played, we—
- Ⓔ went to Sally's house
- Ⓕ played with the dog
- Ⓖ ate some cake
- Ⓗ rode on a bike

C I asked Sally to—
- Ⓐ ride in the car
- Ⓑ come back soon
- Ⓒ make a cake
- Ⓓ read a book

Our block used to have many large oak trees along the street. It was quite shady and cool in the summer. Squirrels would run along the strong branches and birds with bright feathers would make nests among the soft leaves. But last year, some people came in a huge truck and chopped down all the oak trees. They wanted to make the street wider. I hope the squirrels and the birds will return to our block. The other children want them back too, so today we planted six small trees.

1

1 The story tells what things were like in the—
- Ⓐ summer
- Ⓑ spring
- Ⓒ fall
- Ⓓ winter

2 People chopped down the trees to—
- Ⓔ make the street wider
- Ⓕ build a house
- Ⓖ chase away the birds
- Ⓗ get the wood

3 When the trees were standing, the—
- Ⓐ children made tree houses
- Ⓑ birds made nests in them
- Ⓒ children chopped off the branches
- Ⓓ cats climbed in them

4 How many trees did the children plant?
- Ⓔ 5
- Ⓖ 6
- Ⓕ 2
- Ⓗ 1

5 After the trees were cut down, the children missed the—
- Ⓐ trucks
- Ⓒ men
- Ⓑ animals
- Ⓓ noise

6 The children planted new trees so that—
- Ⓔ they could climb the trees
- Ⓕ the animals would return
- Ⓖ they would have wood for fires
- Ⓗ the street would be wider

7 When the truck came, the children must have felt—
- Ⓐ good
- Ⓒ frightened
- Ⓑ excited
- Ⓓ sad

2

Go on to the next page ▶

FIGURE 17-1

vowel sounds, short or unglided vowel sounds, consonant digraphs, diphthongs, vowel digraphs, and phonograms. Such tests also can assess competency in the various aspects of comprehension such as literal comprehension, interpretive comprehension, critical reading, and creative reading. They also can assess mastery of the various study skills.

The major purpose of using criterion-referenced tests is to enable a teacher to individualize reading instruction more effectively. They are designed to help a teacher determine the reading skills in which a student is competent and those in which additional instruction and/or reinforcement are needed. Usually, the student is given a preassessment device when he or she enters the program. The program then usually refers the teacher to a number of instructional reading materials at the appropriate level that should help the student to gain mastery of the reading skills in which he or she has been found to be weak. When the student has completed the material, he or she is given another criterion-referenced test to determine if mastery of that reading skill has been attained. If so, the student proceeds to another instructional objective. If not, the student must practice this reading skill again using another method of study.

Criterion-referenced tests have several *advantages* that may make them useful in an elementary reading program. As a result of using such tests, the student should receive instruction and/or reinforcement only in those reading skills in which he or she lacks competence. Criterion-referenced tests also may help a teacher to know that a student has truly mastered a reading skill before the student is taught other reading skills that may be a source of confusion for him or her. Thus, it seems that criterion-referenced tests may help a teacher to individualize his or her reading program.

Criterion-referenced reading tests have a few limitations that you always should consider before using such a measure. Perhaps one of their major limitations is that they fragment the reading process. For example, one such series of tests assesses competency in 450 different reading skills. In addition, the criterion level of any such test always is set in a rather arbitrary manner. Although the criterion level often is at the *80* percent level of competency, it may be higher or lower. However, it is impossible to say that a student who earned a *75* percent score on a criterion-referenced test lacks competence in a reading skill while a student who earned *80* percent on that test is truly competent.

Another limitation of criterion-referenced tests is the great amount of record keeping that is required by their use. However, this limitation is greatly minimized if the record keeping is computerized as is now sometimes done. (See Chapter 9.) In this case, the preassessment test is scored by computer, and the computer prints out the appropriate reading program for each student. As the student completes the various parts of the reading program, the computer keeps the record of the student's performance.

However, one of the more serious limitations of such tests is that it is difficult for them to assess competency in the higher-level reading skills such as interpretive comprehension, critical reading, and creative reading. Criterion-referenced tests usually stress lower-level reading skills such as phonic analysis and structural analysis. It also is difficult for a criterion-referenced test to evaluate a student's attitudes toward reading and interest in reading.

Here is a comprehensive, but not complete, list of criterion-referenced tests:

Fountain Valley Teacher Support System in Reading. Available from Richard L. Zweig Associates, 20800 Beach Boulevard, Huntington Beach, California 92648.
This reading program consists of 77 tests on cassette tapes and assesses competency in 277 different reading skills.

Harper & Row Classroom Management System. Available from Harper & Row, Publishers, 10 East 53 Street, New York, New York 10022.
This reading program contains assessment tests for word analysis and comprehension skills, a prescriptive reference chart, pupil performance record cards, and a control file.

Individualized Reading Skills Program. Available from Houghton Mifflin Company, 2 Park Street, Boston, Massachusetts 02107.
This reading program contains preassessment tests, postassessment tests, self-teaching and self-scoring reading skill booklets, and class and individual record charts.

Individual Pupil Monitoring System—Reading. Available from Houghton Mifflin Company, 2 Park Street, Boston, Massachusetts 02107.
This reading program can be used in grades 1–6 and contains criterion-referenced tests based on behavioral objectives in the areas of discrimination, decoding, comprehension, and study skills.

Patterns, Sounds, and Meaning. Available from Allyn and Bacon, Inc., 470 Atlantic Avenue, Boston, Massachusetts 02210.
This word analysis program emphasizes decoding skills and vocabulary development.

Prescriptive Reading Inventory. Available from California Test Bureau/McGraw-Hill, Del Monte Research Park, Monterey, California 93940.
This reading program assesses competency in 155 reading skills. The program also contains a Class Diagnostic Map.

Right-to-Read Management System. Available from Winston Press, 430 Oak Grove, Suite 203, Minneapolis, Minnesota 55403.
This reading program contains assessment devices and provisions for record keeping.

SMS: Skills Monitoring System—Reading. Available from Psychological Corporation, 757 Third Avenue, New York, New York 10017.
This reading skills management system contains criterion-referenced tests in the word identification and comprehension skills.

SRA Diagnosis. Available from Science Research Associates, North Wacker Drive, Chicago, Illinois 60606.
This reading program contains survey tests, criterion-referenced tests, and a prescription guide.

Wisconsin Design for Reading Skill Improvement. Available from National Computer Systems, 4401 West 76th Street, Minneapolis, Minnesota 55435.
This reading program contains a rationale, a set of guidelines, teachers' planning guides, resource files, and tests for reading skills assessment. (See Figure 17-2.)

STANDARDIZED DIAGNOSTIC AND WORD IDENTIFICATION TESTS

A standardized diagnostic reading test or a word identification test is used mainly with a student who has not done well on a standardized survey reading test or on the reading subtests of an achievement test battery.

A *standardized diagnostic reading test* is an individually administered or group-administered test that attempts to ascertain a student's reading strengths and weaknesses in the various word identification and comprehension skills. It sometimes also attempts to determine a student's approximate reading level. It can evaluate any aspect of phonic analysis, structural analysis, sight word recognition, or contextual analysis. It also can assess ability in vocabulary knowledge, literal comprehension, interpretive comprehension, and rate of reading.

Normally, a group diagnostic reading test is given to a mildly or moderately disabled reader because it takes more time to give such a test on an individual basis. The individual diagnostic reading test usually is given to a severely disabled reader. However, most individual and group diagnostic reading tests can only evaluate a student's reading strengths and weaknesses through the eighth-grade instructional reading level. Such a test *cannot* help you to determine the causes of a student's reading difficulties, but instead tries to determine his or her reading strengths and weaknesses.

A *standardized word identification test* also can be either group-administered or individually administered. It resembles the word identification subtest on a diagnostic reading test. Thus, you would not give a student a diagnostic reading test and a word identification test.

Test 2
Central Thought—Topic: With Organizer

Example

Bill had a pet dog. Bill's dog was about three feet tall and four feet long. He had soft brown fur and a long tail. His ears were short and pointed.

(A) brown fur
(B) three feet tall
(C) Bill's dog
(D) pointed ears

1. Mailmen do different things. They pick up letters. Some mailmen bring letters to homes. Others sell stamps at the post office. They also drive trucks.

(A) mailmen
(B) letters
(C) driving trucks
(D) selling stamps

2. Rocks may be big or small. Some are hard. Others are soft. Some have sharp points. Others are round and smooth. All rocks are not the same.

(A) round and soft
(B) sharp points
(C) rocks

3. Susan was planting a seed. First she got out a flowerpot. Then she put some black dirt in the pot. Susan put the seed in the dirt. Then she added water to the pot.

(A) adding water
(B) planting a seed
(C) black dirt
(D) a flowerpot

FIGURE 17-2

Both such tests usually are effective in determining a student's reading skill competencies and weaknesses and in establishing a fairly accurate instructional reading level for him or her. Therefore, their use can enable you to teach reading in a more diagnostic-prescriptive manner than might otherwise be possible. (See Chapter 9.) However, they have several limitations of which you should be aware. The individual diagnostic reading test and word identification test take a great deal of time to give and score. Most such tests also evaluate experiential background and, therefore, may discriminate against culturally different students. However, such tests do enable you to diagnose a student's reading difficulties much more specifically than is possible in a survey reading test.

Here is a list of several useful diagnostic reading tests:

Diagnostic Reading Scales, revised edition. Available from California Test Bureau/McGraw-Hill, Del Monte Research Park, Monterey, California 93940.

This is an individual diagnostic reading test that can be used with most students in grades 1–7. It evaluates word recognition, the instructional level of oral reading, the independent level of silent reading, the rate of silent reading, the potential level, and eight phonic skills.

Durrell Analysis of Reading Difficulty, new edition. Available from Psychological Corporation, 757 Third Avenue, New York, New York 10017.

This is an individual diagnostic reading test that is designed for students reading at grades 1–6. It contains a set of reading paragraphs, a cardboard tachistoscope, word lists, and a record blank. It evaluates oral and silent reading, listening comprehension, word analysis, phonics, faulty pronunciation, handwriting, and spelling.

Stanford Diagnostic Reading Test. Available from Psychological Corporation, 757 Third Avenue, New York, New York 10017.

This is a group diagnostic test that evaluates ability in auditory skills, phonic analysis, syllabication, vocabulary, comprehension, and reading rate. It is available in three different levels.

Here are two word identification tests:

McCullough Word-Analysis Test. Available from Personnel Press, 191 Spring Street, Lexington, Massachusetts 02173.

This is a group test designed for use in grades 4–8. It evaluates ability in recognizing initial consonants, comparing vowel sounds, matching symbols with vowel sounds, identifying phonetic respellings, using pronunciation keys, dividing words into syllables, and finding root words.

Sipay Word Analysis Tests. Available from Educators Publishing Service, 75 Moulton Street, Cambridge, Massachusetts 02138.

This is a battery of sixteen individually administered word analysis tests that evaluate ability in one or more of the following three decoding skill areas: visual analysis, phonic analysis, and visual blending.

STANDARDIZED ORAL READING TESTS

An *oral reading test* is used to evaluate a student's competency in oral reading and in literal comprehension. It is an individually administered test that can be used in grades one through eight. It consists of a series of graded paragraphs for the student to read aloud. Copies of the paragraphs that the student reads are found in a separate booklet. The teacher has a copy of each of the paragraphs in another test booklet on which he or she can mark oral reading errors as the student reads each paragraph. Although the marking system for each test varies somewhat, the usual oral reading errors are mispronunciations, substitutions, omissions, insertions, repetitions, and hesitations. Dialect-based oral reading miscues are considered oral reading errors on an oral reading test.

In giving an oral reading test, the teacher asks the student to begin reading aloud a paragraph that is two or more years below the estimated reading grade level. The student then continues reading each paragraph aloud until the *ceiling* or frustration level for the test is reached. After the student has finished reading each paragraph aloud, the teacher asks some literal comprehension questions that are included in the teacher's test booklet. At the conclusion of the test, it is scored, and a reading grade level is determined.

Because an oral reading test must be given on an individual basis, it normally is not given to each student in an elementary classroom. Instead it is given to students who have scored below their expectancy level on a standardized survey reading or achievement test. As it would be repetitious, an oral reading test is rarely given to a student who has been given an individual diagnostic reading test or an Individual Reading Inventory.

The two common oral reading tests are these:

Gilmore Oral Reading Test. Available from Psychological Corporation, 757 Third Avenue, New York, New York 10017.

This test contains ten passages of increasing difficulty that formulate a cohesive story. Reading is evaluated on this test in the areas of accuracy, comprehension, and rate.

Gray Oral Reading Tests. Available from Psychological Corporation, 757 Third Avenue, New York, New York 10017.
This test contains thirteen oral reading passages that determine a grade equivalent for the student.

STANDARDIZED LISTENING COMPREHENSION TESTS

A *standardized listening comprehension test* sometimes is used as one method of determining if a student is reading up to the limits of his or her capacity. Listening comprehension also can be called auditory comprehension or auding. Listening comprehension is said to evaluate language acquisition and reasoning ability.

The standardized listening comprehension tests currently are of two major kinds. Several of them are simply listening comprehension tests in which the teacher reads a series of paragraphs aloud to a group of students. After reading each paragraph aloud, the teacher asks a number of comprehension questions to which the student responds in his or her test booklet. The other type of test combines listening comprehension and reading achievement so that the teacher can obtain a comparison between a student's scores on these two different kinds of tests. The teacher first attempts to determine the student's listening comprehension by reading some words, sentences, or paragraphs aloud. Each student then responds to questions in his or her test booklet. The teacher then establishes a *potential* or *capacity level* for each student. The student next takes a related vocabulary subtest and paragraph comprehension subtest to determine his or her reading achievement. A comparison is then made between each student's potential level and reading achievement to determine if he or she can probably make reading progress with an excellent individually prescribed reading program.

Thus, you can see that a listening comprehension test may be useful in determining a student's probable potential for reading improvement if he or she is disabled in reading. However, the results of such a device always should be used cautiously, for the reading improvement of a disabled reader also depends on other factors such as the teacher-student relationship, the student's emotional adjustment, the student's motivation, and the home environment.

Here are two standardized listening comprehension tests:

Durrell Listening-Reading Series. Available from Psychological Corporation, 757 Third Avenue, New York, New York 10017.
This is a series of three tests designed to be used in the primary

grades, intermediate grades, and junior high school. Each test compares listening and reading performance standardized on the same students.

Sequential Tests of Educational Progress: Listening. Available from Addison-Wesley Publishing Company, Inc., Jacob Way, Reading, Massachusetts 01867.
This listening comprehension test has a form that can be used in the intermediate grades. It evaluates different aspects of listening comprehension skills.

A DESCRIPTION OF AN INDIVIDUAL READING INVENTORY

The *Individual Reading Inventory* sometimes is called an Informal Reading Inventory. It is an informal reading measure in contrast to a standardized reading measure. It is useful in determining a student's independent, instructional, and frustration reading levels and in attempting to determine a student's specific reading skill strengths and weaknesses. Although it can be given to all students in an elementary class, owing to time limitations, it most often is given only to the disabled readers. It normally would be given to a disabled reader during the first few months of the school year. If you give a standardized diagnostic reading test to a student, you normally would not give him or her an Individual Reading Inventory.

The Individual Reading Inventory, as it is known today, undoubtedly originated with Emmett A. Betts and his doctoral student Patsy A. Kilgallon. Kilgallon established criteria for accuracy in word identification and comprehension that were then tested with forty-one students.[5] However, in this informal reading test the students read each passage silently and then orally, which is a different procedure than is usually used when giving such an inventory today. Betts then spelled out his own definitions of the independent, instructional, and frustration reading levels and the listening comprehension level in a textbook that was published in 1946.[6]

Many variations of the Individual Reading Inventory (IRI) are true informal reading tests. However, there are commercial inventories that are considered to be standardized in some ways, which means that

---

[5]Patsy A. Kilgallon, "A Study of Relationships Among Certain Pupil Adjustments in Language Situations," doctoral dissertation, Pennsylvania State College, 1942.

[6]Emmett A. Betts, *Foundations of Reading Instruction* (New York: American Book Company, 1946).

they have been subjected to some field-testing, statistical analysis, and revision. Several commercial inventories are briefly described later in this chapter.

The less formal IRIs vary somewhat according to different reading specialists. The Individual Reading Inventory that is described here is my variation of this informal diagnostic technique.

Establishing Rapport with the Student

Rapport should be established with the student before administering an IRI to enlist the cooperation of the student. You can ask the student informal questions about his or her interests, his or her view of reading, his or her hobbies, and his or her special strengths and weaknesses in reading. You also can tell the student that he or she is going to take an informal reading test that will help you determine the kind of material that he or she can read successfully.

Dictating a Language Experience Story

You may want to have a disabled reader in an elementary class dictate a language experience story to you so that you can determine how well the student can read his or her own language patterns. You then can make a comparison of the student's ability to read about his or her own experiences in his or her own language patterns with his or her ability to read commercial material. Detailed information on how to use the language experience approach was provided in Chapter 4.

Administering a Sight Word Test

The next part of an Individual Reading Inventory may be the giving of a sight word test. This obviously is a test that attempts to determine the number of words that a student can recognize by sight from those words found on a sight word list. Chapter 13 described a number of different sight word lists. Any one of these lists can be used in an IRI.

Giving the Graded Word Lists and Oral Reading Paragraphs

The giving of graded word lists and oral reading paragraphs can be the next part of an IRI. A series of word lists that are formulated from the same basal readers as are the graded oral reading paragraphs normally are given first. From these word lists, you can determine the paragraph a student should begin reading aloud. The graded oral reading paragraphs are a series of passages, often beginning at the primer level and continuing through the twelfth-grade reading level. The passages can be used for oral reading, silent reading, or as a listening comprehension measure. A student usually begins reading a paragraph aloud that is about two grade levels below his or her estimated instructional reading level and continues reading until he or she reaches the frustration reading level.

Giving Inventories in the Word Identification Techniques

The final part of an IRI may be the giving of an informal inventory in the word identification techniques of phonic analysis, structural analysis, contextual analysis, and dictionary usage. Each such inventory should be formulated at the correct instructional level for the student.

PROCEDURES FOR CONSTRUCTING AN INDIVIDUAL READING INVENTORY OR PURCHASING A COMMERCIAL INDIVIDUAL READING INVENTORY

Most teachers undoubtedly will wish to purchase a commercial inventory because of the time that is saved. A number of basal reader series also contain informal inventories that are specific to those basal readers. These obviously are very useful also. However, this textbook provides very brief suggestions for constructing the word lists and graded oral reading paragraphs of an IRI if you wish to do so.

To formulate the graded word list, turn to the vocabulary list or glossary near the end of each book. Then randomly select every nth word so that you have a total of about twenty-five or thirty words in each list. Type the words for the student to pronounce on a stencil or ditto, and then duplicate them. You should have a copy of each word list on which to mark the student's correct or incorrect response to each word on the list.

You then construct each of the graded oral reading paragraphs from the chosen basal reader series or the graded textbook. For each paragraph, you should attempt to use mainly the vocabulary found in that book and in all of the preceding books of that series. You can try to condense an actual story that is found in the reading material, but you also can formulate your own story from the appropriate words if you want to invest the time to do this.

Then you type each of the paragraphs on a sheet of paper so that the student can read from this copy. If it is possible, use a primary typewriter for typing the paragraphs on the primary-grade reading level. Then glue or paste each paragraph on a piece of tagboard or cardboard. The student's copy of each paragraph does not contain the comprehension questions or the provision for determining the reading level. The teacher should also have a copy of each graded oral reading paragraph with the comprehension questions and the method for determining the reading levels. This copy can be duplicated, or an acetate overlay can be used with each typed copy of the paragraphs.

There are a number of commercial Individual Reading Inventories that you can purchase and use in the elementary school. Obviously, each inventory differs considerably in terms of its content and method for determining the different reading levels. Here is a fairly comprehensive, but not inclusive, list of such commercial inventories.

Analytical Reading Inventory. Available from Charles E. Merrill Publishing Co., 1300 Alum Creek Drive, Columbus, Ohio 43216.

Basic Reading Inventory. Available from Kendall/Hunt Publishing Company, 2460 Kerper Boulevard, Dubuque, Iowa 52001.

Classroom Reading Inventory. Available from William C. Brown Company, Publishers, 2460 Kerper Boulevard, Dubuque, Iowa 52001.

Ekwall Reading Inventory. Available from Allyn and Bacon, Inc., 470 Atlantic Avenue, Boston, Massachusetts 02210.

Informal Reading Assessment. Available from Rand McNally, Box 7600, Chicago, Illinois 60680.

Reading Diagnosis Kit. Available from the Center for Applied Research in Education, West Nyack, New York 10994.

Standard Reading Inventory. Available from Klamath Printing Company, 320 Lowell Street, Klamath Falls, Oregon 97601.

Sucher-Allred Reading Placement Inventory. Available from the Economy Company, Box 25308, Oklahoma City, Oklahoma 73125.

DIRECTIONS FOR GIVING AND EVALUATING AN INDIVIDUAL READING INVENTORY

As was stated earlier, have the student begin pronouncing the words aloud on a word list that is at least two reading levels below his or her estimated instructional reading level. The student continues pronouncing the words on the graded word lists until the point where he or she is able to pronounce less than *90* percent of the words on the list. The student then begins reading the graded oral reading paragraphs that correspond to the level at which at least *90* percent of the words on a list were recognized. As the student reads each of the paragraphs orally, mark his or her oral reading miscues on your copy of the paragraph. It usually is very helpful to tape-record a student's reading of the paragraphs. Then you can mark each student's miscues or oral reading errors when the tape recording later is played back. You may have to replay some of the paragraphs several times to locate all the reading errors.

As a student reads each of the paragraphs aloud, you mark his or her oral reading errors on your copy of the paragraph. Although there are a number of different marking systems, here is one that I recommend:

Omissions	Circle the entire word or letter sound. (happy)
Additions	Insert with a caret. ni\^ce
Substitutions or mispronunciations	Draw a line through the word and write in student's usage. ~~then~~ than
Reversals	Use the transposition symbol. been ⌐has⌐
Repetitions	Use a wavy line to indicate a repetition of two or more words. in the house
Words aided	If the student says nothing after about five seconds, give him or her the word and cross it out. ~~osmosis~~

Have the student continue the graded oral reading paragraphs until he or she reaches the frustration reading level. This is the point at which the student makes many oral reading errors, has inadequate comprehension, and appears tense and insecure. You then can use the rest of the oral reading paragraphs as a listening comprehension test, if they seem applicable, to establish a *potential* or *capacity level* for the student. This is the point at which the student can answer about 75 percent of the comprehension questions correctly. This level corresponds to the potential reading level that can be determined from a listening comprehension test as was described earlier in this chapter.

You can use the directions for determining the various reading levels that are found on a commercial inventory, and you can adapt them if you have constructed your own inventory. Some commercial inventories differentiate between major and minor oral reading miscues. A *major oral reading miscue* is one that interferes with comprehension whereas a *minor oral reading miscue* is one that does not. Some commercial inventories do not count *dialect-based oral reading miscues* as errors, but others do so. I believe it to be most logical to differentiate between major and minor oral reading miscues and not to count dialect-based miscues as errors.

I describe the *independent reading level* as the point at which a student can recognize words with *99* percent accuracy and at which he or she has *95* percent or better comprehension. I believe the *instructional reading level* to be the point at which a student can recognize words with about *90* percent or better accuracy and at which he or she has *75* percent or better comprehension. I call the *frustration reading level* the point at which a student has less than *90* percent accuracy in word identification and has less than about *50* percent accuracy in comprehension.

However, you should know that the best-known criteria were developed by Emmett Betts. Betts stated that the independent reading level was the point at which a student can recognize words with *99* percent accuracy and has *95* percent or better comprehension. He described the instructional reading level as the point at which the student can recognize words with *95* percent accuracy or better and has *75* percent or better comprehension. Betts defined the frustration reading level as the point at which the student has less than *90* percent accuracy in word identification and less than *50* percent accuracy in comprehension.[7] Other classification schemes for determining reading levels that have somewhat lower standards have been developed by George Spache[8] and Nila Banton Smith.[9]

A student often should read for pleasure on the independent reading level, which also is called the free reading level. A student usually should read material with teacher guidance on the instructional level and usually should avoid reading material on the frustration reading level.

USING INVENTORIES IN THE WORD IDENTIFICATION TECHNIQUES

Although the final part of an Individual Reading Inventory may be the giving of inventories in the word identification techniques of phonic analysis, structural analysis, contextual analysis, or dictionary usage,

---

[7]Betts, *Reading Instruction.*

[8]George D. Spache and Evelyn B. Spache, *Reading in the Elementary School* (Boston: Allyn and Bacon, Inc., 1977), pp. 339–340.

[9]Nila Banton Smith, *Graded Selections for Informal Reading Diagnosis* (New York: New York University Press, 1959 and 1963).

the teacher also can give an inventory in any of these techniques to a group or an individual whenever it seems useful. An inventory is given in a word identification technique to evaluate a student's strengths and weaknesses in that technique so that correct instruction and reinforcement can be prescribed.

A number of moderately and severely disabled readers in the elementary school lack competence in phonic analysis. They may be especially weak in the knowledge of short vowel sounds. An *inventory in phonic analysis* may be useful in helping to determine a student's specific weaknesses in phonic analysis. Any inventory in phonic analysis can be either individually administered or group-administered. Generally, an individual inventory in phonic analysis is the more useful although it takes longer to administer. An inventory in phonic analysis can evaluate a student's competency in such phonic analysis subskills as understanding of beginning and ending consonant sounds, consonant blends, consonant digraphs, long and short vowel sounds, diphthongs, phonograms, *r*-controlled vowels, auditory blending, and phonic generalizations.

Although you can design your own phonic analysis inventories at the appropriate level by using basal reader materials or phonic workbooks, the *Reading Diagnosis Kit* contains several useful phonic analysis inventories.[10]

An *inventory in structural analysis* can be given in either an individual or a group setting. Such an inventory should be used as a tentative indicator of a student's competency in structural analysis. It can require that a student locate a base or root word in a derivative, locate the prefix or suffix in a derivative, add a prefix to a word, add a suffix to a regular or irregular base word, mark the accent in a word, form a compound word, divide a word into syllables, define an unknown word by the use of a word part, or apply the appropriate structural analysis generalization.

Even though you can formulate your own structural analysis inventory at the appropriate reading level, the *Reading Diagnosis Kit*[11] contains several structural analysis inventories that may be applicable to your situation.

A *contextual analysis inventory* is often a written test that can be given on an individual or group basis. It may be a written test in which the student should underline the one of several options that makes the best sense in sentence context. The *cloze procedure* also can be used as one type of contextual analysis inventory. This procedure

[10]Wilma H. Miller, *Reading Diagnosis Kit* (West Nyack, New York: Center for Applied Research in Education, 1978), pp. 230–233.

[11]Miller, *Reading Diagnosis Kit,* pp. 234–239.

was described in detail in Chapter 13. When the cloze procedure is used for this purpose, any word that makes sense in a blank space should be considered correct even if it is not the exact omitted word. The *Reading Diagnosis Kit*[12] contains a number of examples of inventories in contextual analysis.

As was stated in Chapter 16, dictionary usage can be considered both a study skill and a word identification skill. Normally, an inventory in dictionary usage should be based upon the actual dictionary that the student in the elementary school is using. This type of inventory can evaluate a student's knowledge of such subskills as knowledge of alphabetical sequence, knowledge of the pronunciation key, use of guide words, understanding of synonyms, and selection of the correct dictionary definition for use in context. Usually, a dictionary usage inventory is given to a student who is reading at the intermediate-grade level or higher. There is an inventory contained in the *Reading Diagnosis Kit*[13] that you can use as a model for your own inventories in dictionary usage.

THE USE OF A GROUP READING INVENTORY

A number of students in the intermediate grades have considerable difficulty in comprehending and studying their selected social studies and science textbooks as was explained in Chapter 16. You can use a variation of a *group reading inventory* to determine if your students can comprehend the selected textbooks successfully. Although lower-level textbooks in these content areas should be provided, if possible, for the moderately and severely disabled readers in the intermediate grades, many of the other students need to be taught the special reading skills that are needed for effective comprehension and study in these content areas as was also explained in Chapter 16. A group reading inventory can help you to determine the special reading skills that should be presented in the content areas.

There are several different variations of group reading inventories. One such variation attempts to determine if a group of students can use the various aids included in the selected content textbook. This informal inventory usually is given at the beginning of a course or a semester. To formulate this type of inventory, formulate approximately twenty questions on the use of such textbook aids as the table of contents, the glossary, the maps, the index, the italicized words, the

---

[12]Miller, *Reading Diagnosis Kit,* pp. 240–247.

[13]Miller, *Reading Diagnosis Kit,* pp. 248–249.

diagrams, the pictures, the graphs, and the tables. The students then try to complete the inventory by using their textbook to answer the questions.

Another variation of a group reading inventory is designed to determine if students can comprehend and study a selected content textbook with success. To construct this type of inventory, the teacher selects a passage of about 1,000 to 2,000 words in the middle of the content textbook. The students read the passage from their textbook silently. Each student then responds to an open-ended question such as the following: What was this passage about? Each student also answers some objective questions about the passage. These questions can evaluate a student's competency in such reading skills as literal comprehension, interpretive comprehension, critical reading, specialized vocabulary, the directly stated main idea, significant details, irrelevant details, and the implied main idea.

Another variation of a group reading inventory is based on one specific chapter of a required content textbook. This also is an open-book test, which is given near the beginning of a course or semester. It is supposed to determine if a student possesses the special reading skills that are required to comprehend the chosen content textbook effectively. This informal reading inventory includes a matching vocabulary exercise composed of some of the specialized vocabulary terms contained in the chapter. It also can consist of literal, interpretive, critical, and creative questions from the chapter as well as questions about the main ideas and important details contained in the chapter.

Models of each of these variations of the group reading inventory are found in the *Reading Diagnosis Kit*.[14] These models should help you to formulate your own informal reading inventories in the content areas of social studies and science.

USING AN INTEREST INVENTORY

It has been mentioned many times previously in this textbook that interests can play an extremely important part in motivating elementary-school students to read for pleasure. Many reluctant readers who otherwise would read little will read materials in which they are vitally interested. As an example, a fifth-grade student who is a reluctant reader may be very interested in professional football. If his or her teacher is aware of this interest and provides him or her with relevant materials on this topic that can be read easily, the student may be motivated to read for pleasure.

[14]Miller, *Reading Diagnosis Kit,* pp. 255–260.

An *interest inventory* is a diagnostic device that helps you to determine the interests of a student. This device can be given on either an individual or a group basis. As a child in the early primary grades normally cannot complete an interest inventory himself or herself, you usually must give him or her this device individually. This also may be true for a disabled reader in the intermediate grades. However, must students in the intermediate grades can complete an interest inventory in a group situation.

Normally, you do not have to construct your own interest inventory. Usually, an interest inventory is not specific to a particular classroom. However, if you want to construct your own interest inventory, you can ascertain a student's interests in such areas as the following: favorite television programs, favorite after-school activities, favorite weekend activities, hobbies, favorite types of books, use of the public library, and types of books and magazines that are available in the home.

Each completed interest inventory is evaluated informally. You try to determine each student's special interests so that these interests can be capitalized on in choosing various kinds of reading materials. You then may want to complete an index card for each student, on which you briefly summarize all of his or her special interests. All of these index cards may be filed in a small box for future reference.

Sample interest inventories can be found in a source such as the *Reading Diagnosis Kit*.[15] However, here are five sample questions from such an inventory:

What is the name of the favorite book that you have read for yourself?

What are the names of your two favorite television programs?

What do you really like to do after school?

What do you like to do best on a Saturday?

Do you collect anything? If you do, what kinds of things do you like to collect?

USING SEVERAL SIMPLE PROJECTIVE TECHNIQUES

A *projective technique* is a device that is designed to help a teacher determine how a student views himself or herself and his or her reading difficulties without the student's knowing exactly what the teacher is trying to find out. Thus, the use of a projective technique may help a teacher to learn more about a student and the probable causes of his

---

[15]Miller, *Reading Diagnosis Kit*, pp. 286–293.

or her reading difficulties than otherwise might be possible. The use of a simple projective technique is especially valuable with disabled readers in the elementary school. Although a number of projective techniques, such as the Rorschach Inkblot Test, the Children's Apperception Test, the Goodenough-Harris Draw-a-Man Test, and the Bender Visual-Motor Gestalt Test, must be given by a child psychologist, elementary teachers can give and evaluate some simple projective techniques by themselves.

The *Incomplete Sentences Test* is a most useful projective technique that an elementary-school teacher can give and evaluate. This device consists of the beginning parts of some carefully structured sentences that a student can complete in an oral or written form depending upon his or her reading ability. The evaluation of an Incomplete Sentences Test should tell the teacher more about a student's emotional adjustment, attitudes toward home and family, attitudes toward school, and attitudes towards reading. However, the teacher must be careful not to infer too much from the results of this device but rather to use it only as a tentative indicator. However, the teacher can use the insights gained about a student in the school reading program.

Incomplete Sentences Tests are found in a source such as the *Reading Diagnosis Kit.*[16] However, here are several sample sentences from this device:

> It is hard for me to _____.
> I wish that my father _____.
> It is easy for me to _____.
> I think that school is _____.
> I would like to be able to _____.
> It makes me angry when _____.
> The thing that I like best about school is _____.
> It makes me happy when _____.
> I feel proud of myself when _____.

Another simple projective technique is the *open-ended story*. This is a story beginning that the student finishes in writing. It can be used to determine a student's attitudes toward some kind of problem situation and evaluates his or her attitudes in such areas as honesty, truthfulness, or responsibility. The *sociogram* helps you learn which students are well accepted and which are not well accepted by their classmates. You should use the social structure of a class to provide activities that will maximize each student's feeling of acceptance and belonging. You can also use *story* or *theme assignments* to find out how a student views himself or herself, his or her attitudes toward home

---

[16]Miller, *Reading Diagnosis Kit,* pp. 303–308.

and family, his or her attitudes toward school and reading, and his or her overall emotional adjustment. The *Wish Test* is an adaptation of an Incomplete Sentences Test. It contains a number of incomplete sentences, each of which begins with the words "I wish." It attempts to discover insights about a child's desires and wishes. Examples of all of these simple projective techniques are found in the *Reading Diagnosis Kit.*[17]

SELECTED REFERENCES

Farr, Roger, and Nancy Roser. *Teaching a Child to Read.* New York: Harcourt Brace Jovanovich, Inc., 1979, Chapter 2.

Fry, Edward. "Test Review: Metropolitan Achievement Tests." *The Reading Teacher, 34* (November 1980): 196–201.

Hansell, T. Stevenson. "Four Methods of Diagnosis for Content Areas Reading." *Journal of Reading, 24* (May 1981): 696–700.

Harris, Albert J., and Edward R. Sipay. *How to Increase Reading Ability.* New York: Longman, Inc., 1980, Chapters 8, 9.

Jongsma, Eugene A. "Test Review: Gates-MacGinitie Reading Tests." *Journal of Reading, 23* (January 1980): 340–345.

———. "Test Review: Test of Reading Comprehension." *The Reading Teacher, 33* (March 1980): 703–708.

Jongsma, Kathleen S., and Eugene A. Jongsma. "Test Review: Commercial Informal Reading Inventories." *The Reading Teacher, 34* (March 1981): 697–705.

Kaluger, George, and Clifford J. Kolson. *Reading and Learning Disabilities.* Columbus, Ohio: Charles E. Merrill Publishing Co., 1978, Chapters 6, 7.

Karlin, Robert. *Teaching Elementary Reading.* New York: Harcourt Brace Jovanovich, Inc., 1980, Chapter 2.

Laffey, James L., and Donna Kelly. "Test Review: Woodcock Reading Mastery Tests." *The Reading Teacher, 33* (December 1979): 335–339.

LaPray, Margaret H. *On the Spot Reading Diagnosis File.* West Nyack, New York: Center for Applied Research in Education, 1978.

Schell, Leo M. "Test Review: California Achievement Tests: Reading." *Journal of Reading, 23* (April 1980): 624–628.

Smith, William Earl, and Michael D. Beck. "Determining Instructional Reading Level with the 1978 Metropolitan Achievement Tests." *The Reading Teacher, 34* (December 1980): 313–319.

Spache, George D. *Diagnosing and Correcting Reading Disabilities.* Boston: Allyn and Bacon, Inc., 1981.

Zintz, Miles V. *The Reading Process.* Dubuque, Iowa: William C. Brown Company, Publishers, 1980, Chapter 19.

---

[17]Miller, *Reading Diagnosis Kit,* pp. 309, 313–315.

SUGGESTED ACTIVITIES

1. Analyze one standardized survey reading or achievement test, standardized reading test, or standardized oral reading test in terms of the author, publisher, date, subtests, strengths, weaknesses, and uses.
2. Administer the test you analyzed to one student or a small group of students. Evaluate the results according to the manual of the test.
3. Construct and/or give an Individual Reading Inventory to an elementary-school student. Analyze the results, and make recommendations about a prescribed reading program for that student.
4. Select a content textbook, and construct one of the variations of the group reading inventory described in the chapter. If possible, give this group reading inventory to several students at the appropriate grade level.
5. Construct an interest inventory, and give it to one or several students at the appropriate grade level.
6. Construct an Incomplete Sentences Test, and give it to one student or a small group of students. Analyze the results, and share your findings with other students or teachers.

**Teaching reading
to children with
unique needs**

What Should She Do?

Mrs. Grigalunas was in her first year
of teaching in a third-grade class in a
small suburban city in the Far West.
At the beginning of the school year she
was told that two special children were
going to be attending her regular third-
grade classroom. One of them was a
learning-disabled student, and the
other was a visually impaired or low-
vision student. Mrs. Grigalunas was
very concerned at first because she felt
that she was not competent to do a
good job of teaching reading to these
special children. She had learned about
the concept of mainstreaming in her
reading methods courses at the university from which she had graduated the
previous May. She had learned that
mainstreaming or placing special children into regular classrooms for at
least part of each school day was the
mandate of U.S. Public Law 94-142,
The Education for All Handicapped
Children Act. One of the principles of
this law is that handicapped children
will be placed in the least restrictive
environment in which they can receive
an appropriate education.

However, Mrs. Grigalunas was fairly
relieved to find out that there was help
available from consultants in the
teaching of learning-disabled children
and visually impaired children. Each of
these consultants had prepared an Individualized Educational Program
(IEP) for each of these children. The
consultants were to suggest teaching
strategies and materials for successfully implementing each individually
prescribed reading program.

Paul was the learning-disabled student in Mrs. Grigalunas's classroom,
and he exhibited a number of the behavioral characteristics that are associated with learning disability such as
hyperactivity, distractability, the tendency to perseverate, poor visual perception ability, and a marked discrepancy
between language skills and arithmetic
skills. A few of the teaching strategies
that Mrs. Grigalunas used with Paul
were presenting short and explicit
tasks, eliminating distracting elements
from these tasks, overlearning some of
the important reading skills, the use of
several tracing techniques, and the
provision of many success experiences.

Sandy was the visually impaired
child who was placed in Mrs. Grigalunas's classroom. She had visual acuity
in her better eye no better than 20/120
after correction, which classified her as
a low-vision or partially sighted child.
She could not perform tasks that required detailed vision without an aid
such as large type reading materials or
a magnifier. Because Sandy was reading on about the second reader, second
semester level, Mrs. Grigalunas chose a
basal reader and workbook that were
printed in large type. She also selected
some reading materials that were
available in large type. Sandy experienced considerable success with these
special reading materials.

After you have read this chapter,
you will know many practical strategies for teaching reading to children in
your regular classroom who are visually or auditorily handicapped, learning-disabled, slow-learning, blind or

visually impaired, and deaf or hard-of-hearing. This chapter is not designed for the special education teacher, but rather for the teacher of reading in the regular classroom who may have one or several special children in his or her classroom.

CHARACTERISTICS OF CHILDREN WITH VISUAL PERCEPTION DIFFICULTIES

The typical infant starts to make visual differentiations almost from the beginning of his or her life. Most of the development of visual perception ability, however, takes place in a normal child between the ages of three and a half and seven and a half years. A child should have good ability in visual perception because the discrimination of details in the environment is needed for the intellectual development that affects reading performance.

There are a number of causes of inadequate visual perception ability. One cause may be a visual defect such as myopia (nearsightedness), hyperopia (farsightedness), inadequate binocular coordination, or astigmatism. Inadequate visual perception also can be caused by directional confusion, which is the improper orientation to the left and right in space. Another cause may be improper body posture in relation to a near-point task, in which the child tilts his or her head or body while viewing images, causing distortions. Even emotional problems may cause poor visual perception ability. If a student is very weak in visual perception ability, he or she usually has great difficulty learning words by sight or by wholes.

HOW TO DIAGNOSE A STUDENT'S VISUAL PERCEPTION ABILITY

There are several formal and informal ways of determining a student's probable visual perception ability. Several standardized devices attempt to determine visual perception ability. Most of them should be given mainly to the student who is functioning at the reading readiness or beginning reading level and who appears by teacher observation to be very weak in visual perception ability.

Here are several of the most useful visual perception tests:

Bender Visual-Motor Gestalt Test. Available from the Psychological Corporation, 757 Third Avenue, New York, New York 10017.

Frostig Developmental Test of Visual Perception. Available from Publishers Test Service, 2500 Garden Road, Monterey, California 93940.

Purdue Perceptual-Motor Survey. Available from Charles E. Merrill Publishing Co., 1300 Alum Creek Drive, Columbus, Ohio 43216.

Winter Haven Perceptual Forms Test. Available from Winter Haven Lions Research Foundation, Box 112, Winter Haven, Florida 33880.

SOME TEACHING STRATEGIES FOR IMPROVING VISUAL PERCEPTION ABILITY

There are a number of strategies for improving visual perception ability, most of which are appropriate for students functioning at the primary-grade reading level. For example, construct a balance disk—a heavy plywood base about twenty inches square balanced on a five-inch square or circular piece of wood attached to the center on the bottom of the larger piece. Have the child stand on one foot, balance, or turn in a circle while fixating on a wall target. As another example, suspend a Marsden (swinging) ball from any convenient point at the child's eye level. Swing the ball slowly back and forth, and have the child follow the swinging motion with his or her eyes.

Have the child string beads in various patterns. Give the child drawings or pictures of various patterns, and have the child use each drawing or picture as a model. As another example, get a ring-shaped gelatin mold, and place a very small ball in it. As the ball is rolling, have the child follow the ball's movement with only his or her eyes. As another activity, have the child extend his or her arms about a foot from his or her face and place them about one foot apart. Then have the child jump his or her eyes from the tip of one index finger to the tip of the other one. This is called rotary pursuit training.

All tracing techniques are useful. Some of these are tracing letters and words made of coarse sandpaper, tracing in a sand box, tracing in a salt tray, tracing salt or sugar letters glued on poster board, placing a wire screen under a sheet of manila paper and tracing a letter or word that has been written with a crayon, and tracing letters or words that have been made of glitter sprinkled over glue on poster board. For another activity, have the child make his or her own body into appropriate letter shapes. Finally, place five objects in front of the child, and have him or her study them. Then the child should close his or her eyes while you take away one or two of the items. Have the child open his or her eyes and indicate which item or items are missing.

CHARACTERISTICS OF CHILDREN WITH AUDITORY PERCEPTION DIFFICULTIES

At about the age of two a child begins to attach meanings to sounds and uses words to communicate. A child learns by listening to sounds and imitating words. Any child who does not have good auditory and verbal stimulation at this age may not develop auditory awareness for sounds or good auditory discrimination skills. A child with poorly developed auditory discrimination skills often is slow in acquiring speech accuracy.

There are several different kinds of deficits in auditory discrimination ability and auditory perception ability. For example, a child can have poor auditory acuity (hearing) so that the high tones and the low tones cannot be heard properly. A child can have poor auditory comprehension so that he or she cannot extract meaning from sound patterns. A child can have inadequate auditory memory so that sounds and sound sequences cannot be remembered. He or she may have poor auditory discrimination so that the differentiation between sounds cannot be heard.

If a student has been found to be weak in auditory skills, usually a sight or visual approach is used while the auditory modality is strengthened. As the child develops more ability in auditory discrimination and perception, more phonic analysis skills can be presented.

HOW TO DIAGNOSE A STUDENT'S AUDITORY DISCRIMINATION ABILITY

There are a few formal and informal means of determining a student's auditory discrimination and/or perception ability. Many of the activities included in Chapter 3 for the improvement of auditory discrimination ability also can be used to evaluate auditory discrimination ability. There are several standardized tests that can be used for this purpose. They are most often given to a student who is functioning at the reading readiness or beginning reading level and who appears by teacher observation to be very weak in auditory discrimination ability.

Here are several of the more useful auditory discrimination tests:

Goldman-Fristoe-Woodcock Test of Auditory Discrimination. Available from American Guidance Service, Publishers Building, Circle Pines, Minnesota 55014.

Tenvad. Available from Follett Publishing Company, 1010 West Washington Boulevard, Chicago, Illinois 60607.

Wepman Auditory Discrimination Test. Available from Language Research Associates, P.O. Box 2085, Palm Springs, California 92263.

SOME TEACHING STRATEGIES FOR IMPROVING AUDITORY DISCRIMINATION ABILITY

There are many strategies that can be used for improving auditory discrimination ability, most of which are most appropriate for students functioning at the primary-grade reading level. As one example, tape-record various sounds such as a bell ringing, a whistle blowing, a ball bouncing, a dog barking, or a car horn blowing. Then have the child identify each sound. To increase auditory memory, pronounce a series of digits, beginning with two, and have the child repeat them. A child at the primary-grade reading level probably should be able to remember up to four or five digits in correct order. As another activity, pronounce a series of symbols orally. Then have the child draw each series of symbols on the chalkboard. Here is one example: dash, dash, dot, dot, dash, dot.

Whisper a sentence in a child's ear, and have him or her then whisper it to the next child. This activity can be done by a small group of children. Have the child at the end say the sentence aloud, and then have the children discuss how the sentence has changed. As another activity, have the child listen to and imitate various sound sequences such as clapping and tapping. If you wish, place this activity on a cassette tape. As one more example, pronounce a short sentence containing seven or eight words; then have the child repeat the sentence. Additional activities that can be used for the improvement of auditory discrimination ability were provided in Chapter 3.

CHARACTERISTICS OF LEARNING-DISABLED CHILDREN

At the outset it is important to understand that there is little agreement among the specialists in this area as to how the terms are used. A student who is learning-disabled is often said to exhibit Strauss's syndrome. Learning-disabled students often have an average or above-average intellectual level. However, there usually is a great discrepancy between their expected achievement in one or more school subjects and the actual achievement. They often may be hyperactive and must receive medication so that they can calm down enough in order to learn effectively. They often are distractible and have a very short attention span. They also may perseverate, which means that they may perform the same task over and over in the same way even if the performance is not appropriate.

A student who is learning-disabled may have very poor visual perception ability, very poor auditory perception ability, or very poor visual and auditory perception ability. This type of child may have a maturational or developmental lag that causes difficulty in academic learning. Some specialists believe that learning disability is the result of neurological dysfunction, and a few specialists equate learning disabilities with minimal brain damage. Approximately *90* percent of learning-disabled children have significant reading problems. A few of them instead have difficulty in gross motor or fine motor skills, which makes it difficult for them to learn handwriting, and others may have great difficulty in learning mathematical concepts.

HOW TO DIAGNOSE LEARNING DISABILITY

As was stated earlier, it is very difficult to determine accurately if a child is learning-disabled. This normally requires a careful diagnosis by a neurologist, and even then his or her findings usually must be regarded as tentative.

In a determination of learning disability, the visual perception ability and auditory perception ability of the young child usually are determined by using the standardized measures that were described earlier in this chapter. In addition, such standardized devices as the following may be used: *Weschler Intelligence Scale for Children—Revised (WISC-R), Illinois Tests of Psycholinguistic Abilities, Goodenough-Harris Drawing Test,* and *Harris Tests of Lateral Dominance.*

Careful observation also is used to determine if a student may be learning-disabled. These may be tentative indicators of learning disability: poor oral language, inability to remember names and letter sounds, inability to blend sounds into words, inability to remember sight words, poor spelling ability, poor handwriting, poor arithmetic ability, poor visual perception ability, poor motor coordination, distractibility, hyperactivity, inability to concentrate, inability to control behavior, and excessive moodiness.

SOME TEACHING STRATEGIES FOR IMPROVING THE READING ABILITY OF LEARNING-DISABLED STUDENTS

There are a number of teaching strategies that may be useful for learning-disabled students at both the primary-grade and intermediate-grade levels. It *may* be useful to place the child in a position in the classroom where he or she will receive few extraneous stimuli, as in a screened-off area. However, some parents object greatly to the use of this strategy, so it should be used only with their approval and with the child's approval. Indeed, such a practice may violate a child's constitutional rights.

Always present tasks that are very short and very explicit. To eliminate distractors, use only several examples on an activity sheet. You can cut an activity sheet apart in rows, and then each row can be fastened to a sheet of blank paper. You also can tape-record the instructions for an activity sheet. Have the child replay the instructions as many times as necessary. Use a headset with a tape recorder because the headset shuts out auditory stimuli that might interfere with the essential stimuli.

Combine whole-word and part-to-whole reading instruction by having the child learn the names of a few letters first that can be formed into simple words later. After these letters have been learned, present some words containing these letters, and have the child name each letter. It is also important to present one reading skill at a time and give the child the opportunity to overlearn this reading skill before proceeding to another one. This is especially important in the case of the short vowel sounds, which are very difficult for many learning-disabled children to discriminate.

Use one or several of the tracing techniques to help the child learn letters or simple words. Several such techniques are the use of sandpaper letters, the sand tray, the salt tray, clay letters, or letters made of pipe-stem cleaners glued to cardboard. A device such as the Language Master is very useful with learning-disabled children because it combines visual and auditory stimuli and also provides immediate feedback. It is available from Bell and Howell Company, 7100 McCormick Road, Chicago, Illinois 60645. Another device that can be useful with such children is the Hoffman Reader. It contains a filmstrip that teaches the child specific reading skills. It has auditory input, and the child uses earphones. The child follows in a text or completes a workbook as he or she looks and listens. It is available from Hoffman Information Systems, 5623 Peck Road, Arcadia, California 91006.

Each learning-disabled student always should have many success experiences to fall back on. Such success experiences help to increase the child's ability to accept failure. However, motivation should not be too intense for such a child. Too much motivation may be accompanied by distracting emotions.

CHARACTERISTICS OF SLOW-LEARNING CHILDREN

A slow-learning student usually exhibits some behavioral characteristics that can be used for identification. The two most commonly used are intelligence quotient (IQ) and mental age (MA). The borderline slow learner has an IQ of about 80 to 90, and the educably mentally handicapped child has an IQ of about 60 to 80. A slow-learning student often uses short, simple sentences with few descriptive words. He or she generally learns reading skills and concepts at a slower pace than do students of average or above-average intelligence. The slow-learning student generally has difficulty in learning abstract concepts and finds it easier to learn concrete concepts such as phonic analysis and literal comprehension.

Some slow-learning students have physical problems, such as poor motor coordination, that are not so common in their brighter peers. Many slow-learning students have a negative self-image and feel inadequate. They, therefore, may appear to be withdrawn, passive, and apathetic in the elementary classroom. This mainly results from the fact that they very often are given school tasks at which they cannot succeed. It is important that a student be accurately diagnosed if he or she is a slow learner because the teacher cannot expect better performance from a student than what the student is capable of doing.

HOW TO DIAGNOSE A SLOW-LEARNING STUDENT

There are several formal and informal ways of determining if a student probably is a slow learner. Usually, a trained examiner such as a psychologist gives the child an individual intelligence test. The most common of these were described in Chapter 17 and are as follows: *Wechsler Preschool and Primary Scale of Intelligence (WPPSI), Wechsler Intelligence Scale for Children—Revised (WISC-R),* and *Stanford-Binet Intelligence Scale.*

You can also use teacher observation to determine if a student probably is a slow learner. The behavioral characteristics that were mentioned earlier in this chapter can be used for this purpose. You also can teach the child a concept very carefully. If he or she does not seem to learn this concept as easily and quickly as most of the peer group, he or she *may be* a slow learner. However, this should always be a tentative conclusion because the student's poor performance also may be the result of emotional problems, low motivation, an impoverished home environment, or inadequate nutrition.

SOME TEACHING STRATEGIES FOR IMPROVING THE READING ABILITY OF SLOW-LEARNING STUDENTS

There are many teaching strategies that can be used with slow-learning students at both the primary-grade and intermediate-grade reading levels. Each important reading skill should be overlearned before a succeeding reading skill is presented. As one example, the short /e/ sound should be thoroughly mastered before the short /i/ sound is presented so that confusion on the child's part will be avoided. It is also important to present concrete concepts as much as possible instead of abstract concepts. For example, stress literal comprehension with a slow-learning student while placing minimal stress on interpretive comprehension, critical reading, and creative reading.

It is also important to present such safety words to a slow learner as *stop, look, exit, danger,* and *walk.* These words usually should be presented by sight. Because some slow learners receive a kinesthetic reinforcement from oral reading, I recommend that it be used much more extensively than is typically the case with other students. All types of tracing techniques are very good with slow-learning students also. Some examples are a sand tray, a salt tray, felt letters, sandpaper letters, or glitter letters.

Sometimes *behavior modification* has been successful with slow learners. As an example, when a child performs a reading task correctly, you give him or her a tangible reward such as a candy bar, a cookie, M & Ms, or tokens that can be exchanged for money. It is also important to record the progress of a slow-learning student concretely. Graphs of progress, stickers, or gold stars may be good motivational devices. As was explained earlier, it is exceedingly important to build each slow learner's self-concept by assigning reading tasks with which he or she can experience certain success.

It is also important to present either the basal reader approach or a formal phonic program at a very slow and deliberate rate. You should also provide much concrete, meaningful repetition of the various reading skills. Slow learners need many drill-like activities, especially in the various word identification skills. Older slow-learning students should do as much practical reading as possible. This includes the newspaper, catalogs, the telephone directory, simple job application blanks, and special reading materials that have been written for slow-learning students.

CHARACTERISTICS OF BLIND AND LOW-VISION CHILDREN

All children who have visual problems can be classified as visually handicapped. Blind children have no useful vision or can only distinguish the difference between light and dark. Blind children must rely on auditory and tactile input. A blind chiild is one who has a corrected visual acuity of 20/200 or less in the better eye or a severely restricted field of vision.

A child with low vision may be called visually impaired or partially sighted. This type of child cannot perform tasks that require detailed vision without such special aids as large type, special lighting, or magnifiers. These children usually have poor distance vision but can see objects and materials that are held near their eyes. Their visual efficiency sometimes depends on the amount of light and the amount of contrast available. Low-vision children have visual acuity from 20/70 to 20/200 in the better eye after correction.

HOW TO DIAGNOSE LOW VISION

The teacher can notice evidence of vision difficulties in a child such as watering eyes, rubbing of the eyes, holding a book very close to the face, and squinting. Normally, a child's vision is evaluated by a member of the medical profession such as a school nurse or an ophthalmologist. These personnel generally use one or several devices that evaluate near-point vision, far-point vision, possible astigmatism, and binocular coordination or fusion.

One or several of the following devices are usually considered to be very good in vision testing by specialists in the field: *Keystone Visual Survey Tests, Ortho-Rater, Professional Vision Tester,* or the *Titmus Biopter.*

SOME TEACHING STRATEGIES FOR IMPROVING THE READING ABILITY OF BLIND AND LOW-VISION CHILDREN

As was stated in the introduction to this chapter, a consulting teacher may be a very great help to the regular classroom teacher who is to work with a blind or low-vision child. The language experience approach, the basal reader approach, individualized reading, and a formal phonic approach all have been used successfully to teach reading skills to both blind and low-vision children. It is extremely important to know that most basal reading series, some phonic materials, and some supplementary materials are available in both Braille and large type. These materials often may be obtained from the following address:

American Printing House for the Blind
1839 Frankfort Avenue
Louisville, Kentucky 40206

The Printing House for the Blind also provides cassette tapes of many books for supplementary and recreational reading. It also maintains the Central Catalog, a registry of all volunteer-produced materials that are available for loan.

Blind children should read materials that do not rely very much on visual imagery for meaning. They learn to read Braille, which is drawing meaning from symbols. It is a system of tactual reading and writing based on a cell of six possible raised dots in an array with a maximum of two dots across and three dots down. Various arrangements of dots represent letters, part words, whole words, numbers, and punctuation. Children may write Braille with a brailler or with a slate and stylus. New words should be introduced in context with blind children. Structural analysis is a useful word identification technique in reading Braille, but phonic analysis is not always valuable with Braille because of the characteristics of Braille. The teacher of the blind child may have to make special efforts to develop word meanings and comprehension because of the somewhat limited experiential background of blind children.

Most low-vision children can use regular print material as well as large type material. They also sometimes use magnifiers, including those that attach to eyeglasses, that are hand-held, or that stand alone on a base over the printed page. A closed circuit television system that projects the image of a page onto a desk model television monitor also can be used with low-vision children.

Contextual analysis is especially useful as a word identification technique with low-vision children. If the child is going to use a hand-held magnifier, he or she must learn how to move it across a word as it is being decoded. Low-vision children also need to have their background of experiences improved for effective comprehension.

CHARACTERISTICS OF DEAF AND HARD-OF-HEARING CHILDREN

A profoundly deaf child is unable to hear, and a hard-of-hearing child usually has approximately a thirty-decibel hearing loss as determined by an audiometer. This child usually needs a hearing aid. Approximately 5 percent of children in the elementary school have a significant hearing loss. A significant hearing loss affects communication, can result in poor speech, or can hinder learning to read. Most hearing losses occur in the middle ear or in a ruptured eardrum. Hearing loss also can be caused by brain damage, and such a loss is called auditory aphasia.

Losses in acuity of the high tones affect the child's ability to deal with some consonant sounds and blends. Because English vocabularies are distinguished by their consonant sounds, high-tone losses present a real problem in learning to read. Losses in acuity of the low tones affect the child's discrimination of the vowel sounds. Therefore, low-tone losses usually do not affect reading performance as much as do high-tone losses if the teacher does not make an issue of vowels that are mispronounced.

Obviously, a deaf child cannot rely on phonic analysis as a word identification technique, but a hard-of-hearing child may be able to do so fairly well. However, such children must be able to use their own sound-symbol association correctly in this instance.

HOW TO DIAGNOSE AUDITORY ACUITY

The determination of a child's auditory acuity usually is left to medical personnel such as the school nurse or an otologist. An audiometer usually is used to test a child's auditory acuity. This involves placing headphones on the child, having the child sit where he or she cannot see the dials being manipulated, and giving him or her a buzzer or other signal device to use in indicating when a sound can be heard. As the testing continues at each pitch level through the range of loudness back and forth from loud to soft and in reverse, an interrupter switch is employed.

The examiner marks the lowest level of loudness at which the child can hear each pitch on a chart called an audiogram. When the test is complete, these points are joined by a line, and a graph of the hearing is made. Audiometers are made by such companies as the following: *Beltone, Eckstein, Maico,* and *Zenith.*

SOME TEACHING STRATEGIES FOR IMPROVING THE READING ABILITY OF DEAF AND HARD-OF-HEARING CHILDREN

As has been stated earlier, a consulting teacher should be of great help to the regular classroom teacher who is to work with a deaf or hard-of-hearing child. Many different reading methods have been used fairly successfully with both types of children. However, research has indicated that only *10* percent of hearing-impaired eighteen-year-olds are able to read at or above the eighth-grade level.[1] The basal reader approach, the language experience approach, individualized reading, and programmed readers have all been used with deaf and hard-of-hearing children. Although the basal reader approach has been the

---

[1]Raymond J. Trybus and Michael A. Karchmer, "School Achievement Scores of Hearing Impaired: National Data on Achievement Status and Growth Patterns," *American Annals of the Deaf, 122* (April 1977): 62–69.

most commonly used, it may not be the best approach because of the syntactic ability of hearing-impaired students. For example, such students often omit connectives such as *and, but,* and *or.* Obviously, hearing-impaired children should use sight word recognition as a major word identification technique. Deaf children should receive minimal emphasis on phonic analysis as a word identification technique, but hard-of-hearing children may be able to use phonic analysis if they can use their own sound-symbol associations, even though they are not the traditional ones. For example, if a child consistently says *lenf* for *length,* it is not very important if the child can recognize the word by sight and has established a meaning for it.

The language experience approach has been used fairly effectively with hearing-impaired children. American Sign Language (ASL) can be used in the dictation of language experience stories. It is a language that possesses a vocabulary of signs to represent concepts and experiences. The language experience approach is considered to be an excellent approach because it is an active approach and uses the child's language, knowledge, and experiences. The word bank also can be used with hearing-impaired children (see Chapter 4). A student-dictated sentence can be written on the back of the card with the target word underlined. The other side of the card can contain the target word in isolation. If the child is unable to recognize the word on sight, he or she can turn the card around and use context for its identification.

It is also essential that hearing-impaired children have great exposure to written language. The stories should be presented in the language communication mode that is most comfortable for the hearing-impaired child.

SELECTED REFERENCES

Bockmiller, Patricia R., and Joan D. Coley. "A Survey of Methods, Materials, and Teacher Preparation Among Teachers of Reading to the Hearing Impaired." *The Reading Teacher, 34* (February 1981): 526–529.

Burg, Leslie, and Maurice Kaufman. "Laws About Special Education: Their Impact on the Use of Reading Specialists." *The Reading Teacher, 34* (November 1980): 187–191.

Curry, Rebecca Gavurin. "Using LEA to Teach Blind Children to Read." *The Reading Teacher, 29* (December 1975): 272–279.

Fein, Ruth L., and Adrienne H. Ginsberg. "Realistic Literature About the Handicapped." *The Reading Teacher, 31* (April 1978): 802–805.

Gormley, Kathleen A., and Leo D. Geoffrion. "Another View of Using Language Experience to Teach Reading to Deaf and Hearing Impaired Children." *The Reading Teacher, 34* (February 1981): 519–525.

Kaluger, George, and Clifford J. Kolson. *Reading and Learning Disabilities*. Columbus, Ohio: Charles E. Merrill Publishing Co., 1978.

Niensted, Serena. "Talking with LD Teachers." *The Reading Teacher, 28* (April 1975): 662–665.

Spache, George D. *Diagnosing and Correcting Reading Disabilities*. Boston: Allyn and Bacon, Inc., 1981, Chapters 2, 3.

Stauffer, Russell G. "The Language Experience Approach to Reading Instruction for Deaf and Hearing Impaired Children." *The Reading Teacher, 33* (October 1979): 21–24.

———. *The Language-Experience Approach to the Teaching of Reading*. New York: Harper & Row, Publishers, 1980, Chapter 12.

Vernon, McCay, and Joan D. Coley. "The Sign Language of the Deaf and Reading-Language Development." *The Reading Teacher, 32* (December 1978): 297–301.

Ward, Marjorie, and Sandra McCormick. "Reading Instruction for Blind and Low Vision Children in the Regular Classroom." *The Reading Teacher, 34* (January 1981): 434–444.

SUGGESTED ACTIVITIES

1. Examine one of the visual perception and/or auditory discrimination tests that were mentioned in the chapter. You may want to give the *Frostig Developmental Test of Visual Perception* or the *Wepman Auditory Discrimination Test*.

2. If possible, use one of the teaching strategies that were mentioned in the chapter for improving ability in visual perception or auditory discrimination with one child or a small group of children.

3. If possible, visit a class of learning-disabled children. What type of teaching strategies are used with these children in the area of reading?

4. If possible, select a slow learner, and present an appropriate reading skill to him or her.

5. If possible, examine some large type reading materials that have been designed for low-vision children.

6. If possible, examine one of the devices for testing vision or hearing that were mentioned in the chapter.

The Instant Words
First Hundred*

First 25 Group Ia	Second 25 Group Ib	Third 25 Group Ic	Fourth 25 Group Id
the	or	will	number
of	one	up	no
and	had	other	way
a	by	about	could
to	word	out	people
in	but	many	my
is	not	then	than
you	what	them	first
that	all	these	water
it	were	so	been
he	we	some	call
was	when	her	who
for	your	would	oil
on	can	make	now
are	said	like	find
as	there	him	long
with	use	into	down
his	an	time	day
they	each	has	did
I	which	look	get
at	she	two	come
be	do	more	made
this	how	write	may
have	their	go	part
from	if	see	over

Common suffixes: s, ing, ed

*Edward Fry, "The New Instant Word List," *The Reading Teacher*, 34 (December 1980): 287–288.

The Instant Words
Second Hundred

First 25 Group 2a	Second 25 Group 2b	Third 25 Group 2c	Fourth 25 Group 2d
new	great	put	kind
sound	where	end	hand
take	help	does	picture
only	through	another	again
little	much	well	change
work	before	large	off
know	line	must	play
place	right	big	spell
year	too	even	air
live	mean	such	away
me	old	because	animal
back	any	turn	house
give	same	here	point
most	tell	why	page
very	boy	ask	letter
after	follow	went	mother
thing	came	men	answer
our	want	read	found
just	show	need	study
name	also	land	still
good	around	different	learn
sentence	form	home	should
man	three	us	America
think	small	move	world
say	set	try	high

Common suffixes: s, ing, ed, er, ly, est

The Instant Words
Third Hundred

First 25 Group 3a	Second 25 Group 3b	Third 25 Group 3c	Fourth 25 Group 3d
every	left	until	idea
near	don't	children	enough

First 25 Group 3a	Second 25 Group 3b	Third 25 Group 3c	Fourth 25 Group 3d
add	few	side	eat
food	while	feet	face
between	along	car	watch
own	might	mile	far
below	close	night	Indian
country	something	walk	real
plant	seem	white	almost
last	next	sea	let
school	hard	began	above
father	open	grow	girl
keep	example	took	sometimes
tree	begin	river	mountain
never	life	four	cut
start	always	carry	young
city	those	state	talk
earth	both	once	soon
eye	paper	book	list
light	together	hear	song
thought	got	stop	leave
head	group	without	family
under	often	second	body
story	run	late	music
say	important	miss	color

Common suffixes: s, ing, ed, er, ly, est

APPENDIX II

240 Starter Words
A Basic Reading/Writing Vocabulary†

*a	*all	*an	*are	*away	*before
*about	almost	*and	*around	*back	*best
*after	*also	*another	*as	*be	*better
*again	*always	*any	*ask	*because	*big
air	*am	anything	*at	*been	black

book	*for	*is	*my	*school	*told
both	*found	*it	*name	*see	*too
*boy	*four	it's	need	*she	*took
brought	*from	*just	*never	*should	town
*but	gave	*keep	*new	*show	*two
*by	*get	*kind	*next	side	*under
*came	girl	knew	*night	*small	until
*can	*give	*know	*no	*so	*up
*car	*go	land	*not	*some	*us
*children	gone	*last	*now	*something	*use
city	*good	*left	*of	*soon	*very
*come	*got	*let	*off	*still	*want
*could	great	life	*old	sure	*was
*day	*had	light	*on	table	*water
*did	half	*like	*once	*take	*way
*didn't	hard	*little	*one	*tell	*we
different	*has	*long	*only	*than	*well
*do	*have	*look	open	*that	*went
done	*he	*made	*or	*the	*were
*don't	*head	*make	*other	*their	*what
door	heard	*man	*our	*them	*when
*down	*help	*many	*out	*then	*where
*each	*her	*may	*over	*there	*which
end	*here	*me	part	*these	*while
enough	high	*men	*people	*they	*white
even	*him	might	*place	*thing	*who
ever	*his	money	*play	*think	*why
*every	*home	*more	*put	*this	*will
family	*house	morning	red	*thought	*with
father	*how	*most	*right	*three	*work
few	*I	mother	*room	*through	*world
*find	*if	*Mr.	*said	*time	*would
fire	I'm	Mrs.	*same	*to	*year
*first	*in	*much	*saw	today	*you
five	*into	*must	*say	together	*your

* = 190 most important words

†Robert L. Hillerich, "Word Lists—Getting it Altogether," *The Reading Teacher*, 27 (January 1974): 367.

INDEX